Basic Creo Parametric 5.0 in 20 Lessons

Louis Gary Lamit
Silicon Valley, California
USA

WWW.CAD-RESOURCES.COM

Dedication

This book is dedicated to my teacher:

Thich Phap Chon   *gate gate pāragate pārasagate bodhi svāhā*

ISBN: 9781070553801
ISBN: 9781071253793 *Color Version*

About the author

Louis Gary Lamit taught at De Anza College (1984-2018) in Cupertino, CA. Mr. Lamit has worked as a drafter/detailer, designer, numerical control (NC) programmer, technical illustrator, and engineer in the automotive, aircraft, and piping industries. Most of his work experience is in mechanical and piping design. He started as a drafter in the Detroit area (as a job shopper) in the automobile industry, doing tooling, dies, jigs and fixture layout, and detailing at Koltanbar Engineering, Tool Engineering, Time Engineering, and Premier Engineering for Chrysler, Ford, AMC, and Fisher Body. Mr. Lamit has worked at Pacific Pipe Company, Remington Arms. and Pratt & Whitney Aircraft as a designer, and at Boeing Aircraft and Kollmorgan Optics as an NC programmer and aircraft engineer. Mr. Lamit has taught at (Melby Junior High School, Warren, Mi.; Carroll County Vocational Technical School, Carrollton, Ga.; Heald Engineering College, San Francisco, Ca.; Cogswell Polytechnical College, San Francisco and Cupertino, Ca.; Mission College, Santa Clara, Ca.; Santa Rosa Junior College, Santa Rosa, Ca.; Northern Kentucky University, Highland Heights, Ky.; and De Anza College, Cupertino, Ca.). He owns and operates his own consulting business (Vavni, ImpactXoft) and training firm (CAD-Resources.com- Lamit and Associates), and has been involved with advertising, and patent illustration. He has trained Google, BAE, and Stryker employees at their facilities in Silicon Valley on Pro/E and Creo Parametric.

He is the author of: Industrial Model Building (1981), Piping Drafting and Design (1981), Descriptive Geometry (1983), Pipe Fitting and Piping Handbook (1984), Drafting for Electronics (1986), CADD (1987), Technical Drawing and Design (1994), Principles of Engineering Drawing (1994), Fundamentals of Engineering Graphics and Design (1997), Engineering Graphics and Design with Graphical Analysis (1997),Basic Pro/ENGINEER in 20 Lessons (1998) (Revision 18), Basic Pro/ENGINEER (with references to PT/Modeler) (1999), Pro/ENGINEER 2000i (1999), Pro/ENGINEER 2000i2 (Pro/NC and Pro/SHEETMETAL) (2000), Pro/ENGINEER Wildfire (2003) Introduction to Pro/ENGINEER Wildfire 5.0 (2004), Moving from 2D to 3D CAD for Engineering Design (2007), Pro/ENGINEER Wildfire 3.0 (2007), Pro/ENGINEER Wildfire 4.0 (2008), Pro/ENGINEER Wildfire 5.0 (2010), Creo Parametric (2012), PTC Creo Parametric 2.0 (2015), PTC Creo Parametric 3.0 (2016), PTC Creo Parametric 4.0 (Part 1- Lessons 1-12) (2017). PTC Creo Parametric 4.0 (Part 2- Lessons 13-22) (2017), Creo Parametric 5.0 (Part 1- Lessons 1-12) (2018), and Creo Parametric 5.0 (Part 2- Lessons 13-22) (2018), Basic Creo Parametric 5.0 in 20 Lessons (2019), Mastering Creo Parametric, 6.0 (2019)

Mr. Lamit also owns and writes for books and journals though WalkingFish Books Amazon-CreateSpace: Fishing Journals, Golfing Journals, Bird Watching Journals, Garden Journals and the Wally the WalkingFish children's book series.

Table of Contents

Preface

Creo Parametric CAD/CAM software program is used throughout the world for small design requirements (medical devices, consumer products, consumer products, electronic components) to large assembly projects (airline, automobile, and manufacturing facilities). An aspiring or employed engineer will benefit from the knowledge contained in the book. This book guides you through *parametric design* using Creo Parametric. While using this text, you will create individual components, assemblies, and drawings. Parametric can be defined as any set of physical properties whose values determine the characteristics or behavior of an object. Parametric design enables you to generate a variety of information about your design: its mass properties, a drawing, or a base model. The text involves creating a parts, assemblies, and drawings, using a set of commands that systematically walk you through the design process.

Who this book is for

This book is intended for those students or professionals wishing to master Creo Parametric as a new CAD design tool.

In order to use this book:

To complete the projects in this text, you will need the following:

- Creo Parametric [Student (free download)], [Academic (license from your educational institution), or [commercial version (through your company)].
- An engineering workstation, PC or laptop with Windows 7, 8, or 10.
- Creo Parametric will not run on Apple products without supplemental software.

Resources

Extra projects (downloadable PDF) can be downloaded at: www.cad-resources.com

Creo Parametric Free Schools Edition software is available at **www.ptc.com**.

If you wish to contact the author concerning questions, changes, additions, suggestions, comments, or to get on our email list, please send an email:

Email: lgl@cad-resources.com
Author Web Site: www.cad-resources.com

Using the Text

The text employs command sequences and descriptions to guide you through construction sequences. Icons, symbols, shortcut keys, and conventions are used:

Click: **View** tab > **Display Style** > **Shading** > **Model** tab > **Extrude** > **Placement** tab > **Define** > **Sketch Plane---** Plane: select datum plane **Top**

Commands:

- **>** Continue with command sequence or screen picks using **LMB**

-  Selections using **LMB** popup menu displays options

Mouse or keyboard terms used in this text:

- **LMB**   Left Mouse Button
  - or **"Pick"**   term used to direct an action (i.e., "Pick the edge")
  - or **"Click"**   term used to direct an action (i.e., "Click on the icon")
  - or **"Select"**   term used to direct an action (i.e., "Select the feature")

- **MMB**   Middle Mouse Button
  (accept the current selection or value)
  - or **Enter**   press **Enter** key to accept entry
  - or ☑   Click on this icon to accept entry

- **RMB**   Right Mouse Button
  Click (toggles to next selection)
  Press and hold (displays a list of available commands)

Shortcut Keys:

Keystroke	Action
ALT	• Temporarily disables filters during selection when the pointer is in the graphics window. Hold down the ALT key during selection. • Activates Key Tips on the Ribbon. With your pointer anywhere in the Ribbon, Graphics Window, Model Tree, etc., press the ALT key.

CTRL	Temporarily hides the Live Toolbar in 3D part and assembly modes.
CTRL+A	Activates a window.
CTRL+C	Copies the selection to the clipboard.
CTRL+D	Displays a model in standard view.
CTRL+N	Opens the **New** dialog box.
CTRL+O	Opens the **File Open** dialog box.
CTRL+R	Repaints a window.
CTRL+S	Opens the **Save Object** dialog box.
CTRL+V	Pastes the clipboard contents to the selected location.
CTRL+Y	Performs a single step redo operation.
CTRL+Z	Performs a single step undo operation.
ESC	• Cancels an operation • Clears the selection in the graphics window • Cancels a dragger operation • Closes the Live Toolbar • Cancels the currently active tool
ENTER	Accepts the changes and closes the Live Toolbar in 3D and assembly modes. Also clears the selection in the graphics window.
F1	Opens **Help** for the current context.
G	Hides the current guide for the geometry in 2D mode.
L	Locks or unlocks the current guide in 2D mode.
P	Shows or hides precision panels in 2D mode temporarily.
S	Switches between the Line and Arc Creation modes in 2D mode.
TAB	Pre-highlights surface sets for selection based on shape selection rules.

Introduction

Parametric means *any set of physical properties whose values determine the characteristics or behavior of an object.* **Parametric design** enables you to generate a variety of information about your design: its mass properties, a drawing, or a base model. To get this information, you must first model your part design. Parametric modeling philosophies used in Creo Parametric comprise:

- *Feature-Based Modeling* solid models as combinations of engineering features.
- *Construction of Assemblies* just as features are combined into parts, parts may be combined into assemblies.
- *Capturing Design Intent* the capability to incorporate engineering knowledge into the solid model is an essential aspect of parametric modeling.

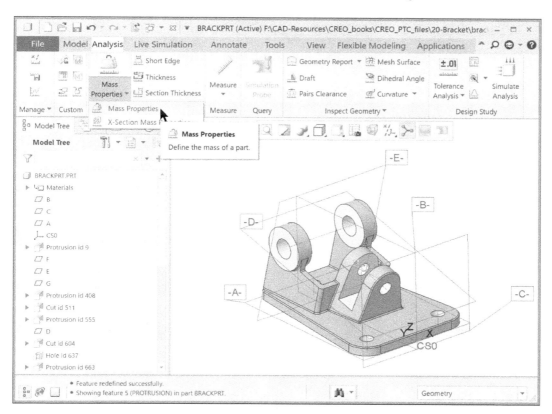

Parametric Design

Parametric design models are not drawn so much as they are *formed* from solid volumes of materials. To begin the design process, analyze your design.

Break down the overall design into its basic components, building blocks, or primary features. Identify the most fundamental feature of the object to sketch as the first, or base, feature. Varieties of **base features** can be modeled using extrude, revolve, sweep, and blend tools.

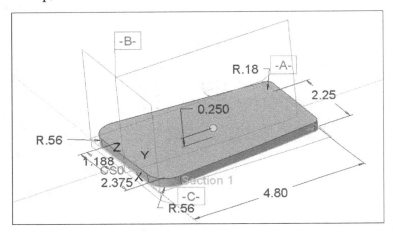

Sketched features (*extrusions, sweeps, etc.*) and pick-and-place features called **referenced features** (*holes, rounds, chamfers, etc.*) are required in most designs. With the SKETCHER, you use 2D entities (points, lines, rectangles, circles, arcs, splines, and conics)

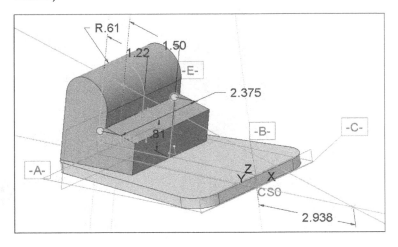

14

Geometry assumptions and constraints will close ends of connected lines, align parallel lines, and snap sketched lines to horizontal and vertical (orthogonal) orientations. Additional constraints are added by means of **parametric dimensions** to control the size and shape of the sketch.

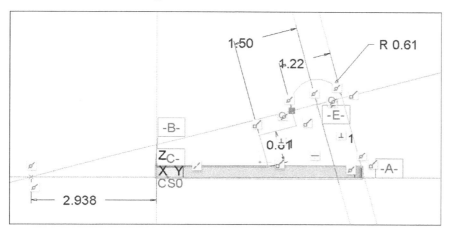

Features are the basic building blocks you use to create an object. Features "understand" their fit and function as though "smarts" were built into the features themselves. For example, a hole or cut feature "knows" its shape and location and the fact that it has a negative volume. As you modify a feature, the entire object automatically updates after regeneration. The idea behind feature-based modeling is that the designer constructs an object so that it is composed of individual features that describe the way the geometry is supposed to behave if its dimensions change. This happens quite often in industry, as in the case of a design change.

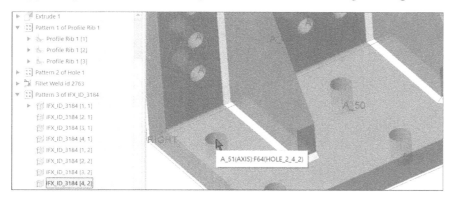

Parametric modeling is the term used to describe the capturing of design operations as they take place, as well as future modifications and editing of the design. The order of the design operations is important. As an example; a designer specifies two surfaces must be parallel. Therefore, if surface one moves, surface two moves along with surface one to maintain the specified design relationship. The surface two is a **child** of surface one in this example. Parametric modeling software allows the designer to **reorder** the steps in the object's creation. Various types of features are used as building blocks in the progressive creation of solid objects.

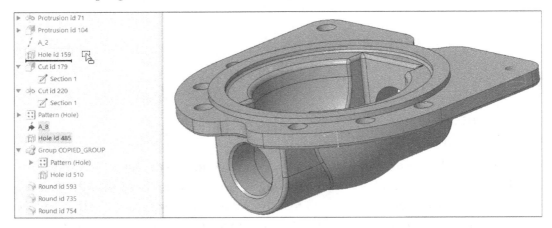

The "hunks" of solid material from which parametric design models are constructed are called **features**. Features generally fall into one of the following categories:

Base Feature The base feature is normally a set of datum planes referencing the default coordinate system. The base feature is important because all future model geometry will reference this feature directly or indirectly; it becomes the root feature. Changes to the base feature will affect the geometry of the entire model.

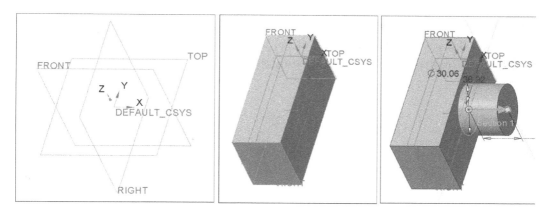

Datum Features Datum features (planes, lines, axes, curves, and points) are generally used to provide sketching planes and contour references for sketched and referenced features. Datum features do not have volume or mass and may be visually hidden without affecting solid geometry.

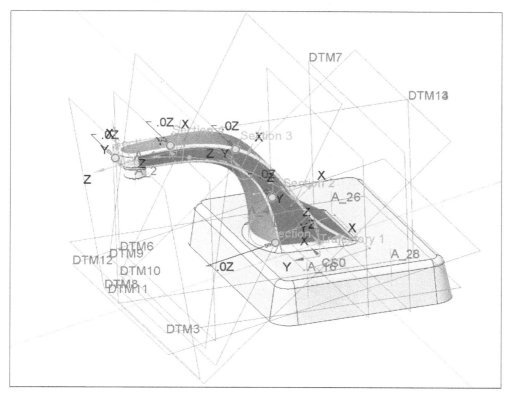

17

Sketched Features Sketched features are created by extruding, revolving, blending, or sweeping a sketched cross section. Material may be added or removed by protruding or cutting the feature from the existing model.

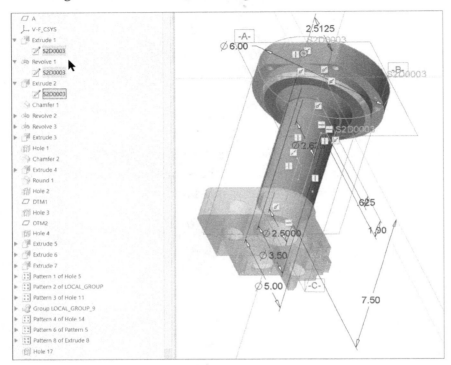

Referenced Features Referenced features (rounds, holes, shells) use existing geometry for positioning and employ an inherent form; they do not need to be sketched.

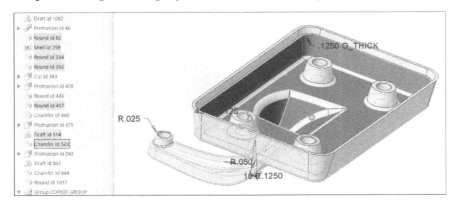

Fundamentals

The design of parts and assemblies, and the creation of related drawings, forms the foundation of engineering graphics. When designing with Creo Parametric, many of the previous steps in the design process have been eliminated, streamlined, altered,

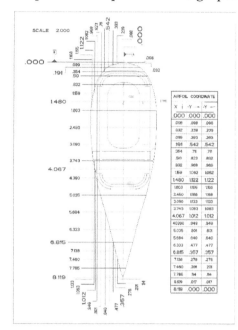

AIRFOIL COORDINATE		
X	-Y -	-Y -
.000	.000	.000
.008	.098	.098
.032	.239	.239
.099	.393	.393
.191	.542	.542
.364	.711	.711
.510	.823	.812
.832	.969	.969
1.159	1.062	1.062
1.480	1.122	1.122
1.803	1.156	1.156
2.460	1.168	1.168
3.090	1.133	1.133
3.743	1.083	1.083
4.067	1.012	1.012
4.0290	.949	.949
5.035	.801	.801
5.684	.640	.640
6.333	.477	.477
6.815	.357	.357
7.138	.278	.278
7.460	.201	.201
7.786	.114	.114
8.109	.017	.017
8.119	.000	.000

refined, or expanded. The model you create as a part forms the basis for all engineering and design functions.

The part model contains the geometric data describing the part's features, but it also includes non-graphical information embedded in the design itself. The part, its associated assembly, and the graphical documentation (drawings) are parametric. The physical properties described in the part drive (determine) the characteristics and behavior of the assembly and drawing. Any data established in the assembly mode, in turn, determines that aspect of the part and, subsequently, the drawings of the part and the assembly. All the information contained in the part, the assembly, and the drawing is interrelated, interconnected, and parametric.

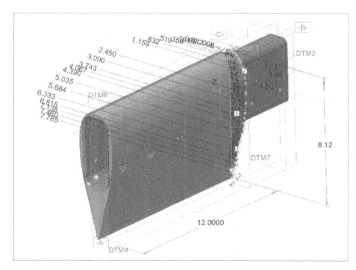

19

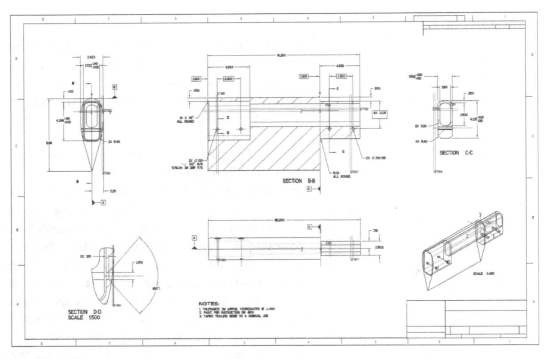

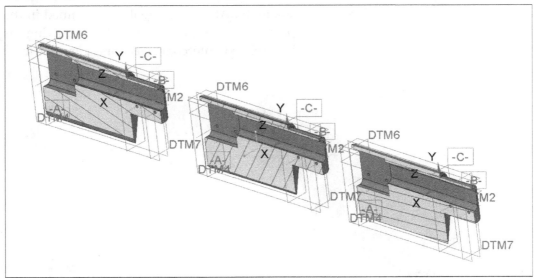

Parent-Child Relationships

Solid modeling is a cumulative process, therefore certain features precede others. Features that follow must rely on previously defined features for dimensional and geometric references. The relationships between features and those that reference them are termed *parent-child relationships*. Because children reference parents, parent features can exist without children, but children cannot exist without their parents. This type of CAD modeler is called a history-based system. Using information commands will provide a list of a model's parent-child references and dependencies.

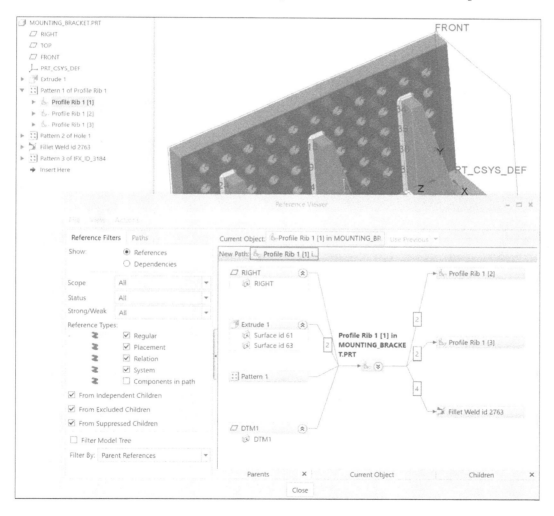

The parent-child relationship is one of the most powerful aspects of parametric design. When a parent feature is modified, its children are automatically recreated to reflect the changes in the parent feature's geometry. It is essential to reference feature dimensions so that design modifications are correctly propagated through the model/part. Any modification to the part is automatically propagated throughout the model and will affect all children of the modified feature.

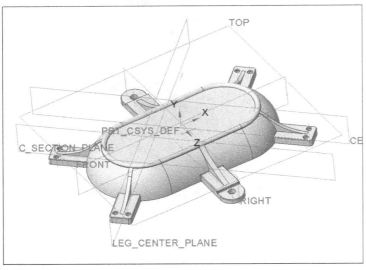

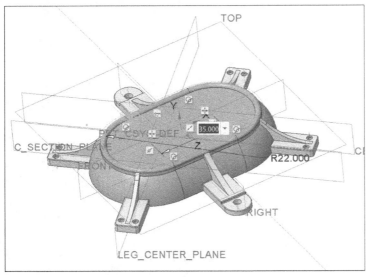

Capturing Design Intent

A valuable characteristic of any design tool is its ability to *render* the design and at the same time capture its *intent.* Parametric methods depend on the sequence of operations used to construct the design. The software maintains a *history of changes* the designer makes to specific parameters. The point of capturing this history is to keep track of operations that depend on each other.

Whenever Creo Parametric is instructed to change a specific dimension it will update all operations that are referenced to that dimension. As an example, a circle representing a bolt hole circle may be constructed so that it is always concentric to a circular slot. If the slot moves, so does the bolt circle. Parameters are usually displayed in terms of dimensions or labels and serve as the mechanism by which geometry is changed. The designer can change parameters manually by modifying a dimension or can reference them to a variable in an equation (**relation**) that is solved either by the modeling program itself or by external programs such as spreadsheets.

Features can also store non-graphical information. This information can be used in activities such as drafting, numerical control (NC), finite-element analysis (FEA), and kinematics analysis.

Capturing design intent is based on incorporating engineering knowledge into a model by establishing and preserving certain geometric relationships. For example, the wall thickness of a pressure vessel should be proportional to its surface area and should remain so, even as its size changes.

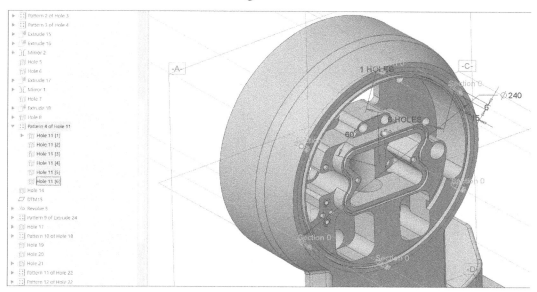

Navigation Window

Besides using the File command and corresponding options, the *Navigation window* can be used to directly access other functions. As previously mentioned, the working directory is a directory that you set up to contain Creo Parametric files. You must have read/write access to this directory. You usually start Creo Parametric from your working directory. A new working directory setting is not saved when you exit the current Creo Parametric session. By default, if you retrieve a file from a non-working directory, rename the file and then save it, the renamed file is saved to the directory from which it was originally retrieved, if you have read/write access to that directory.

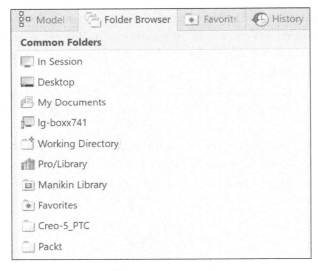

The navigation area is located on the left side (default) of the Creo Parametric

main window. It includes tabs for the 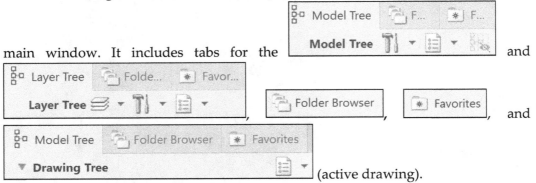 and

, , , and

(active drawing).

Folder Browser

The **Folder browser** is an expandable tree that lets you browse the file systems and other locations that are accessible from your computer. As you navigate the folders, the contents of the selected folder appear in the Creo Parametric browser as a Contents page. The Folder browser contains top-level nodes for accessing file systems and other locations that are known to Creo Parametric:

- **In Session** Creo Parametric objects that have been retrieved into local memory.
- **Desktop** Files and programs on the Desktop. Only Creo Parametric items can be opened.
- **My Documents** Files created and saved in Windows *My Documents* folder.
- **Working Directory** Directory linked with the Select Working Directory command. All work will be accessed and saved in this location.
- **Network** *(only for Windows)* The navigator shows computers on the networks to which you have access.
- **Manikin Library** A Manikin model is a standard assembly that can be manipulated and positioned within the design scenario.
- **Favorites** Saved folder locations for fast retrieval.

Manipulating Folders

To work with folders, use the **Browser** to accomplish file management requirements. The Browser's **Views** drop-down menu includes **List, Thumbnails,** and **Details:**

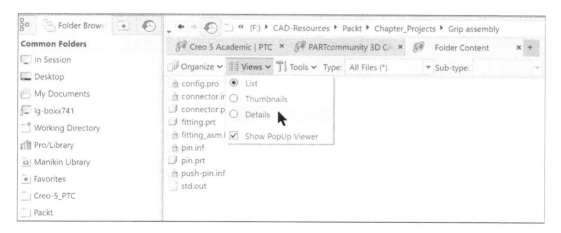

You can perform a variety of tasks from the Browser's **Organize** drop-down menu including **New Folder**, **Rename**, **Cut**, **Copy**, **Paste**, **Delete**, and **Add to common folders**:

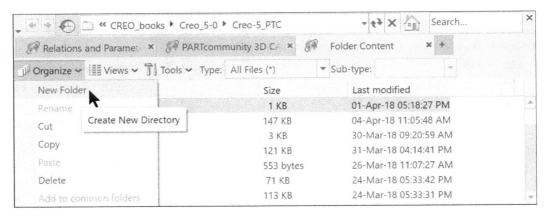

The Browser's **Tools** drop-down menu includes **Sort By**, go **Up One Level**, **Add to Favorites**, **Remove from Favorites**, **Organize Favorites**, show **All Versions**, **Show Instances**, and **Send to Mail Recipient (as Zipped Attachment)**:

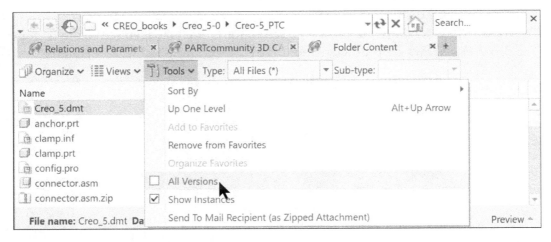

Do not change your working directory from your default system work folder unless instructed to do so.

From the Browser's **Type** field, you can limit the search to one of Creo Parametric's file types:

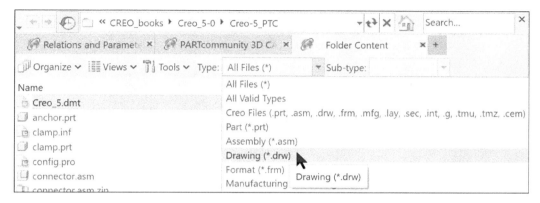

To set a working directory using the Browser, pick on the desired folder > *RMB* > *Set Working Directory*:

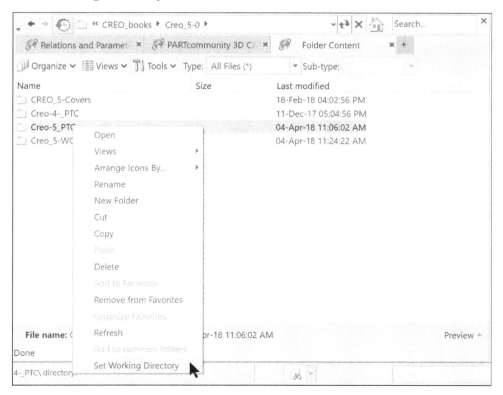

After you set (select) the working directory, pick on the object to preview:

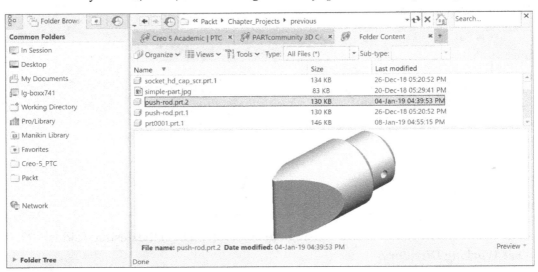

Within the preview window, dynamically reorient the model using the **MMB** by itself (**Spin**- press and hold the **MMB** as you move the mouse) or in conjunction with the **Shift** key (**Pan**) or **Ctrl** key (**Zoom, Turn**). A mouse with a thumbwheel (as the middle button) can be rolled to zoom in/out on the object. Double-clicking on the file name will open the part. After you complete this lesson you will have this same part in your working directory. From the Browser's toolbar you can also navigate to other directories or computer areas:

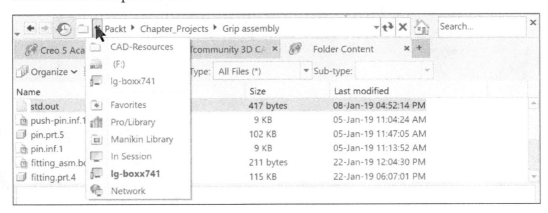

PART 1: Creo Parametric interface and commands

Part 1 will enable you to experience the three primary modes for Creo Parametric: part, assembly, and drawing by modeling a few parts, assembling them, and creating drawings of the parts and the assembly. System interface and environment settings are introduced along with basic features and editing of models.

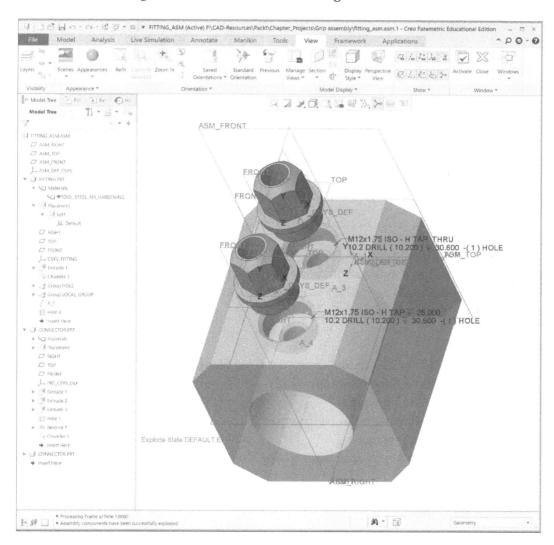

CHAPTER 1: System Interface, Settings and Customization

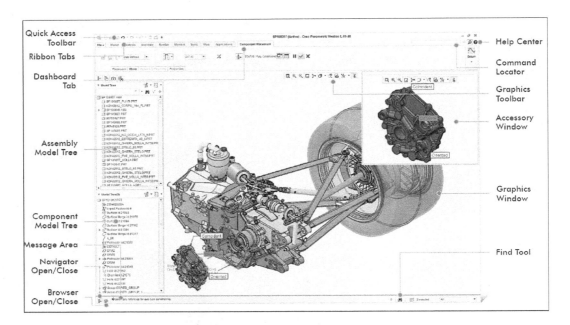

This chapter will introduce you to the Creo Parametric working environment. The interface consists of a navigation window, an embedded Web browser, toolbars, information areas, and a graphics window. An assortment of interface and menu customizations will be introduced.

Objectives
1. Download 3D CAD models from the Creo Standard Parts Library
2. Experience the Creo Parametric Browser
3. Master the File Functions
4. Become familiar with the Help center
5. Alter Display Settings
6. Investigate an object with Information Tools
7. Experience the Model Tree functionality
8. Understand and customize the User Interface (UI)
9. Create a Mapkey

Interface

The Creo Parametric interface encompasses a navigation window, an embedded Web browser, toolbars, information areas, and the graphics window. Each Creo Parametric object opens in its own window. You can perform many operations from the Ribbon in multiple windows without canceling pending operations. The Creo Parametric window consists of the following elements:

Browser A Web browser is located to the right of the navigator window. This browser provides you access to internal or external Web sites.

Graphics Window The graphics window is the main working space (main window).

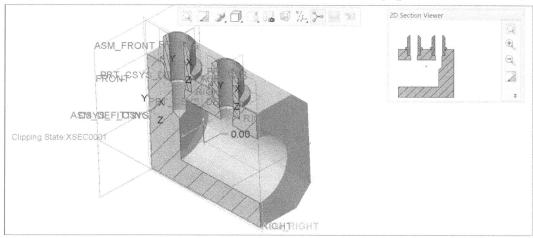

Navigation Area The navigation area is located on the left side of the Graphics Window. It includes tabs for the Model Tree and Layer Tree, Folder Browser, Favorites, History and Connections.

on the status bar/message area (lower left corner of the window) controls the display of the navigator.

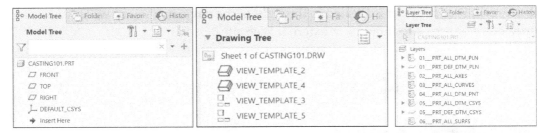

Quick Access Toolbar The Quick Access toolbar is available regardless of which Ribbon tab is selected. By default, it is located at the top of the window. It provides quick access to frequently used commands which are represented by icons or buttons, such as buttons for opening and saving files, undo, redo, regenerate, close window, switch windows, and so on. In addition, you can customize the Quick Access toolbar to include other frequently used buttons and cascading lists.

Graphics Toolbar The Graphics toolbar contain icons to speed up access to commonly used View tab commands. By default, the Graphics toolbar consist of a row of buttons located directly under the Ribbon. The Graphics toolbar can be positioned on the top, left, bottom, and right of the graphics window, or in the status bar, or turned off. Graphics toolbar buttons can be added or removed to customize the layout.

File Menu The File button in the upper-left corner of the window opens a menu that contains commands for managing files, models, preparing models for distribution, and for setting the environment and configuration options.

Ribbon The Ribbon contains command buttons organized in a set of tabs. On each tab, the related buttons are grouped. You can minimize the Ribbon to make more space available on your screen. You can customize the Ribbon by adding, removing, or moving buttons.

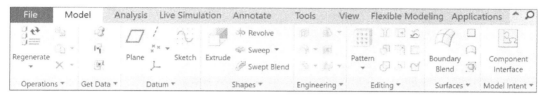

Tabs Tabs are available when you are in a mode or application. The Model, Analysis, Annotate, Tools, View, Applications tabs are commonly available tabs when you are in part mode. Tabs related to a context open or close automatically when you activate or deactivate the context. Tabs that contain tools of an application or controls of a tool have specific buttons to open and close them.

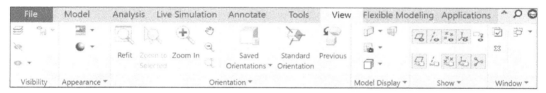

Screen Tips The status bar messages also appear in small boxes near the menu option or dialog box item or toolbar button that the mouse pointer is passing over.

Message Area Each window has a status bar/message area located at the bottom of the Creo Parametric window.

Command Locator The Command Locator will quickly locate and initiate any command by opening the Ribbon and group associated with the command and listing optional locations.

Accessory Window When you place a component or use a tool that includes an accessory component or feature, you can open the accessory component and its Model Tree in a new window, even if it is already open in another window. An accessory window can be docked in the graphics window or opened separately.

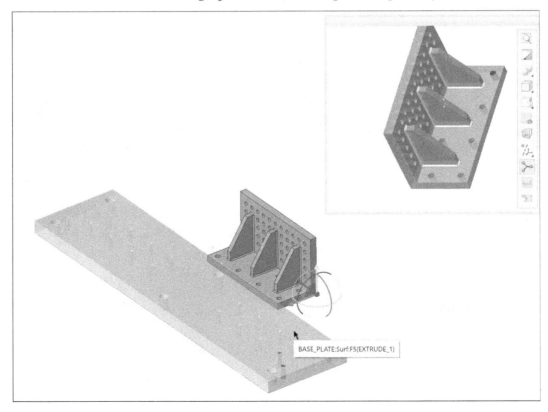

Chapter 1 STEPS

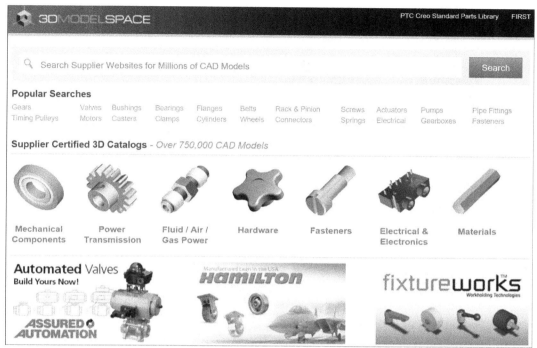

Figure 1.1 3DMODELSPACE Catalog

Catalog Parts

In order to see and use the Creo Parametric UI, we must have an active object. You will download an existing 3D standard component using the Browser (Fig. 1.1). You will also experience using the Catalog of parts from PTC. You can access online catalogs from the **3DModelSpace** link. The home page for the catalog lists catalogs of standard components.

You can browse catalogs, search for a component, view the details of the components, and download the selected component in Creo Parametric. You can also add a shortcut to a catalog.

Note: The PTC website may change names of certain items as they update.

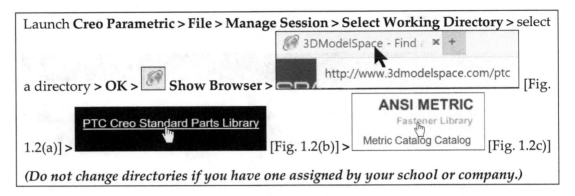

Launch **Creo Parametric > File > Manage Session > Select Working Directory** > select a directory > **OK** > Show Browser > [Fig. 1.2(a)] > PTC Creo Standard Parts Library [Fig. 1.2(b)] > ANSI METRIC Fastener Library Metric Catalog Catalog [Fig. 1.2c)]

(Do not change directories if you have one assigned by your school or company.)

Figure 1.2(a) 3DModelSpace

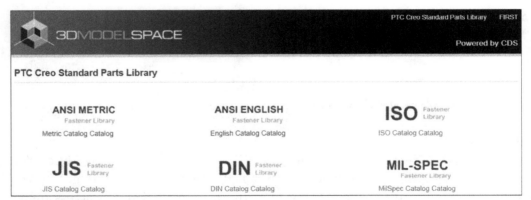

Figure 1.2(b) Parts Library

Figure 1.2(c) ANSI METRIC Fastener Library

Scroll to the bottom of the PTC Catalog Directory page and click:

| I ACCEPT the Terms and Conditions Stated Above. | [Fig. 1.2(d)] > | Show All Categories | [Fig. 1.2(e)] |

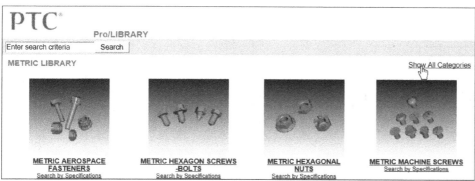

Figure 1.2(d) METRIC LIBRARY Category Images

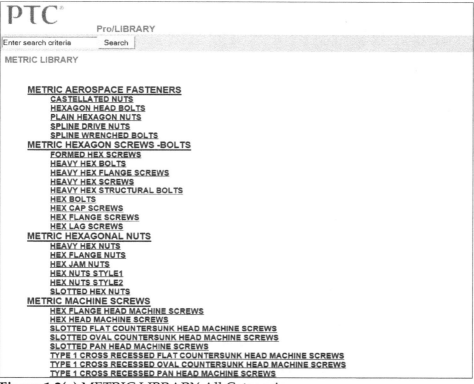

Figure 1.2(e) METRIC LIBRARY All Categories

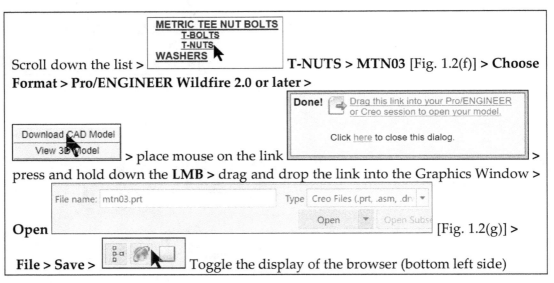

Scroll down the list > T-NUTS > MTN03 [Fig. 1.2(f)] > **Choose Format > Pro/ENGINEER Wildfire 2.0 or later >**

Done! Drag this link into your Pro/ENGINEER or Creo session to open your model.

Click here to close this dialog.

Download CAD Model
View 3D Model > place mouse on the link > press and hold down the **LMB** > drag and drop the link into the Graphics Window >

File name: mtn03.prt   Type Creo Files (.prt, .asm, .dr ▼

Open   Open Subse [Fig. 1.2(g)] >

File > Save > Toggle the display of the browser (bottom left side)

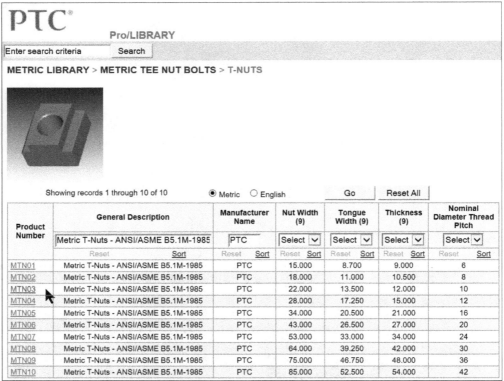

Product Number	General Description	Manufacturer Name	Nut Width (9)	Tongue Width (9)	Thickness (9)	Nominal Diameter Thread Pitch
	Metric T-Nuts - ANSI/ASME B5.1M-1985	PTC	Select ✓	Select ✓	Select ✓	Select ✓
	Reset Sort	Reset Sort	Reset Sort	Reset Sort	Reset Sort	Reset Sort
MTN01	Metric T-Nuts - ANSI/ASME B5.1M-1985	PTC	15.000	8.700	9.000	6
MTN02	Metric T-Nuts - ANSI/ASME B5.1M-1985	PTC	18.000	11.000	10.500	8
MTN03	Metric T-Nuts - ANSI/ASME B5.1M-1985	PTC	22.000	13.500	12.000	10
MTN04	Metric T-Nuts - ANSI/ASME B5.1M-1985	PTC	28.000	17.250	15.000	12
MTN05	Metric T-Nuts - ANSI/ASME B5.1M-1985	PTC	34.000	20.500	21.000	16
MTN06	Metric T-Nuts - ANSI/ASME B5.1M-1985	PTC	43.000	26.500	27.000	20
MTN07	Metric T-Nuts - ANSI/ASME B5.1M-1985	PTC	53.000	33.000	34.000	24
MTN08	Metric T-Nuts - ANSI/ASME B5.1M-1985	PTC	64.000	39.250	42.000	30
MTN09	Metric T-Nuts - ANSI/ASME B5.1M-1985	PTC	75.000	46.750	48.000	36
MTN10	Metric T-Nuts - ANSI/ASME B5.1M-1985	PTC	85.000	52.500	54.000	42

Showing records 1 through 10 of 10   ● Metric ○ English   Go   Reset All

Figure 1.2(f) METRIC LIBRARY > METRIC TEE NUT BOLTS > T-NUTS

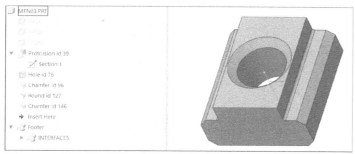

Figure 1.2(g) Drag and Drop the Link into the Graphics Window - Library Part

ALTERNATE MODEL- *If your system cannot access the Standard Parts Library; in the embedded web Browser > www.cad-resources.com > Enter*

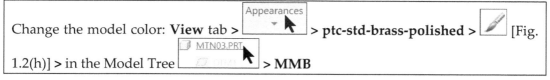

> click on the appropriate book cover icon *> place your mouse cursor on the part icon > drag and drop the link into the Graphics Window*

Change the model color: **View** tab > Appearances > **ptc-std-brass-polished** > [Fig. 1.2(h)] > in the Model Tree MTN03.PRT > **MMB**

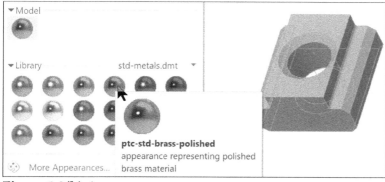

Figure 1.2(h) Appearances

Click: close the Browser [Fig. 1.2(i)] > ▶ to expand the Model Tree features and Footer [Fig. 1.5(j)] > **Ctrl+LMB** and select the hidden datum planes in the Model Tree > 👁 Show **Show > RMB** on Interfaces **INTFC001 > Information > Feature Information** [Fig. 1.2(k)] > ✕ close the Browser > **Ctrl+D**

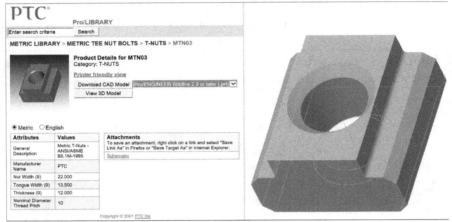

Figure 1.2(i) Close the Browser

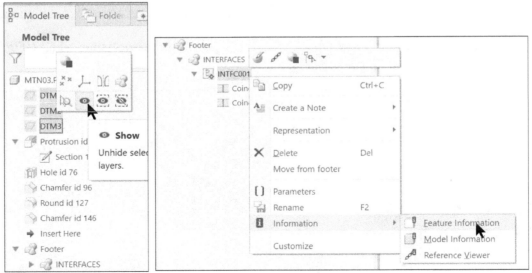

Figure 1.2(j) Expand Model Tree   **Figure 1.2(k)** INTFC001 Feature Information

Click: **File > Save As >** New Name-- *type* **metric-t-nut** [Fig. 1.2(l)] **> OK > File > Close > Ctrl+O** open an existing model **> metric-t-nut.prt** [Fig. 1.2(m)] **> Open >** [▶] to expand Model Tree items [Fig. 1.2(n)]

File name	MTN03.PRT
New file name	metric-t-nut
Type	Part (*.prt)

Figure 1.2(l) Save As metric-t-nut

Figure 1.2(m) File Open Dialog Box

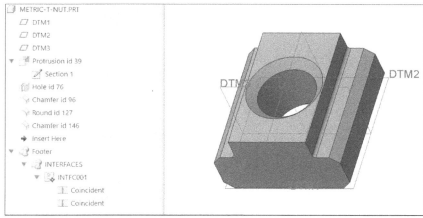

Figure 1.2(n) metric-t-nut.prt

File Functions

The **File** tab provides options for opening, creating, saving, renaming, backing up files, and printing. Before using any File tool, make sure you have set your working directory to the folder where you wish to save objects for the project. The Working Directory is a directory that you set up to contain Creo Parametric files. You can save a file using **Save** [Fig. 1.3(a)] or **Save As** from the File tab. The default folder to save or back up a file is determined as follows: The **My Documents** folder if you have not set

a Working Directory. The **Working Directory** you have set for your current session. The folder you last accessed to open, save, save a copy, or back up your file. Each time you save a file, it creates a new version; *nut.prt.1*, *nut.prt.2*, etc. Save fifty times and you have fifty more files; *nut.prt.50.* To purge old versions: **File > Manage File > Delete Old Versions > Enter**. The last (highest number- last saved) version will be the remaining file and the one that opens the next time you access the file.

Save As [Fig. 1.3(b)] is the exportation of Creo Parametric files to different formats, and to save files as images. Since the name already exists in session, you cannot save or Rename a file using the same name as the original file name, even if you save the file in a different directory. Creo Parametric forces you to enter a unique file name by displaying the message: *An object with that name exists in session. Choose a different name.*

Creo Parametric file names are restricted to a maximum of 31 characters and have no spaces. A file can be a part, assembly, or drawing. Each is considered an "object" or "model".

Figure 1.3(a) Save

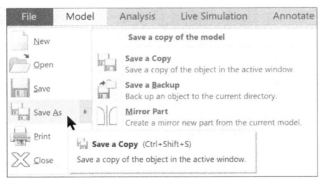

Figure 1.3(b) Save As

Help Center

Accessing the  Help function [Fig. 1.4(a)] is one of the best ways to learn any CAD software. Use the Help Center [Fig. 1.4(b)] as often as possible to understand the tool or command you are using at the time and to expand your knowledge of the capabilities provided by Creo Parametric. Use the **Help** menu to gain access to online information, release information, and customer service information.

Figure 1.4(a) Activate the Help Center

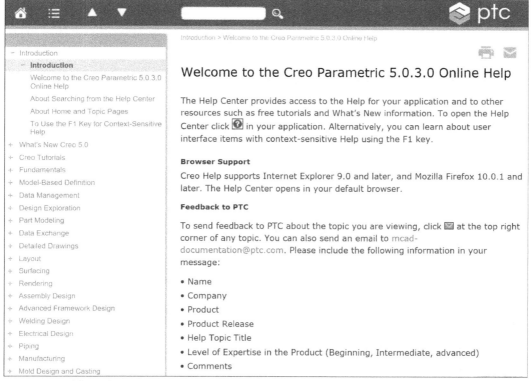

Figure 1.4(b) Online Help Center

For **Context sensitive help**, move your pointer over the icon, dialog box, or menu command for which you want help and press the **F1** key on the keyboard. Click:

Model tab > move the mouse pointer over  > press **F1** > **About the Extrude Feature** [Figs. 1.5(a-b)] > investigate other commands > **Close** PTC Help browser

ECAD
About the Extrude Tool

Feature Recognition Tool
About the Extrude Feature

Figure 1.5(a) Creo Parametric Help

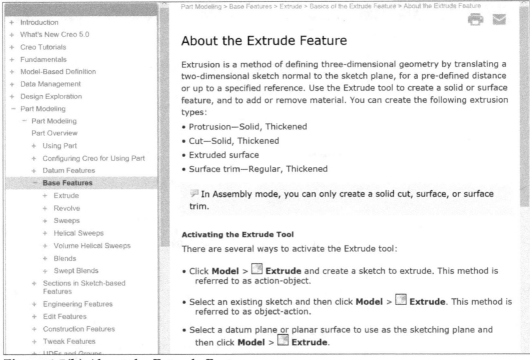

Figure 1.5(b) About the Extrude Feature

Command Locator

The command search tool enables you to find known commands faster and preview the location of the command on the user interface. You can preview the location only if the command is located on the Ribbon, Quick Access toolbar, Graphics toolbar, or File menu. You can also run a command by clicking the command in the search list. The tool displays commands not in the Ribbon under the **Commands not in the ribbon** category in the search list. The tool searches within the current mode.

Click: 🔍 **Command Search** in the upper top right-hand side of your **screen** [Fig. 1.6(a)] > [_____ 🔍] Command Locator opens > *type* **view** [view ✕] [Fig. 1.6(b)] > 📦 **Perspective View** [Fig. 1.6(c)] > select 📦 **Perspective View** *(toggle off)* [Fig. 1.6(d)] > 🔍 toggle shut

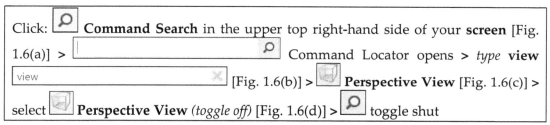

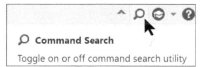

Figure 1.6(a) Command Search

Figure 1.6(b) View Commands

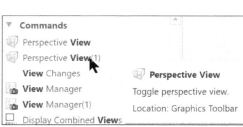

Figure 1.6(c) Perspective View

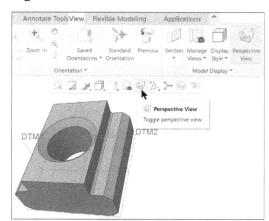

Figure 1.6(d) Perspective View

View and Display Functions

Using the **View** tab [Fig. 1.7(a)] you can adjust the model view, orient the view, hide and show entities, create and use advanced views, and set model display options.

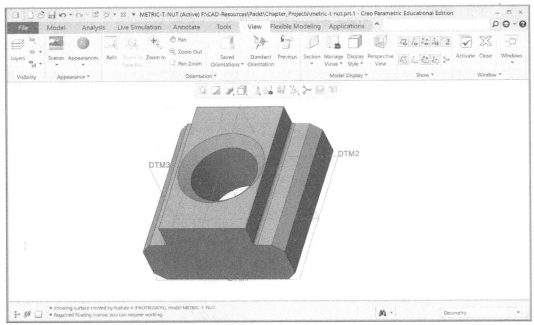

Figure 1.7(a) View tab

The following list includes some of the View operations you can perform:

- Orient the model view in the following ways, spin, pan, and zoom models and drawings, display the default orientation, revert to the previously displayed orientation, change the position or size of the model view, change the orientation, and create new orientations
- Toggle display style; shading with edges, shading with reflections, shading, hidden line, no hidden line, and wireframe.
- Highlight items in the graphics window when selected in the Model Tree
- Explode or un-explode an assembly view
- Repaint the graphics window
- Refit the model to the window after zooming in or out on the model
- Update drawings of model geometry
- Hide and unhide entities, and hide or show items during spin or animation

Click: **View** tab > [icons] *off* > [icons] *off* > | Display Style ▼ | >

| ☐ Wireframe | *(Ctrl+6)* > | Display Style ▼ | > | ☐ Hidden Line | *(Ctrl+5)* > | Display Style ▼ | > | ☐ No Hidden |

(Ctrl+4) > | Display Style ▼ | > | ☐ Shading | *(Ctrl+3)* > | Display Style ▼ | > | ☐ Shading With Reflections | *(Ctrl+1)*

> | Display Style ▼ | > | ☐ Shading With Edges | *(Ctrl+2)* [Fig. 1.7(b)]

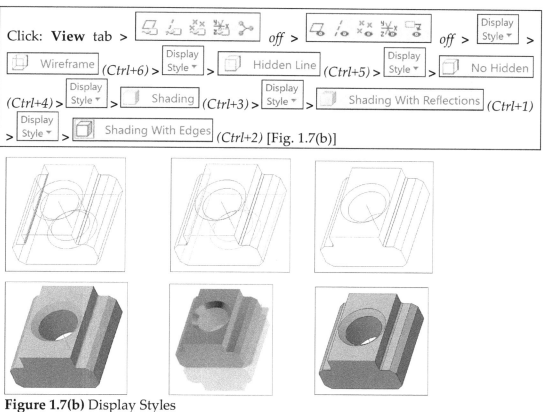

Figure 1.7(b) Display Styles

Click: [icons] [icons] *on* > [🔍] **Refit** > press and hold the

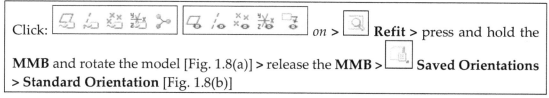

MMB and rotate the model [Fig. 1.8(a)] > release the **MMB** > [icon] **Saved Orientations** > **Standard Orientation** [Fig. 1.8(b)]

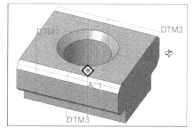

Figure 1.8(a) Rotated View

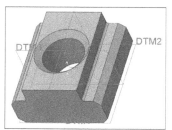

Figure 1.8(b) Standard Orientation

View Tools

Creo Parametric provides various view tools, including:

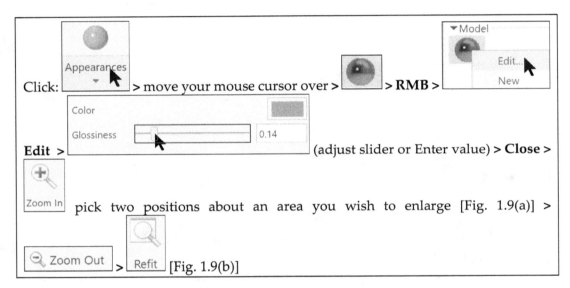 **Refit** Adjust the zoom level to fully display the object on the screen, 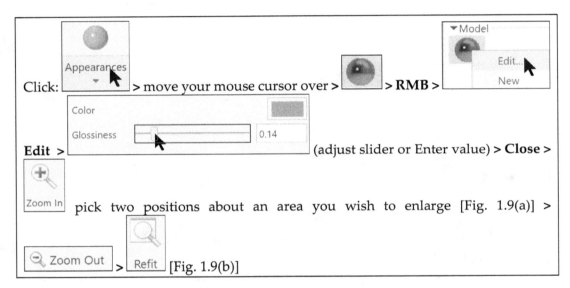 **Zoom In** Zoom in on the model, 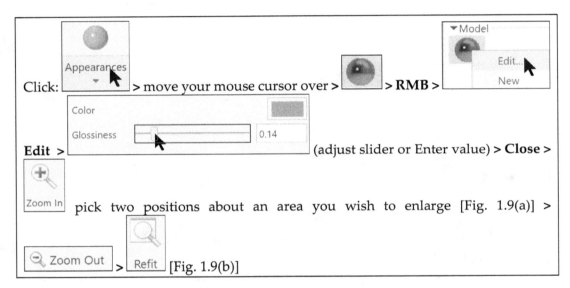 **Zoom Out** Zoom out from the model, 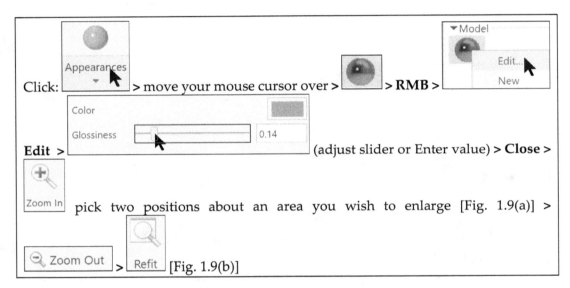 **Reorient** Configure model orientation preferences, **View Normal**, **Perspective.**

Click: > move your mouse cursor over > > **RMB** >

Edit > (adjust slider or Enter value) > **Close** >

 pick two positions about an area you wish to enlarge [Fig. 1.9(a)] >

 > [Fig. 1.9(b)]

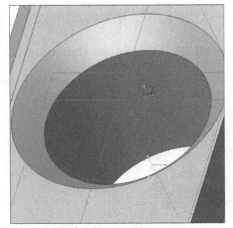

Figure 1.9(a) Zoom In

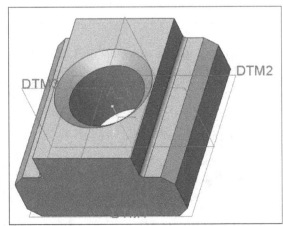

Figure 1.9(b) Refit

Using Mouse Buttons to Manipulate the Model

You can also dynamically reorient the model using the **MMB** by itself (**Spin**) or in conjunction with the **Shift** key (**Pan**) or **Ctrl** key (**Zoom, Turn**).

Click: [icons] *off* > hold down **Ctrl** key and **MMB** in the Graphics Window near the model and move the cursor up (zoom out) [Fig. 1.10(a)] > release the **Ctrl** key and **MMB** > hold down **Shift** key and **MMB** in the Graphics Window near the model and move the cursor about the screen (pan) [Fig. 1.10(b)] > release the **Shift** key and **MMB** > hold down **MMB** in the Graphics Window near the model and move the cursor around (spin) [Figs. 1.10(c-d)] > release the **MMB** > **Ctrl+D** > [icons] [icons] *on*

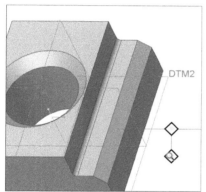

Figure 1.10(a) Zoom

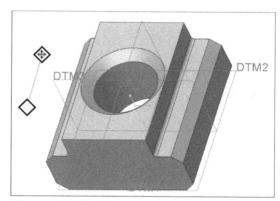

Figure 1.10(b) Pan

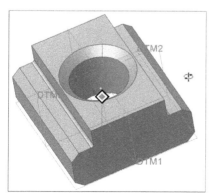

Figure 1.10(c) Spin

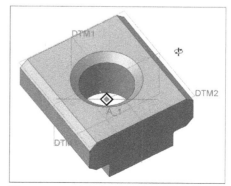

Figure 1.10(d) Spin Again

System Display Settings

A number of changes can be made to the default colors by customizing them including: define, save, and open color schemes, customize colors used in the user interface, redefine basic colors used in models, assign colors to be used by an entity, store a color scheme so you can reuse it, and open a previously used color scheme.

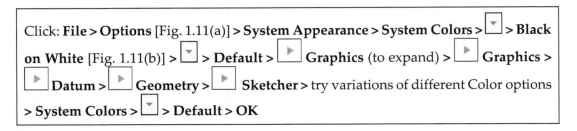

Click: **File > Options** [Fig. 1.11(a)] > **System Appearance > System Colors >** ⬜ > **Black on White** [Fig. 1.11(b)] > ⬜ > **Default >** ⬜ **Graphics** (to expand) > ⬜ **Graphics >** ⬜ **Datum >** ⬜ **Geometry >** ⬜ **Sketcher >** try variations of different Color options > **System Colors >** ⬜ > **Default > OK**

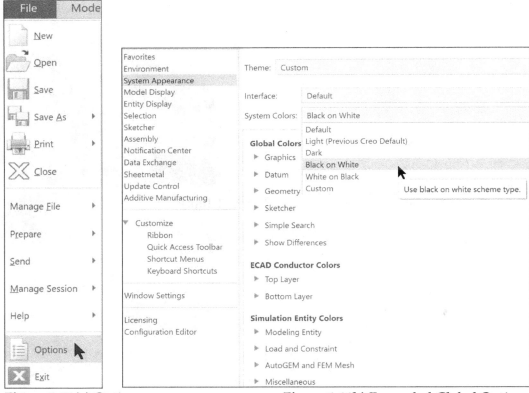

Figure 1.11(a) Options   **Figure 1.11b)** Expanded Global Options

Information Tools

At any time during the design process you can request model, feature, or other information. Picking on a feature in the graphics window or Model Tree and then **RMB > Information** will provide information about that feature in the Browser. Both feature and model information can be obtained using this method. A variety of information can also be extracted using the **Tools** tab in the Ribbon.

Click: **Model** tab > in the Model Tree, pick once on the chamfer > **RMB > Information** > **Feature Information** [Figs. 1.12(a-b)] > ☒ upper right corner of Browser or ⊚ lower left of screen to close the Browser > **File > Save > OK > File > Manage File > Delete Old Versions > Yes > Ctrl+D**

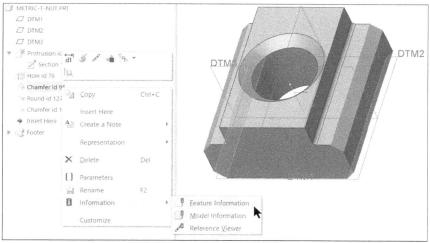

Figure 1.12(a) Information > Feature Information from the Model Tree

Figure 1.12(b) Feature Information: Chamfer, Displayed in the Browser

51

In the Model Tree, select: **METRIC-NUT.PRT** > **RMB** > **Information** > **Model Information** [Figs. 1.12(c-d)] > 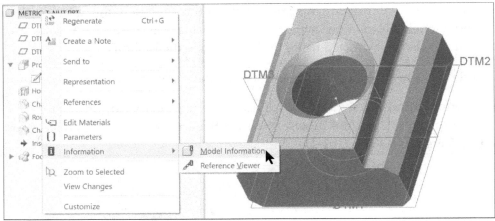 close Browser

Figure 1.12(c) Model Information

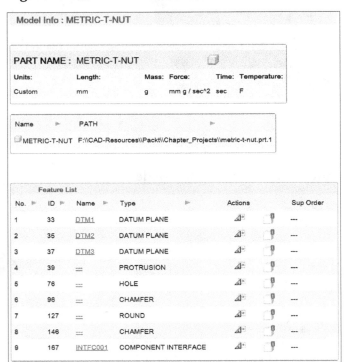

Figure 1.12(d) Information from the Model

The Model Tree

The **Model Tree** is a tabbed feature on the Creo Parametric Navigator that displays a list of every feature or part in the current part, assembly, or drawing.

The model structure is displayed in hierarchical (tree) format with the root object (the current part or assembly) at the top of its tree and the subordinate objects (parts or features) below. If you have multiple Creo Parametric windows open, the Model Tree contents reflect the file in the current active window. The Model Tree lists the related feature and part level items in a current object and does not list the entities that comprise the features. Model Tree items contain an icon that reflects its object type, for example, hidden, assembly, part, feature, or datum plane (also a feature). The icon can also show the display status for a feature, part, or assembly.

Selection in the Model Tree is object-action oriented; you select objects in the Model Tree without first specifying what you intend to do with them. You can select components, parts, or features using the Model Tree. You cannot select the individual geometry that makes up a feature (entities). To select an entity, you must select it in the graphics window. With the **Settings** tab 🔲 you can control what is displayed in the Model Tree. You can add informational columns to the Model Tree window, such as **Tree Columns** containing parameters and values, assigned layers, or feature name.

Click: Settings **Settings >** Tree Filters... Control display of model tree items by type and status > Display (toggle *on* all Display options and Feature Types) [Fig. 1.13(a)] > **Apply > OK**

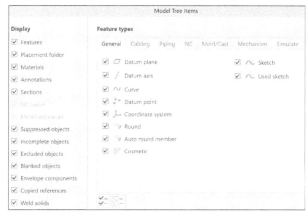

Figure 1.13(a) Model Tree Items

Click: 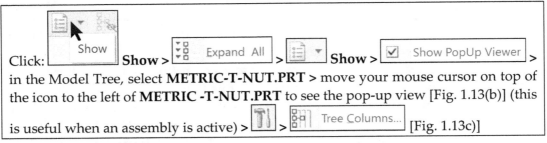 **Show** > Expand All > **Show** > ☑ Show PopUp Viewer >
in the Model Tree, select **METRIC-T-NUT.PRT** > move your mouse cursor on top of
the icon to the left of **METRIC -T-NUT.PRT** to see the pop-up view [Fig. 1.13(b)] (this
is useful when an assembly is active) > [TI] > Tree Columns... [Fig. 1.13c)]

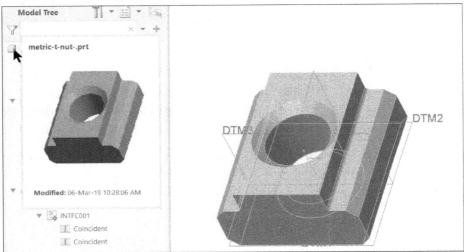

Figure 1.13(b) Pop-up Viewer

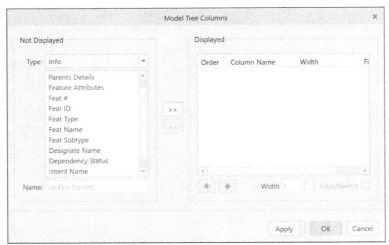

Figure 1.13(c) Model Tree Columns Dialog Box

Click: **Feat #** > [>>] (or double-click) > **Feat ID** > [>>] (or double-click) > **Feat Type** > **Enter** > **Feat Name** > **Apply** > **OK** [Fig. 1.13(d)] > press **LMB** and drag ⊞ the Model

	Feat #	
☐ METRIC-T-NUT.PRT		⊣⊪
▱ DTM1	1	

Tree Panel to see all the Columns [above] [Fig. 1.13(e)] > press **LMB** and pull the panel back until only the Model Tree and **Feat** # is displayed

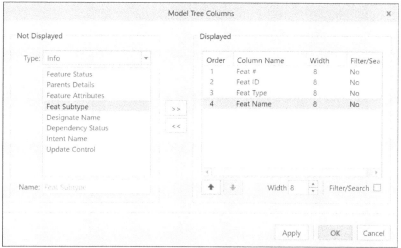

Model Tree Columns ✕

Not Displayed

Type: Info ▼

Feature Status
Parents Details
Feature Attributes
Feat Subtype
Designate Name
Dependency Status
Intent Name
Update Control

>>
<<

Displayed

Order	Column Name	Width	Filter/Sea
1	Feat #	8	No
2	Feat ID	8	No
3	Feat Type	8	No
4	Feat Name	8	No

Name: Feat Subtype

↑ ↓ Width 8 ▲▼ Filter/Search ☐

Apply   OK   Cancel

Figure 1.13(d) Adding Displayed Columns

	Feat #	Feat ID	Feat Type	Feat Name
☐ METRIC-T-NUT.PRT				
▱ DTM1	1	33	Datum Plane	DTM1
▱ DTM2	2	35	Datum Plane	DTM2
▱ DTM3	3	37	Datum Plane	DTM3
▼ Protrusion id 39	4	39	Protrusion	
Section 1	<None>			
Hole id 76	5	76	Hole	
Chamfer id 96	6	96	Chamfer	
Round id 127	7	127	Round	
Chamfer id 146	8	146	Chamfer	
→ Insert Here				
▼ Footer	<None>			
▼ INTERFACES	<None>			
▼ INTFC001	9	167	Component Inte	INTFC001
Coinc				
Coinc				

Figure 1.13(e) Model Tree and Model Tree Columns

Customizing the User Interface (UI)

You can customize the Creo Parametric user interface, according to your needs or the needs of your group or company, to include the following:

- Create keyboard macros (*mapkeys*), and add them to the menus and toolbars
- Add or remove existing toolbars
- Move or remove commands from the menus or toolbars
- Add options to the Menu Manager
- Customize popup menus
- Blank (make unavailable) options in the Menu Manager
- Set default command choices for Menu Manager menus

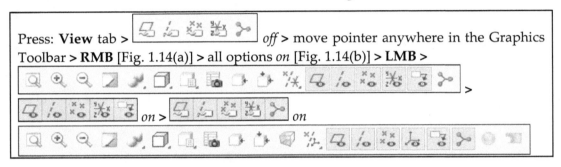

Press: **View** tab > [icons] *off* > move pointer anywhere in the Graphics Toolbar > **RMB** [Fig. 1.14(a)] > all options *on* [Fig. 1.14(b)] > **LMB** >

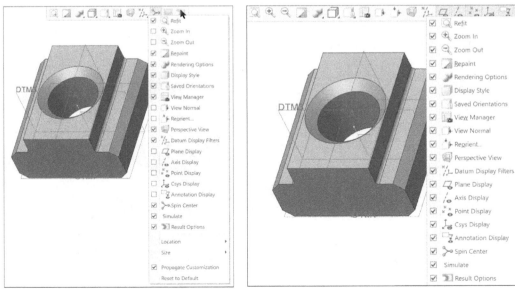

Figure 1.14(a) Customize Graphics Toolbar   Figure 1.14(b) All Options On

To change the location of the Graphics Toolbar, click: **RMB** within the Graphics Toolbar > **Location** [Fig. 1.14(c)] > **Size** [Fig. 1.14(d)] > **Large** [Fig. 1.14(e)] > **RMB** within the Graphics Toolbar > **Reset to Default** [Fig. 1.14(f)]

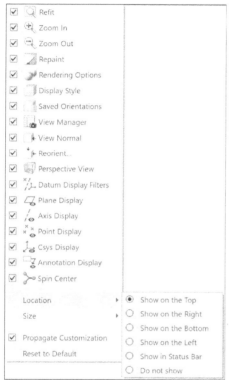

Figure 1.14(c) Graphics Toolbar Location

Figure 1.14(d) Graphics Toolbar Size

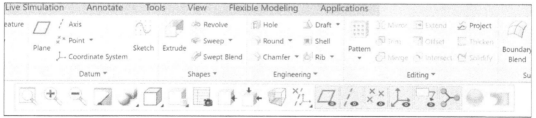

Figure 1.14(e) Graphics Toolbar Size Large

Figure 1.14(f) Reset to Default

Place your pointer inside the active **View** tab in the Ribbon > **RMB** [Fig. 1.15(a)] > 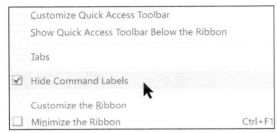 check **Hide Command Labels** > > place your pointer anywhere inside the Ribbon > **RMB** > check **Minimize the Ribbon** [Fig. 1.15(b)] > place your pointer inside the Ribbon tabs > **RMB** > uncheck **Minimize the Ribbon** > place your pointer inside the **View** tab > **RMB** > uncheck **Hide Command Labels** > place your pointer inside the Ribbon tabs > **RMB** > **Tabs** [Fig. 1.15(c)] > **LMB**

Figure 1.15(a) Customize the Ribbon via the View tab

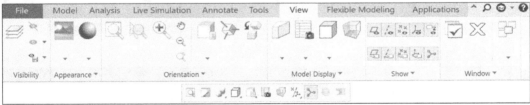

Figure 1.15(b) Minimized Ribbon

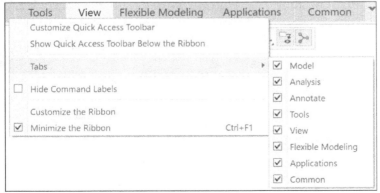

Figure 1.15(c) All Ribbon Tabs On

Click: **Model** tab > **Datum** Group *(Groups that have a* ⊡ *indicate that there are overflow commands for that Group- more commands which are not typically placed on the Ribbon)* > **RMB** > **Groups** [Fig. 1.16(a)] > **Customize the Ribbon** > move the Creo Parametric Options dialog box down if needed > **Datum** Group [Fig. 1.16(b)] > pick on **Curve** > **Curve through Points** > drag and drop [Fig. 1.16(c)] into the Ribbon [Fig. 1.16(d)] > **OK** to close the Creo Parametric Options dialog box

(After you are familiar with Creo Parametric's default UI, you can customize the interface based on your or your companies' productivity requirements Do not make changes now since the text and the PTC Help assume the default of commands and colors, etc.)

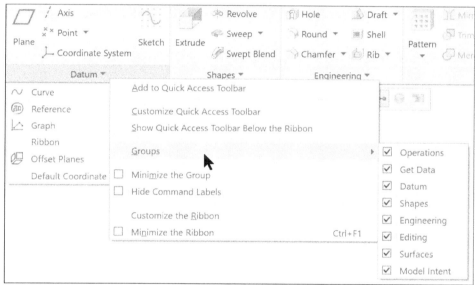

Figure 1.16(a) Groups

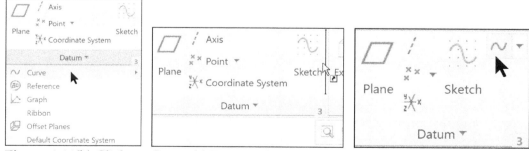

Figure 1.16(b) Click on Curve **(c)** Drag and Drop **(d)** Curve

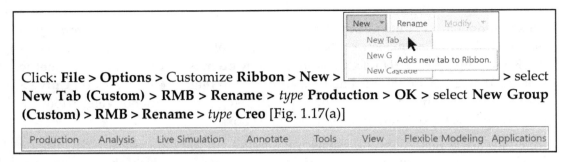

Click: **File > Options >** Customize **Ribbon > New >** 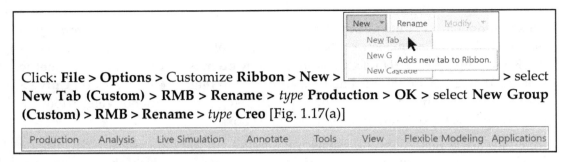 **> select New Tab (Custom) > RMB > Rename >** *type* **Production > OK >** select **New Group (Custom) > RMB > Rename >** *type* **Creo** [Fig. 1.17(a)]

| Production | Analysis | Live Simulation | Annotate | Tools | View | Flexible Modeling | Applications |

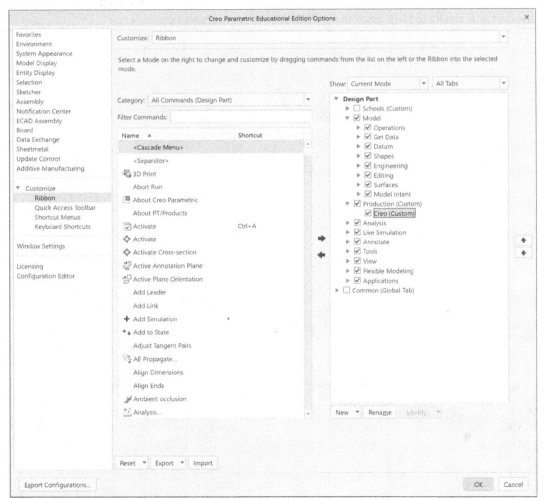

Figure 1.17(a) Customize Ribbon

Click: **Edit Definition** > ⬛ [Fig. 1.17(b)] > Category: **All Commands (Design Part)**
[Fig. 1.17(c)] > **Delete Old Versions** > ⬛ [Fig. 1.17(d)] > **OK** > **Production** tab >
Delete Old Versions [Fig. 1.17(e)] > **Yes** [Fig. 1.17(f)] > **Model** tab
(Customize your Production tab after you see what commands you would like to access faster.)

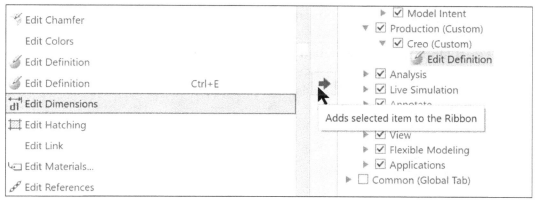

Figure 1.17(b) Edit Definition > Add

Figure 1.17(c) Category: **Figure 1.17(d)** Command **Figure 1.17(e)** Delete Old Versions

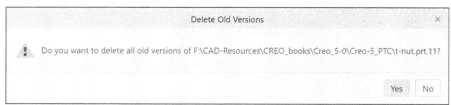

Figure 1.17(f) Delete Old Versions Confirmation

Mapkeys

A **Mapkey** is a macro that maps frequently used command sequences to certain keyboard keys or sets of keys. Mapkeys are saved in the configuration file, and are identified with the option *mapkey*, followed by the identifier and then the macro. You can define a unique key or combination of keys which, when pressed, executes the mapkey macro. You can create a mapkey for virtually any task you perform frequently. By adding mapkeys to your Ribbon or Toolbars, you can run mapkeys with a single mouse click or menu command and therefore streamline your workflow.

Click: **File > Options > Environment > Mapkeys Settings** [Fig. 1.18(a)] **> New** from the Mapkeys dialog box [Fig. 1.18(b)] (Record Mapkey dialog box opens) > Key Sequence, *type* **$F3** > Name, *type* **Display** > Description, *type* **Change display** [Fig. 1.18(c)] **> Record**

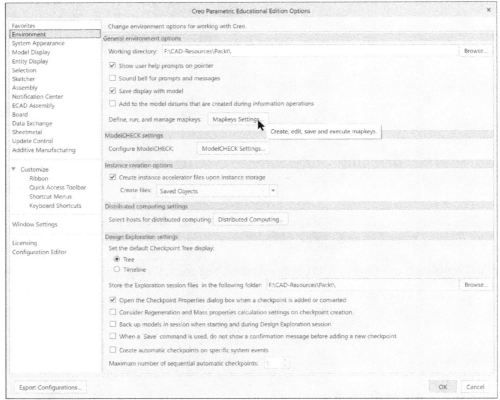

Figure 1.18(a) Option Dialog Box > Environment > Mapkeys Settings

Click: **File > Options > Model Display > Isometric > Apply > OK > No > View** tab >  toggle *off* > **Ctrl+D > Stop** (from Record Mapkey dialog box) > **OK > Save** (from Mapkeys dialog box) > File name: *type* **Creo_textbook.pro > OK > Close** (from Mapkeys dialog box) > press **F3 > Ctrl+D > Ctrl+S** [Fig. 1.18(d)]

Figure 1.18(b) Mapkeys

Figure 1.18(c) Record Mapkey

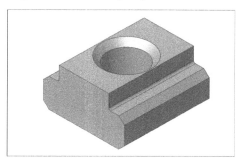

Figure 1.18(d) New Display

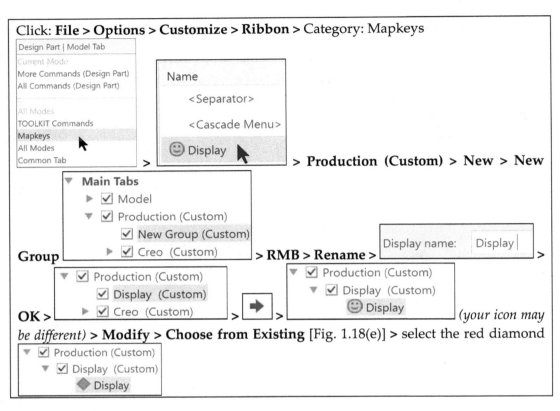

Click: **File > Options > Customize > Ribbon >** Category: Mapkeys

> **Production (Custom) > New > New**

Group **> RMB > Rename >**

OK > *(your icon may be different) >* **Modify > Choose from Existing** [Fig. 1.18(e)] > select the red diamond

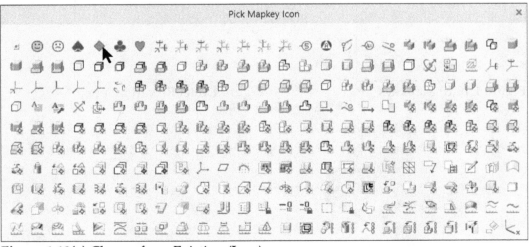

Figure 1.18(e) Choose from Existing (Icon)

Click: **Modify > Edit Button Image** [Fig. 1.18(f)] > click on a color block and edit the

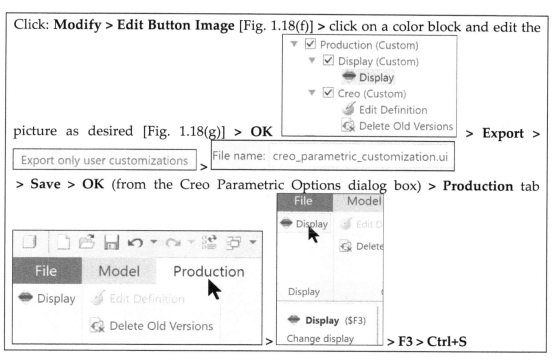

picture as desired [Fig. 1.18(g)] > **OK** > **Export >**

> **Save > OK** (from the Creo Parametric Options dialog box) > **Production** tab

> **F3 > Ctrl+S**

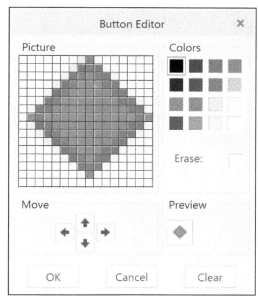

Figure 1.18(f) Button Editor

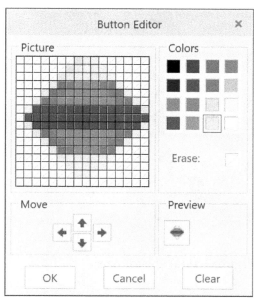

Figure 1.18(g) Edit the Picture

Customizing the Mini Toolbar will be next. Select the Protrusion in the Model Tree or in the Graphics Window **> RMB > Customize > All Commands (Design Part) > Mapkeys** [Fig. 1.19(a)] **>** Display drag and drop into Mini Toolbar [Fig. 1.19(b)]

> More Commands (Design Part) > Standard Orientation drag and drop into Mini Toolbar **OK >** click on any feature in the Model Tree **> RMB**

> RMB > **> Save** [Fig. 1.20]]

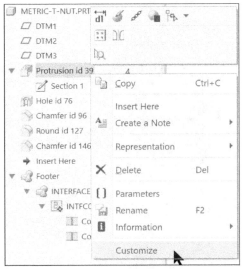

Figure 1.19(a) Customize

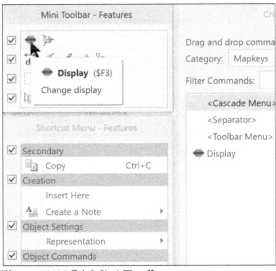

Figure 1.19(b) Mini Toolbar

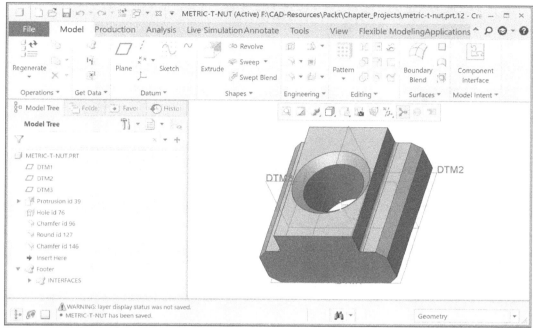

Figure 1.20 Completed Project

Quiz

1. What is the Standard Parts catalog?
2. Name three items that you cane initiate from the File drop down menu.
3. If you save a part file six times how many parts are now in the Working Directory?
4. What happens when you Delete Old Versions?
5. What are three things that can be done directly from the Model Tree?
6. Where is the Command Locator on the screen?
7. Name three keyboard shortcuts and what they do.
8. Name two ways of getting Information about a feature.
9. What is a Mapkey?

This completes Chapter 1.

CHAPTER 2: Creating components

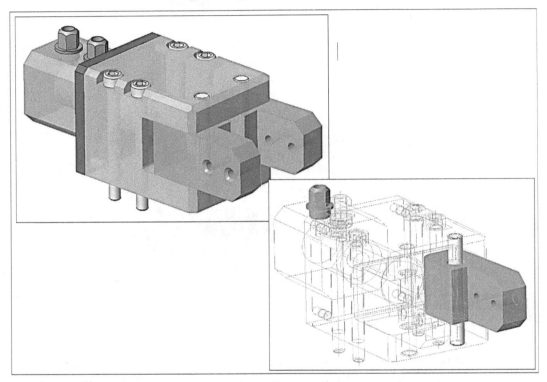

The purpose of this Chapter is to introduce you to basic Feature and Engineering Tools. You will model components using default selections. Modeling simple components will introduce you to the power and capability of Creo Parametric. The design of a part starts with the creation of base features and a sketched solid protrusion. Other solid and cut extrusions are then added in sequence as required by the design. Holes, rounds, chamfers, and other pick and place features are added as the design progresses.

Objectives
1. Model components
2. Sample Feature Tools
3. Utilize a variety of Engineering Tools: Hole, Shell, Round, and Chamfer
4. Sketch simple sections
5. Sketch in 2D

Part Design

Before you begin any part, you must plan the design. The **design intent** will depend on several things that are out of your control and many that you can establish. Asking yourself a few questions will clear up the design intent you will follow: Is the part a component of an assembly? If so, what surfaces or features are used to connect one part to another? Will geometric tolerancing be used on the part and assembly? What units are being used in the design, SI or decimal inch? What is the part's material? What is the primary part feature? How should I model the part, and what features are best used for the primary protrusion (the first solid mass)? On what datum plane should I sketch to model the first protrusion?

In many cases, the part will be the first component of this interconnected process. The *part* function in Creo Parametric is used to design components. During part design, you can accomplish the following:

- Create the base feature
- Define and redefine construction features to the base feature
- Modify the dimensional values of part features
- Embed design intent into the model using tolerance specifications and dimensioning schemes
- Create pictorial and shaded views of the component
- Create part families (Family Tables)
- Perform mass properties analysis and clearance checks
- List part, feature, layer, and specific required model information
- Measure and calculate model features

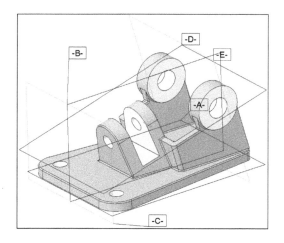 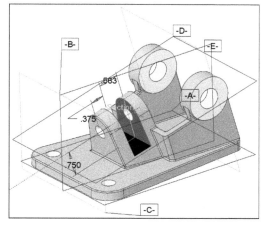

Establishing Features

The design of any part requires that the part be *confined, restricted, constrained,* and *referenced.* In parametric design, the easiest method to establish and control the geometry of your part design is to use datum planes. Creo Parametric automatically creates the three **primary datum planes**. The default datum planes (**RIGHT**, **TOP**, and **FRONT**) constrain your design in all three directions.

      Datum planes are infinite planes located in 3D model mode and are associated with the object that was active at the time of their creation. To select a datum plane, you can pick on its name or anywhere on the perimeter edge.

      Datum planes are *parametric*--geometrically associated with the part. Parametric datum planes are associated with and dependent on the edges, surfaces, vertices, and axes of a part. Datum planes are used to create a reference on a part that does not already exist. For example, you can sketch or place features on a datum plane when there is no appropriate planar surface. You can also dimension to a datum plane as though it were an edge.

      Three **default datum planes** and a **default coordinate system** are created when a new part is started using the default template. Note that in the **Model Tree** window, they are the first four features of the part, which means that they will be the *parents* of the features that follow.

      Note that the Z axis is pointing up. If your system has it pointing outwards-towards you, then that is OK. If you do not have the Options file for Templates that use the Z axis up version, it can be downloaded from cad-resources.com.

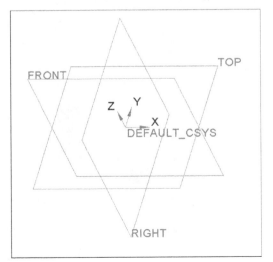
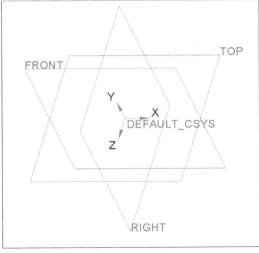

Datum Features

Datum features are planes, axes, and points you use to place geometric features on the active part. Datums other than defaults can be created at any time during the design process. As we have discussed, there are three (primary) types of datum features: **datum planes**, **datum axes**, and **datum points** (there are also *datum curves* and *datum coordinate systems*). You can display all types of datum features, but they do not define the surfaces or edges of the part or add to its mass properties.

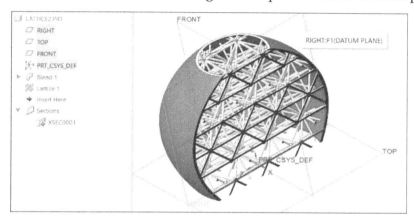

Specifying constraints that locate it with respect to existing geometry creates a datum. For example, a datum plane might be made to pass through the axis of a hole and parallel to a planar surface. Chosen constraints must locate the datum plane relative to the model without ambiguity. You can also use and create datums in assembly mode. Besides datum planes, datum axes and datum points can be created to assist in the design process. You can also automatically create datum axes through cylindrical features such as holes and solid round features by setting this as a default in your Creo Parametric configuration file.

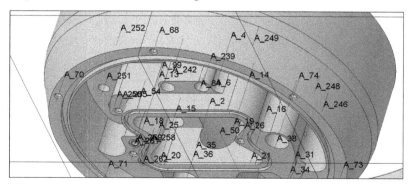

71

Chapter 2 STEPS

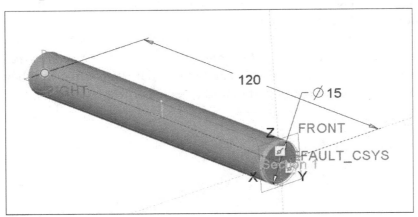

Figure 2.1 Pin

Creating the Pin

In Chapter 2 you will model two simple parts that will be used in the assembly. The Pin (dowel) [Fig. 2.1] component will be modeled first.

Open **Creo Parametric** on your computer. Click: **Select Working Directory**

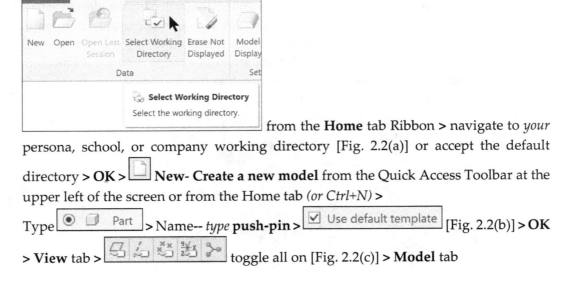

from the **Home** tab Ribbon > navigate to *your* persona, school, or company working directory [Fig. 2.2(a)] or accept the default directory > **OK** > ☐ **New- Create a new model** from the Quick Access Toolbar at the upper left of the screen or from the Home tab *(or Ctrl+N)* >

Type ◉ ☐ Part > Name-- *type* **push-pin** > ☑ Use default template [Fig. 2.2(b)] > **OK**

> **View** tab > ⬡⬡⬡⬡⬢ toggle all on [Fig. 2.2(c)] > **Model** tab

Figure 2.2(a) Select Working Directory Dialog Box (*your directory will be different*)

New

Type	Sub-type
○ Layout	● Solid
○ Sketch	○ Sheetmetal
● Part	○ Bulk
○ Assembly	
○ Manufacturing	
○ Drawing	
○ Format	
○ Notebook	

File name: push-pin

Common name:

☑ Use default template

OK   Cancel

Figure 2.2(b) New Dialog Box

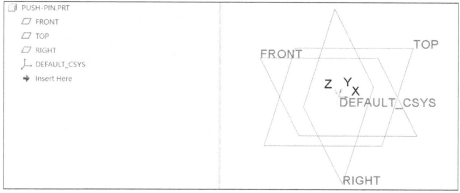

Figure 2.2(c) Default datum planes and default coordinate system

From keyboard: **Ctrl+S** (saves the active object) **> OK >**  **Extrude** from Model tab Ribbon **> Placement** tab in the Dashboard [Fig. 2.3(a)] **> Define...** Define an Internal Sketch [Fig. 2.3(b)]

Figure 2.3(a) Extrude Placement Tab

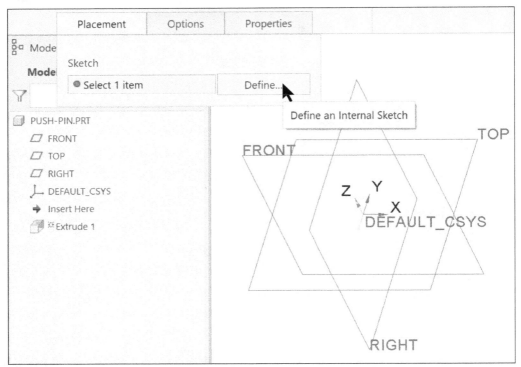

Figure 2.3(b) Placement Panel/Tab, Define an Internal Sketch

Select the **FRONT** datum plane from the Graphics Window (or Model Tree) [Fig. 2.3(c)]. The FRONT datum plane is the Sketch Plane and the RIGHT datum plane is automatically selected as the Sketch Orientation Reference with an Orientation of Right [Fig. 2.3(d)].

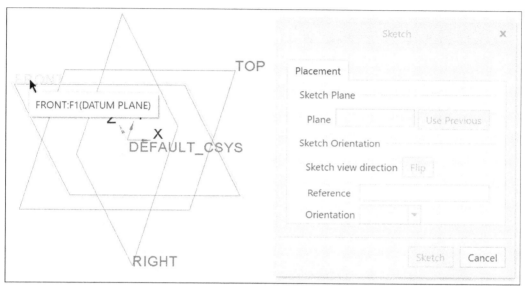

Figure 2.3(c) Select the FRONT Datum Plane

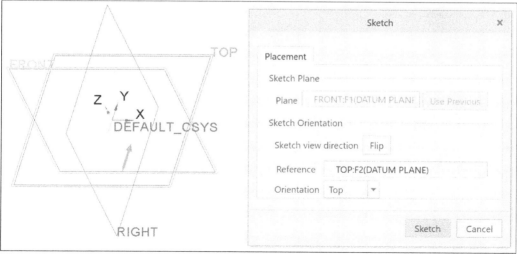

Figure 2.3(d) Sketch Dialog Box

Click: **Sketch** to close the Sketch dialog box [Fig. 2.3(e)] > [icon] **Center and Point- Create a circle by picking the center and a point on the circle** from the Sketch tab in the Ribbon [Fig. 2.3(f)]

Figure 2.3(e) Activate the Sketcher

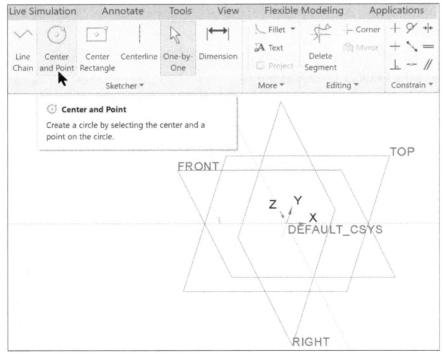

Figure 2.3(f) Select the Circle Tool

Pick the origin for the circle's center [Fig. 2.3(g)] > drag the pointer away from the center point and pick a point on the circle's edge [Fig. 2.3(h)] > move the pointer off the circle's edge > **MMB** (**M**iddle **M**ouse **B**utton) [Figs. 2.3(i-j)] > double-click on the dimension > *type* **15** > **Enter** [Figs. 2.3(k-l)] > **Ctrl+D** (or roll **MMB** to zoom)

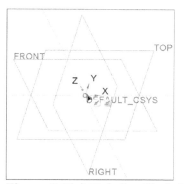

Figure 2.3(g) Pick the Circle's Center

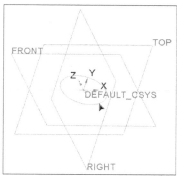

Figure 2.3(h) Pick a Point on the Circle's Edge

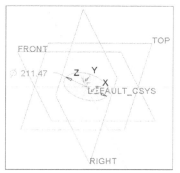

Figure 2.3(i) Circle and Dimension

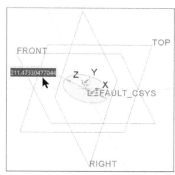

Figure 2.3(j) Double-click on the Dimension

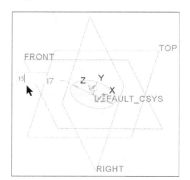

Figure 2.3(k) Type 15

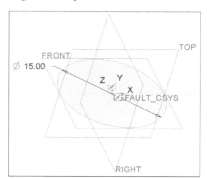

Figure 2.3(l) Completed Sketch

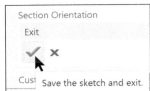

Click: **RMB (Right Mouse Button)** > [Fig. 2.3(m)] > click in the depth value field [Fig. 2.3(n)] > *type* **120** [Fig. 2.3(o)] > **Enter** > checkmark in the Dashboard [Fig. 2.3(p)] *or MMB*

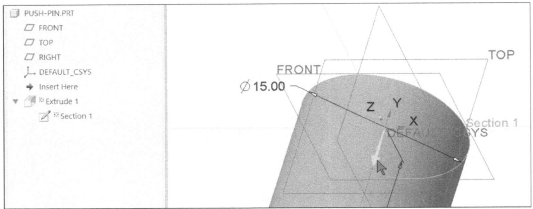

Figure 2.3(m) Dynamic Preview of Geometry

Figure 2.3(n) Extrude Dashboard Depth Value Field

Figure 2.3(o) New Depth Value

Figure 2.3(p) Complete the Extrusion

78

Click: **Refit** from the Graphics Toolbar > **Edge Chamfer** [Fig. 2.3(q)] > press and hold the **Ctrl key** and select *both* ends of the extrusion [Figs. 2.3(r-t)] > double-click on the default size and change to **1mm** [Figs. 2.3(u-v)] > **Enter** > **Ctrl+S**

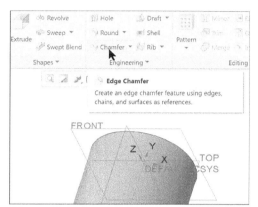

Figure 2.3(q) Edge Chamfer

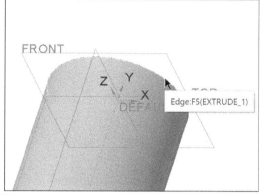

Figure 2.3(r) Select edge

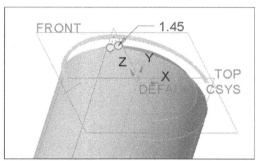

Figure 2.3(s) Default Chamfer

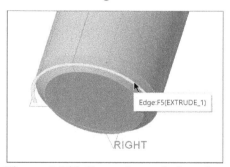

Figure 2.3(t) Opposite end chamfer

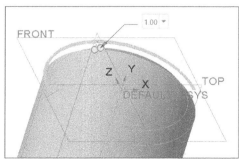

Figure 2.3(u) Modify

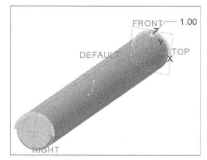

Figure 2.3(v) Chamfer

To complete the component, change its name and units. Click: **File > Prepare > Model Properties >** Units **change > millimeter Newton Second (mmNs) >** [→ Set...] [Fig. 2.4(a)] **> Interpret** [Fig. 2.4(b)] **> OK > Close** [Fig. 2.4(c)] **> Close > File > Prepare > File > Manage File > Rename** [Fig. 2.4(d)] **>** type **PIN** [Fig. 2.4(e)] **> OK > Tools** tab **> Model Information**[Fig. 2.4(f)] **> Save > File > Close** *[(or* [⊠] *from the Quick Access Toolbar)*

Figure 2.4(a) Set

Figure 2.3(b) Interpret

Figure 2.3(c) Millimeter units

Figure 2.4(d) Rename

Figure 2.4(e) Rename

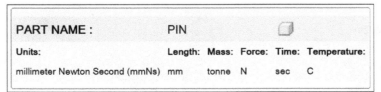

PART NAME :	PIN				
Units:	**Length:**	**Mass:**	**Force:**	**Time:**	**Temperature:**
millimeter Newton Second (mmNs)	mm	tonne	N	sec	C

Figure 2.4(f) Model Information showing new name and metric units

You have completed your first Creo Parametric component.

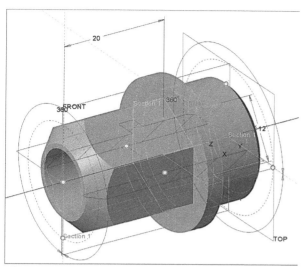

Figure 2.5 Connector

Creating the Connector

The second part (Fig. 2.5) will include new commands along with ones used previously in the Pin. Revolved features will be used in this component design including revolve extrude and the hole tool. Throughout the book each Chapter has repeated and new commands to reinforce what you have already learned and add new capabilities to increase your experience with the software. Since there are normally 3 to 4 ways of doing almost every command, the book will introduce alternative ways of accomplishing each activity. As an example, to end a command such as Extrude, you can click the ***check mark*** on the Dashboard, press ***Enter*** on the keyboard, or click the ***MMB*** *(Middle Mouse Button)*.

Click: from the Home tab Ribbon **>** select *your* working directory or accept the default directory [Fig. 2.6(a)] **> OK**

(Do not change directories if you have one assigned as a default by your school or company.) If you create subdirectories, then make sure all files (parts, drawings, assemblies) associated in that Chapter or project are in the same folder.

Click: 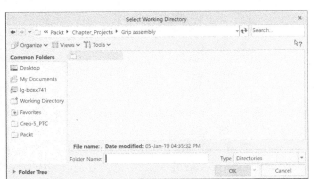 **Create a new model** > Type ⊙ ⊡ Part > Sub-type **Solid** [Fig. 2.6(b)] > Name-- *type* **connector** > ☑ Use default template > click the **MMB** (Middle Mouse Button) *(or press Enter or pick OK)* [Fig. 2.6(c)] > **File** tab > **Prepare** > **Model Properties** > Units **change** > **millimeter Newton Second (mmNs)** > ⇥ Set... > **OK** > **Close** > **Close** > slowly click twice on the coordinate system in the model tree ⌐ DEFAULT_CSYS **I** > *type* **connector** *(Creo will change to uppercase)* > **Ctrl+S** > **OK**

(Creo Parametric does NOT automatically save for you. Save after creating each feature.)

Figure 2.6(a) Working Directory   **Figure 2.6(b)** Type New, Sub-type Solid

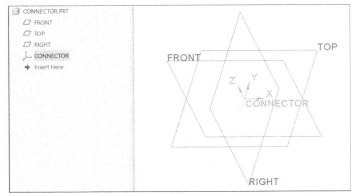

Figure 2.6(c) Note that the Z axis is pointing up. *If your system has it pointing outwards-towards you, then that is OK. Or you can download Template files from cad-resources.com. The orientation of the default coordinate will not influence any the book's instructions.*

Click: **File** tab **> Options** [Fig. 2.6(d)] **> Sketcher >** scroll down if necessary **>**

☑ Show the grid

☑ Snap to grid [Fig. 2.6(e)] **> OK > No**

(Will keep these settings for just this session. Upon starting a new Creo session the settings will revert to the default settings and values.)

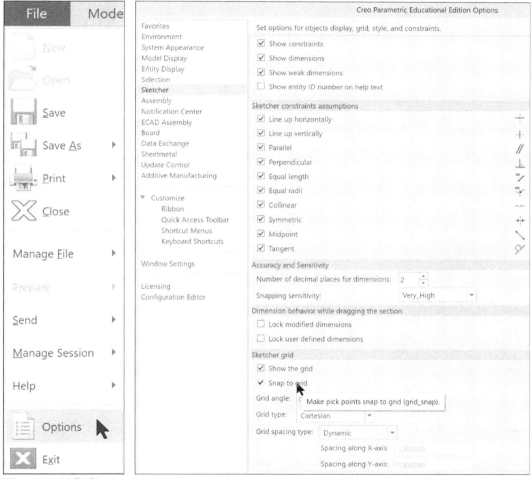

Figure 2.6(d) Options   **Figure 2.6(e)** Sketcher Options

Click: **Model** tab > pick datum **RIGHT** to sketch on > **Revolve** > **Sketch View** > press: **RMB** > **Create Axis of Revolution** [Fig. 2.7(a)] > create horizontal axial centerline by picking twice along the edge of the FRONT datum [Fig. 2.7(b)] > **MMB** [Fig. 2.7(c)]

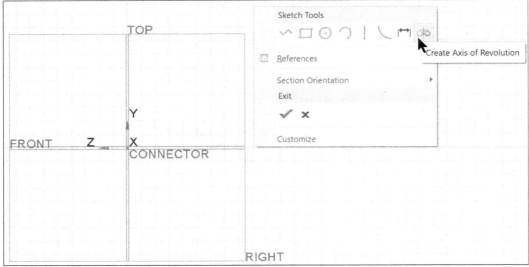

Figure 2.7(a) Create Axis of Revolution

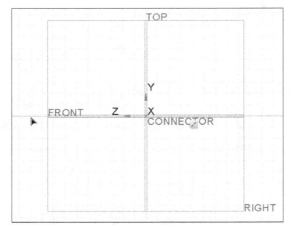

Figure 2.7(b) Select two points

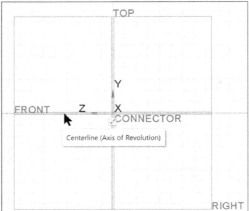

Figure 2.7(c) Axis of Revolution

Press **RMB >** 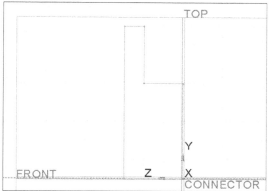 **>** starting at the coordinate system's origin sketch *(vertical line first)* the outline of the closed section with 6 non-intersecting lines *(Note that there are sketched entities only on one side of the Axis of Revolution)* [Fig. 2.7(d)] **> MMB** to end the current line **> MMB** to end the current tool and to display the *weak* dimensions [Fig. 2.7(e)] **>** click on each dimension and reposition [Fig. 2.7(f)]

Figure 2.7(d) Sketch six lines

Figure 2.7(e) Sketch with dimensions

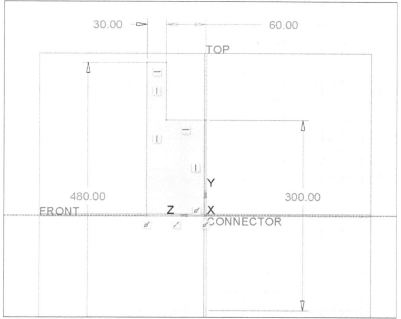

Figure 2.7(f) Weak dimensions (keep your dimensions, do not change)

Capture all the lines and dimensions with a window [Fig. 2.7(g)] > **RMB** > ⊟ **Modify** [Fig. 2.7(h)] > ☑ Lock Scale [Fig. 2.7(i)] > change the large diameter dimension to **28mm** [Fig. 2.7(j)] > **Enter** *leave all other dimensions "weak"* > **OK** > 🔍 **Refit** [Fig. 2.7(k)]

Weak dimensions are automatically generated as you create an entity. When you modify a weak dimension, it becomes a strong dimension. If you create other geometry, modify the geometry or other dimensions that relate to it, a weak dimension may disappear.

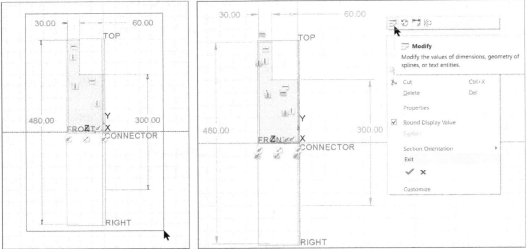

Figure 2.7(g) Capture all entities with a window   **Figure 2.7(h)** RMB Modify

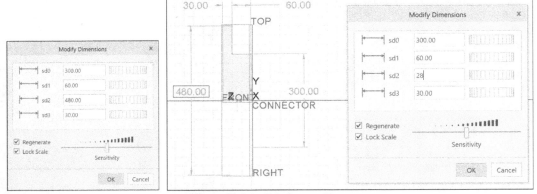

Figure 2.7(i) Lock Scale   **Figure 2.7(j)** Modify large diameter

File > Options > Sketcher > ☐ Show the grid ☐ Snap to grid **> Number of Decimal Places > 0 > Enter > OK > No >** reposition the dimensions for clarity and modify to design sizes [Fig. 2.7(l)] **> RMB >** ✓ **OK** [Fig. 2.7(m)] > use the **MMB** to rotate the model [Fig. 2.7(n)] > ✓ to complete the feature > **Ctrl+D** Standard Orientation > **Ctrl+S** Save

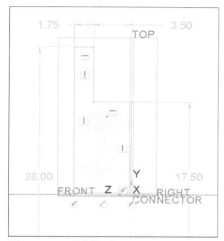

Figure 2.7(k) Refit

Figure 2.7(l) Move and modify the dimensions

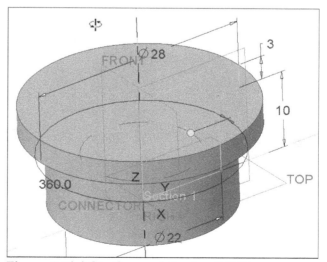

Figure 2.7(m) Feature preview   **Figure 2.7(n)** Sip the model using MMB

Pick on the bottom edge > ⬜ **Edge Chamfer** [Fig. 2.7(o)] > double-click on the default dimension and change to **1mm** [Fig. 2.7(p)] > **Enter** > **MMB** completes the command > in the Graphics Window, **LMB** to deselect > spin the model with your **MMB** [Fig. 2.7(q)] > **Ctrl+D** (*or* ⬜ *Standard Orientation from Graphics toolbar*) > **File** > **Save**

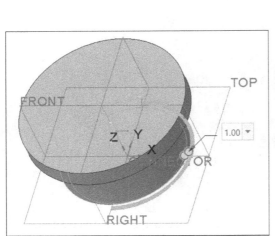

Figure 2.7(o) Edge Chamfer

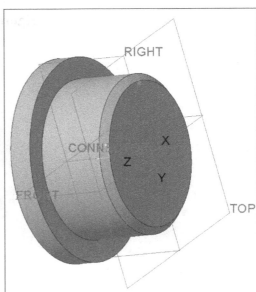

Figure 2.7(p) Chamfer

Figure 2.7(q) Completed chamfer

Pick the upper surface of the connector [Fig. 2.8(a)] > Extrude from the Model tab Ribbon > **Sketch View- Orient the sketching plane parallel to the screen** from the Graphics Toolbar or Sketch tab Ribbon Setup Group [Figs. 2.8(b-c)] > type **pal** in the Command Locator [Fig. 2.8(d)] > **Pal**ette... > Sketcher Palette opens [Fig. 2.8(e)]

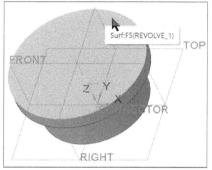

Figure 2.8(a) Select the top surface

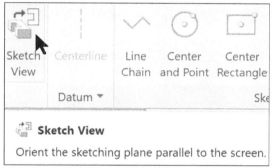

Figure 2.8(b) Sketch View from the Sketch tab

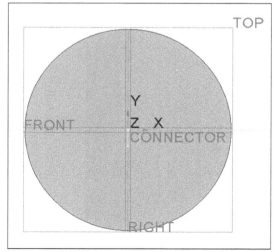

Figure 2.8(c) Sketch View

Figure 2.8(d) Palette

89

Click: **View** tab > from the Ribbon, 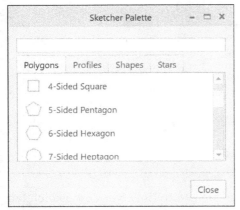 all should be toggled on > 🔍
Refit from the Graphics Toolbar > within the Polygons tab (default selection), scroll

down to see the octagon ⬡ 6-Sided Hexagon > double-click on **6-Sided Hexagon** *(or drag & drop)* [Figs. 2.8(f-g)]

Figure 2.8(e) Sketcher Palette   **Figure 2.8(f)** Polygons tab: 6-Sided Hexagon

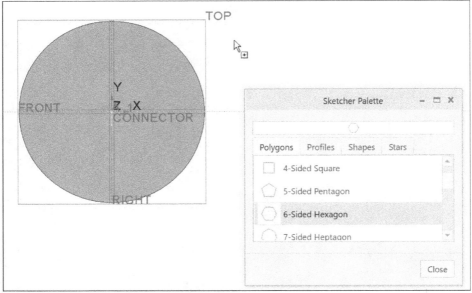

Figure 2.8(g) Drag the cursor to locate the hexagon

Click: **LMB** to place the octagon on the sketch (pick a position **not** on the CYSY) [Fig. 2.8(h)] > place the pointer at the center of the octagon > press and hold down the **LMB** to drag (move) the octagon > drop (release the **LMB** at) the Center Point of the hexagon at the origin [Fig. 2.8(i)] > ⬜ > ⬜ Hidden Line > modify the Scaling Factor value to **10** ⬜ 10.000000 > **Enter** > ✓ in the Ribbon > **Close** from the Sketcher Palette

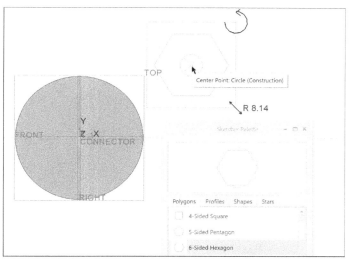

Figure 2.8(h) Place the Hexagon anywhere on the Sketch by picking a position

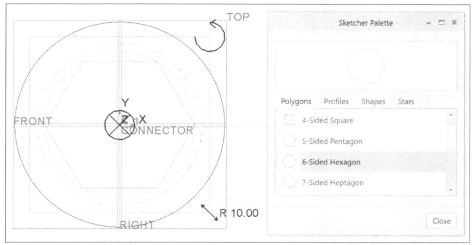

Figure 2.8(i) Hexagon at the Origin of the Part (PRT_CSYS_DEF)

Click: [icon] **Refit** [Fig. 2.8(j)] > **RMB** > [icon] **Create dimensions** > add a dimension for *"across flats"* by picking (**LMB**) the top and bottom line of the hexagon and then the position for the dimension (**MMB**) [Fig. 2.8(k)] > **Delete** the **10** dimension [Fig. 2.8(l)] > double-click on the default dimension > type **19** [Fig. 2.8(m)] > **Enter**

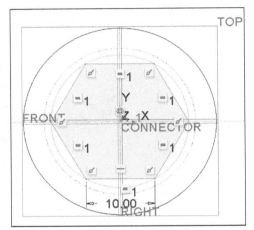

Figure 2.8(j) Hexagon Sketch

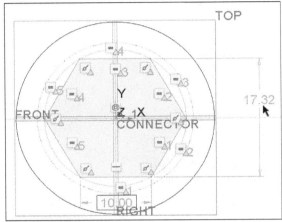

Figure 2.8(k) New dimension

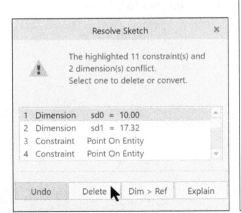

Figure 2.8(l) Delete

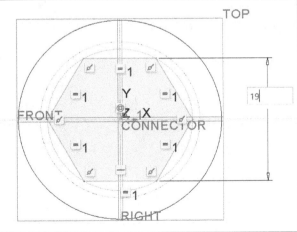

Figure 2.8(m) Enter the design dimension

Pick: [image] **Saved orientations** from the Graphics Toolbar > **Standard Orientation** [Fig. 2.8(n)] > [image] > [image] Shading With Edges > **RMB** > [image] ✓ ✗ [Fig. 2.8(o)] > modify the depth value in the Dashboard to **20mm** [Fig. 2.8(p)] > **Enter** > [image] ✓ from the Dashboard [Fig. 2.8(q)] > **LMB** to deselect [Fig. 2.8(r)] > **Ctrl+S**

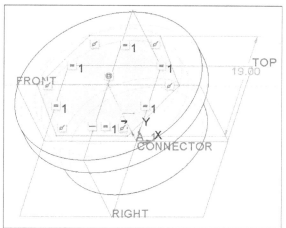

Figure 2.8(n) Hexagon Sketch   **Figure 2.8(o)** Hexagon feature preview

Figure 2.8(p) Modify Depth to **20**

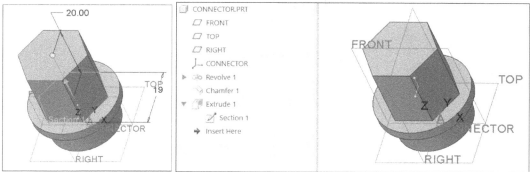

Figure 2.8(q) Depth Preview   **Figure 2.8(r)** Extruded Hexagon

Press: **View** tab > 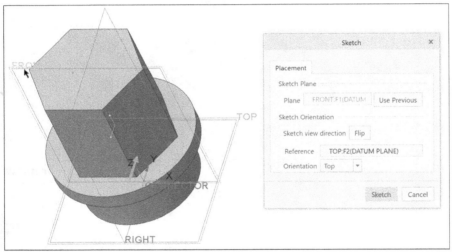 **ptc-std-gold** (or a color of your choice) > ✏ > click on the object name in the Model Tree > **MMB** > ⬛ **Display Style > Hidden Line > Model** tab > ⟳ Revolve > **RMB > Remove Material > RMB > Define Internal Sketch** > select the **FRONT** datum plane as sketching plane [Fig. 2.9(a)] > **Sketch** > 🔲 **Sketch View > RMB > References** > select the top edge/surface [Fig. 2.9(b)] > select the right vertical edge [Fig. 2.9(c)] > **Solve > Close**

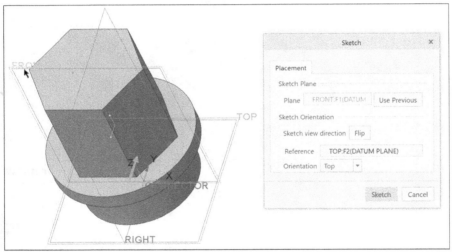

Figure 2.9(a) Select FRONT datum plane

Figure 2.9(b) Select the top edge/surface as a reference

94

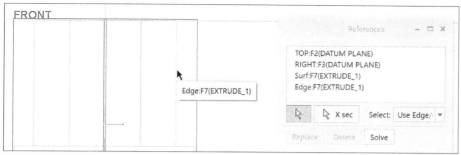

Figure 2.9(c) Select the right edge as a reference

Press: **RMB >** **Line Chain >** sketch the three lines [Fig. 2.9(d)] **> MMB > MMB >** [Fig. 2.9(e)] **> LMB >** press **RMB >** **Equal** Constrain [Fig. 2.9(f)]

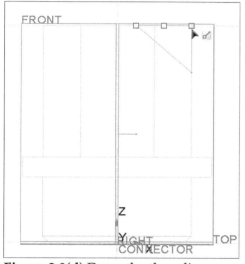

Figure 2.9(d) Draw the three lines

Figure 2.9(e) Move the dimensions

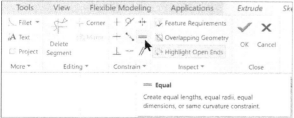

Figure 2.9(f) Equal constraint

Select both legs of the triangle sketch [Fig. 2.9(g)] > double-click on the remaining dimension > **4** [Fig. 2.9(h)] > **Enter** > **RMB** > 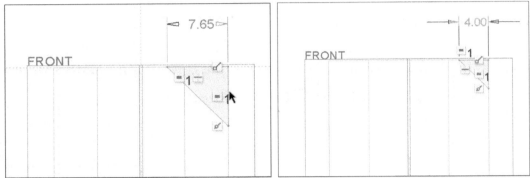 **Create axis of revolution** > pick two points along the vertical axis [Fig. 2.9(i)] > **MMB** [Fig. 2.9(j)] > **RMB** > ✓ [Fig. 2.9(k)] > ▢ **Shading with edges** [Fig. 2.9(l)]

Figure 2.9(g) Select the vertical and horizontal lines **Figure 2.9(h)** Modify

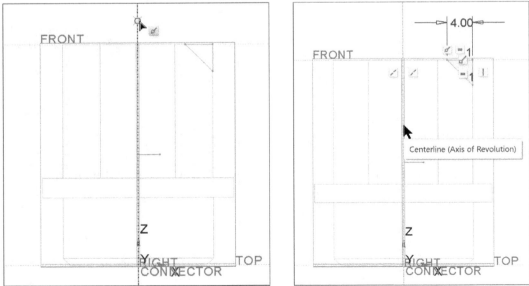

Figure 2.9(i) Create a vertical axis of revolution **Figure 2.9(j)** Axis

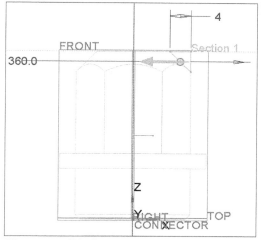

Figure 2.9(k) Cut preview hidden line

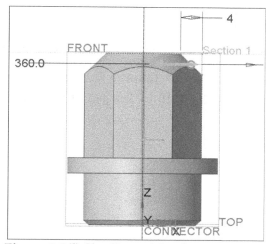

Figure 2.9(l) Shading with edges

Ctrl+D Standard orientation [Fig. 2.9(m)] **> MMB** to end command **> Ctrl+S** [Fig. 2.9(n)]

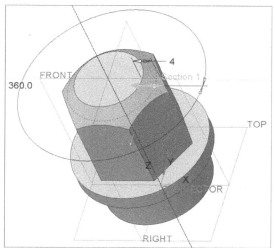

Figure 2.9(m) Standard orientation

Figure 2.9(n) Completed feature

Select axis **A_1** or **A_2** from the model [Fig. 2.10(a)] > ☐ Hole **Hole** > hold down the **Ctrl** key and pick datum **TOP** from the model or the Model Tree [Fig. 2.10(b)] > modify the diameter to **12mm** > ⊟⊟ [Fig. 2.10(c)] > **RMB** > **Flip** > **MMB** to complete the command > **LMB** to deselect > **Ctrl+D** > **Ctrl+S**

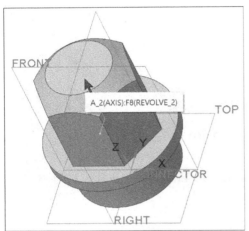

Figure 2.10(a) Select the axis   **Figure 2.10(b)** Select Datum TOP

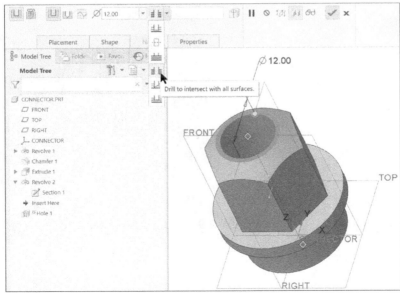

Figure 2.10(c) Through all hole

98

Click: 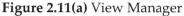 **View Manager** > **Sections** tab > **New** [Fig. 2.11(a)] > **Planar** > *type* **A** > **Enter**

> select datum **RIGHT** [Fig. 2.11(b)] > 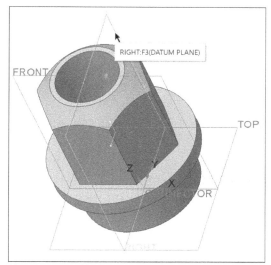 > □ > ⊞ > ✓ >
RMB [Fig. 2.11(c)] > **Close** > **File** > **Save** [Fig. 2.11(d)] > **File** > **Close**

Figure 2.11(a) View Manager

Figure 2.11(b) Select RIGHT Datum Plane

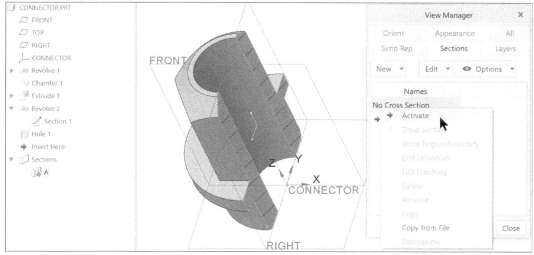

Figure 2.11(c) Section

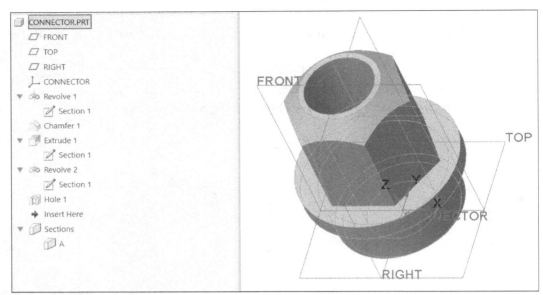

Figure 2.11(d) Connector

Quiz

1. What is a base feature and why is it important?
2. What is design intent?
3. Name three datum features.
4. What is the Working Directory and why should you have all components in one folder for an assembly?
5. What is the difference between weak and strong dimensions?
6. What is an Axis of Revolution?
7. In the Sketcher, what is the Palette functionality?
8. How do you create a section?

This completes Chapter 2.

 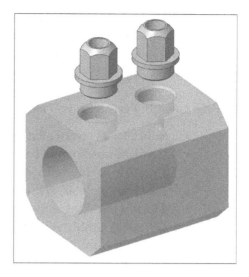

Assembly mode allows you to place together components and subassemblies to create an assembly. Assemblies can be modified, reoriented, documented, or analyzed. An assembly can be assembled into another assembly, thereby becoming a subassembly. *Bottom-up design* means that existing parts are assembled, one by one, until the assembly is complete. *Top-down design* is the design of an assembly where one or more component parts are created in Assembly mode as the design unfolds.

This assembly will be used in a later chapter where it will be assembled into larger assembly therefore becoming a "sub-assembly".

Objectives
1. Create a Group
2. Use copy, paste, and paste special to replicate and move geometry and components
3. Assemble components to create an assembly using Bottom-Up Design
4. Understand and use a variety of Assembly Constraints
5. Modify a component constraint
6. Use the 3D Dragger to position components
7. Generate a BOM
8. Understand Regeneration

Assemblies

Just as parts are created from related features, **assemblies** are created from related parts. The progressive combination of subassemblies, parts, and features into an assembly creates parent-child relationships based on the references used to assemble each component. The *Assembly* functionality is used to assemble existing parts and subassemblies.

During assembly creation, you can:

- Simplify a view of a large assembly by creating a simplified representation
- Perform automatic or manual placement of component parts
- Create an exploded view of the component parts
- Perform analysis, such as mass properties and clearance checks
- Modify the dimensional values of component parts
- Define assembly relations between component parts
- Create assembly features
- Perform automatic interchange of component parts
- Create parts in Assembly mode
- Create documentation drawings of the assembly

Just as features can reference part geometry, parametric design also permits the creation of parts referencing assembly geometry. **Assembly mode** allows the designer both to fit parts together and to design parts based on how they should fit together.

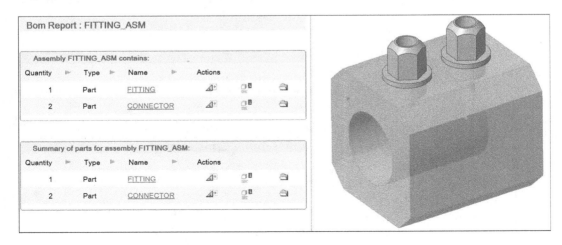

Chapter 3 STEPS

Before using assembly tools, the Fitting component needs to be modeled [Fig. 3.1].

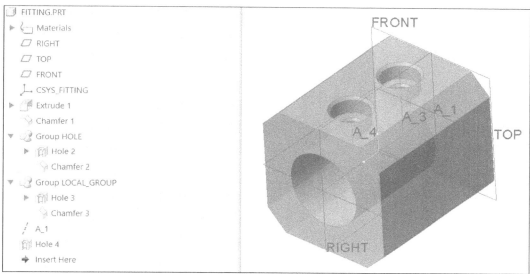

Figure 3.1 Fitting

Press: **Ctrl+N** > File name: **fitting** > **OK** > **RMB** in the Ribbon > **Customize the Ribbon** > move the Creo Parametric Options dialog down if needed > **RMB** on the Extrude button in the Shapes group ⌊ Shapes ▼ ⌋ of the Model tab Ribbon > **Small Button**

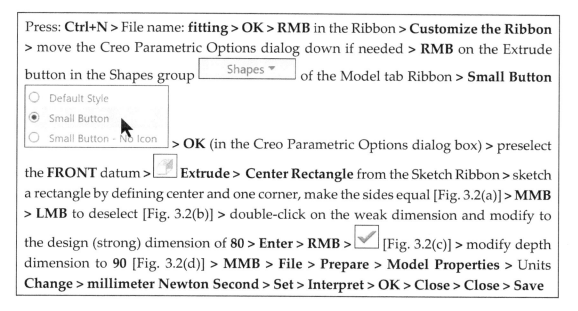 > **OK** (in the Creo Parametric Options dialog box) > preselect the **FRONT** datum > Extrude > **Center Rectangle** from the Sketch Ribbon > sketch a rectangle by defining center and one corner, make the sides equal [Fig. 3.2(a)] > **MMB** > **LMB** to deselect [Fig. 3.2(b)] > double-click on the weak dimension and modify to the design (strong) dimension of **80** > **Enter** > **RMB** > [Fig. 3.2(c)] > modify depth dimension to **90** [Fig. 3.2(d)] > **MMB** > **File** > **Prepare** > **Model Properties** > Units Change > **millimeter Newton Second** > **Set** > **Interpret** > **OK** > **Close** > **Close** > **Save**

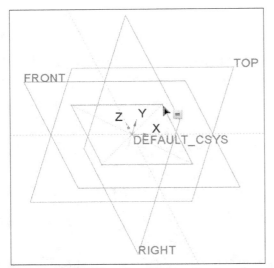

Figure 3.2(a) Sketch a Center Rectangle

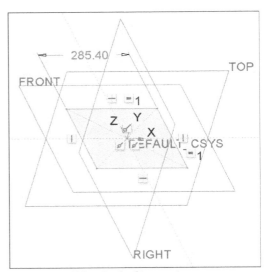

Figure 3.2(b) Weak dimension

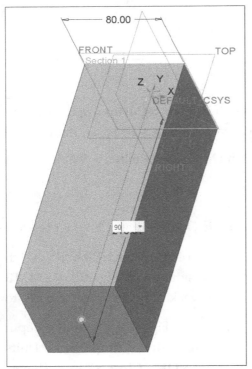

Figure 3.2(c) Depth Preview

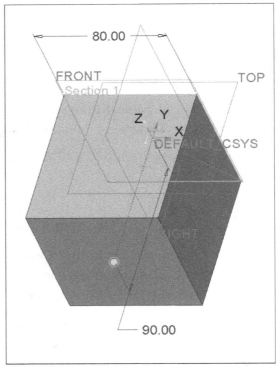

Figure 3.2(d) Modify the depth

Chamfers

Chamfers are created between abutting edges of two surfaces on the solid model. An edge chamfer removes a flat section of material from a selected edge to create a beveled surface between the two original surfaces common to that edge. Multiple edges can be selected. There are four basic dimensioning schemes for edge chamfers [Fig. 3.3]:

- **45 x d** Creates a chamfer that is at an angle of 45° to both surfaces and a distance **d** from the edge along each surface. The distance is the only dimension to appear when edited. **45 x d** chamfers can be created only on an edge formed by the intersection of two *perpendicular* surfaces.
- **d x d** Creates a chamfer that is a distance **d** from the edge along each surface. The distance is the only dimension to appear when edited.
- **d1 x d2** Creates a chamfer at a distance **d1** from the selected edge along one surface and a distance **d2** from the selected edge along the other surface. Both distances appear along their respective surfaces.
- **Ang x d** Creates a chamfer at a distance **d** from the selected edge along one adjacent surface at an **Angle** to that surface.

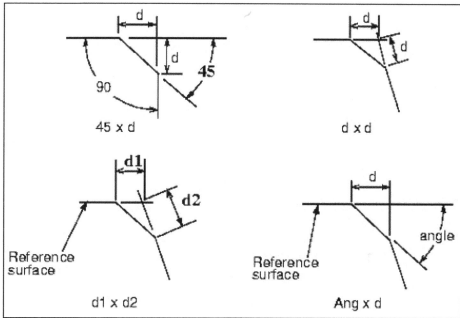

Figure 3.3 Chamfers

105

Select: **Model** tab > **Chamfer** > **Sets** tab > press and hold the Ctrl key and select all four horizontal edges *(No need to spin the model to select the edge not shown. Place the cursor near the hidden edge until it highlights or click your RMB to filter through to the proper selection.)* [Fig. 3.4(a)] > click in the **D** value field (or double-click directly on the dimension) > *type* **12** > **Enter** [Fig. 3.4(b)] > **MMB** > **LMB** > **Ctrl+S** > **OK**

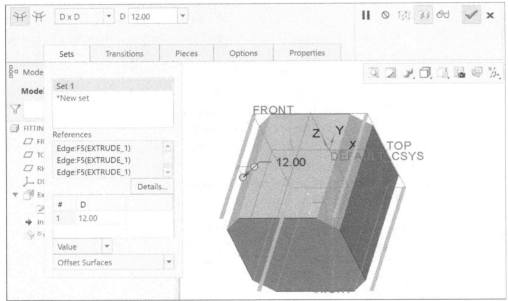

Figure 3.4(a) Select the four edges

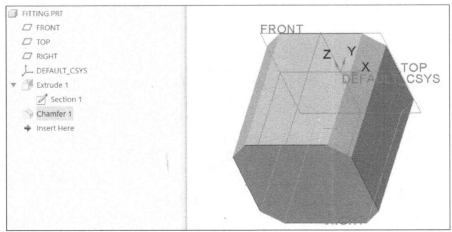

Figure 3.4(b) Chamfer

Hold down the **Ctrl** key and select the **TOP** and **RIGHT** datum planes from the model or Model Tree > 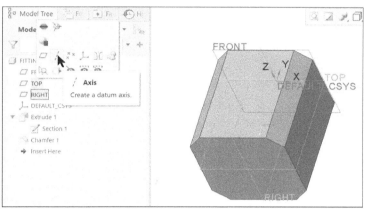 **Axis** [Fig. 3.5(a)] > **Model** tab > **Hole** > **Placement** tab > **Ctrl+** select the front face as the start surface [Fig. 3.5(b)]

					⌀ 45.00	▼	⟂ ▼	65.00	▼	

> **MMB**

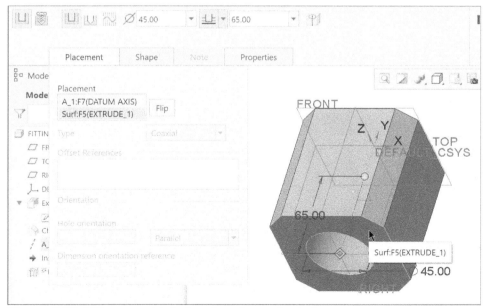

Figure 3.5(a) Axis will be created at intersection of datums TOP and RIGHT

Figure 3.5(b) Placement tab, front surface selected

107

With the hole *still selected*; in the Graphics Window, press: **RMB > Hole Representation** [Fig. 3.5(c)] **> Convert to Lightweight** [Fig. 3.5(d)] **> Undo > LMB > Ctrl+S > File > Manage File > Delete Old Versions > Yes**

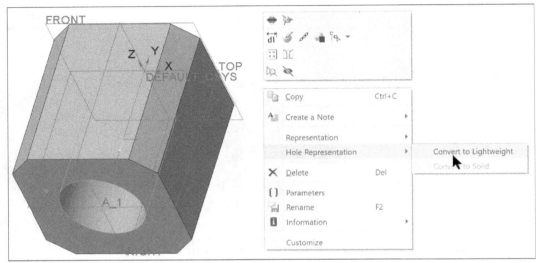

Figure 3.5(c) Convert the Hole Display to Lightweight

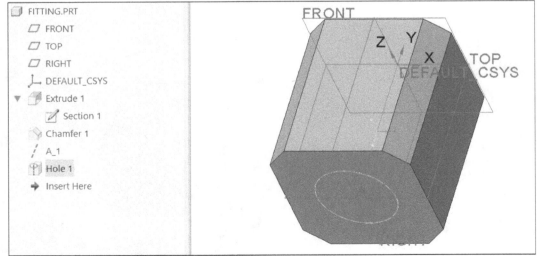

Figure 3.5(d) Lightweight Display of Hole. Note the change in the Model Tree Representation of the Hole Symbol. Lightweight speeds regeneration.

Standard Holes

Hole charts are used to lookup diameters for a given fastener size. You can create custom hole charts and specify their directory location with the configuration file option *hole_parameter_file_path.* UNC, UNF and ISO hole charts are supplied.

Click: 🔲 Hole > select options as shown:

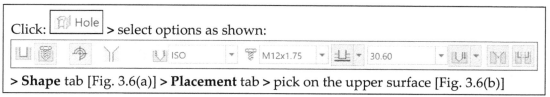

> **Shape** tab [Fig. 3.6(a)] > **Placement** tab > pick on the upper surface [Fig. 3.6(b)]

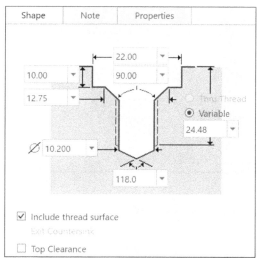

Figure 3.6(a) Standard Hole Shape

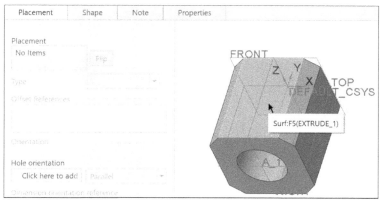

Figure 3.6(b) Placement

Click inside the **Offset References** field [Fig. 3.6(c)] > press and hold **Ctrl** key > select the **FRONT** and **RIGHT** datums from the graphics window or Model Tree > change the **Offset References** values as shown [Fig. 3.6(d)]

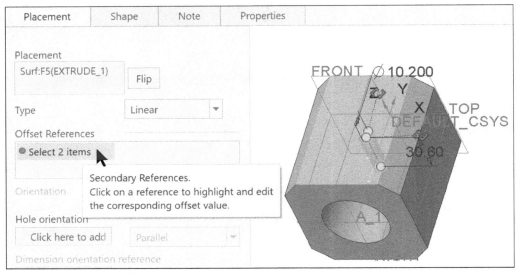

Figure 3.6(c) Offset References

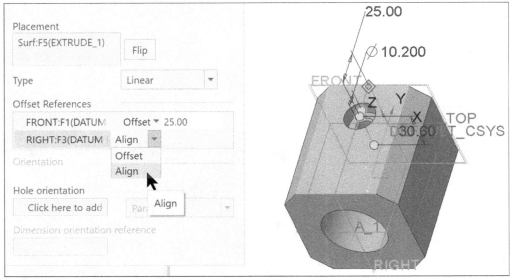

Figure 3.6(d) Placement (0) or Align

Click: **Note** tab [Fig. 3.6(e)] > **Properties** tab [Fig. 3.6(f)] > ✓ > if closed: ▯ to open the Model Tree *(lower left-hand corner)* > click ▶ next to Hole 2 in the Model Tree > **Note_1** [Fig. 3.6(g)] > 🗎 **Properties** (or double-click on Note_0) [Fig. 3.6(h)]

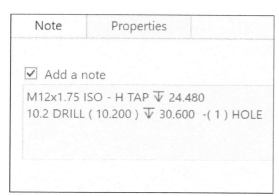

Figure 3.6(e) Note tab

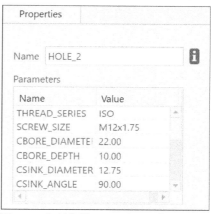

Figure 3.6(f) Properties tab

Figure 3.6(g) Note Properties

Figure 3.6(h) Note Text

In the Note Dialog Box, modify the Name and Text fields [Fig. 3.6(i)]. Move the mouse pointer within the Text field in front of &DIAMETER, click: **Symbols** > [⌀] add the diameter symbol [Fig. 3.6(j)] > **Close** > **OK** from the Note dialog box > **View** tab > **Appearances** > select a new color > pick **fitting** in the Model Tree > **MMB** > spin the model [Fig. 3.6(k)] > **Ctrl+S**

Figure 3.6(i) Modified Note

Figure 3.6(j) Text Symbol Dialog Box

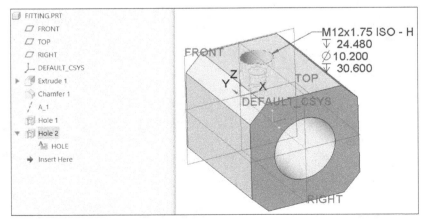

Figure 3.6(k) Annotation

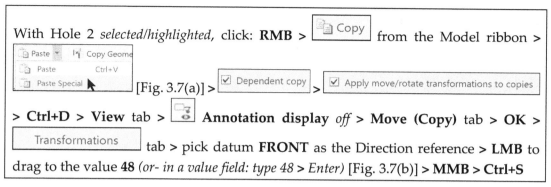

With Hole 2 *selected/highlighted*, click: **RMB >** [Copy] from the Model ribbon > [Fig. 3.7(a)] > ☑ Dependent copy > ☑ Apply move/rotate transformations to copies **> Ctrl+D > View** tab > **Annotation display** *off* **> Move (Copy)** tab **> OK >** Transformations tab **>** pick datum **FRONT** as the Direction reference **> LMB** to drag to the value **48** *(or- in a value field: type 48 > Enter)* [Fig. 3.7(b)] **> MMB > Ctrl+S**

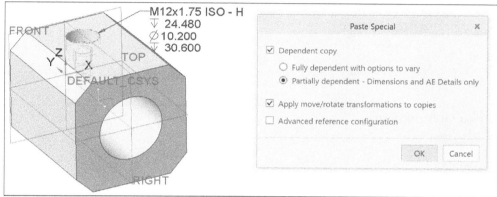

Figure 3.7(a) Paste Special

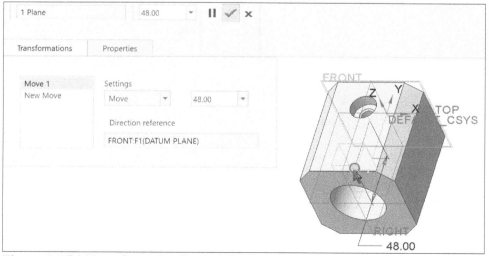

Figure 3.7(b) Transform the Copied Feature

113

Select the **Moved Copy 1** in the Model Tree [Fig. 3.7(c)] **> RMB > Information > Feature Information** [Fig. 3.7(d)] **>** 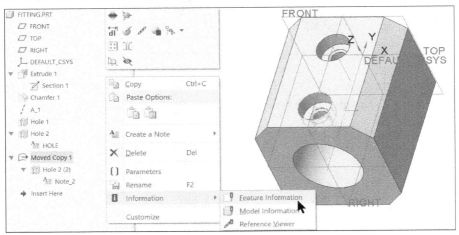 **Show Browser** *close (or* ⊠ *close)* **> Ctrl+S > File > Close**

Figure 3.7(c) Information

Feature info : MOVE

PART NAME : FITTING
FEATURE NUMBER : 10
INTERNAL FEATURE ID : 390

Parents

No.	Name	ID	Actions
1	FRONT	7	

Feature Element Data - Move

No.	Element Name	Info
1	Feature Name	Defined
2	Move Transformations	Defined
2.1	Single Transformation	Defined
2.1.1	Direction	Defined
2.1.1.1	Direction Reference	FRONT:F1(DATUM PLANE)
2.1.1.2	Direction Side	Along
2.1.2	Movement Type	Translate
2.1.3	Movement Value	48.00

Figure 3.7(d) Feature information

Assembly Mode

Assembly mode allows you to place together components and subassemblies. Assemblies can be modified, reoriented, documented, or analyzed. An assembly can be assembled into another assembly [Fig. 3.8], thereby becoming a subassembly.

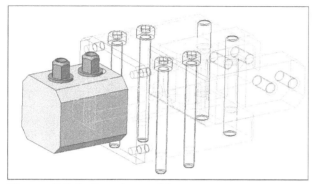

Figure 3.8 Active Assembly

Placing Components

The 3D Dragger is a graphical tool for precision handling of assembly components. The *axes* are called **draggers**. Pull or rotate the draggers to make changes to the components position and orientation. The draggers enable movement in one or more *degrees of freedom* (DOFs). They support linear, planar, free, translation, and angular movements. You can pull a dragger along a 2D or 3D trajectory. When you move a geometric entity using a dragger, the relative distances from the start point of the entity appear in the graphics window as you pull the dragger. You can hold down the SHIFT key while pulling a dragger to snap the dragger to a geometric reference.

To assemble components, use: Assemble **Add a component to the assembly**. After selecting a component from the Open dialog box, the dashboard (opens and the component appears in the assembly window. Alternatively, you can select a component from a browser window and drag it into the graphics window. If there is an assembly in the window, Creo Parametric will begin to assemble the component into the current assembly. Using icons in the dashboard, you can specify the screen window in which the component is displayed while you position it. You can change window options at any time using: **Show component in a separate window** or **Show component in the assembly window**

Creating the Assembly

Using the two parts just modeled you will now create an assembly. Just as you can combine features into parts, you can also combine parts into assemblies. The Assembly mode in Creo Parametric enables you to place component parts and subassemblies together to form assemblies.

As with a part, an assembly starts with default datum planes and a default coordinate system. To create a subassembly or an assembly, you must first create datum features. You then create or assemble additional components to the existing component(s) and datum features.

Click: 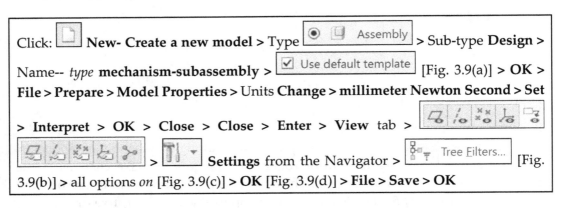 **New- Create a new model** > Type [Assembly] > Sub-type **Design** > Name-- *type* **mechanism-subassembly** > [Use default template] [Fig. 3.9(a)] > **OK** > **File** > **Prepare** > **Model Properties** > Units **Change** > **millimeter Newton Second** > **Set** > **Interpret** > **OK** > **Close** > **Close** > **Enter** > **View** tab > [icons] > [icons] > Settings from the Navigator > [Tree Filters...] [Fig. 3.9(b)] > all options *on* [Fig. 3.9(c)] > **OK** [Fig. 3.9(d)] > **File** > **Save** > **OK**

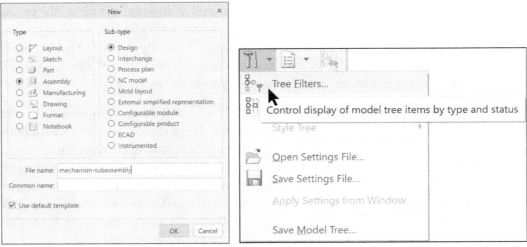

Figure 3.9(a) New Dialog Box, Assembly   **Figure 3.9(b)** Tree Filters

116

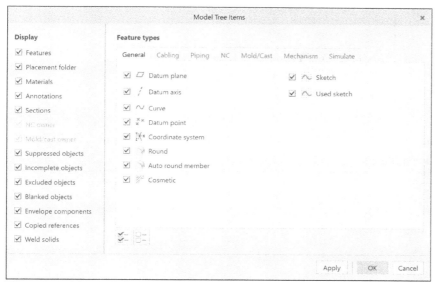

Figure 3.9(c) Model Tree Items Dialog Box

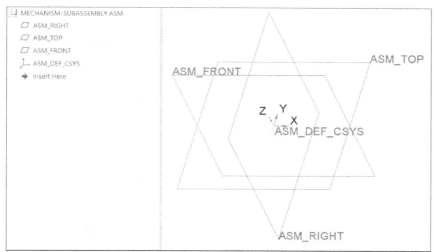

Figure 3.9(d) Assembly Default Datums and Coordinate System

If your screen shows the Z axis in a different orientation, you can use it or go to cad-resources.com and download the start template with the vertical Axis as an option. You will have to delete your file and start again loading the new start template. You will have to start the assembly model over. In reality, t is not necessary to do this since Creo Parametric is a non-coordinate-based system.

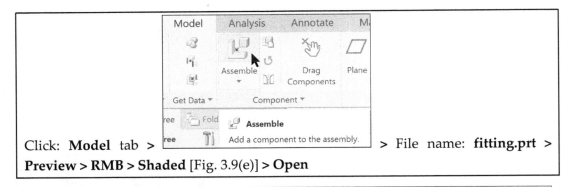

Click: **Model** tab > 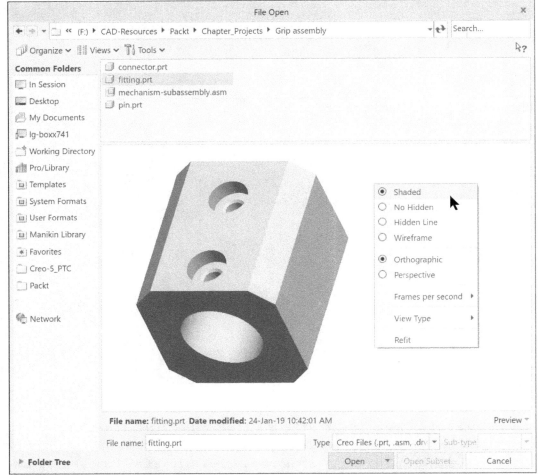 > File name: **fitting.prt** > **Preview > RMB > Shaded** [Fig. 3.9(e)] > **Open**

Figure 3.9(e) Open Dialog Box, Type Creo Files

Click: **LMB** to drop the component > [⚡ Automatic ▾] > [⊡ Default] [Fig. 3.9(f)] > **Placement** tab (Fully Constrained) [Figs. 3.9(g-h)] > **MMB** > **Save**

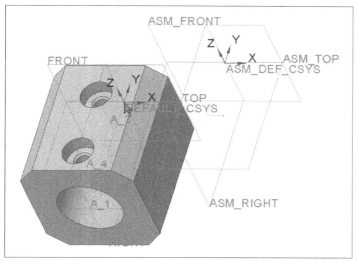

Figure 3.9(f) Assembly preview

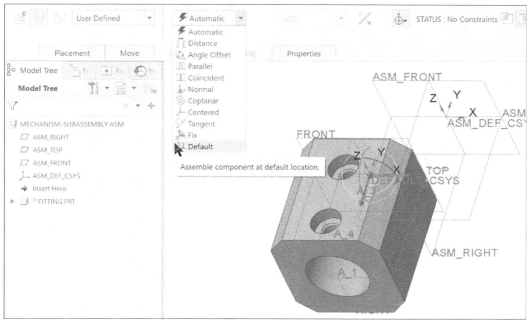

Figure 3.9(g) Default Constraint

119

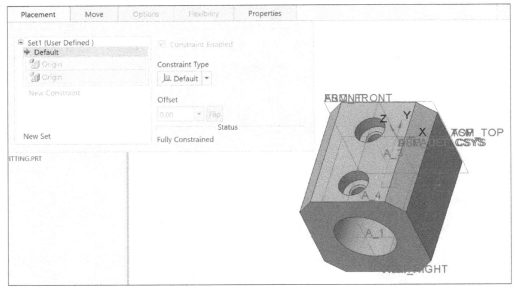

Figure 3.9(h) Fully Constrained

In the Model Tree, expand **Placement** and **Set** [Fig. 3.9(i)] *(Default = coordinate system to coordinate system)* > ✓ from the Dashboard > **LMB > Ctrl+D > Ctrl+S**

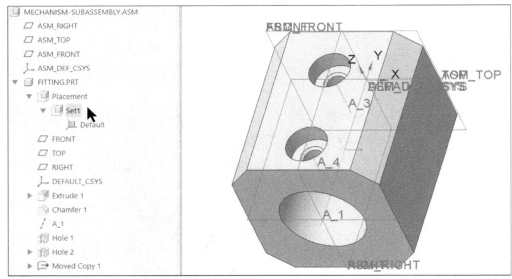

Figure 3.9(i) Fully Constrained Component at the Default Position

Click: **Model** tab > **Assemble** > **connector.prt** [Fig. 3.10(a)] > **Open** [Fig. 3.10(b)]

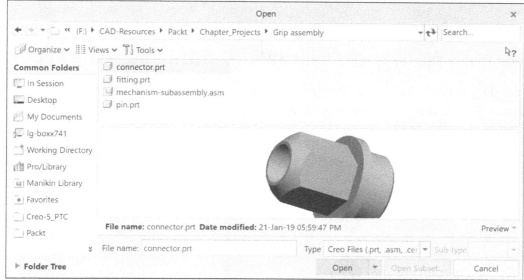

Figure 3.10(a) Select connector.prt

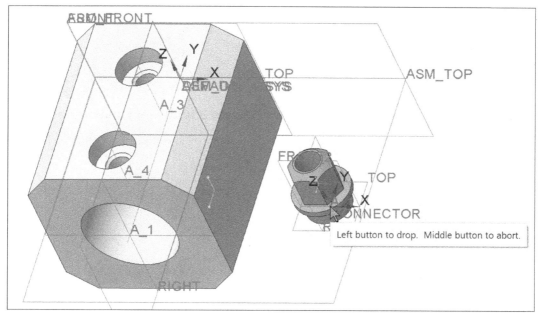

Figure 3.10(b) Component Shown in Assembly Window

Click: **Datum Display Filters > Select All** [Fig. 3.10(c)] **> LMB** to drop [Fig. 3.10(d)] **>** 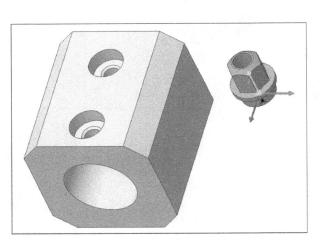 **3D dragger** *off* **>** pick on the Connector's lower cylindrical surface [Fig. 3.10(e)] **>** pick on the Fitting's cylindrical hole surface [Fig. 3.10(f)]

☐ (Select All)
☐ Axis Display
☐ Point Display
☐ Csys Display
☐ Plane Display

Figure 3.10(c) Select the 3D Dragger center

Figure 3.10(d) Move and drop as shown

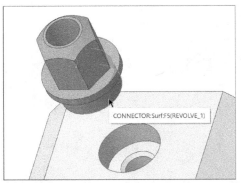

Figure 3.10(e) Select the Connector's Surface

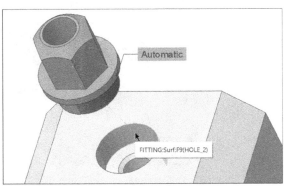

Figure 3.10(f) Select the Hole

122

Click: **Placement** tab > **New Constraint** [Fig. 3.10(g)] > pick on the Fitting's top surface > **MMB** and spin the model > pick on the Connector's flange surface [Fig. 3.10(h)]

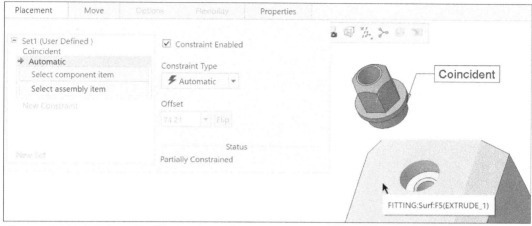

Figure 3.10(g) Select the Fitting's surface

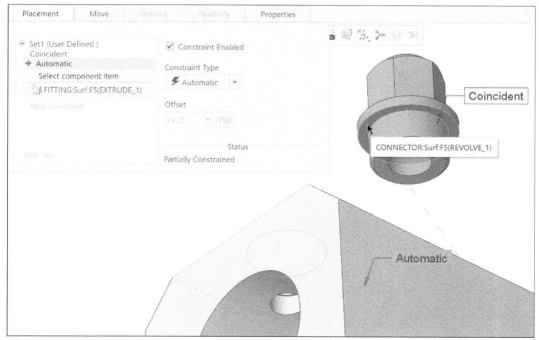

Figure 3.10(h) Select the Connector's flange bearing surface

Press: **Ctrl+D** > Constraint Type > **Coincident** [Fig. 3.10(i)] Fully Constrained [Fig. 3.10(j)] > click **MMB** to complete the command > **File** > **Save**

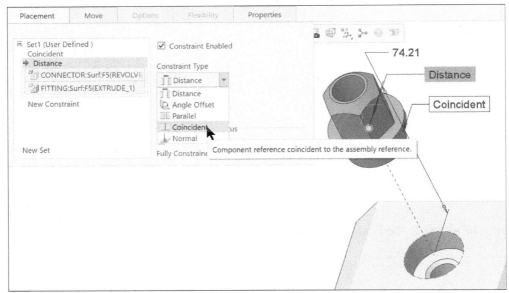

Figure 3.10(i) Coincident constraint

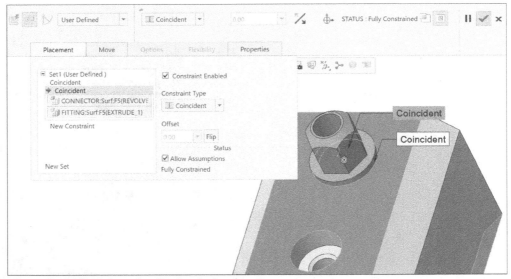

Figure 3.10(j) Select the Fitting's Surface

Select the **Connector** in the **Model Tree** > **Ctrl+C** > **Ctrl+V** > **LMB** to drop the component [Fig. 3.11(a)] > pick on the Fitting's hole surface [Fig. 3.11(b)] > pick the top surface of the Fitting [Fig. 3.11(c)]

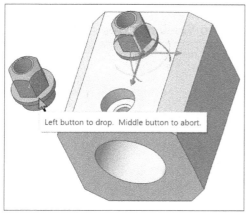

Figure 3.11(a) Drop the component

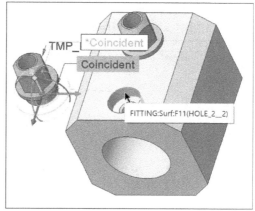

Figure 3.11(b) Select the hole's surface

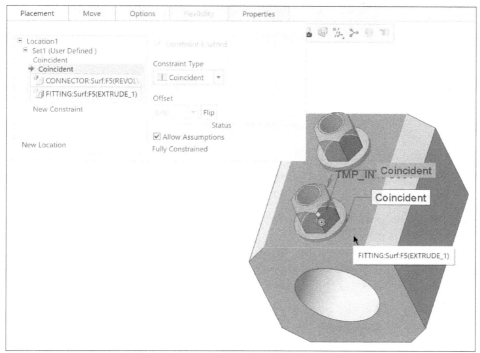

Figure 3.11(c) Select the top of the Fitting

Click: [✓] from the Dashboard > [≡ ▾] > **Expand all** > [✗⃰] **Datum Display Filters** from the Graphics Toolbar > [✓ (Select All)] > **Model** tab > [⇄ ▾] **Regenerate** > **Regenerate Manager > OK > Cancel > Tools** tab > **Bill of Materials** [Fig. 3.12(a)] > **OK** [Fig. 3.12(b)] > [⌖] > **File > Manage File > Delete Old Versions > Yes > File > Save**

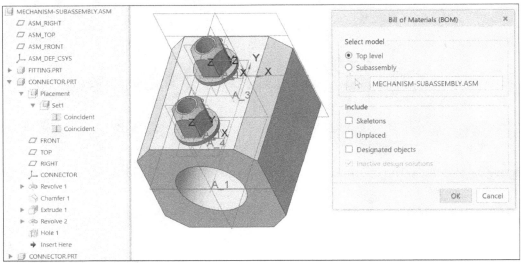

Figure 3.12(a) BOM

Bom Report : MECHANISM-SUBASSEMBLY

Assembly MECHANISM-SUBASSEMBLY contains:

Quantity	Type	Name	Actions		
1	Part	FITTING			
2	Part	CONNECTOR			

Summary of parts for assembly MECHANISM-SUBASSEMBLY:

Quantity	Type	Name	Actions		
1	Part	FITTING			
2	Part	CONNECTOR			

Figure 3.12(b) BOM Report

Layers

Regardless of the design methodology, the assembly datum planes and coordinate system should be on their own separate *assembly layer*. Each part should also be placed on separate assembly layers; the part's datum features should already be on *part layers*. Look over the default template for assembly layering.

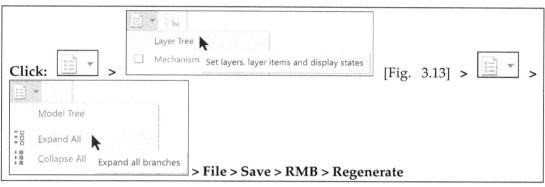

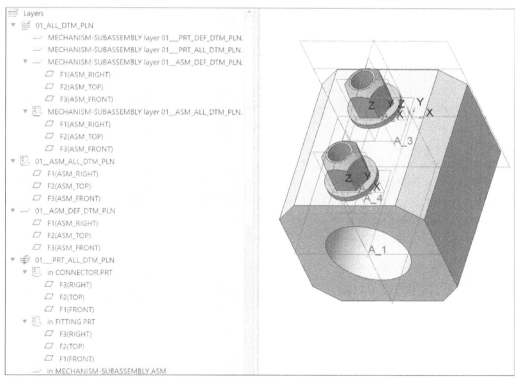

Figure 3.13 Default Template for Assembly Layering

127

Regenerating Models

You can use **Regenerate** to find bad geometry, broken parent-child relationships, or any other problem with a part feature or assembly component.

When Creo Parametric regenerates a model, it recreates the model feature by feature, in the order in which each feature was created, and according to the hierarchy of the parent-child relationship between features.

In an assembly, component features are regenerated in the order in which they were created, and then in the order in which each component was added to the assembly. Creo Parametric regenerates a model automatically in many cases, including when you open, save, or close a part or assembly or one of its instances, or when you open an instance from within a Family Table. You can also use the Regenerate command to manually regenerate the model.

Regenerate, lets you recalculate the model geometry, incorporating any changes made since the last time the model was saved. If no changes have been made, Creo Parametric informs you that the model has not changed since the last regeneration. The **Regeneration Manager** opens the Regeneration Manager dialog box if there are features or components that have been changed that require regeneration. A column next to the Regeneration List indicates each entries Status (Regenerated or Unregenerated). In the Regeneration Manager dialog box, you can:

- Select all features/components for regeneration, select **Show Checked > Check All > Regenerate**.
- Omit all features/components from regeneration, select **Show Checked > Uncheck All > Regenerate**.
- Determine the reason an object requires regeneration, select an entry in the **Regeneration List > RMB > Feature Info**.

Click: **View** tab > **Model Display** Group > **Temporary Shade** > **Ctrl+1** [Fig. 3.14] >
Ctrl+3 > **File** > **Save**

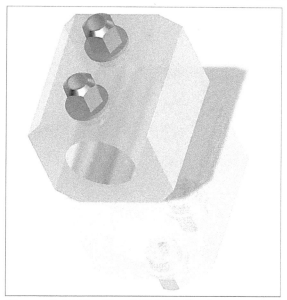

Figure 3.14 Shading With Reflections

You have completed your first Creo Parametric assembly. Next you will create a set of drawings for the assembly and one component.

Quiz

1. What is a base component and why is it important?
2. What is design intent?
3. What is a 3D Dragger?
4. What is the Working Directory and why should you have all components in one folder for an assembly?
5. What are assembly constraints used for??
6. Why are Layers important?
7. What is a BOM?
8. Explain Regeneration

This completes Chapter 3

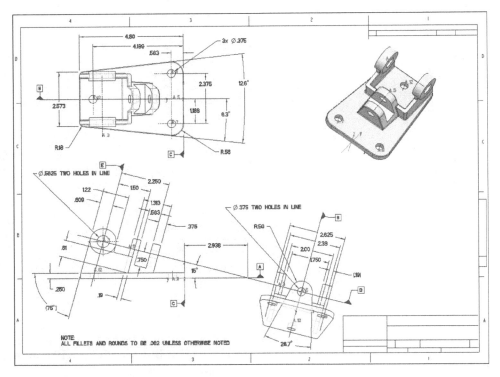

You can create drawings of all parametric design models. All model views in the drawing are *associative:* if you change a dimensional value in one view, other drawing views update accordingly. Moreover, drawings are associated with their parent models. Any dimensional changes made to a drawing are automatically reflected in the model. Any changes made to the model (e.g., addition of features, deletion of features, dimensional changes, and so on) in Part, Sheet Metal, Assembly, or Manufacturing modes are automatically reflected in their corresponding drawings.

Objectives
1. Create part and assembly drawings
2. Display standard views using the template
4. Add, Move, Erase, and Delete views
4. Retrieve a standard format
5. Display centerlines, and dimensions
6. Specify and retrieve standard Format paper size and units

Drawings

The **Drawing** functionality is used to create annotated drawings of parts and assemblies. You can annotate the drawing with notes, manipulate the dimensions, and use layers to manage the display of different items on the drawing. During drawing creation, you can:

- Add views of the part or assembly
- Show existing dimensions
- Incorporate additional driven or reference dimensions
- Create notes on the drawing
- Display views of additional parts or assemblies
- Add sheets to the drawing
- Create draft entities on the drawing
- Balloon components on an assembly drawing
- Create an associative BOM

Drawing mode in parametric design provides you with the basic ability to document solid models in drawings that share a two-way associativity. Changes that are made to the model in Part mode or Assembly mode will cause the drawing to update automatically and reflect the changes. Any changes made to the model in Drawing mode will be immediately visible on the model in Part and Assembly modes.

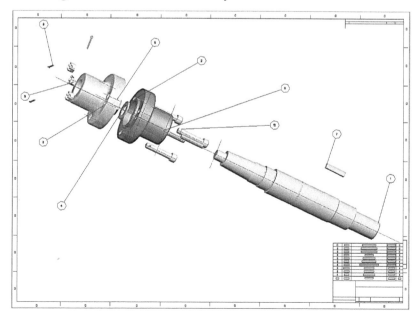

Chapter 4 STEPS

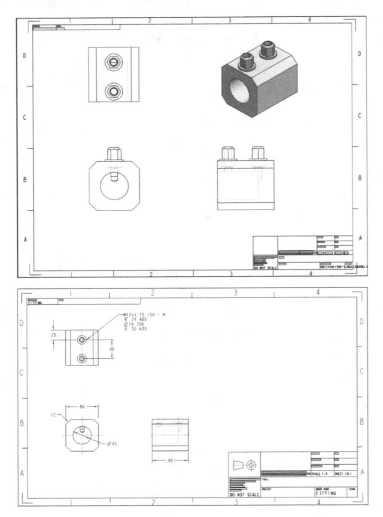

Creating Drawings

Using the part and the assembly just created, you will now create an assembly drawing of the Mechanism-subassembly and a part drawing of the Fitting.

The Drawing mode in Creo Parametric enables you to create and manipulate engineering drawings that use the 3D model (part or assembly) as a geometry source. You can pass dimensions, notes, and other elements of design between the 3D model and its views on a drawing.

Set your working directory to the folder where the mechanism-subassembly and components are stored. Click: **Ctrl+N** > Type  > Name-- *type* **mechanism-subassembly** > ☑ Use default template [Fig. 4.2(a)] > **OK** [Fig. 4.2(b)] > Default Model **Browse > Preview** *on* > **mechanism-subassembly.asm** [Fig. 4.2(c)]

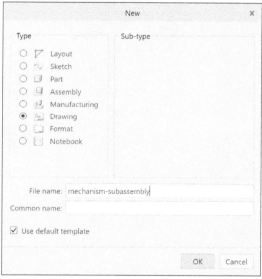

Figure 4.2(a) New Dialog Box, Drawing

Figure 4.2(b) New Drawing Template

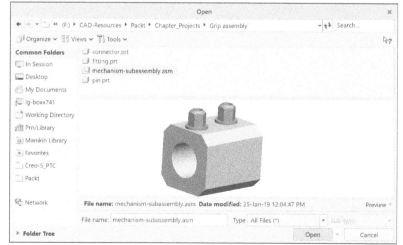

Figure 4.2(c) mechanism-subassembly.asm

Click: **Open** > Template **Browse** > **4-templates** *(if you do not have this folder of templates, you can download into your Working Directory from cad-resources.com, or use a similar format from your list)* > **c_drawing.drw** [Fig. 4.2(d)] > **Open** > **OK** [Fig. 4.2(e)]

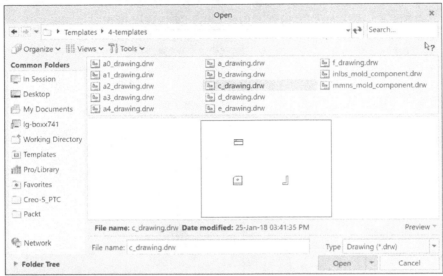

Figure 4.2(d) Templates

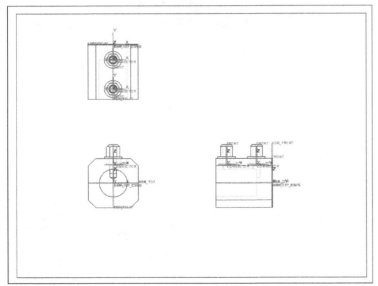

Figure 4.2(e) Assembly drawing

Click: [×/×] *toggle off* [Fig. 4.2(f)] **> Layout** tab **>** in the Graphics Window **RMB > Sheet Setup** from the short cut menu [Fig. 4.2(g)]

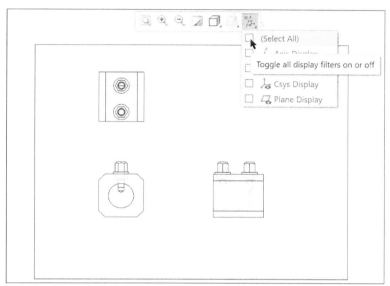

Figure 4.2(f) Drawing

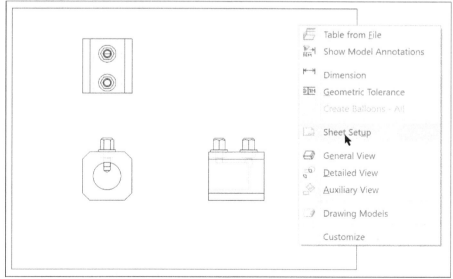

Figure 4.2(g) Drawing Sheet Setup

Sheet Setup dialog box displays > click in **C Size** field [Fig. 4.2(h)] > ⬜▾ > **Browse** > **Preview** > double-click on **c_format.frm** [Fig. 4.2(i)] > **OK** > **Ctrl+S** > **OK**

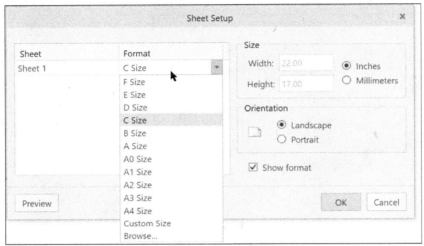

Figure 4.2(h) Sheet Setup Dialog Format Options

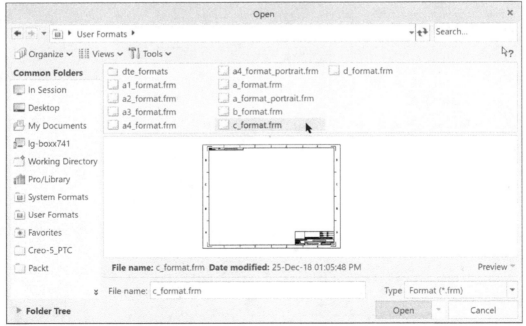

Figure 4.2(i) c_format.frm

In the Graphics Window, press and hold: **RMB > General View** [Fig. 4.2(j)] > **No Combined State** *(selected by default)* > **OK** > pick a position for the new view [Fig. 4.2(k)]

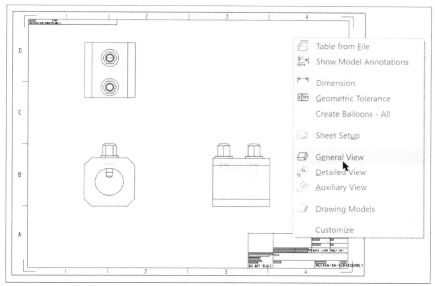

Figure 4.2(j) General View

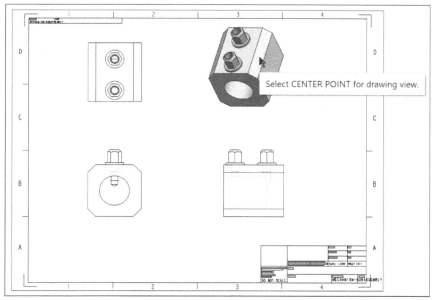

Figure 4.2(k) Place General View

Click: **Trimetric** > **Isometric** [Fig. 4.2(l)] > Categories: **View Display** > Display style **Shading With Edges** > **OK** > **Ctrl+S** [Fig. 4.2(m)] > **File** > **Close**

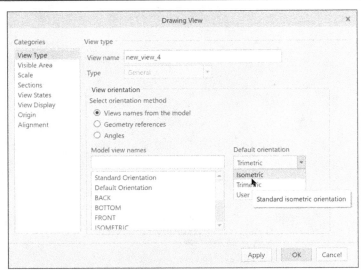

Figure 4.2(l) Isometric

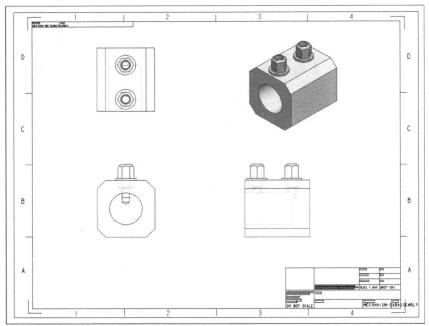

Figure 4.2(m) Completed Assembly drawing

138

Next, we will create a detailed part drawing of the Fitting.

Click: **Ctrl+N > Drawing >** Name--**fitting > Browse > fitting.prt > Open** [Fig. 4.3(a)] > **b_drawing** [Fig. 4.3(b)] > **OK** [Fig. 4.3(c)] > **Ctrl+S > Enter**

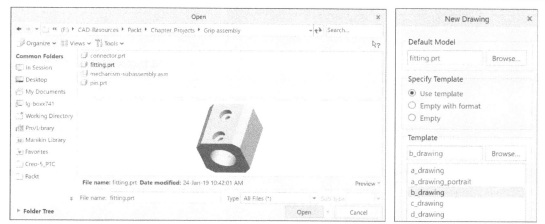

Figure 4.3(a) Fitting Preview   **Figure 4.3(b)** b_drawing

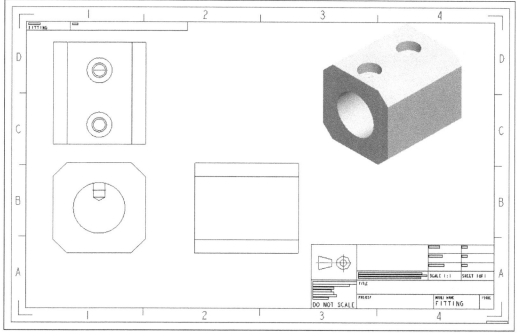

Figure 4.3(c) Fitting Drawing

Select the pictorial view > **Delete** [Fig. 4.3(d)] > from the Layout ribbon click **Lock View Movement** *toggle off* > double-click on **SCALE: 1:1** at bottom left of Graphics

Window > **1/2** > **Enter** [Fig. 4.3(e)]

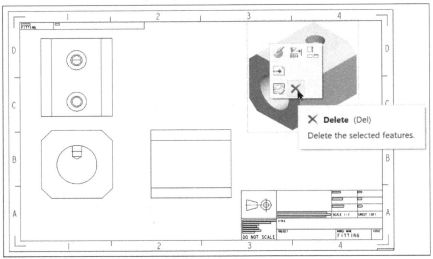

Figure 4.3(d) Delete the Isometric view

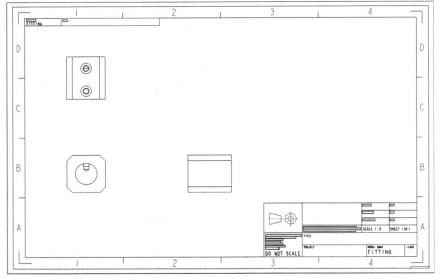

Figure 14.3(e) New drawing view scale

Select the Front view > **LMB** > move the pointer and reposition the view as desired [Fig. 4.4(f)] > **LMB** to deselect the view > window-in (capture) all three views > **RMB** > **Show Model Annotations** [Fig. 4.4(g)]

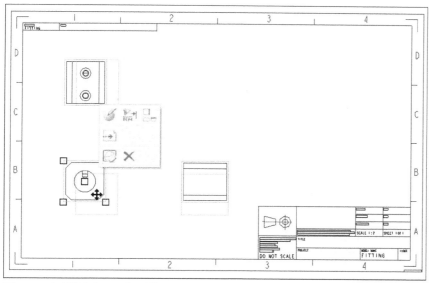

Figure 4.4(f) Move the View

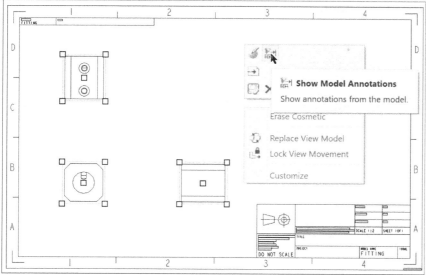

Figure 4.4(g) Show Model Annotations

141

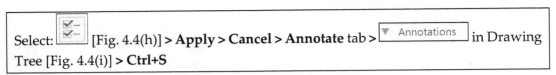

Select: [checkbox icon] [Fig. 4.4(h)] > **Apply** > **Cancel** > **Annotate** tab > [Annotations icon] in Drawing Tree [Fig. 4.4(i)] > **Ctrl+S**

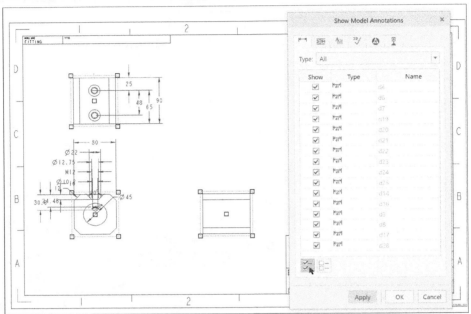

Figure 4.4(h) Show Model Annotations

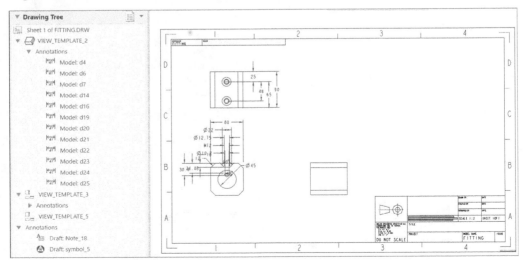

Figure 4.4(i) Annotations display in Model Tree

Capture all views with a window > **Show Model Annotations** > **Show the model datums** > ☑ [Fig. 4.4(j)] > **Apply** > **Show the model notes** > ☑ > **Apply** [Fig. 4.4(k)] > **Cancel** > **Ctrl+S**

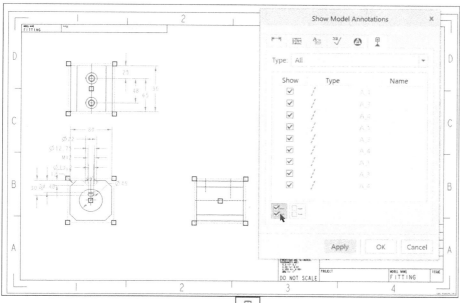

Figure 4.4(j) Show the model datums

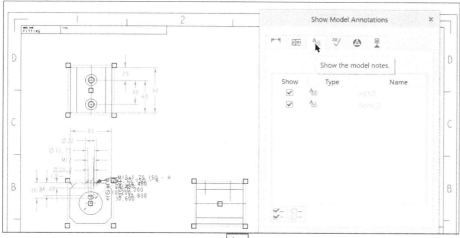

Figure 4.4(k) Show the model notes

Select the Diameter **45** note and move [Fig. 4.4(l)] and drop > select **Model Note_2** from the Model Tree > **Delete** [Fig. 4.4(m)] > **Apply** > **Ctrl+S**

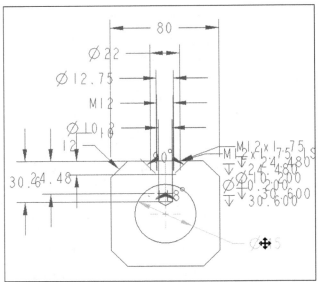

Figure 4.4(l) Select and move Diameter 45 note

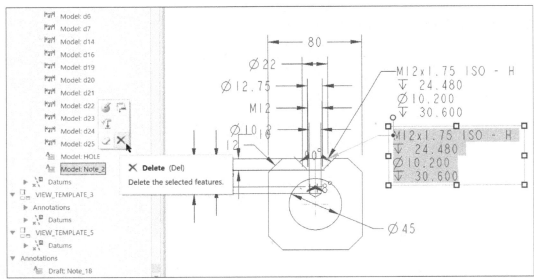

Figure 4.4(m) Delete the extra note

Select the note from the drawing or Model Tree > **Move to View** [Fig. 4.4(n)] > select the Top view and reposition as needed [Fig. 4.4(o)] > **LMB** > select and delete the **65mm** dimension in the Top view (you can use the keyboard **Delete** key) > select the **90mm** dimension > **Move to View** > select the Right Side view > **Ctrl+S**

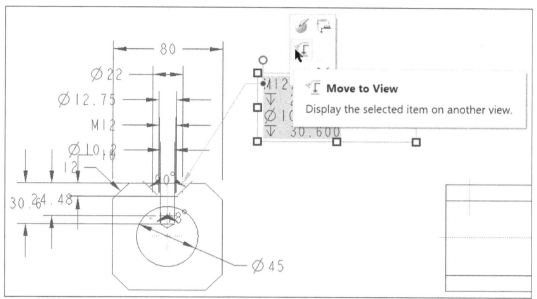

Figure 4.4(n) Move to View

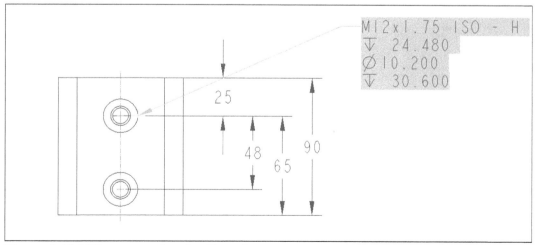

Figure 4.4(o) Note moved to the Top view

From the Model Tree, or press and hold **Ctrl** and select the hole's dimensions in the Front view **>** press the **Delete** key [Fig. 4.4(p)] **>** select the hole's axes in the Front view and extend the axis lines as needed [Fig. 4.4(q)] **> LMB**

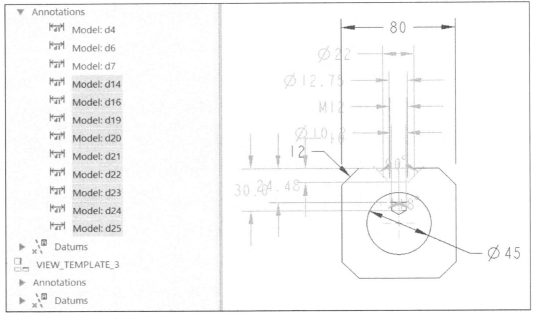

Figure 4.4(p) Delete the Hole's dimensions in the front View

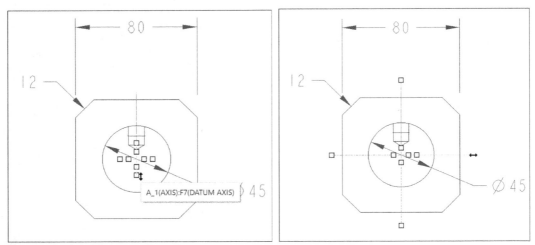

Figure 4.4(q) Cleanup drawing

Double-click on the Right Side view [Fig. 4.4(r)] > **View Display > Hidden > Apply** [Fig. 4.4(s)] > **OK > LMB**

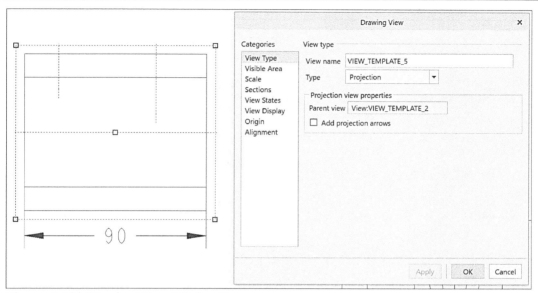

Figure 4.4(r) Display View Dialog Box

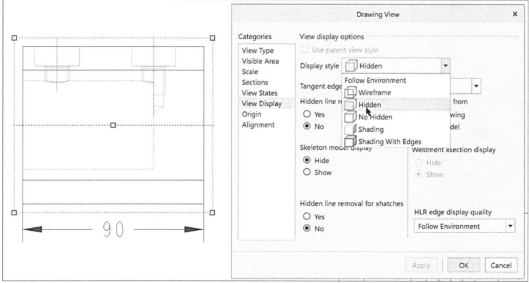

Figure 4.4(s) Display style Hidden

Select the **90mm** dimension **>** drag the extension lines to establish a gap between the extension line and the object [Figs. 4.4(t-u)] **> LMB >** cleanup the drawings dimensions as needed [Fig. 4.4(v)]

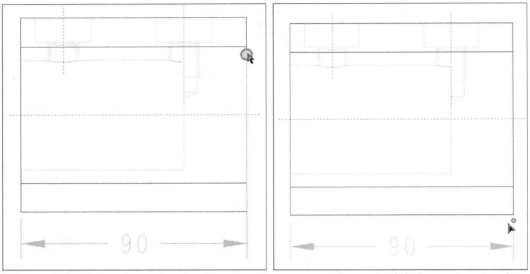

Figure 4.4(t) Select the extension lines' end   **Figure 4.4(u)** Gap extension line

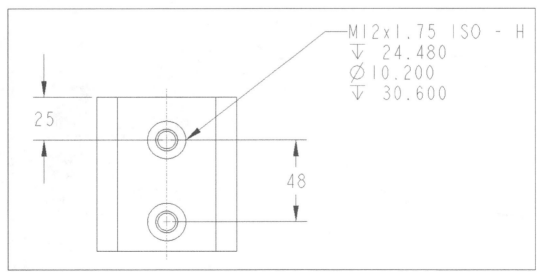

Figure 4.4(v) Cleanup

Click: **Ctrl+S** [Fig. 4.5] > **File** > **Manage File** > **Delete Old Versions** > **Yes** > **File** > **Close** > **File** > **Manage Session** > **Erase Not Displayed** > **OK** > **File** > **Exit** > **Yes**

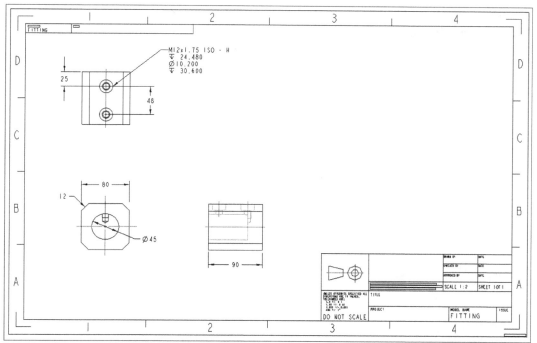

Figure 4.5 Completed Detail drawing

Quiz

1. Name five things that drawing can contain.
2. How do you display dimension, notes and centerlines?
3. What is a Drawing Format?
4. What are some of the items displayed in the Drawing Tree?
5. View Display allows for what changes to a drawing view?
6. How do you trim extension lines?

This completes Chapter 4

PART 2: Editing and evolving design options

Part 2 covers a wide range of Creo Parametric capabilities including: Sketching, Modeling, Editing, Copy and Paste Special, Group, Pattern, Relations, Parameters, Failures, Family Tables, and the Shell Tool.

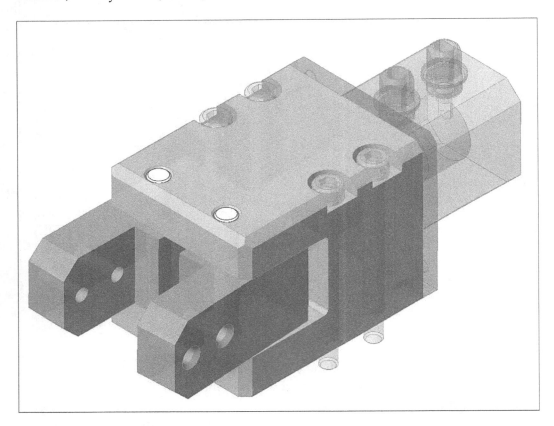

Modeling and redefining features

In this chapter we will create a complex model using a variety of tools and edit and redefine the component's features as needed.

It is tempting to directly start creating models. Nevertheless, in order to build value into a design, you need to create a product that can keep up with the constant design changes associated with the design-through-manufacturing process. Flexibility must be integral to the design. Flexibility is the key to a friendly and robust product design while maintaining design intent, and you can accomplish it through planning. To plan a design, you need to understand the overall function, form, and fit of the product. This understanding includes the following points:

- Overall size of the part
- Basic part characteristics
- The way in which the part can be assembled
- Approximate number of assembly components
- The manufacturing processes required to produce the part

Redefining, known as "editing the definition" of a model's feature is one of the most important steps in engineering design. Few if any designs require no changes, ECOs or, design variations from start to finish. Being able to edit every aspect of your project is as important as the actual modeling phase. Sometimes model geometry cannot be constructed because features that have been modified or created conflict with or invalidate other features. This will happen when flexing the model. A process where you edit and regenerate dimensions to see if the model holds up or fails.

Objectives

1. Learn how to set properties of material and units for a part
2. Editing the definition of a model
3. Become familiar with sketching constrains
4. Understand Creo Parametric file structure
5. Group features together
6. Pattern a feature/group
7. Change the display of the model

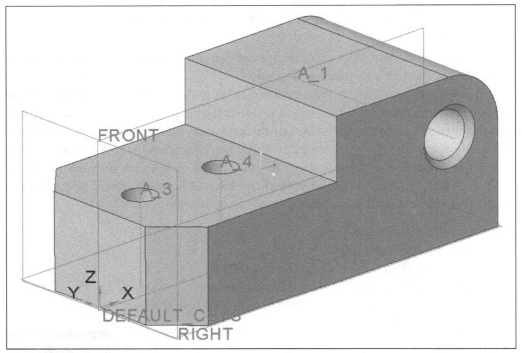

Figure 5.1 Gripper

Extrusions

The design of a part using Creo Parametric starts with the creation of base features (normally datum planes), and a solid extrusion. Other extrusions and cuts are then added in sequence as required by the design. You can use various types of features as building blocks in the progressive creation of solid parts [Fig. 5.1]. Certain features, by necessity, precede other more dependent features in the design process. Those dependent features rely on the previously defined features for dimensional and geometric references. The progressive design of features creates these dependent feature relationships known as *parent-child relationships*. The actual sequential history of the design is displayed in the Model Tree.

The parent-child relationship is one of the most powerful aspects of Creo Parametric and parametric modeling in general. It is also very important as you modify a part. After a parent feature in a part is modified, all children are automatically modified to reflect the changes in the parent feature. It is therefore essential to reference feature dimensions so that Creo Parametric can correctly propagate design modifications throughout the model.

A **protrusion/extrusion** is a feature that adds or removes material. An extrusion is *the first solid feature created* after base feature of datum planes. Figure 5.2 shows four common extrusions.

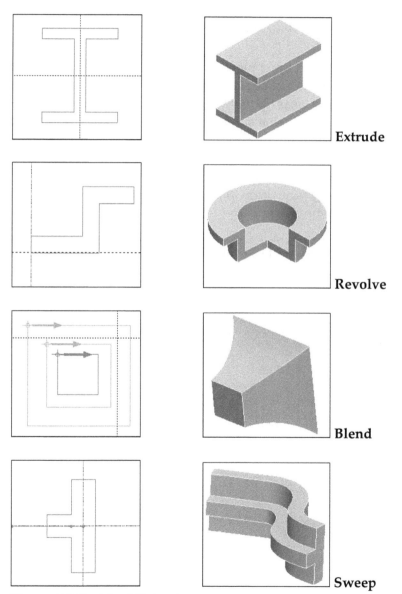

Extrude

Revolve

Blend

Sweep

Figure 5.2 Sketched Extrusions

Chapter 5 STEPS

The Gripper is composed of an extrusion created from a sketch with lines and a fillet, and three holes. Several things need to be established before you start modeling. These include setting up the *environment*, selecting the *units*, and establishing the *material* for the part.

Before you begin any part, you must plan the design. The **design intent** will depend on several things that are out of your control and many that you can establish. Asking yourself a few questions will clear up the design intent you will follow: Is the part a component of an assembly? If so, what surfaces or features are used to connect one part to another? Will geometric tolerancing be used on the part and assembly? What units are being used in the design, SI or decimal inch? What is the part's material? What is the primary part feature? How should I model the part, and what features are best used for the primary protrusion (the first solid mass)? On what datum plane should I sketch to model the first protrusion?

Launch **Creo Parametric > Select Working Directory > OK > Ctrl+N >** Name-- **gripper > Enter > File > Prepare > Model Properties** [Fig. 5.3(a)] **> Units change > millimeter Newton Second (mmNs) >** $\boxed{\text{→ Set...}}$ **> Close**

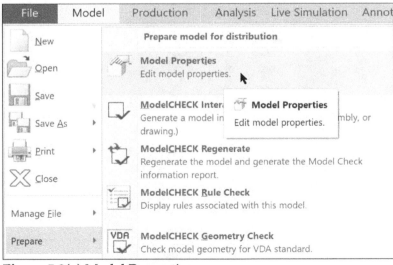

Figure 5.3(a) Model Properties

Click: Mass Properties 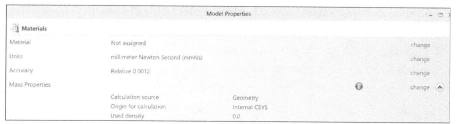 [Fig. 5.3(b)] > Material **change** > double-click on **metal_steel_high_carbon.mtl** [Fig. 5.3(c)] > **Yes > OK > Close > Ctrl+S > Enter > Tools** tab > ⬜ **Model Information** [Fig. 5.3(d)] > ☒ close the Browser

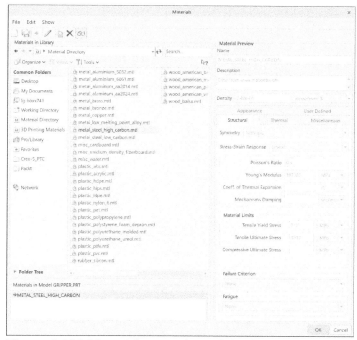

Figure 5.3(b) Model Properties

Figure 5.3(c) Materials- metal_steel_high_carbon.mtl

PART NAME :	GRIPPER				
MATERIAL FILENAME: METAL_STEEL_HIGH_CARBON					
MATERIAL HARDNESS: 297.000000					
Units:	Length:	Mass:	Force:	Time:	Temperature:
millimeter Newton Second (mmNs)	mm	tonne	N	sec	C

Figure 5.3(d) Materials & Units

155

Since **Use Default Template** was selected, the default datum planes and the default coordinate system are displayed in the Graphics Window and in the Model Tree. *The **default datum planes** and the **default coordinate system** will be the first features on all parts and assemblies.* The datum planes are used to sketch on and to orient the part's features. Having datum planes as the first features of a part, instead of the first extrusion, gives the designer more flexibility during the design process.

Up to this point you have been creating sketches internal to the feature tool selected. Here, you will create an external sketch and use it for a subsequent feature.

Click: > **View** tab > [toolbar icons] *toggle all on* > **Model** tab > Sketch > select datum **FRONT** [Fig. 5.4(a)] > **Sketch** > pick on **FRONT** in the Model Tree [Fig. 5.4(b)]

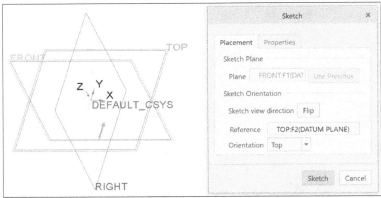

Figure 5.4(a) Sketch Dialog Box, Sketch Plane FRONT datum

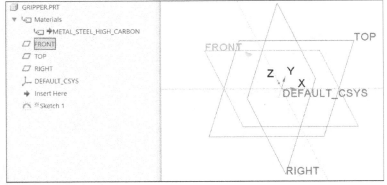

Figure 5.4(b) FRONT datum selected as sketch plane

Click: 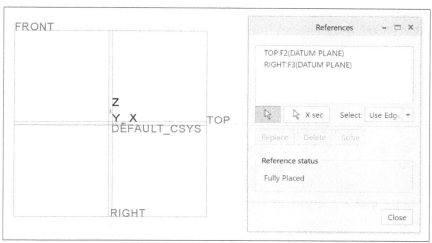 **Sketch View >** in the Graphics Window, press **RMB > References** [Fig. 5.4(c)] *(the TOP and RIGHT datum planes are the positional/dimensional references)* > **Close > File > Options > Sketcher >** Number of decimal places for dimensions **2** [Fig. 5.4(d)] > **OK > No > Shift+MMB** (pan) and **Ctrl+MMB** (zoom) to reposition and resize

Figure 5.4(c) References Dialog Box

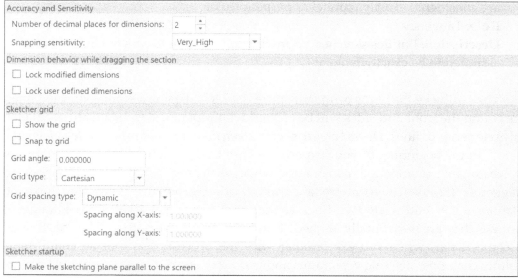

Figure 5.4(d) Sketcher Options

The sketch is now displayed and oriented in 2D. The coordinate system is at the middle of the sketch (facing up or front depending on the template file that was used) where datum RIGHT and datum TOP intersect. The square box you see is the limited display of datum FRONT. This is like sketching on a piece of paper. Creo Parametric is not coordinate-based software, so you need not enter geometry with X, Y, and Z coordinates.

Because this is a sketch in the true sense of the word, you need only create geometry that *approximates* the shape of the feature; the sketch does not have to be accurate as far as size or dimensions are concerned. No two sketches will be the same between those using these steps, unless you count each grid space (which is unnecessary). Even with the grid snap off, Creo Parametric constrains the geometry according to rules, which include but are not limited to the following:

- **Rule:** Symmetry
  Description: Entities sketched symmetrically about a centerline are assigned equal values with respect to the centerline
- **Rule:** Horizontal and vertical lines
  Description: Lines that are approximately horizontal or vertical are considered exactly horizontal or vertical
- **Rule:** Parallel and perpendicular lines
  Description: Lines that are sketched approximately parallel or perpendicular are considered exactly parallel or perpendicular
- **Rule:** Tangency
  Description: Entities sketched approximately tangent to arcs or circles are assumed to be exactly tangent

The outline of the part's primary feature is sketched using a set of connected lines. The cut on the front and sides will be created with separate sketched features. Sketch only one series of lines. ***Do not create sketch elements on top of other sketch elements.***

In the beginning of your experience with Creo Parametric it is important not to create any unintended constraints while sketching. Therefore, remember to exaggerate the sketch geometry and not to align geometric items that have no relationship. If you draw two lines at the same horizontal level, Creo Parametric assumes they are horizontally aligned. Two lines the same length will be constrained as equal. Later, when you are familiar with the process, you will be comfortable adding, changing, deleting constraints and geometry on the fly. At this point, be more careful with your sketch elements and geometry constraints.

Select: [⌇] **Line Chain** > beginning at the origin of the coordinate system sketch six lines starting with a horizontal line *(watch the constraints as they appear- make each segment a different length)* [Fig. 5.4(e)] > **MMB** to end the line sequence [Fig. 5.4(f)] >

MMB If the sketch is valid it will be shaded > *(If the sketch is not to your liking, click* [↺] *Undo and try again) (do not change your weak dimension values. Your sketch should have the same shape but different dimension values)* > **RMB** > [✓] > **File > Save > Enter**

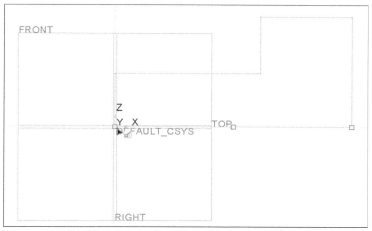

Figure 5.4(e) Sketching the Closed Outline *(do not make unwanted constraints)*

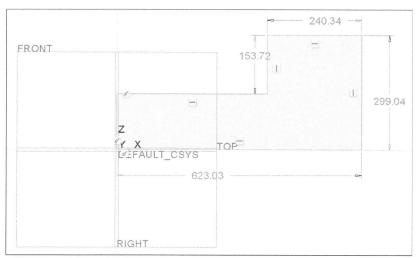

Figure 5.4(f) Default *"weak"* Dimensions Display *(your sketch should appear "similar")*.

Sketcher constraint symbols ═1 ┃ , ╱ appear next to an entity that is controlled by that constraint. Sketcher constraints can be turned on or off (enabled or disabled) while sketching. Simply click the RMB as you sketch- before picking the position- and the constraint that is displaying will have a slash imposed over it. This will disable it for that entity. An // next to a line means parallel; a ⌀ means tangent. Dimensions display, as they are needed according to the references selected and the constraints. Seldom are they the same as the required dimensioning scheme needed to manufacture the part. The dimensioning scheme is important, not the dimension value, which can be modified.

Place and create the dimensions as required. Do not be concerned with the perfect positioning of the dimensions, but in general, follow the spacing and positioning standards found in the **ASME Y15.5** standards. This saves you time when you create a drawing of the part. Dimensions placed at this stage of the design process are displayed on the drawing document by simply showing all the dimensions.

To dimension between two lines, pick the lines (LMB) and place the dimension value (MMB). To dimension a single line, pick on the line (LMB), and place the dimension with MMB.

Select: **Sketch 1** from the Model Tree > 🖌 **Edit Definition** [Fig. 5.4(g)] > **LMB** to deselect > **RMB** > **Dimension** > to create a dimension—pick the line[s] > move the pointer > **MMB** to place the dimension > **MMB** *(to accept the initial value)* > **MMB** *(to end the dimensioning tool)* > to move a dimension—pick on a dimension > hold down the **LMB** > move it to a new position

---

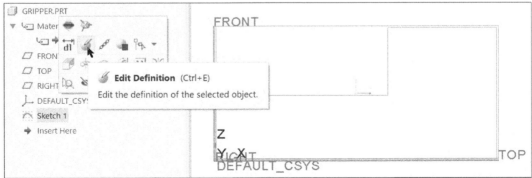

Figure 5.4(g) Edit Definition

160

Light colored dimension values are called "weak" dimensions. If a weak dimension matches your dimensioning scheme, you can make it "strong" (darker)—pick on a weak dimension, highlights. > press **RMB** > **Strong** [Fig. 5.4(h)] > **Enter** > **MMB** *(do not make the "sketch dimensions" Strong since they are not design values)*

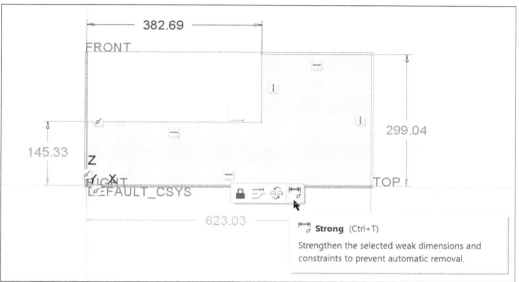

Figure 5.4(h) Edited sketch (dimension scheme must be the same, not the values)

Click: `Select` > Window-in the sketch (place the cursor at one corner of the window; with the **LMB** depressed, drag the cursor to the opposite corner of the window and release the **LMB**) to capture all *four* dimensions, which will *highlight*. > `Modify` from **Ribbon** *or RMB > Modify [Fig. 5.4(i)]* > ☑ Regenerate ☑ Lock Scale > lengthen the Modify Dimensions dialog box *(so that you can see all four dimensions)* [Fig. 5.4(j)] > in the Modify Dimensions dialog box, locate the dimension for the overall width *(your dimension value may be different)*, double-click in that length dimension value field and *type* in the design value at the prompt (**120**) [Fig. 5.4(k)] > **Enter**

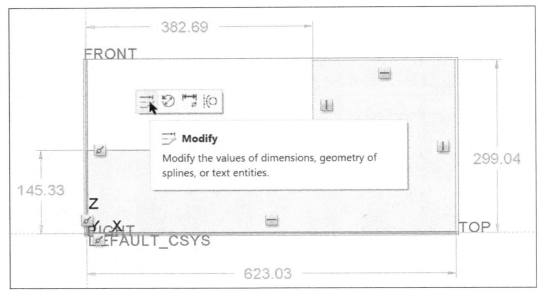

Figure 5.4(i) Modify

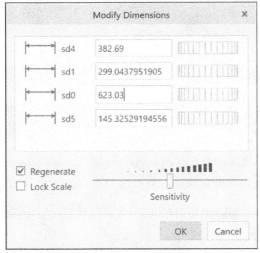

Figure 5.4(j) Modify Dimensions

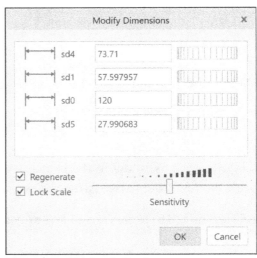

Figure 5.4(k) Lock Scale

Click: **OK** Save the sketch and exit [Fig. 5.4(l)] > 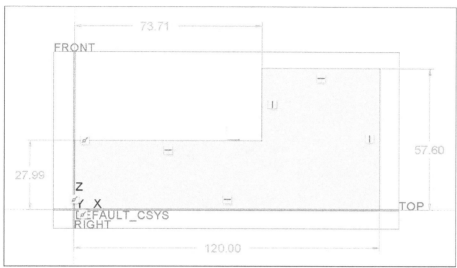 ⊞ **Refit** > double-click on another dimension on the sketch (in the Graphics Window) and modify the value > **Enter** > continue until all the values are changed to the design sizes [Fig. 5.4(m)] *(your sketch **must** have these dimensions and dimension values)* > **LMB**

Figure 5.4(l) Modify each Dimension individually

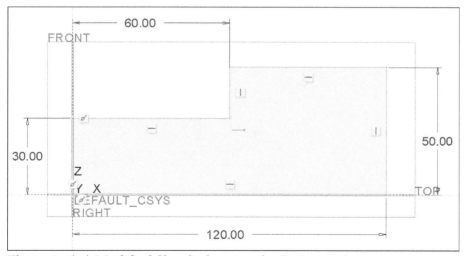

Figure 5.4(m) Modified Sketch showing the Design Values
(your sketch must have these dimensions and dimension values)

Press: **Ctrl+D > RMB >** [✓] **OK > Save >** select the **Sketch** from the **Model Tree >** [⬚]
Extrude [Fig. 5.5(a)] **>** the extrusion will preview [Fig. 5.5(b)]

The external sketch is used by the extrude tool instead of sketching after the tool was selected.

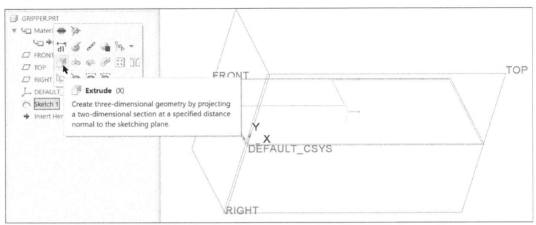

Figure 5.5(a) Extrude using Sketched Curve *("Datum Curve")*

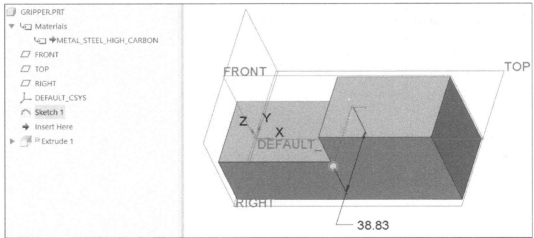

Figure 5.5(b) Extrusion preview

Double-click on the depth value on the model > **60** [Fig. 5.5(c)] > **Enter** > place the pointer over the square drag handle 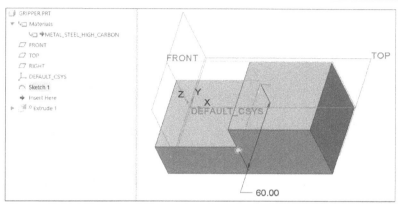 *(it will change color)* [Fig. 5.5(d)] > press **RMB** > **Symmetric** [Fig. 5.5(e)] > **MMB** > **LMB** [Fig. 5.5(f)]

Figure 5.5(c) Depth of Extrusion Previewed

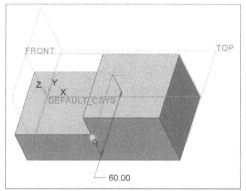

Figure 5.5(d) Modify the Depth Value

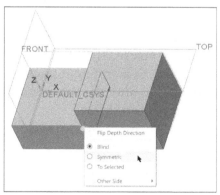

Figure 5.7(e) RMB > Symmetric

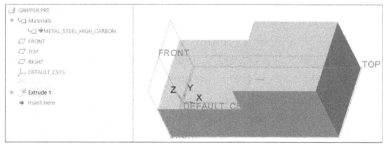

Figure 5.5(f) Completed Extrusion *(Sketch is grayed-out, hidden in the Model Tree)*

Click: **File > Options > Model Display > Trimetric > Isometric** [Fig. 5.5(g)] **> OK > No > File > Manage File > Delete Old Versions > Yes**

Figure 5.5(g) Isometric

Creo Parametric files

Storing an object on the disk does not overwrite an existing object file. To preserve earlier versions, Creo Parametric saves the object to a new file with the same object name but with an updated version number. Every time you store an object using **Save**, you create a new version of the object in memory and write the previous version to disk. Creo Parametric numbers each version of an object storage file consecutively (for example, box.sec.1, box.sec.2, box.sec.3). If you save 25 times, you have 25 versions of the object, all at different stages of completion. You can use *File > Manage File > Delete Old Versions* after the *Save* command to eliminate previous versions of the object that may have been stored.

When opening an existing object file, you can open any version that is saved. Although Creo Parametric automatically retrieves the latest saved version of an object, you can retrieve any previous version by entering the full file name with extension and version number (for example, partname.prt.5). If you do not know the specific version number, you can enter a number relative to the latest version. For example, to retrieve a part from two versions ago, enter partname.prt.3 *(or partname.prt.-2)*.

You use *File > Manage Session > **Erase Current** to* remove the object and its associated objects from memory. If you close a window before erasing it, the object is still in memory. In this case, you use *File > Manage Session > **Erase Not Displayed** to* remove the object and its associated objects from memory. This does not delete the object. It just removes it from active memory. *File > Manage File > Delete All Versions* removes the file from memory and from disk completely. You are prompted with a Delete All Confirm dialog box when choosing this command. Be careful not to delete needed files.

Select the edge of the extrusion > **Round** [Fig. 5.6(a)] > drag the handle until the radius is **18mm** [Fig. 5.6(b)] > **MMB** [Fig. 5.6(c)]

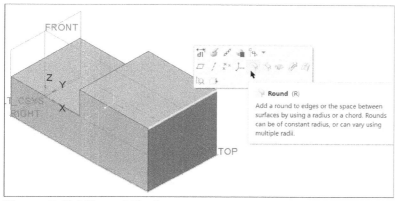

Figure 5.6(a) Round Tool

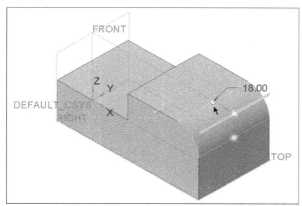

Figure 5.6(b) Round

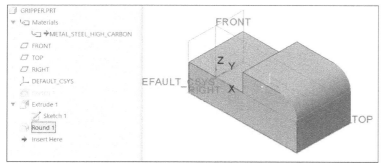

Figure 5.6(c) Completed Round

167

The Model Tree has two features; the extrusion and the round. Since the "Round" is really a large radius curve it should be incorporated into the extrusion.

Click: **Undo** > select **Sketch 1** > **RMB** > **Edit Definition** [Fig. 5.7(a)] > **RMB** > **Fillet** [Fig. 5.7(b)] > select the two lines [Fig. 5.7(c)] > double-click on radius value > **18** > **Enter** > add the **50** height dimension back on the sketch Fig. 5.7(d)]

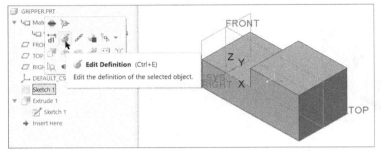

Figure 5.7(a) Edit Definition

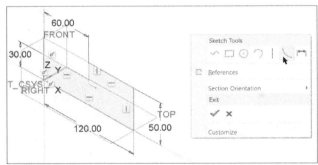

Figure 5.7(b) Select Fillet

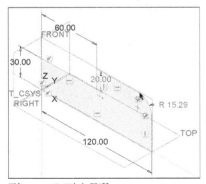

Figure 5.7(c) Fillet

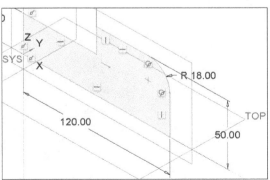

Figure 5.7(d) R18 Fillet (and 50mm height)

168

Click: **RMB >** ☑ **OK > LMB** [Fig. 5.7(e)] **>** select the fillet's curved surface **> Axis** [Fig. 5.7(f)] **> Hole** tool from Ribbon [Fig. 5.8(a)] **>** press **Ctrl** and select the **FRONT** datum plane [Fig. 5.8(b)]

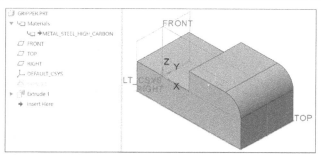

Figure 5.7(e) Model Tree shows one solid feature

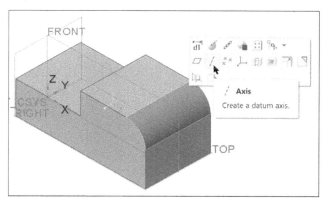

Figure 5.7(f) Axis

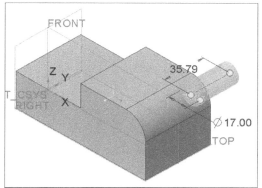

Figure 5.8(a) Hole centered on the Axis

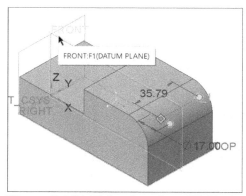

Figure 5.8(b) Hole placed on FRONT

Click: **Placement** tab > diameter **15** > **Enter** [Fig. 5.8(c)] > **Shape** tab > **Though All** on both sides [Fig. 5.8(d)] > **MMB** > select the edge of the hole > **Edge Chamfer** [Fig. 5.9(a)

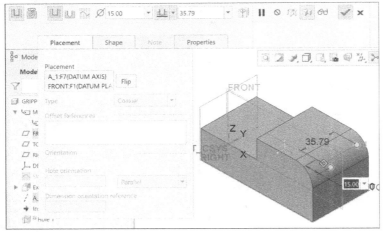

Figure 5.8(c) Placement

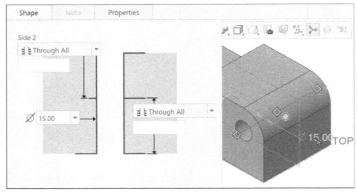

Figure 5.8(d) Through All both sides

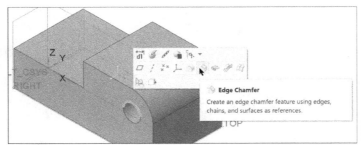

Figure 5.9(a) Edge Chamfer

170

Ctrl+ select the opposite edge of the hole [Fig. 5.9(b] **> 2** [Fig. 5.9(c) **> Enter > MMB > LMB >** add **12mm** chamfers to the short vertical edges [Fig. 5.9(d)] **> Ctrl+D > Save**

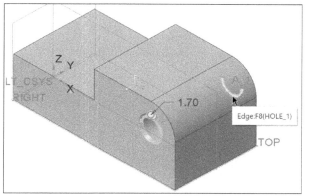

Figure 5.9(b) Chamfer both ends

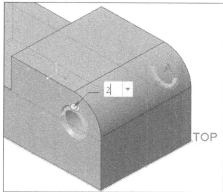

Figure 5.9(c) Chamfers

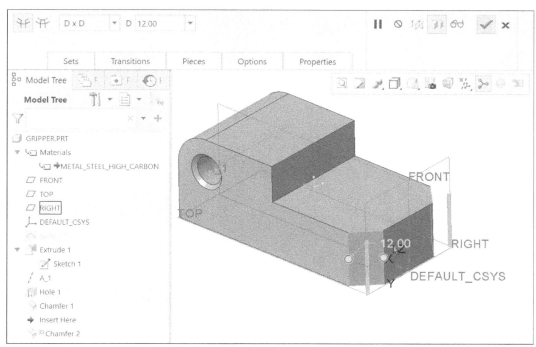

Figure 5.9(d) Corner Chamfers

Spin the model > **Hole** > **Placement** tab > pick on the ledge surface [Fig. 5.10(a) > **RMB** > **Offset Reference Collector** > press **Ctrl** key and select **FRONT** datum and **RIGHT** datums > FRONT Offset **0** *(or Align)* > RIGHT Offset **15** [Fig. 5.10(b) > **MMB**

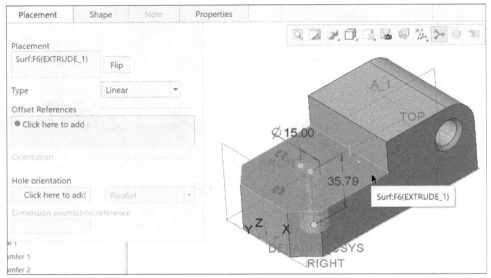

Figure 5.10(a) Hole Placement Surface

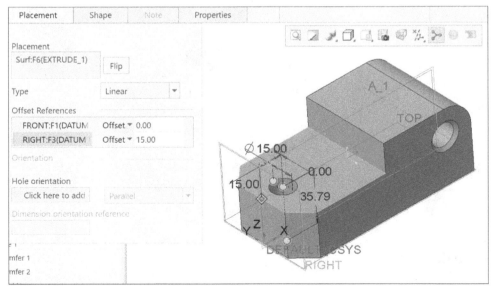

Figure 5.10(b) Hole preview

With the **Hole** still selected > **Ctrl+E** Edit Definition > **Shape** tab > **Through All** > **16** [Fig. 5.10(c) > **Enter** > **MMB** > add a **2mm** chamfer to the hole [Fig. 5.10(d] > **MMB**

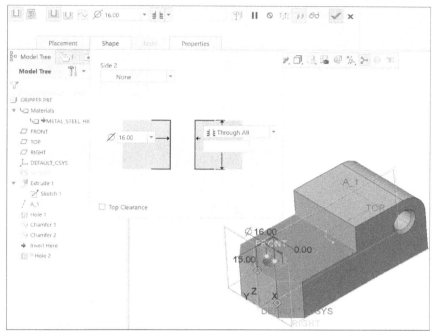

Figure 5.10(c) Hole Shape

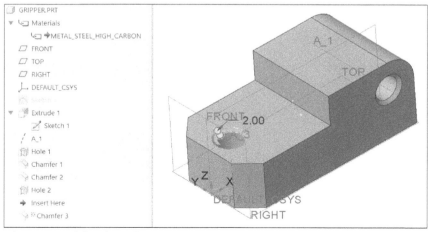

Figure 5.10(d) Chamfer on Hole

173

Press **Ctrl** and select the **Hole 2** and the **Chamfer** from the Model Tree > 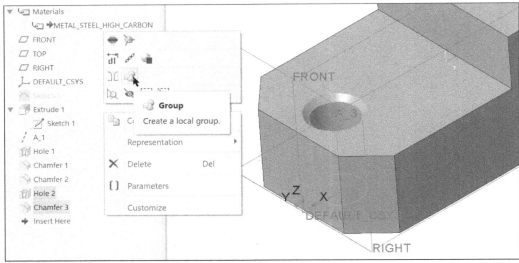 **Group** [Fig. 5.11(a)] > **RMB** > **Pattern** [Fig. 5.11(b)]

Figure 5.11(a) Group

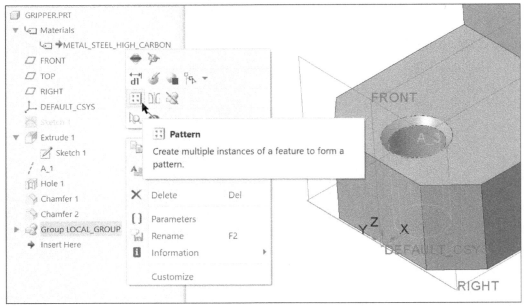

Figure 5.11(b) Pattern

Dimensions tab > select **15** [Fig. 5.11(c)] > **30** > **Enter** [Fig. 5.11(d)] > **MMB** [Fig. 5.11(e)]

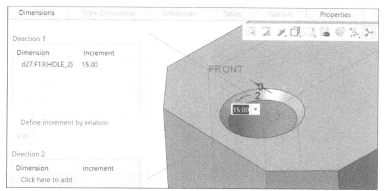

Figure 5.11(c) Select dimension

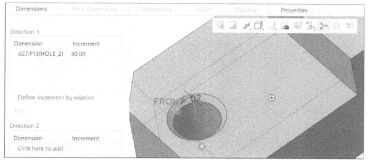

Figure 5.11(d) Increment

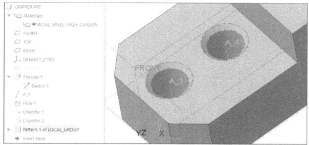

Figure 5.11(e) Patterned Hole

The chamfer is on wrong side of the part and the hole's and chamfer dimension are incorrect. In most cases, the edits to a feature are simple dimensional changes. When the references need changing, Edit Definition is used to go back into the feature's setup and configuration.

Select the **Chamfer** from the Model Tree > **Edit Definition** [Fig. 5.12(a)] > **Sets** > in the References field **RMB** > **Remove** [Fig. 5.12(b)] > spin the model > pick the hole's edge on the bottom of the part > change the size to **4** > **Enter** [Fig. 5.12(c)] > **MMB** > **Save**

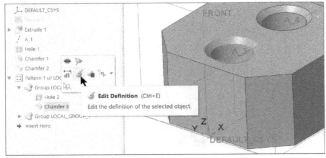

Figure 5.12(a) Edit Definition

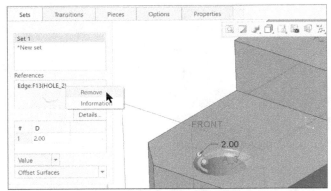

Figure 5.12(b) Remove Edge Reference

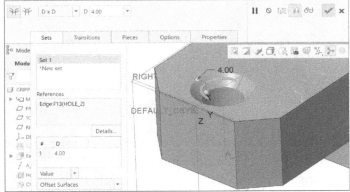

Figure 5.12(c) Add the edge reference to opposite side of hole

Double-click on the **Hole** > double-click on the **16mm** dimension and change to **10.2mm** > **MMB** > **LMB** > **LMB** [Fig. 5.13(a)] > **Sets** > **RMB** > **Remove** [Fig. 5.13(b)] > **MMB** to spin the model > pick the hole's edge on the bottom of the part > change the size to **4mm** > **Enter** > **LMB** > **LMB** > **Ctrl+D** > **Save**

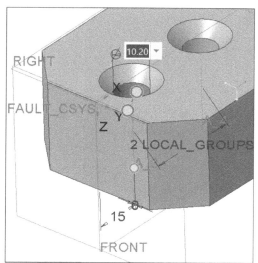

Figure 5.13(a) Viewing bottom of part

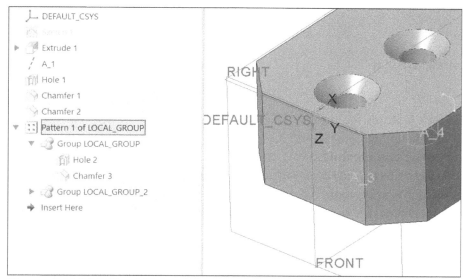

Figure 5.13(b) Edited Holes (viewing bottom of part)

Select: **View** tab > **Appearances** > select a new color > **Display Style** > **Model Display** Group drop down menu > **Temporary Shade** > **Ctrl+1** [Fig. 5.14] > **Ctrl+R** *repaint* > **Save** > **File** > **Manage File** > **Delete Old Versions** > **Yes** > **File** > **Close**

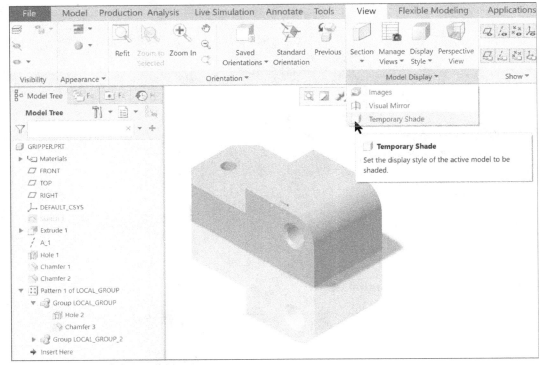

Figure 5.14 Model Display

Quiz

1. Name four features that use sketches.
2. What are sketching constraints?
3. Name three datum features.
4. What is the difference between weak and strong dimensions?
5. What elements are considered important in design intent control?
6. When you save a file does it overwrite the previous save?

This completes Chapter 5

Organizing and editing

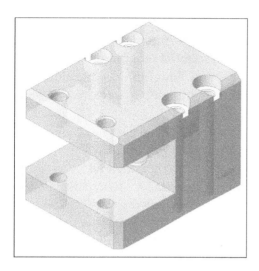

Datums and layers are two of the most useful mechanisms for creating and organizing your design. Features such as *datum planes* and *datum axes* are essential for the formation of complex parts, assemblies, and drawings. Though default datum planes have been sufficient in previous Chapters, here the part incorporates the creation of user-defined datums and the assignment of datums to layers. The datum planes will be set as geometric tolerance features and put on a separate layer.

Objectives
1. Creating and editing sketches of features
2. Editing, adding, and changing references for sketch dimensions
3. Create datums to locate features
4. Mirror features
5. Use copy and paste special to replicate and move geometry
6. Pattern features
7. Add relations to control features
8. Set datum planes for geometric tolerancing
9. Learn how to change and edit the color of models
10. Use layers to organize features
11. Use information commands to extract relations information

Layers and Datum Planes

Most companies have a layering scheme that serves as a *default standard* so that all projects follow the same naming conventions and objects/items are easily located by anyone with access. Layer information such as display status, is stored with each individual part, assembly, or drawing. Layers are an essential tool for grouping items and performing operations on them, such as selecting, hide/unhide, plotting, and suppressing. Any number of layers can be created. User-defined names are available, so layer names can be easily recognized.

Default datum planes and the default coordinate system are automatically placed on two layers each. For the datum planes; the *part default datum plane layer* and the *part all datum plane layer*. The coordinate system will also be layered in a similar fashion. The *part all datum coordinate system layer* for the coordinate system displays the new name created for the coordinate system. It is considered good practice to rename the default coordinate system to something like the components name. If an assembly has 25 components, it will have 25 default coordinate systems. Renaming the coordinate systems of each component will make them easier to visually identify

Editing

For sketched features you can roll the model back to the feature and edit its parametric sketch. Upon regeneration the model will update or fail depending on what extent the changes attempt to make to the component. If a feature fails, Creo Parametric will roll back the model to the last regenerated feature. You can edit or undo the definition of the failed feature at this juncture.

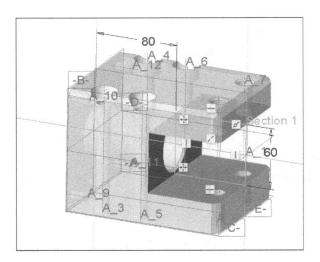

Chapter 6 STEPS

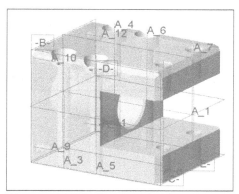

Figure 6.1 Mechanism-body

Launch **Creo Parametric > Select Working Directory** > navigate to your directory >
OK > Ctrl+N > Name-- *type* **mechanism-body** [Fig. 6.1] **> Enter > File > Options >**
Configuration Editor > Options: **Import/Export > Import configuration file >**
Creo_textbook.pro *(created previously)* **> Open > OK > No > File > Prepare > Model**
Properties > Units **change > millimeter Newton Second > Set > Interpret > Close >**
Material **change >** double-click on **metal_steel_high_carbon.mtl > OK > Yes > Close >**
select the coordinate system on the model or in the Model Tree-- **PRT_CSYS_DEF >**
RMB [Fig. 6.2(a)] **> Rename >** *type* **csys_mechanism-body** in the Model Tree **> Enter**
(automatically becomes uppercase) [Fig. 6.2(b)] **> LMB > Ctrl+S > OK**

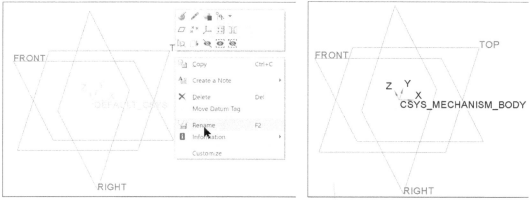

Figure 6.2(a) Rename the Default Coordinate System   **Figure 6.2(b)** Renamed CSYS

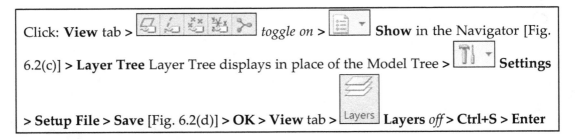

Click: **View** tab > [icons] *toggle on* > [icon] **Show** in the Navigator [Fig. 6.2(c)] > **Layer Tree** Layer Tree displays in place of the Model Tree > [icon] **Settings** > **Setup File** > **Save** [Fig. 6.2(d)] > **OK** > **View** tab > [Layers icon] **Layers** *off* > **Ctrl+S** > **Enter**

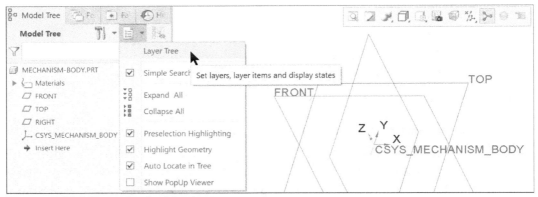

Figure 6.2(c) Show in the Navigator

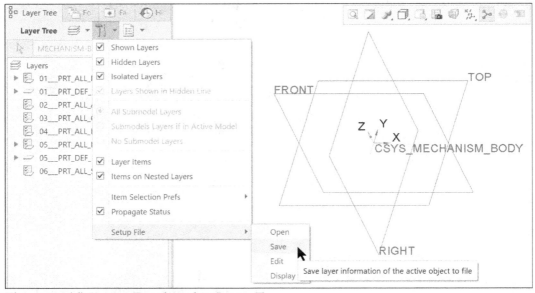

Figure 6.2(d) Layers Displayed in Layer Tree

Click: **Model** tab > [Extrude icon] Extrude **Extrude** *(or type x)* > **Placement** from the Dashboard > **Define** [Fig. 6.3(a)] > in the Sketch dialog box: Sketch Plane--- Plane: select datum

FRONT from the model or Model Tree [Fig. 6.3(b)] > **Sketch > RMB >**

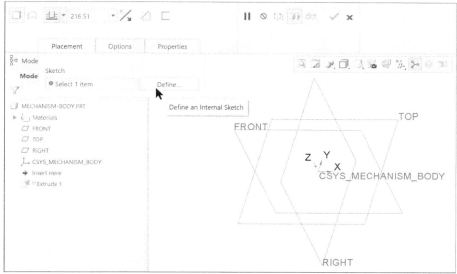

Figure 6.3(a) Define an Internal Sketch

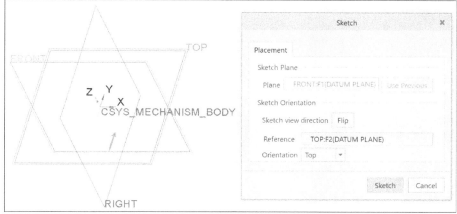

Figure 6.3(b) Select Datum FRONT

Starting at the coordinate system, sketch a rectangle with equal sides [Fig. 6.3(c)] > **MMB** > modify the dimension to a **120mm** square > **RMB** > ✓ > drag the handle to **150mm** [Fig. 6.3(d)] > **MMB** > **LMB** > **Ctrl+S**

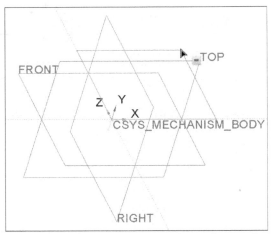

Figure 6.3(c) Sketch rectangle with equal sides

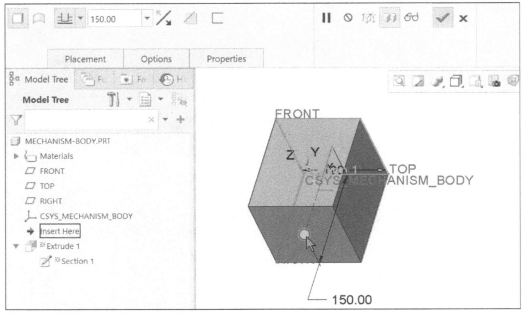

Figure 6.3(d) First Extrusion Feature

Apearances

Colors are used to define material and light properties. Avoid the colors that are used as Creo Parametric defaults for selection. It is up to you to select colors that work with the type of project you are modeling. If the parts will be used in an assembly, each component should have a unique color scheme. In general, using *light pastel colors* are preferred over bright dark ones.

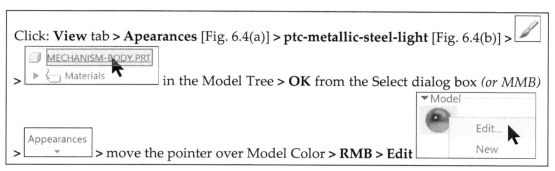

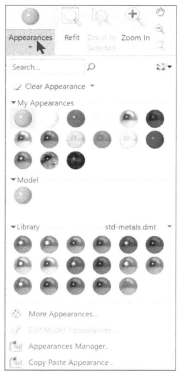

Figure 6.4(a) Appearance Gallery

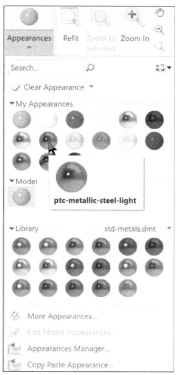

Figure 6.4(b) ptc-metallic-steel-light

Click on the color button in the Model Appearance Editor dialog, Properties, Class Metal > **Generic** [Fig. 6.4(c)] > (color swatch) to open the Color Editor dialog box > move the **RGB/HSV sliders** bars to create a new color (or type new values) > you can also use the **Color wheel** **Color Wheel** > or the **Blending palette** **Blending Palette** > adjust the colors [Fig. 6.4(d)] > **OK** from the Color Editor dialog box > Highlight Color > adjust as desired [Fig. 6.4(e)] > **OK** > set **Transparency** to

Transparency 20.00

Adjust Transparency of selected appearance

20 percent > **Close**

Color selection may be different depending on PTC license and graphics card.

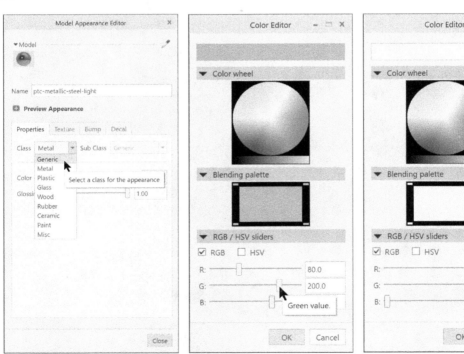

Figure 6.4(c) Appearance   **Figure 6.4(d)** Color   **Figure 6.4(e)** Highlight Color

Click: 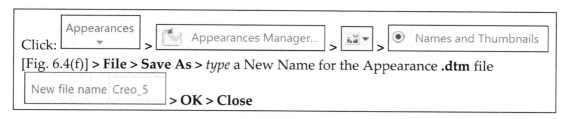 > **File > Save As >** *type* a New Name for the Appearance **.dtm** file

New file name Creo_5 > **OK > Close**

[Fig. 6.4(f)]

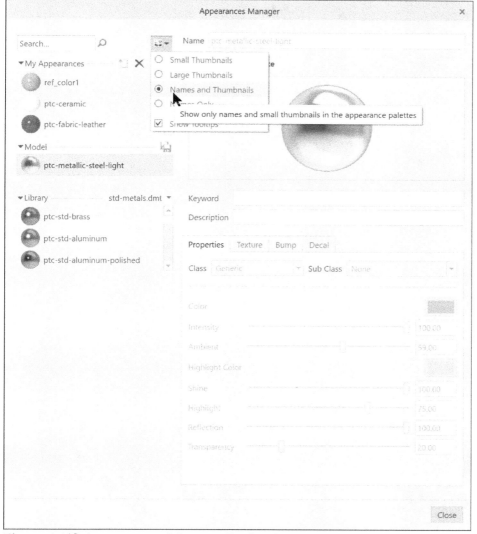

Figure 6.4(f) Appearances Manager Dialog Box

Click: **File > Options > Model Display >** Default model orientation: **Trimetric > Isometric** [Fig. 6.5(a)] **> Sketcher >** Number of decimal place **1** [Fig. 6.5(b)] **> OK > No > Ctrl+D > Ctrl+S** [Fig. 6.5(c)]

	Creo Parametric Educational Edition Options
Favorites	Change how the model is displayed.
Environment	
System Appearance	Model orientation
Model Display	Default model orientation: Isometric

Figure 6.5(a) Model Display Isometric

	Creo Parametric Educational Edition Options
Favorites	Set options for objects display, grid, style, and constraints.
Environment	☑ Tangent
System Appearance	
Model Display	Accuracy and Sensitivity
Entity Display	Number of decimal places for dimensions: 1
Selection	
Sketcher	Snapping sensitivity: Very_High

Figure 6.5(b) Sketcher Number of decimal places (1)

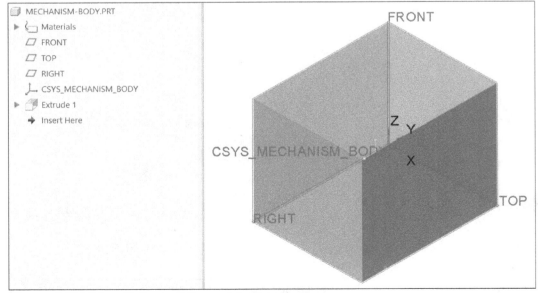

MECHANISM-BODY.PRT
▶ Materials
FRONT
TOP
RIGHT
CSYS_MECHANISM_BODY
▶ Extrude 1
→ Insert Here

Figure 6.5(c) New Color and Isometric Orientation

Pick: **RMB** on the Graphics Toolbar [Fig. 6.5(d)] > toggle all on > **Location > Show on the Right** [Fig. 6.5(e)] > **OK > No > Ctrl+D > Ctrl+S**

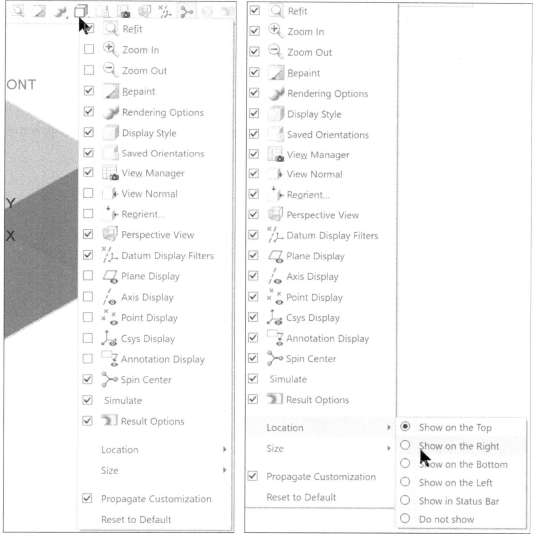

Figure 6.5(d) Graphics Toolbar   **Figure 6.5(e)** Graphics Toolbar Location

For the next feature, two datum planes will be created. New part datum planes are by default numbered sequentially, DTM1, DTM2, and so on. Also, a datum axis will be established through the intersection of the two datums for he large hole's placement. Note that holes and circular features automatically have axes when they are created. Features created with arcs, fillets and so on need to have an axis added if needed as a design reference.

Click: [icon] **Datum Display Filters** from the Graphics Toolbar > [☐ Csys Display] *off* > select the **TOP** datum > [icon] **Plane** [Fig. 6.6(a)] > drag the handle to between *50-70mm*, the size is not important since a *relation* will be created to determine the actual distance [Fig. 6.6(b)] > **OK** > **Save**

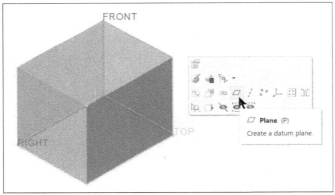

Figure 6.6(a) Offset Datum

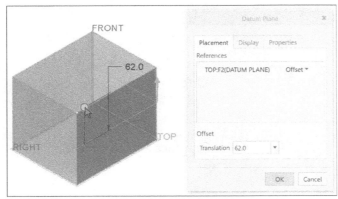

Figure 6.6(b) Drag the handle

Select the **RIGHT** datum > ⬜ **Plane** > Translation- anything number between *50-70mm*, a *relation* will be created to lock the actual distance [Fig. 6.6(c)] > **OK** > press **Ctrl** > select **DTM1** and **DTM2** > **RMB** > ⬜ **Axis** [Fig. 6.6(d)]

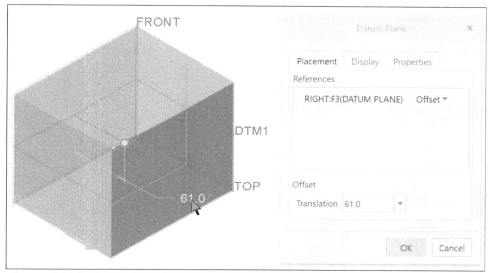

Figure 6.6(c) New offset datum

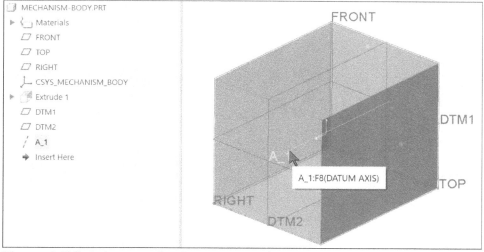

Figure 6.6(d) Axis created at intersection of DTM1 and DTM2

Relations

Parametric relations are user-defined equations written between symbolic dimensions and parameters. Relations capture design relationships between features which control the effects of modifications on models. Relations will be created to ensure that datum DTM1 and DTM2 are centered. Your **"d"** values may be different.

> Select: **Tools** tab > **Relations** > select **DTM1** [Fig. 6.7(a)] > pick **d6** *(Note: your "d" values may be different)* [Fig. 6.7(b)] > select or type **=**

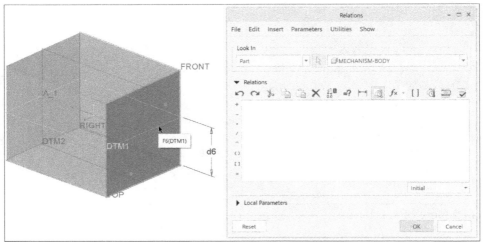

Figure 6.7(a) Select DTM1

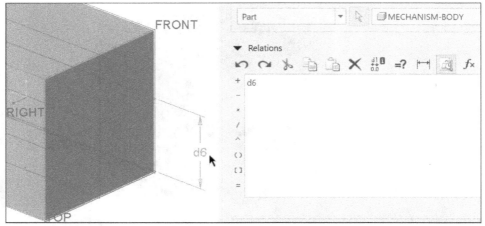

Figure 6.7(b) Select d6 (you may have a different number)

Select the extrude feature from the model > pick **d4** [Fig. 6.7(c)] > type **/2** in the Relations field *(your "d" values may be different)* [Fig. 6.7(d)] > [✓] **Execute/Verify Relations > OK > RMB > Regenerate >** double-click **DTM1** and then double-click on the **60** dimension > ⚠️ Dimension in MECHANISM-BODY is driven by relation d6=d4/2. displays in the Message Log area at bottom left of the Graphics Window > **LMB > LMB > Ctrl+S**

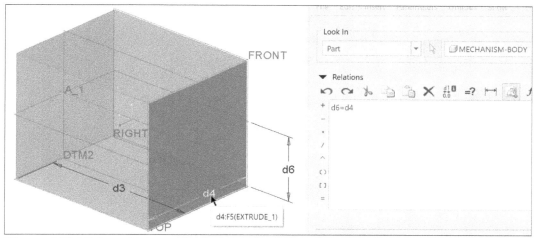

Figure 6.7(c) Select d4 *(your d values may be different)*

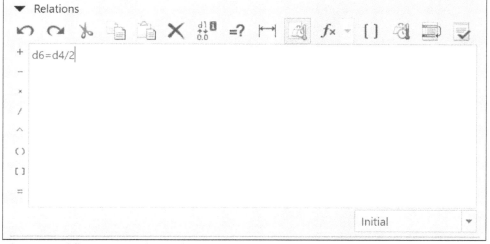

Figure 6.7(d) Relation d6=d4/2 *(your d values may be different)*

193

Repeat: **Tools** tab > **Relations** > start another line > select **DTM2** [Fig. 6.7(e)] > pick **d7** *(Note: your "d" values may be different)* [Fig. 6.7(f)] > select or type =

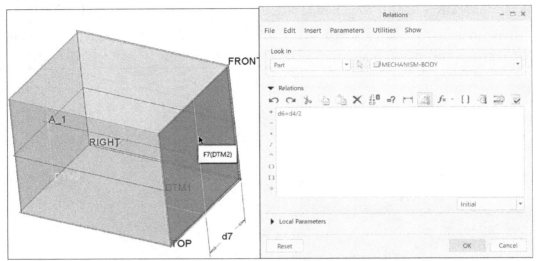

Figure 6.7(e) Select DTM2 *(your d values may be different)*

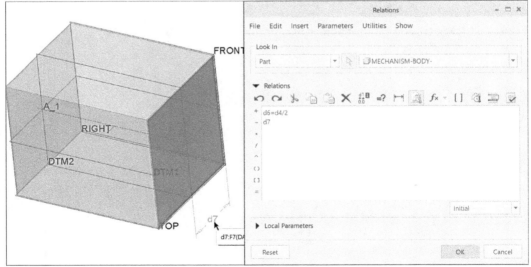

Figure 6.7(f) Select d7 *(your d values may be different)*

Select the extrude feature > pick **d4** [Fig. 6.7(g)] > **/2** in the Relations field > [✓] > **OK** [Fig. 6.7(h)] > **OK** > **RMB** > **Regenerate** > double-click **DTM2** and then double-click on the **60** dimension > ⚠ Dimension in MECHANISM-BODY is driven by relation d7=d4/2. > **Ctrl+D**

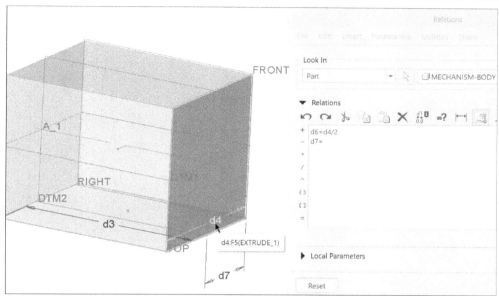

Figure 6.7(g) Select d4 *(your d values may be different)*

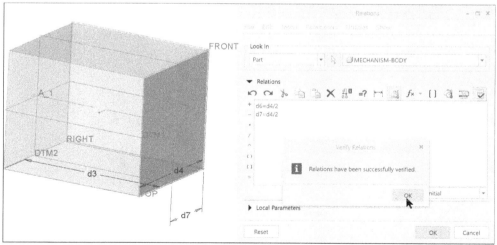

Figure 6.7(h) Relation d7=d4/2 *(your d values may be different)*

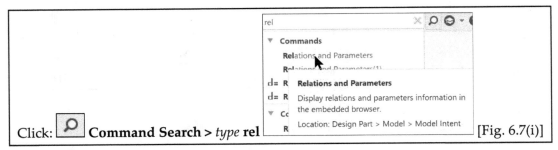

Click: 🔍 **Command Search >** *type* **rel** [Fig. 6.7(i)]

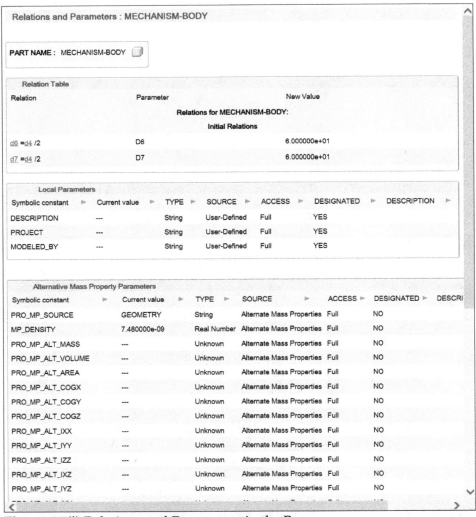

Figure 6.7(i) Relations and Parameters in the Browser

Select **d6**, and **d7** *(your **d** values may be different)* in the Browser to display them in the Graphics Window [Fig. 6.7(j)] > ☒ or 🔄 to close the Browser > in the Graphics Window, **LMB > RMB > Regenerate > Ctrl+R > Ctrl+D > Ctrl+S**

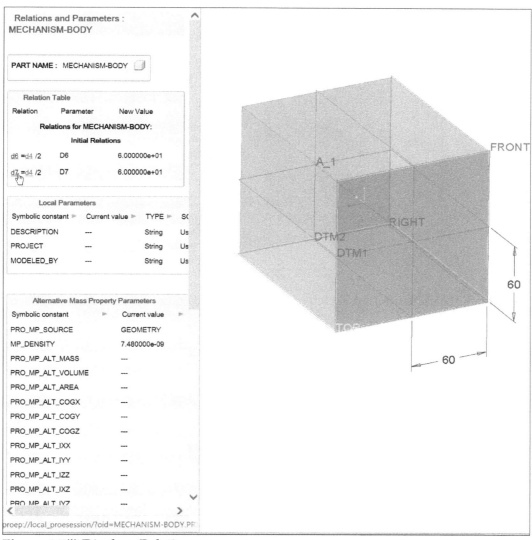

Figure 6.7(j) Displays Relation

Click: [Extrude] **Extrude > RMB > Remove Material > RMB > Define Internal Sketch** [Fig. 6.8(a)] > Sketch Plane--- Plane: select datum **DTM2** as the sketch plane > **Sketch** [Fig. 6.8(b)]

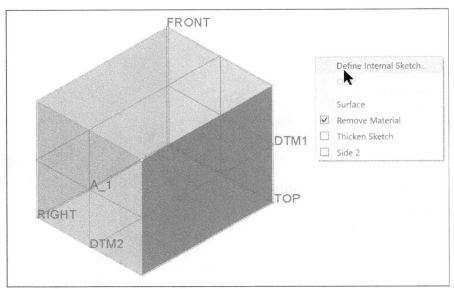

Figure 6.8(a) Define Internal Sketch

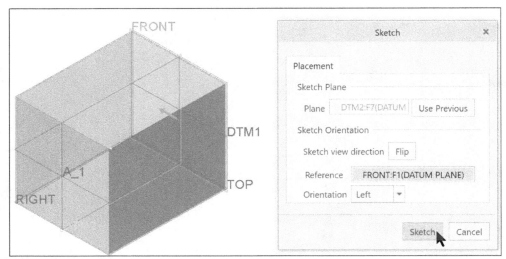

Figure 6.8(b) DTM2 Selected as Sketch Plane

In the Graphics Window, press: **RMB > References >** pick DTM1 and the upper surface and the left vertical surface of the part to add it to the References dialog box > **Solve** [Fig. 6.8(c)] > **Close >** ⟨icon⟩ **Sketch View**

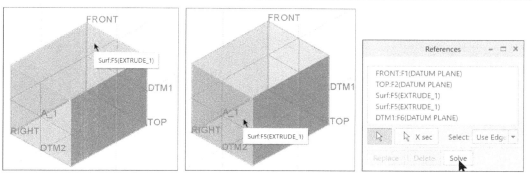

Figure 6.8(c) Add References

Click: **View** tab > **Display Style >** ⟨icon⟩ Hidden Line *(or Ctrl+5)* > **Sketch** tab > in the Graphics Window, press **RMB >** ⟨icon⟩ **Construction Centerline** [Fig. 6.8(d)] > create a *horizontal* centerline through the center of the part by picking two positions along the edge of DTM1 > **MMB > LMB**

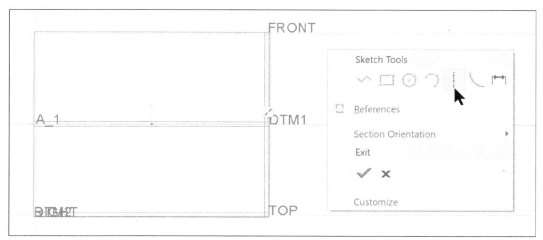

Figure 6.8(d) Centerline

Press: **RMB >** ⬚ **Corner Rectangle** [Fig. 6.8(e)] > click **LMB** to sketch a rectangle symmetrical to the centerline [Fig. 6.8(f)] > **LMB** to complete the current rectangle > **MMB** to end the rectangle tool [Fig. 6.8(g)] > modify the dimensions to **60** and **80** > **LMB** [Fig. 6.8(h)]

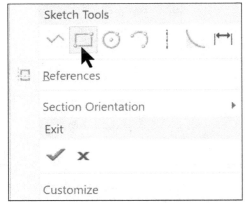

Figure 6.8(e) RMB > Corner Rectangle

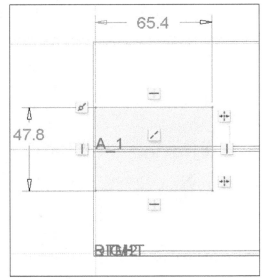

Figure 6.8(g) Weak Dimensions

Figure 6.8(f) Sketch the Rectangle

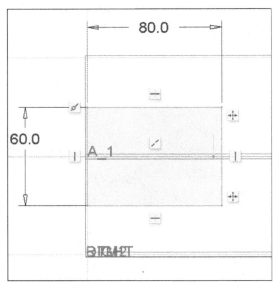

Figure 6.8(h) Design Dimensions

Press: **Ctrl+D** [Fig. 6.8(i)] **> RMB >** ✓ **> Ctrl+2** [Fig. 6.8(j)] **> Extrude** tab **> Options** tab **>** Side 1 **Through All >** Side 2 **Through All** [Fig. 6.8(k)] **> MMB > Save**

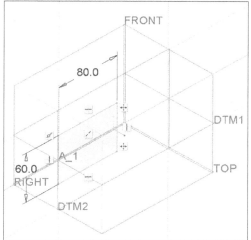

Figure 6.8(i) Through All

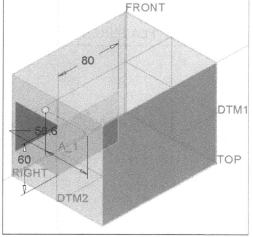

Figure 6.8(j) Shaded With Edges

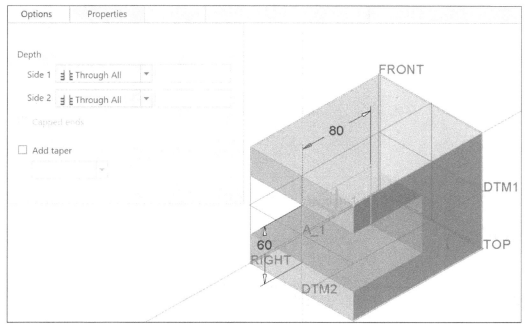

Figure 6.8(k) Cut Preview

Create a new layer and add **DTM1, DTM2, A_1** to it, click: **View** tab > [⊟ **Layers**]

(Layer Tree displays in place of the Model Tree in the Navigator) > [▶] > [▶] [Fig. 6.9(a)] >

[**Layer Tree** ⊟ ▾] > **New Layer** [Fig. 6.9(b)] > In the Layer Properties dialog box, Name:

type **DATUM_FEATURES** *(do not press Enter)* as the name for new layer

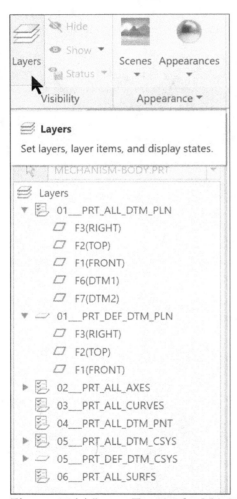

Figure 6.9(a) Layer Tree in the Navigator

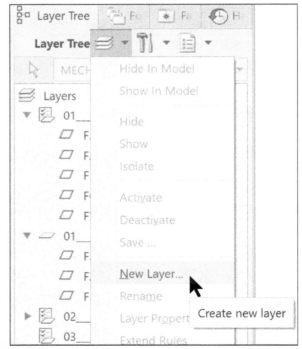

Figure 6.9(b) Create New Layer

Pick **DTM1, DTM2,** and **A_1** from the model [Fig. 6.9(c)] > **OK** [Fig. 6.9(d)] > **LMB** > **Save** > **Layers** closes > **Save**

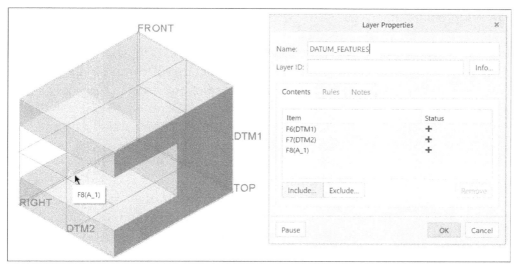

Figure 6.9(c) Layer Properties

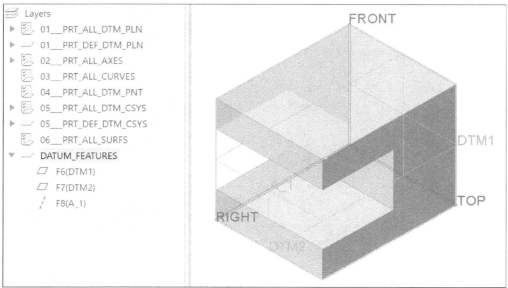

Figure 6.9(d) DATUM_FEATURES

Geometric tolerances

Before continuing with the modeling of the part, the datums used and created thus far will be "set" for geometric tolerancing. Geometric tolerances (GTOLs) provide a comprehensive method of specifying where on a part the critical surfaces are, how they relate to one another, and how the part must be inspected to determine if it is acceptable. They provide a method for controlling the location, form, profile, orientation, and run out of features. When you store a GTOL in a solid model, it contains parametric references to the geometry or feature it controls—its reference entity—and parametric references to referenced datums and axes. In Assembly mode, you can create a GTOL in a subassembly or a part. A GTOL that you create in Part or Assembly mode automatically belongs to the part or assembly that occupies the window; however, it can refer only to set datums belonging to that model itself, or to components within it. It cannot refer to datums outside of its model in some encompassing assembly, unlike assembly created features.

You can add GTOLs in Part or Drawing mode, but they are reflected in all other modes. Creo Parametric treats them as annotations, and they are always associated with the model. Unlike dimensional tolerances, though, GTOLs do not affect part geometry. Before you can reference a datum plane or axis in a GTOL, you must set it as a reference. Creo Parametric encloses its name using the set datum symbol. After you have set a datum, you can use it in the usual way to create features and assemble parts. You enter the set datum command by picking on the datum plane or axis in the Model Tree or on the model itself > RMB > Properties. Creo Parametric encloses the datum name in a feature control frame. If needed, type a new name in the **Name** field of the **Datum** dialog box. Most datums will follow the alphabet, A, B, C, D, and so on. You can hide (not display) a set datum by placing it on a layer and then hiding the *layer (or selecting on the item in the Model Tree > RMB > Hide).*

Icon	Datum Types	Description
-A-	Set	Use to mark planes and axes. You can place it on datum planes and on dimensions.
	Set Datum Tag annotation	This annotation is similar to a datum feature symbol. It is recognized by GTOL annotations in the same way that datum feature symbols are recognized by GTOL annotations. You can place a set datum tag annotation on datum planes, on dimensions, in GTOLs, or on geometry.

Select datum **TOP** in the Model Tree > **RMB** > ⬚ **Properties** [Fig. 6.10(a)] > double-click in the Name field > *type* **a** (lowercase will automatically change to uppercase) > ⬚-A- [Fig. 6.10(b)] > **OK** in the Datum dialog box [Fig. 6.10(c)] > repeat the process and set datum FRONT as **B** and datum RIGHT as **C**.

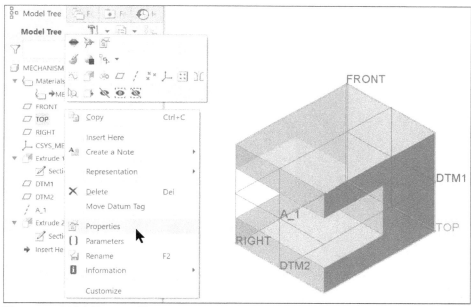

Figure 6.10(a) Datum Properties

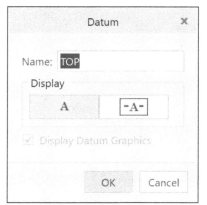

Figure 6.10(b) Datum Dialog Box

Figure 6.10(c) Set

You can also set datums directly on the model. Pick **DTM1** on the model >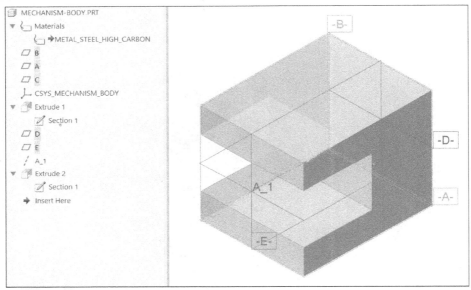
Properties > Name- **D** > [-A-] > **OK** > pick **DTM2** > Properties > Name- **E** > [-A-]
> **OK** [Fig. 6.10(d)] > **LMB** > **Ctrl+S** > pick datum **D** from the Model Tree > **RMB** >
Information > **Feature information** [Fig. 6.10(e)] > *close*

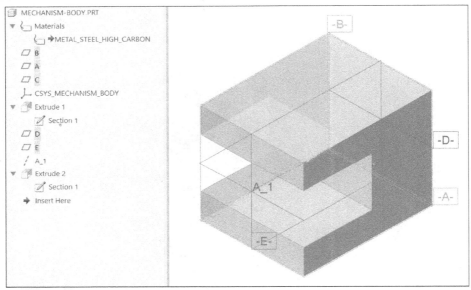

Figure 6.10(d) Datums Set on the Model

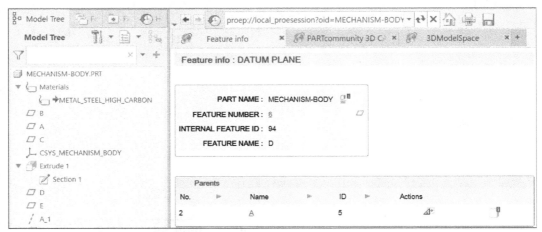

Figure 6.10(e) Feature information

Spin the model > **Model** tab > 📰 Hole **Hole** > **Placement** tab > **Ctrl+** pick on **A_1** [Fig. 6.11(a)] and the **B** datum [Fig. 6.11(b)] > **Flip** > **Ctrl+D**

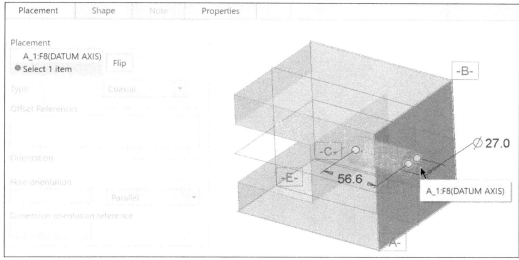

Figure 6.11(a) Select Axis

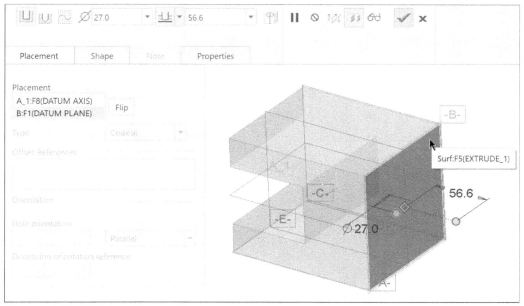

Figure 6.11(b) Select Datum B

Place the pointer over the drag handle > **RMB** > **Through Until** [Fig. 6.11(c)] > pick the surface of the cut [Fig. 6.11(d)] > drag the diameter to **50** [Fig. 6.11(e)] > **MMB** > **Ctrl+S**

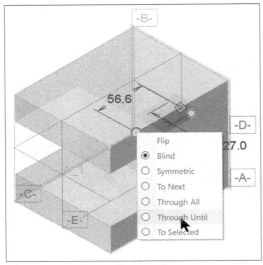

Figure 6.11(c) Through Until   **Figure 6.11(d)** Select Surface

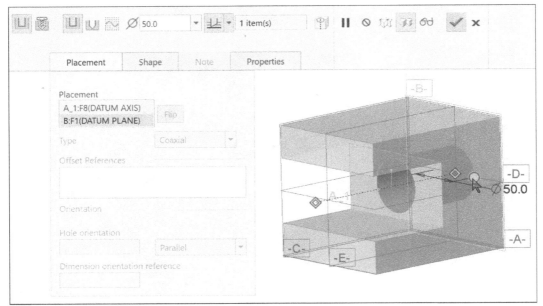

Figure 6.11(e) Diameter 50mm

Select the circle's edge > **Edge Chamfer** [Fig. 6.12(a)] > modify to **2mm** [Fig. 6.12(b)] > **MMB > Ctrl+S**

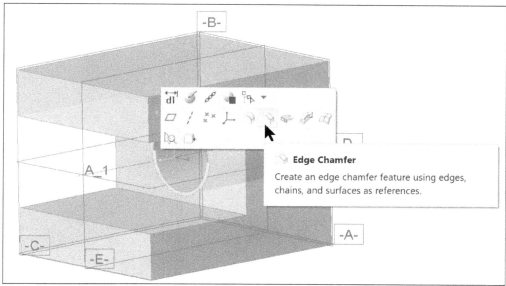

Figure 6.12(a) Edge Chamfer

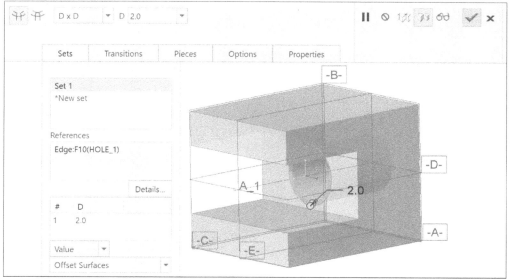

Figure 6.12(b) 2mm Chamfer

Select: **Chamfer** from the Model Ribbon > D **6** > **Sets** tab > **Ctrl+** select the three horizontal and four vertical edges [Fig. 6.12(c)] > **MMB** > **Ctrl+S** [Fig. 6.12(d)] > **Ctrl+D**

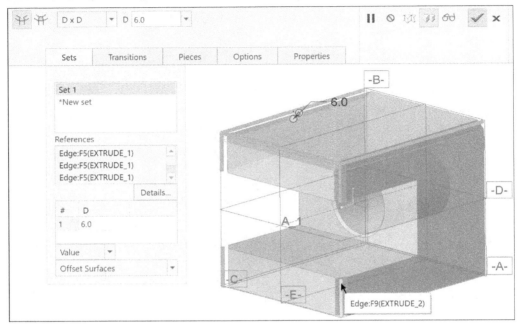

Figure 6.12(c) Chamfers Preview

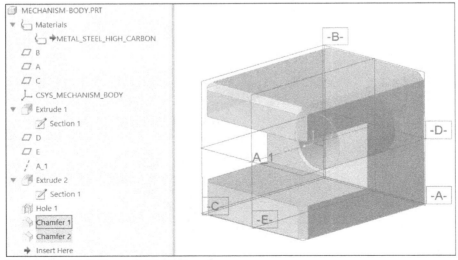

Figure 6.12(d) Completed Chamfers

Click **Hole > Create Standard Hole > No Tapping > Create clearance hole > Placement tab > M12x1.5 > Drill to intersect all surfaces > Adds countersink > Adds counterbore**

| ⊔ | 🗐 | | 🔔 | ⊔ ⊐⊏ | 🔩 ISO | ▼ | ⬛ M12x1.5 | ▼ | ⊟⊟ ▼ | | ⋈ | ⨝⨝ |

> select the placement surface [Fig. 6.13(a)] > drag the location handles to datum **B** and datum **E** [Fig. 6.13(b)]

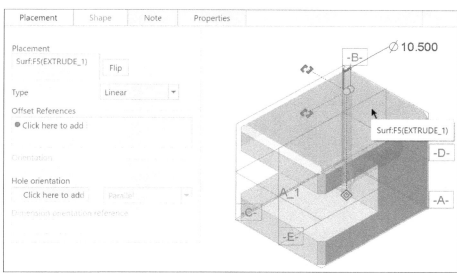

Figure 6.13(a) Select the Placement Surface

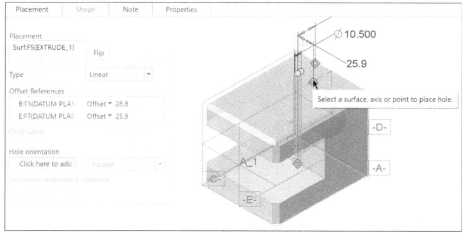

Figure 6.13(b) Drag Handles to Datum B and E

Offset from Datum B > **30** > Offset from Datum E > **48** [Fig. 6.13(c)] > **Shape** tab > modify the dimensions [Fig. 6.13(d)] > **MMB** > **Save**

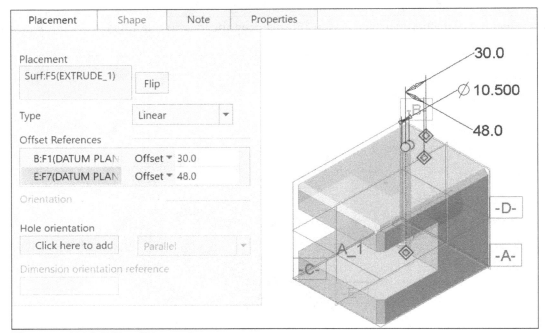

Figure 6.13(c) Offset Dimensions

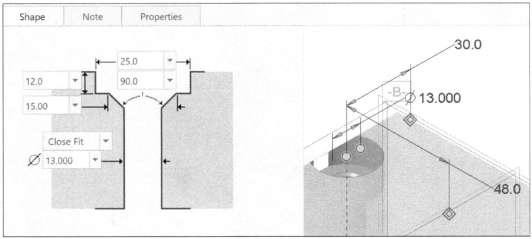

Figure 6.13(d) Modify Dimensions

Select the Hole in the Model Tree > **Mirror** [Fig. 6.13(e)] > **References** tab > select datum
E as the mirror plane [Fig. 6.13(f)] > **MMB** > **Save**

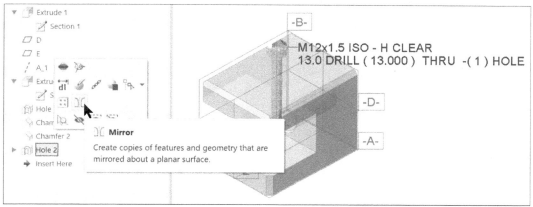

Figure 6.13(e) Mirror

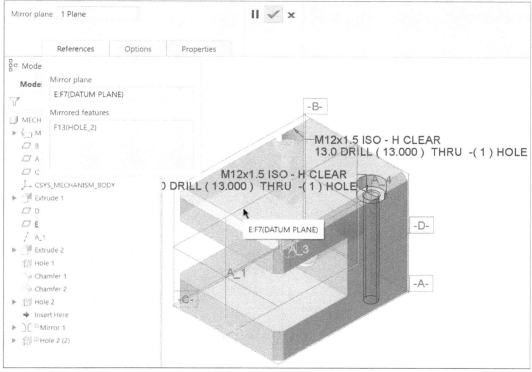

Figure 6.13(f) Mirror Plane Datum E

From the Graphics Toolbar > 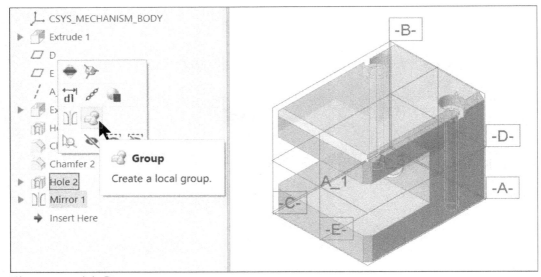 **Annotation Display** *off* > **Ctrl+** select the **Hole 2** and **Mirror 1** features in the Model Tree > **Group** [Fig. 6.13(g)] > **RMB** > **Copy** [Fig. 6.13(h)] > **RMB** > **Paste Special** [Fig. 6.13(i)]

Figure 6.13(g) Group

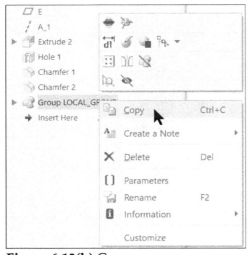

Figure 6.13(h) Copy

Figure 6.13(i) Paste Special

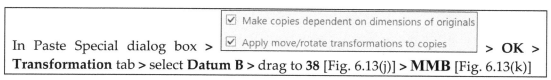

In Paste Special dialog box > ☑ Make copies dependent on dimensions of originals ☑ Apply move/rotate transformations to copies > **OK** > **Transformation** tab > select **Datum B** > drag to **38** [Fig. 6.13(j)] > **MMB** [Fig. 6.13(k)]

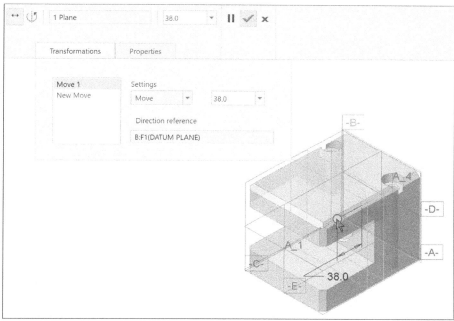

Figure 6.13(j) Transformation

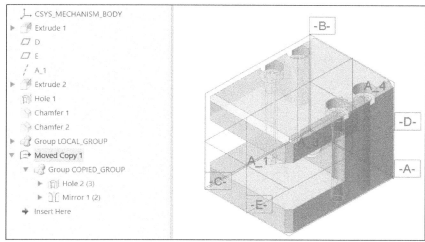

Figure 6.13(k) Moved Copy

Two of the holes break through the cut's wall [Fig. 6.14(a)]. Edit Definition will be used to redefine the cuts dimensions and dimension scheme. The **80mm** dimension should reference Datum B not the front face of the part [Fig. 6.14(b)].

In the Model Tree pick the **Extrude 2** cut **> Edit Definition** [Fig. 6.14(c)]

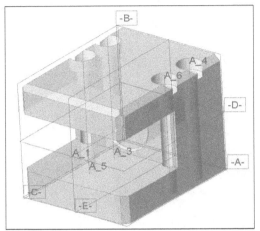

Figure 6.14(a) Holes break through wall

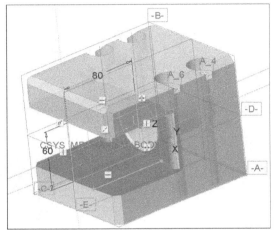

Figure 6.14(b) Dimension References

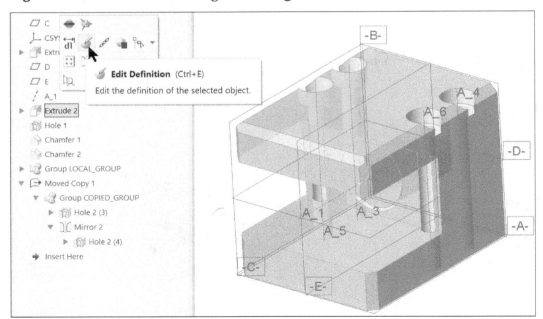

Figure 6.14(c) Edit Definition *(note: hole surfaces have been assigned a new color)*

Click: **Placement** tab > **Edit** Edit the Internal Sketch [Fig. 6.14(d)] > 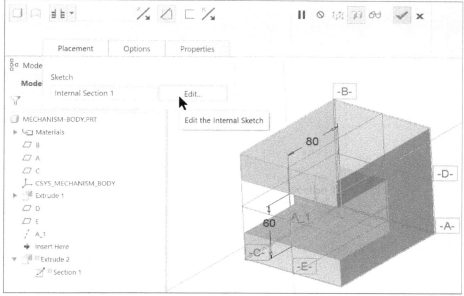 [Fig. 6.14(e)]

Figure 6.14(d) Placement tab

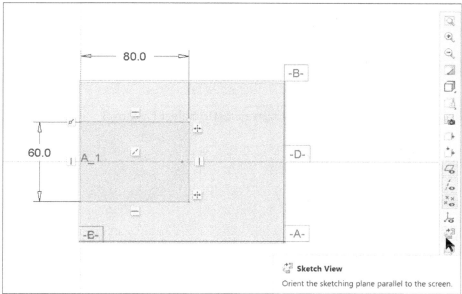

Figure 6.14(e) Sketch View

Click: select **80** > **RMB** > **Delete** [Fig. 6.14(f)] *(changes from strong to weak dimension)* > **RMB** > [⊢→⊣] **Dimension** > pick the line [Fig. 6.14(g)] > pick **Datum B** [Fig. 6.14(h)] > **MMB** to place dimension [Fig. 6.14(i)] > modify to **80** [Fig. 6.14(j)]

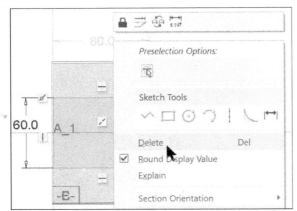

Figure 6.14(f) Delete the 80mm Dimension

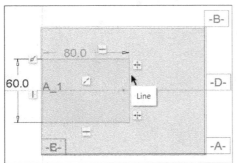

Figure 6.14(g) Select the Line

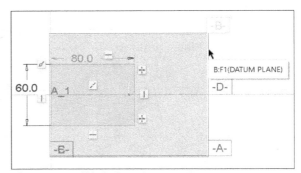

Figure 6.14(h) Select Datum B

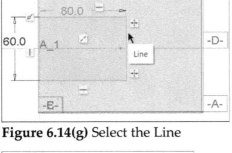

Figure 6.14(i) MMB to place dimension

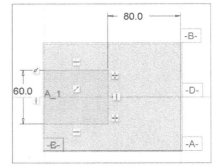

Figure 6.14(j) Modify to 80mm

Press **Ctrl+D** [Fig. 6.14(k)] > **RMB** > ✓ [Fig. 6.14(l)] > **MMB** > double-click on the cut [Fig. 6.14(m)] > **LMB** > **Save**

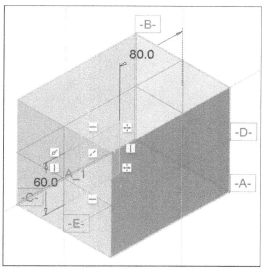

Figure 6.14(k) New Dimension Scheme **Figure 6.14(l)** Cut Preview

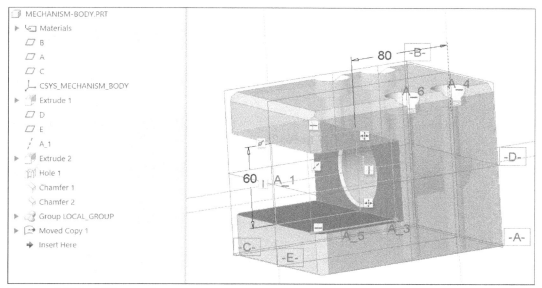

Figure 6.14(m) Dimensions

Select 🔲 Hole **Hole > 15** diameter > ▤▤ through all > **Placement** tab > pick on the upper surface [Fig. 6.15(a)] > **Offset References > Ctrl+** select datum **B** and datum **E >** change the dimensions to **135** and **29** [Fig. 6.15(b)] > **MMB > Ctrl+D > Save**

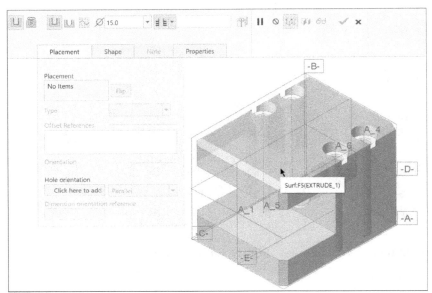

Figure 6.15(a) Select Placement Surface

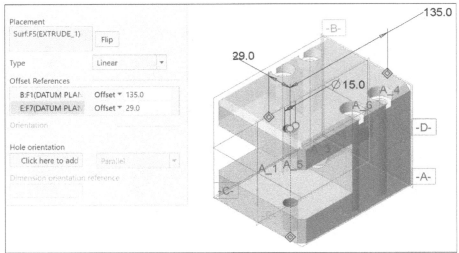

Figure 6.15(b) Select Datum B and Datum E

Select the circle's edge > **Edge Chamfer** > modify to **1.5** [Fig. 6.15(c)] > **MMB** > **Ctrl+** select the **Hole** and **Chamfer** [Fig. 6.15(d)] > **Enter** > **Group** [Fig. 6.15(e)] > **LMB**

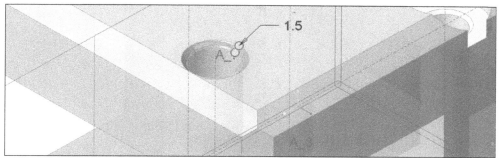

Figure 6.15(c) Edge Chamfer

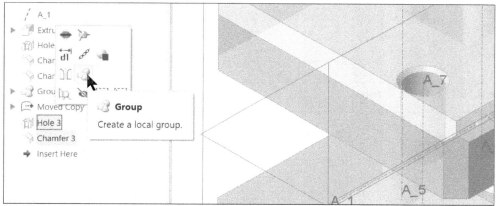

Figure 6.15(d) Group the Chamfer and Hole

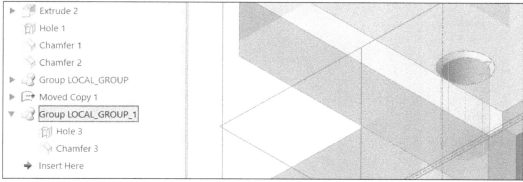

Figure 6.15(e) Local Group

Select the Group from the Model Tree > **Mirror** [Fig. 6.15(f)] > **References** tab > select datum **E** as the Mirror plane [Fig. 6.15(g)] > **MMB > LMB > Ctrl+S**

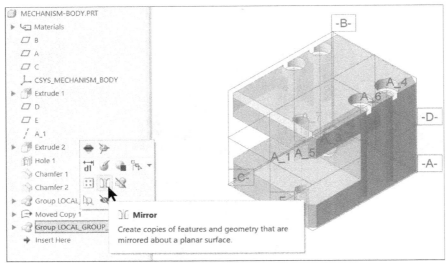

Figure 6.15(f) Edge Chamfer

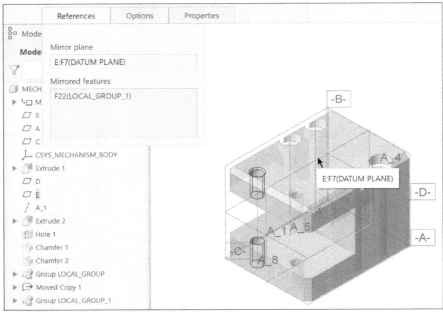

Figure 6.15(g) Select Datum E as Mirror Plane

Spin the model > **Hole** > **Create Standard Hole** > **Adds tapping** > **M10x1.5** > **15** depth

> **Placement** tab > select the placement surface [Fig. 6.16(a)] > **RMB** > **Offset Reference Collector** > **Ctrl+** datum **D** and datum **E** > Offset: **48** in both directions [Fig. 6.16(b)] > **MMB** > **Ctrl+D** > **Save**

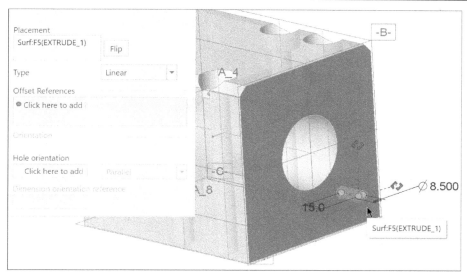

Figure 6.16(a) Select the Placement Surface

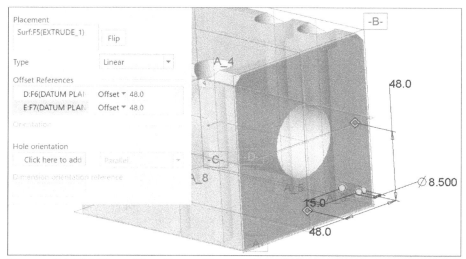

Figure 6.16(b) Drag Handles to Datum D and Datum E

223

With the Hole selected > **RMB > Pattern > Dimensions** tab > Dimension 1 > select the *vertical* **48** dimension > modify to **-96 > Enter > RMB > Direction 2 Dimension >** select the *horizontal* **48** dimension > modify to **-96** [Fig. 6.16(c)] **> Enter > MMB** [Fig. 6.16(d)]

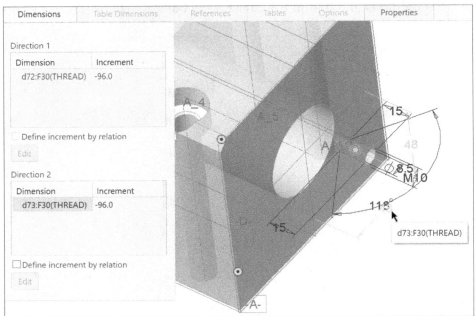

Figure 6.16(c) Direction Dimensions

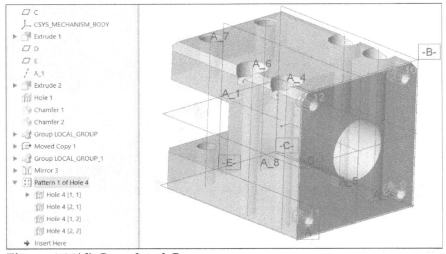

Figure 6.16(d) Completed Component

Press: **Ctrl+D > View** tab > **Model Display > Temporary Shade > Ctrl+1** [Fig. 6.17] > **Ctrl+R > Ctrl+1 > Ctrl+S > File > Manage File > Delete Old Versions > Enter > File > Close > File > Exit > Yes**

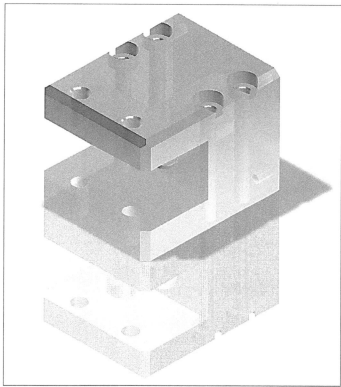

Figure 6.17 Shading With Reflections

Quiz

1. Name three ways of replicating features.
2. What are Layers used for?
3. Name three uses for datum planes.
4. What is a set datum plane?
5. Can you have a model color and colors for model surfaces?
6. What is the purpose of a Relation?
7. Why is Edit Definition important?

This completes Chapter 6.

CHAPTER 7: Revolved Features, Sections, and Annotations

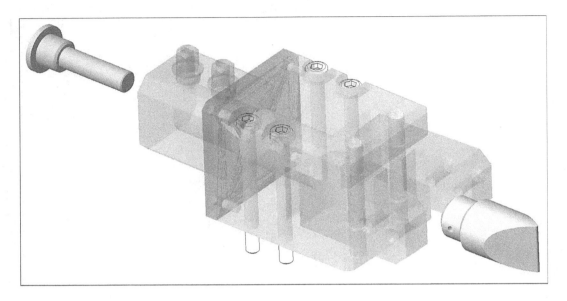

The **Revolve Tool** creates a *revolved solid (or surface)* or a *revolved cut* by revolving a sketched section around a centerline from the sketching plane.

Objectives

1. Model components using revolved features
2. Understand and use the Navigation browser
3. Alter and set the Items and Columns displayed in the Model Tree
4. Edit Dimension Properties
5. Create Sections of the model
6. Use the Model Player to extract information and dimensions
7. Understand the functions and capabilities of the model Annotations
8. Get a hard copy using the Print command

Revolved Features

You can have any number of centerlines in your sketch/section, but only one will be used to rotate your section geometry. Rules for sketching a revolved feature include:

- A section to be revolved must reference an axis
- By default, Creo Parametric allows only one *axis of revolution* per sketch (within a sketch, you may select from different construction centerlines to be designated as the one *axis of revolution*)
- The geometry must be sketched on only one side of the *axis of revolution*
- The section must be closed for a solid but can be open for a cut or a protrusion with assigned thickness

A variety of geometric shapes and constructions are used on revolved features. For instance, hole **chamfers** are created at selected edges of the part. Chamfers are *pick-and-place* features.

Threads can be a *cosmetic feature* representing the *nominal diameter* or the *root diameter* of the thread. Information can be embedded in the feature. Threads show as a unique color. By putting cosmetic threads on a separate layer, you can hide and unhide them.

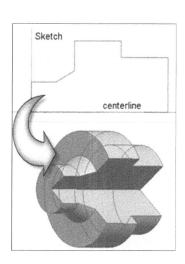

Revolved Solid Protrusion- closed section	
Revolved Protrusion with an assigned thickness- closed section	
Revolved Protrusion with an assigned thickness- open section	
Revolved Cut- open section	
Revolved Surface- open section	

Navigation Window

Besides using the File command and corresponding options, the *Navigation window* can be used to directly access other functions.

As previously mentioned, the working directory is a directory that you set up to contain Creo Parametric files. You must have read/write access to this directory. You usually start Creo Parametric from your working directory. A new working directory setting is not saved when you exit the current Creo Parametric session. By default, if you retrieve a file from a non-working directory, rename the file and then save it, the renamed file is saved to the directory from which it was originally retrieved, if you have read/write access to that directory.

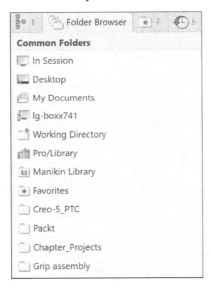

The navigation area is located on the left side (default) of the Creo Parametric main window. It includes tabs for the [Model Tree] and [Layer Tree], [Folder Browser], [Favorites], and [Drawing Tree] (active drawing).

Folder Browser

The Folder browser is an expandable tree that lets you browse the file systems and other locations that are accessible from your computer. As you navigate the folders, the contents of the selected folder appear in the Creo Parametric browser as a Contents page. The Folder browser contains top-level nodes for accessing file systems and other locations that are known to Creo Parametric:

- **In Session** Creo Parametric objects that have been retrieved into local memory.
- **Desktop** Files and programs on the Desktop. Only Creo Parametric items can be opened.
- **My Documents** Files created and saved in Windows *My Documents* folder.
- **Working Directory** Directory linked with the Select Working Directory command. All work will be accessed and saved in this location.
- **Network** *(only for Windows)* The navigator shows computers on the networks to which you have access.
- **Manikin Library** A Manikin model is a standard assembly that can be manipulated and positioned within the design scenario.
- **Favorites** Saved folder locations for fast retrieval.

Manipulating Folders

To work with folders, you can use the **Browser** to accomplish most file management requirements. The Browser's **Views** drop-down menu includes a (simple) **List**, **Thumbnails**, and **Details**:

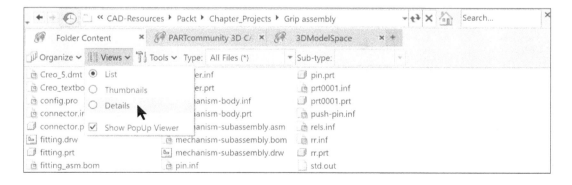

You can perform a variety of tasks from the Browser's **Organize** drop-down menu including **New Folder, Rename, Cut, Copy, Paste, Delete**, and **Add to common folders**:

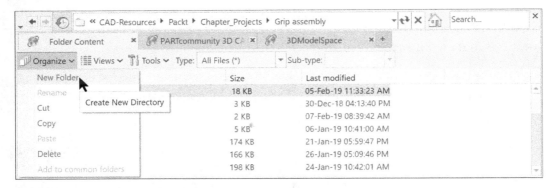

The Browser's **Tools** drop-down menu includes **Sort By**, go **Up One Level**, **Add to Favorites, Remove from Favorites, Organize Favorites**, show **All Versions**, **Show Instances,** and **Send to Mail Recipient (as Zipped Attachment)**:

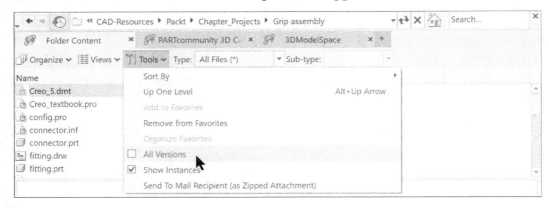

Do not change your working directory from your default system work folder unless instructed to do so.

From the Browser's **Type** field, you can limit the search to one of Creo Parametric's file types:

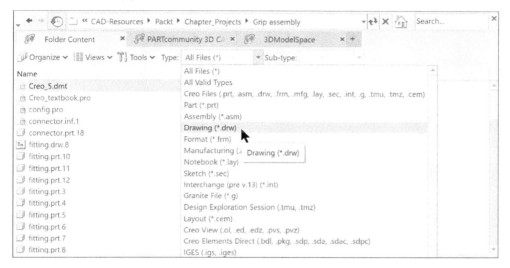

To set a working directory using the Browser, pick on the desired folder > *RMB* > *Set Working Directory*:

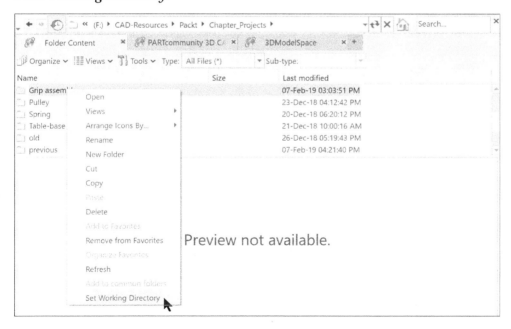

After setting the default working directory, pick on the object to preview:

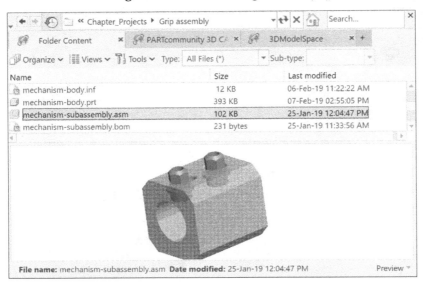

Within the preview window, dynamically reorient the model using the **MMB** by itself (**Spin-** press and hold the **MMB** as you move the mouse) or in conjunction with the **Shift** key (**Pan**) or **Ctrl** key (**Zoom, Turn**). A mouse with a thumbwheel (as the middle button) can be rolled to zoom in/out on the object. Double-clicking on the file name will open the part. After you complete this Chapter you will have this same part in your working directory. From the Browser's toolbar you can also navigate to other directories or computer areas:

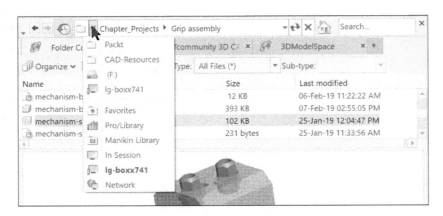

Chapter 6 STEPS

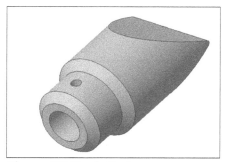

Figure 7.1 Push Rod

Push Rod
The Push Rod (Fig. 7.1) is the first of two revolved parts to be created in this Chapter. The Push Rod, and Piston are revolved parts needed for the mechanism assembly and drawings later in the text. These parts require revolved features including extrusions, holes, cuts and chamfers.

Launch **Creo Parametric > Select Working Directory >** navigate to your directory > **OK > Ctrl+N >** *type* **push_rod > OK > File > Prepare > Model Properties >** Units **change > millimeter_Newton_Second > Set > Interpret > OK >** Material **Change >** double-click on **metal_steel_high_carbon.mtl > Yes > OK > Close > File > Options >**

Configuration Editor > [Options: Import/Export ▾] lower right corner > **Import configuration file >** select your Working Directory > select **Creo_textbook.pro** [Fig. 7.2(a)] *(your file name may be different)* > **Open**

Figure 7.2(a) Import configuration file

Click: **Show:** > **All options** [Fig. 7.2(b)] > Slide the vertical scroll bar *(right side of Creo Parametric Options dialog box)* down to the option **default_dec_places**. To the right of **default_dec_places**, click in the Value field > *type* **1** [Fig. 7.2(c)] > **Enter** (note that the Status has changed ⊡)

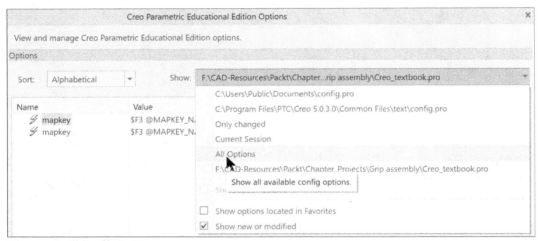

Figure 7.2(b) All Options

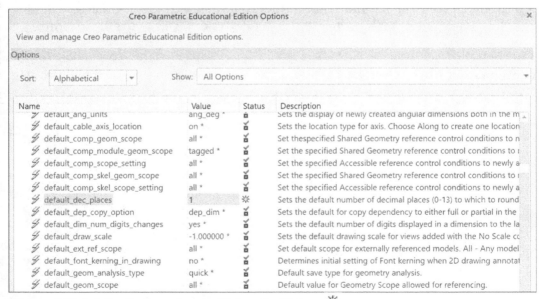

Figure 7.2(c) default_dec_places   Value: 1   Status: ※

Click: **Add … >** in the Add Option name field, *type*: **def_layer** *(you must type this with the keyboard, **but do not press Enter**)* [Fig. 7.2(d)] > Option value: ⬜ > **layer_axis >** move the mouse pointer to the right side of the text: layer_axis, click in the Option value field > type *(space)* **datum_axes > OK** [Fig. 7.2(e)]

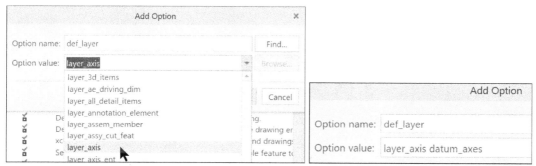

Figure 7.2(d) Option: def_layer layer_axis datum_axes

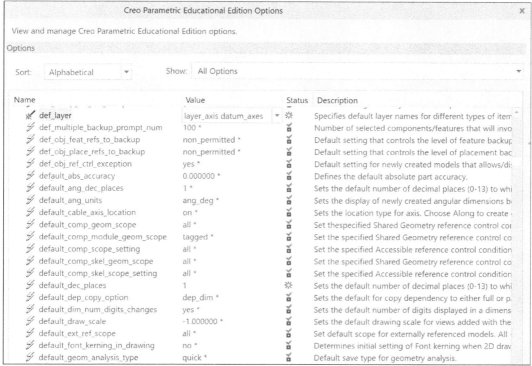

Figure 7.2(e) def_layer: layer_axis datum_axes

Click: 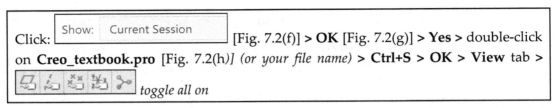 [Fig. 7.2(f)] > **OK** [Fig. 7.2(g)] > **Yes** > double-click on **Creo_textbook.pro** [Fig. 7.2(h*)] (or your file name)* > **Ctrl+S** > **OK** > **View** tab > *toggle all on*

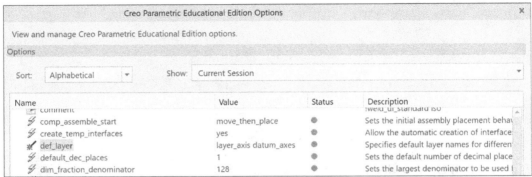

Figure 7.2(f) Showing current session options with def_layer selected

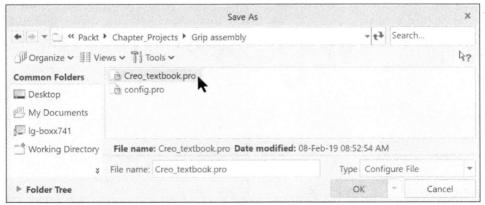

Figure 7.2(g) Creo Parametric Options Confirmation Dialog Box

Figure 7.2(h) Configure File

Click: **File > Options > Model Display > Trimetric > OK > OK > No > Model** tab > ▢ Revolve **Revolve > Placement** tab > **Define** > Sketch Plane--- Plane: select datum **RIGHT** [Fig. 7.3(a)] > Orientation **Left > Sketch >** ▢ **Sketch View >** to change the Graphics Toolbar location click **RMB** anywhere inside the Graphics Toolbar > **Location >** select an option [Fig. 7.3(b)]

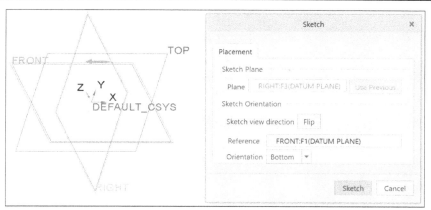

Figure 7.3(a) Sketch Plane and Reference

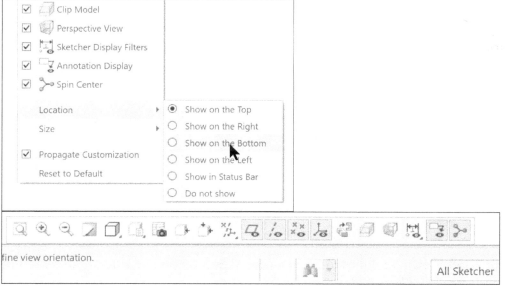

Figure 7.3(b) Location

237

Click: **Centerline** *from the Datum Group in the Ribbon not the Sketching Group (or RMB >* ⊕ *Axis of Revolution) >* sketch a *horizontal* centerline through the default coordinate system > **MMB** > place your cursor over the completed centerline: Centerline (Axis of Revolution) [Fig. 7.3(c)] > **MMB** > **RMB** > ⌵ **Line Chain** [Fig. 7.3(d)] > sketch six lines > adjust the position of the dimensions > **MMB** > **MMB** the sketch will shade if a closed section was properly created > **LMB** [Fig. 7.3(e)]

Do not change your dimensions to those shown here! These are sketch weak dimensions and everyone's will be different. If the shape is incorrect, ↩ ***Undo*** *and re-sketch*

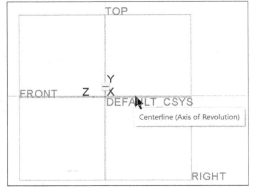

Figure 7.3(c) Construction Centerline

Figure 7.3(d) RMB > Line Chain

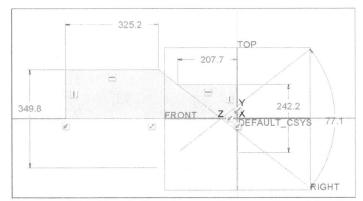

Figure 7.3(e) Sketch Six Lines to Form a Closed Section on one side of the centerline *(your values will be different, do not change)*

Press **RMB** > 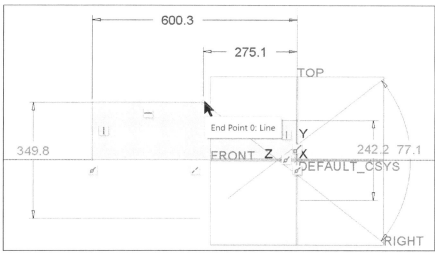 **Dimension** > add an overall horizontal dimension by picking the line > **MMB** to place the dimension > **MMB** > add a horizontal dimension from **Datum TOP** and the point [Fig. 7.3(f)] > **LMB** > capture all of the sketch and dimensions with a window > press **RMB** > **Modify** > **Lock Scale** [Fig. 7.3(g)] > modify the overall dimension to **100** > **Enter** > **OK** > [Fig. 7.3(h)]

Figure 7.3(f) Add dimensions *(your values will be different)*

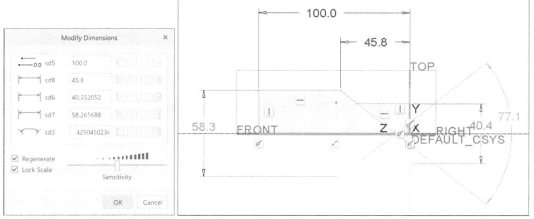

Figure 7.3(g) Modify Dimensions Dialog Box   **Figure 7.3(h)** 100 length dimension

Double-click on and modify dimensions to the design values > **LMB** > reposition
dimensions [Fig. 7.3(i)] > **RMB** > ✓ > **Options** tab Fig. 7.3(j)]

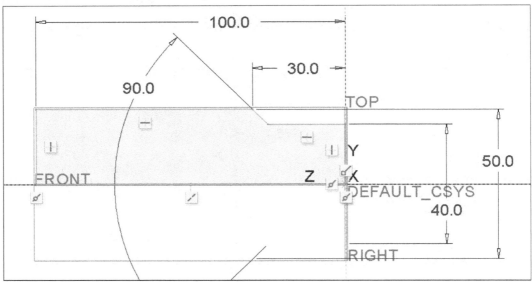

Figure 7.3(i) Design Value Dimensions

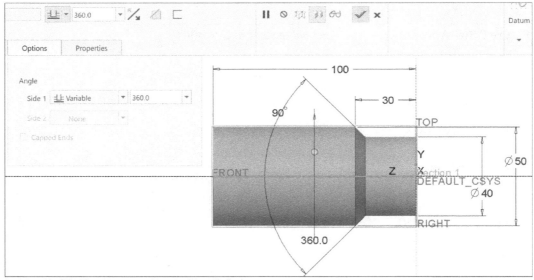

Figure 7.3(j) Show Section Dimensions

Spin the model [Fig. 7.3(k)] > **Zoom in** pick two corners > > **Refit** > double-click on the model [Fig. 7.3(l)] > **LMB** > **Save**

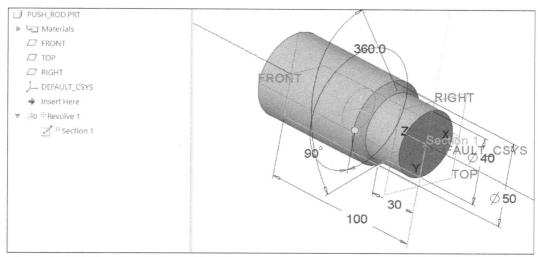

Figure 7.3(k) Revolve Feature Preview

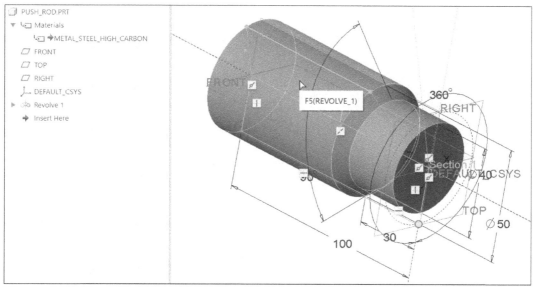

Figure 7.3(l) Revolved Extrusion

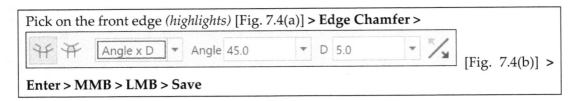

Pick on the front edge *(highlights)* [Fig. 7.4(a)] > **Edge Chamfer >**

Angle x D ▾   Angle 45.0 ▾   D 5.0 ▾   [Fig. 7.4(b)] >

Enter > MMB > LMB > Save

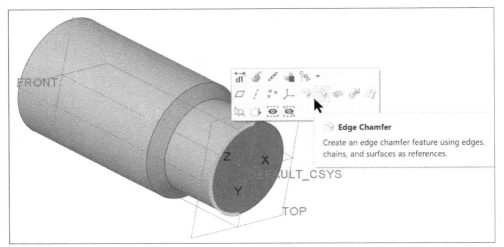

Figure 7.4(a) Pick on the Edge

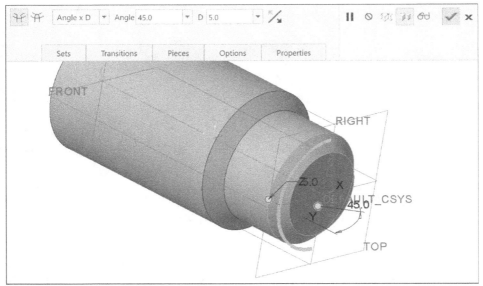

Figure 7.4(b) Chamfer Preview

Select: **Hole > 20** Dia **> 30** depth **> Placement** tab **> Ctrl+ >** pick **Axis A_1** [Fig. 7.5(a)] and the end surface [Fig. 7.5(b)] **> MMB > LMB > Save**

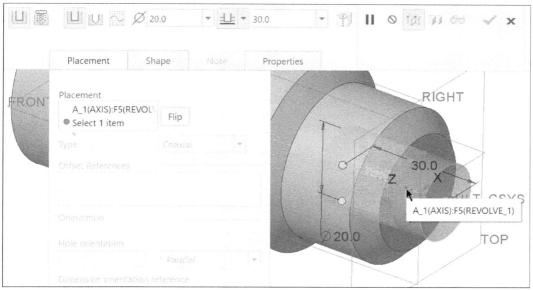

Figure 7.5(a) Select Axis

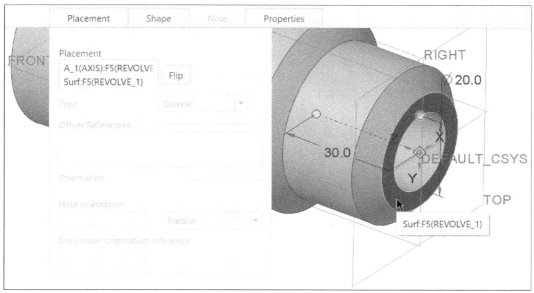

Figure 7.5(b) Select Surface

Select: **Hole > 6** Dia **> Through All > Placement** tab > pick Datum **RIGHT** [Fig. 7.6(a)] **> Offset References > Ctrl+** select datum **TOP** (Offset **-15**) and datum **FRONT** (**Align**) [Fig. 7.6(b)] **> Shape** tab > ▤▤ **Through All > Through All > MMB > LMB > Save**

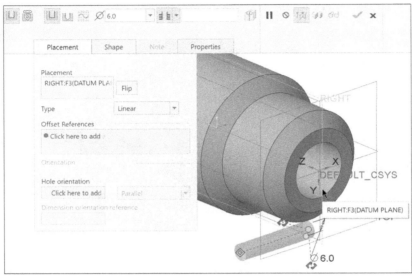

Figure 7.6(a) Select RIGHT Datum

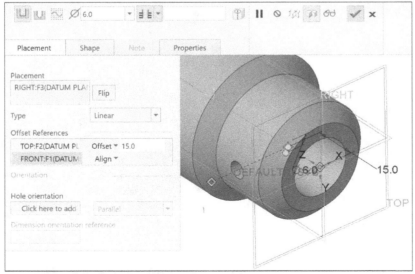

Figure 7.6(b) Select Datum TOP and Datum FRONT

244

Select: **Shape** tab > **Through All** > **Through All** [Fig. 7.6(c)] > **MMB** > **RMB** > **Information** > **Feature Information** [Fig. 7.6(d)] > 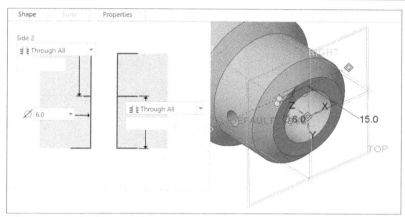 close Browser > **LMB** > **Save**

Figure 7.6(c) Shape tab

Parents					
No.	Name	ID	Actions		
3	RIGHT	3			
2	TOP	5			
1	FRONT	7			

Feature Element Data - HOLE			
No.	Element Name	Info	
1	Hole	Defined	
1.1	Hole Type	Straight hole	
1.2	Hole Make	Regular	
1.3	Diameter	6.0	

Layers		
Layer	Status	
FEATURE IS IN LAYER(S) :		
02___PRT_ALL_AXES	OPERATION = SHOWN	
DATUM_AXES	OPERATION = SHOWN	

FEATURE'S DIMENSIONS:		
Dimension ID	Dimension Value	Displayed Value
d14	6.0 (0.1, -0.1)	6 Dia
d16	15.0 (0.1, -0.1)	15

Figure 7.6(d) Feature Information

Pick: **Extrude > RMB > Remove Material > Placement** tab > **FRONT** as sketching plane [Fig. 7.7(a)] > 🔲 **Sketch View > RMB >** create horizontal **Centerline** [Fig. 7.7(b)]

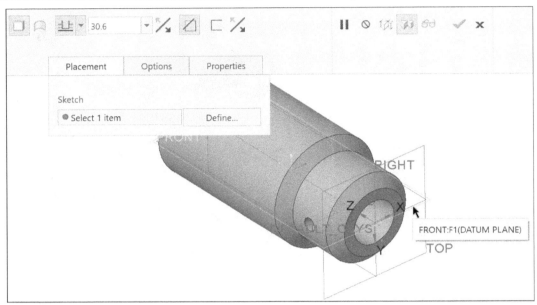

Figure 7.7(a) Sketch Plane

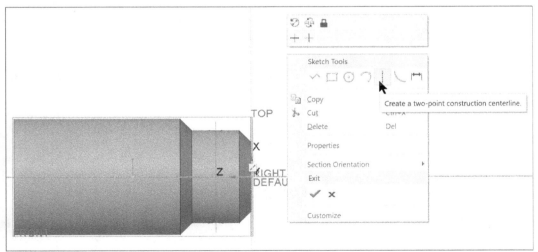

Figure 7.7(b) Centerline

Press: **RMB > References >** select the left edge/surface [Fig. 7.7(c)] **> Solve > Close > Ctrl+5 > RMB >** ⌣ **Line Chain** **> MMB >** sketch the triangle [Fig. 7.7(d)] **>** window-in the sketch **>** 🪞 Mirror **>** select the centerline [Fig. 7.7(e)]

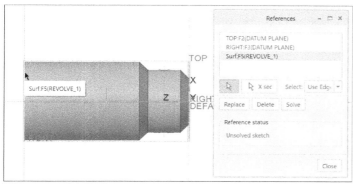

Figure 7.7(c) References

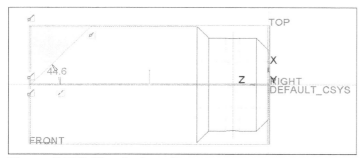

Figure 7.7(d) Sketch three lines

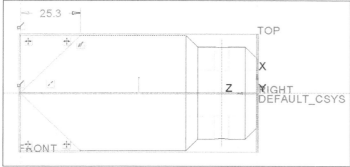

Figure 7.7(e) Mirrored sketch

Press: **RMB** > **Fillet** > select the two angled lines [Fig. 7.7(f)] > **R 2** > **Dimension** > select the two angled lines and place the dimension with **MMB** [Fig. 7.7(g)] > spin the model > **Ctrl+2** > **RMB** > ✓ > **Options** tab > Side 1 **Through All** > Side 2 **Through All** [Fig. 7.7(h)] > **MMB** > **LMB** > **Ctrl+D** > **Save**

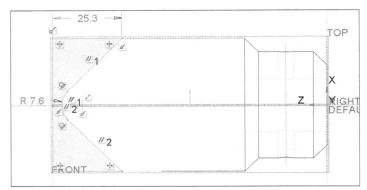

Figure 7.7(f) Radius 2

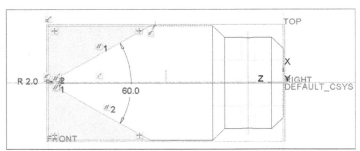

Figure 7.7(g) Angle 60

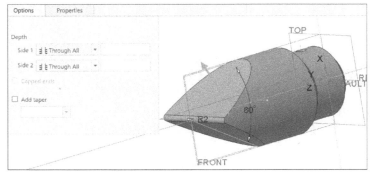

Figure 7.7(h) Mirrored sketch

248

Reordering Features

You can move features forward or backward in the feature creation (regeneration) order list, thus changing the order in which features are regenerated. You can reorder features in the Model Tree by dragging one or more features to a new location in the feature list. If you try to move a child feature to a higher position than its parent feature, the parent feature moves with the child feature in context, so that the parent/child relationship is maintained. You can reorder multiple features in one operation, as long as these features appear in *consecutive* order. Feature reorder *cannot* occur under the following conditions:

- **Parents** Cannot be moved so that their regeneration occurs after the regeneration of their children
- **Children** Cannot be moved so that their regeneration occurs before the regeneration of their parents

You can select the features to be reordered by choosing an option:

- **Select** Select features to reorder on the screen and/or from the Model Tree
- **Layer** Select all features from a layer by selecting the layer
- **Range** Specify the range of features by entering the regeneration numbers of the starting and ending features

---

Select: **Extrude 2** [Fig. 7.7(i)] > drag to below **Chamfer 1** [Fig. 7.7(j)] > **LMB** > **Ctrl+D** > **Save** > **View** tab > **Appearances** > set a new color for the part > **Ctrl+S**

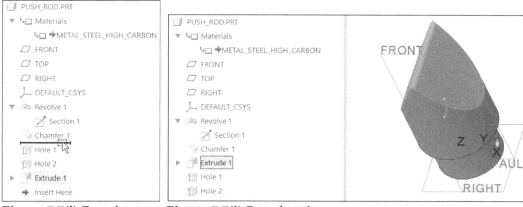

Figure 7.7(i) Reorder   **Figure 7.7(j)** Reordered

Cross Sections

There are six types of cross sections: **Planar, X Direction, Y Direction, Z Direction, Offset**, and **Zone**. You will be creating a planar cross section. Creo Parametric can create standard planar cross sections of models (parts or assemblies), offset cross sections of models (parts or assemblies), planar cross sections of datum surfaces or quilts (Part mode only) and planar cross sections that automatically intersect all quilts and all geometry in the current model.

Open: **View** tab > 📷 **View Manager** View Manager dialog box displays [Fig. 7.8(a)] > **Sections** tab [Fig. 7.8(b)] > **New** [Fig. 7.8(c)] > **Planar** [Fig. 7.8(d)] > *type* **A** [Fig. 7.8(e)] > **Enter** > ⊕ [Fig. 7.8(f)]

Figure 7.8(a) View Manager

Figure 7.8(b) Sections

Figure 7.8(c) New

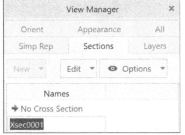

Figure 7.8(d) Default name

Figure 7.8(e) Section A

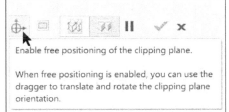

Figure 7.8(f) Enable Dragger

Open: **References** tab > **Section reference** [Fig. 7.8(g)] > select **Front** [Fig. 7.8(h)]

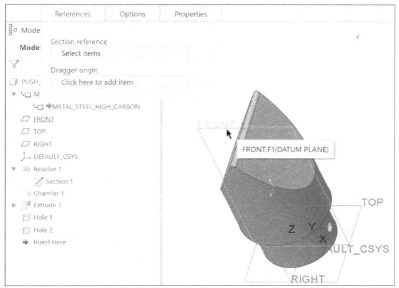

Figure 7.8(g) Section Reference

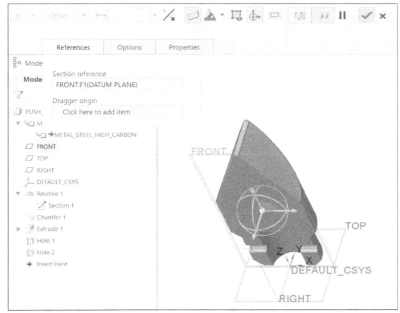

Figure 7.8(h) Section A

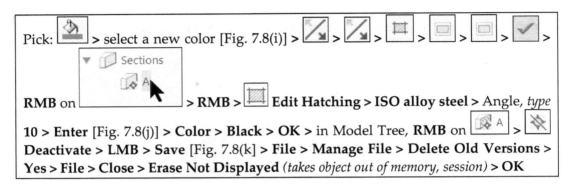

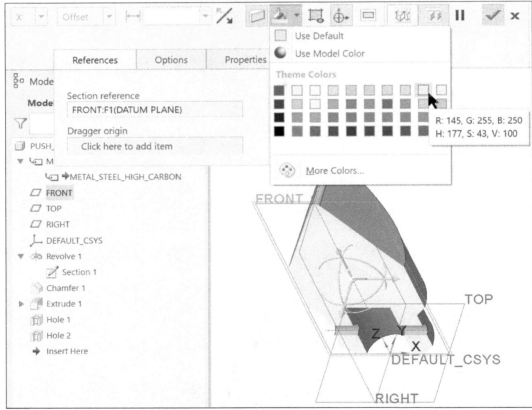

Figure 7.8(i) Section Color

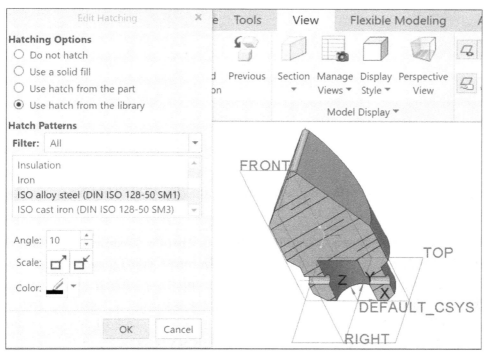

Figure 7.8(j) Edit Hatching

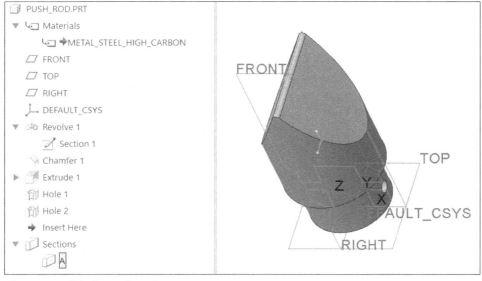

Figure 7.8(k) Completed part

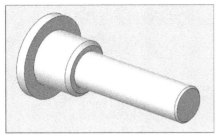

Figure 7.9 Piston

Piston

The second component for this chapter is the Piston (Fig. 7.9). The Piston can be modeled with two features.

Click: **Ctrl+N** > Name-- **Piston** > **OK** > **File** > **Options** > **Model Display** > **Trimetric** > **Configuration Editor** > **Import/Export** > **Import configuration file** > **Creo_textbook.pro** [Fig. 7.10(a)] from your working directory > **Open** > **OK** > **No** > **File** > **Prepare** > **Model Properties** > Units **change** > **millimeter_Newton** > **Set** > **Interpret** > **OK** > Material **Change** > double-click on **metal_steel_high_carbon.mtl** [Fig. 7.10(b)] > **Yes** > **OK** > **Close** > **File** > **Options** > **OK** > **Yes** > **OK**

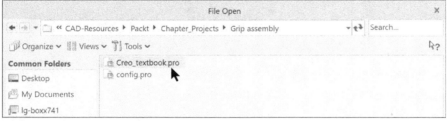

Figure 7.10(a) Configuration File

Figure 7.10(b) Material (your available materials may be different)

Model Tree

The Model Tree is a tabbed feature on the Creo Parametric navigator that contains a list of every feature (or component) in the current part, assembly, or drawing. The model structure is displayed in hierarchical (tree) format with the root object (the current feature, part or assembly) at the top of its tree and the subordinate objects (features, parts, or assemblies) below.

If you have multiple Creo Parametric windows open, the Model Tree contents reflect the file in the current "active" window. The Model Tree lists only the related feature- and part-level objects in a current file and does not list the entities (such as edges, surfaces, curves, and so forth) that comprise the features.

Each Model Tree item displays an icon that reflects its object type, for example, assembly, part, feature, or datum plane (also a feature). The icon can also show the display status for a feature, part, or assembly, for example, suppressed or hidden.

You can save the Model Tree as a **.txt** file. Selection in the Model Tree is object-action oriented; you select objects in the Model Tree without first specifying what you intend to do with them. Items can be added or removed from the Model Tree column display using Settings in the Navigator:

- Select objects and perform object-specific operations using the shortcut menu.
- Filter the display by item type, for example, hiding or un-hiding datum features.
- Open a part within an assembly file by right-clicking the part in the Model Tree.
- Create or modify features and perform operations such as deleting and redefining.
- Search the Model Tree for model properties or feature information.
- Show the display status for an object, for example, suppressed or hidden.

Click: ⬚ in the **Navigator** > **Tree Filters** [Fig. 7.11(a)] > *toggle all on* [Fig. 7.11(b)] >

Apply > **OK** > ⬚ in the **Navigator** > **Tree Columns** [Fig. 7.11(c)]

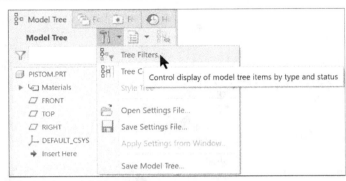

Figure 7.11(a) Tree Filters

Figure 7.11(b) Model Tree Items Dialog Box

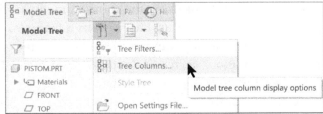

Figure 7.11(c) Model Tree Columns

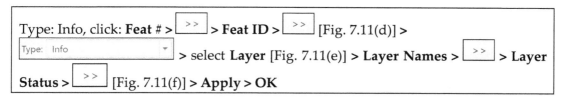

Type: Info, click: **Feat #** > `>>` > **Feat ID** > `>>` [Fig. 7.11(d)] >
Type: Info > select **Layer** [Fig. 7.11(e)] > **Layer Names** > `>>` > **Layer**
Status > `>>` [Fig. 7.11(f)] > **Apply** > **OK**

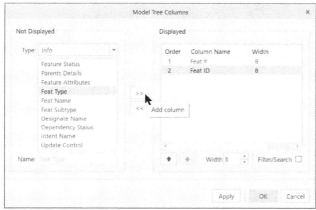

Figure 7.11(d) Model Tree Columns Dialog Box

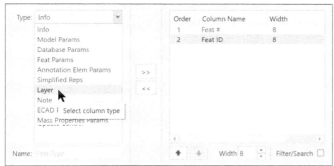

Figure 7.11(e) Model Tree Columns Dialog Box, Type: Layer

Not Displayed		Displayed		
Type: Layer		Order	Column Name	Width
		1	Feat #	8
		2	Feat ID	8
		3	Layer Names	8
		4	Layer Status	8

Figure 7.11(f) Model Tree Columns Dialog Box, Displayed

Press: **LMB** on the sash ⊞ and drag to expand the Model Tree [Fig. 7.11(g)] > adjust the width of each column by dragging the column divider | Feat ID ✛Layer Names | > ⊞ drag the sash to the left to decrease the Model Tree size [Fig. 7.11(h)]

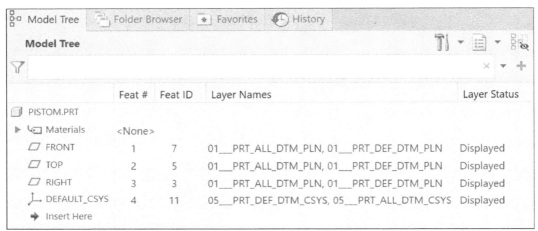

Figure 7.11(g) Expand the Model Tree and Adjust the Width of the Columns

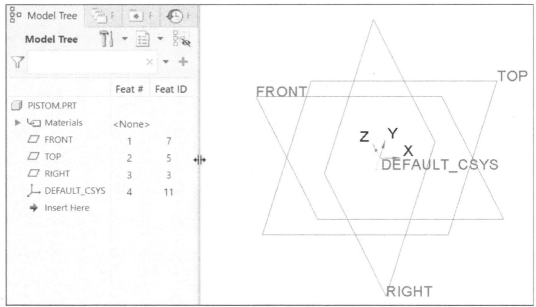

Figure 7.11(h) Decrease the Model Tree Width

Click: **Model** tab > **Revolve** > **Placement** tab > **Define** > Sketch Plane--- Plane: select datum **RIGHT** > **Sketch** > [icon] **Sketch View** > **RMB** > **Centerline** > sketch a *horizontal construction centerline* through the default coordinate system > **MMB** > place your cursor over the completed construction centerline > **RMB** > **Designate Axis of Revolution** [Fig. 7.12(a)] > **OK** [Fig. 7.12(b)] > **MMB**

A "construction centerline" must designated as an axis of revolution for a revolved feature.

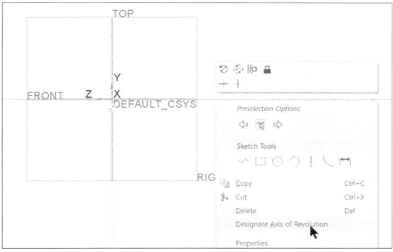

Figure 7.12(a) Designate Axis of Revolution

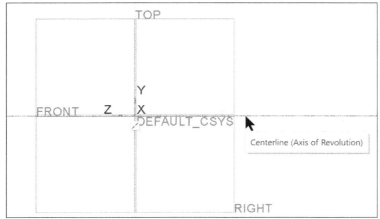

Figure 7.12(b) Centerline (Axis of Revolution)

Click: 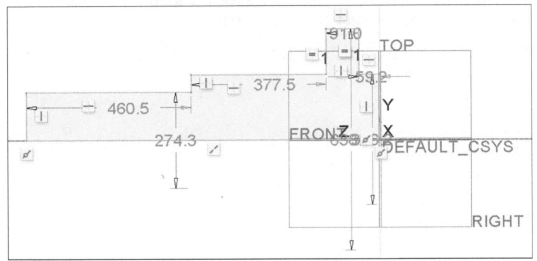 **Line Chain** > sketch ten lines [Fig. 7.12(c)] > adjust the position of the dimensions [Fig. 7.12(d)] > **MMB** > **MMB** the sketch should shade if a closed section was created > **LMB** *(your values will be different, do not change)*

Figure 7.12(c) Sketch Six Lines to Form a Closed Section (on one side of the centerline)

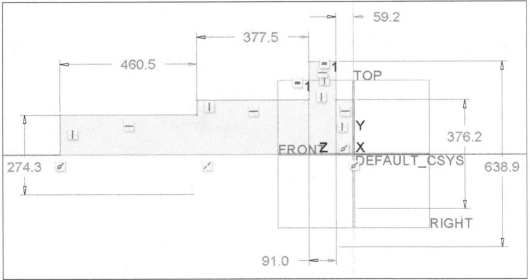

Figure 7.12(d) Adjust dimension positions *(your values will be different)*

Press **RMB** > ⟷ **Dimension** > add an overall horizontal dimension by picking **Datum TOP** and the left vertical side of the sketch > **MMB** to place the dimension > **MMB** [Fig. 7.12(e)] > **LMB** > capture all of the sketch and dimensions with a window > ✎ **Modify** > **Lock Scale** > select the overall dimension [Fig. 7.12(f)] > *type* **100** > **Enter** > **OK** > 🔍

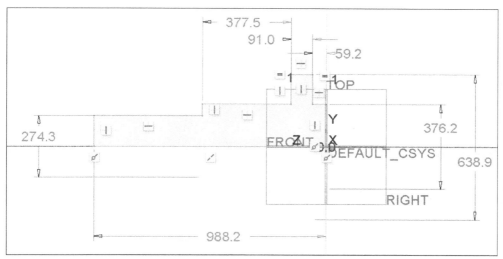

Figure 7.12(e) Add dimensions *(your values will be different)*

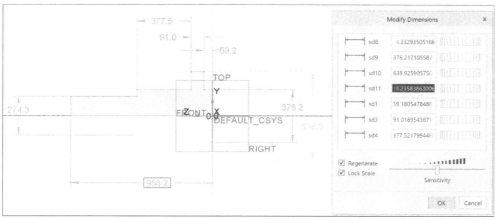

Figure 7.12(f) Modify Dimensions Dialog Box

261

Double-click on and modify dimensions to the design values > **LMB** > reposition dimensions [Fig. 7.12(g)] > **File > Options > Sketcher** > Decimal Places **0 > OK > No > RMB >** ☑ Fig. 7.12(h)]

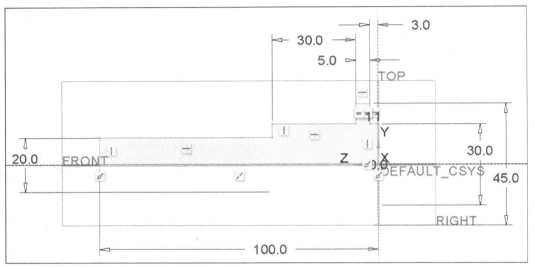

Figure 7.12(g) Design Value Dimensions

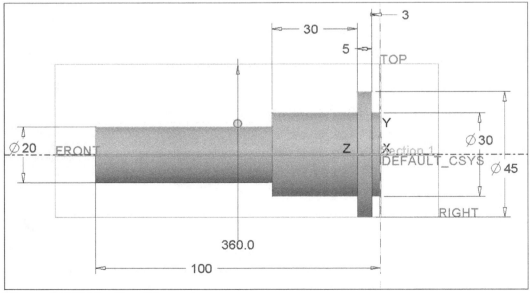

Figure 7.12(h) Section Dimensions

Spin the model [Fig. 7.12(i)] > 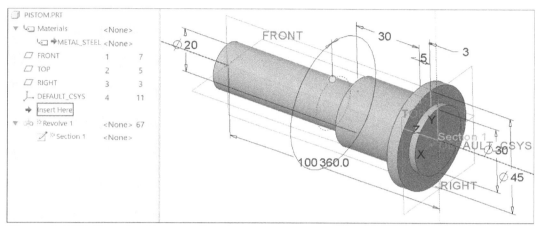 **Zoom in** pick two corners > ✓ > 🔍 **Refit** > ⟋⟍
all off > double-click on the model [Fig. 7.12(j)] > **LMB > Save > OK > View** tab >
Appearances > select a new color

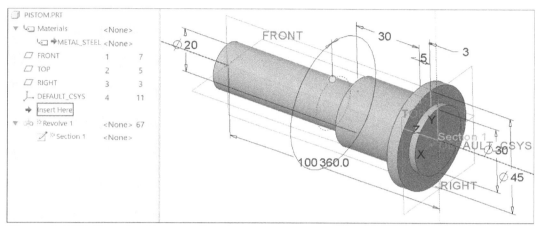

Figure 7.12(i) Revolve Feature Preview

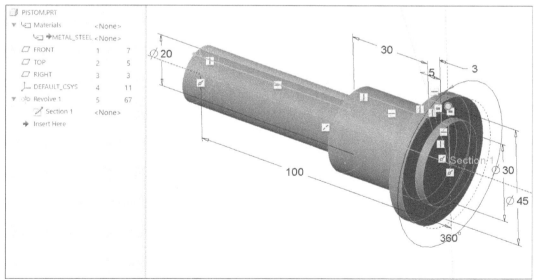

Figure 7.12(j) Revolved Extrusion

263

Select: **Model** tab > **Ctrl+** pick the two edges > **Edge Chamfer** [Fig. 7.13(a)] > D **2** > **Enter** [Fig. 7.13(b)]

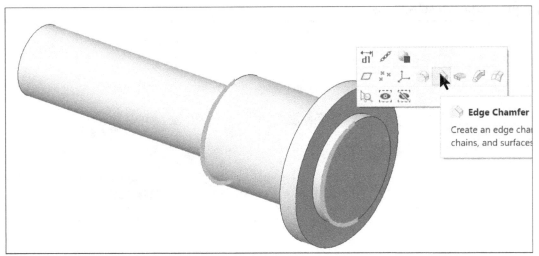

Figure 7.13(a) Pick on the two edges

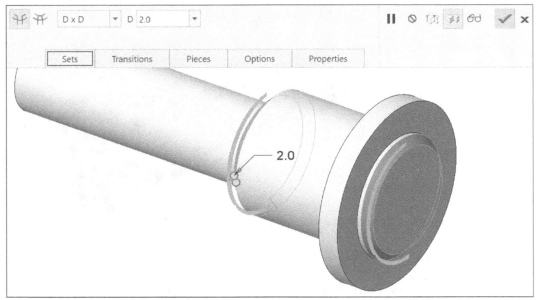

Figure 7.13(b) Chamfers Preview

Select: **Sets** tab > **New set** [Fig. 7.13(c)] > spin the model and pick the edge > D **1** > **Enter** [Fig. 7.13(d)] > **Enter** > **MMB** > **LMB** > **File** > **Options** > **Model Display** > **Default model orientation** > **Isometric** > **Apply** > **OK** > **No** > **Save**

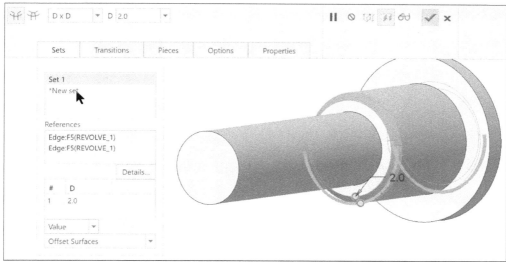

Figure 7.13(c) New set

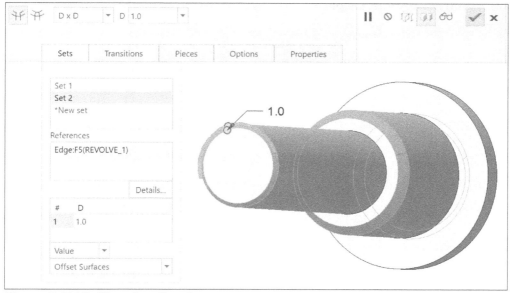

Figure 7.13(d) Chamfers Preview

Click: 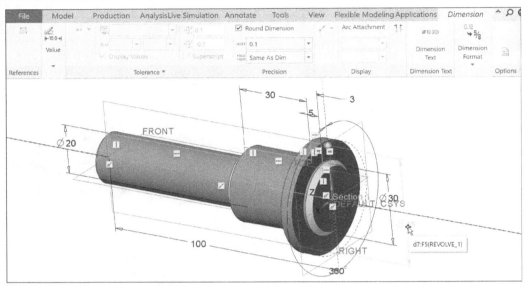 *all on* > spin the model > double-click on the model to display the dimensions for the protrusion > pick on the Ø**45** dimension, Dimension tab displays [Fig. 7.14(a)] > **Display** [Fig. 7.14(b)] Display and Arrow options

Figure 7.14(a) Dimensions Display

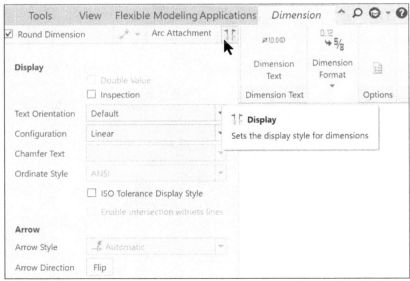

Figure 7.14(b) Dimension tab

Click: **Dimension Text** tab [Fig. 7.14(c)] provides options for Text and Symbols > **Dimension Format** [Fig. 7.14(d)] > **Dual Dimensions** [Fig. 7.14(e)] > **Options** shows Dependencies [Fig. 7.14(f)] > **LMB > LMB > Save**

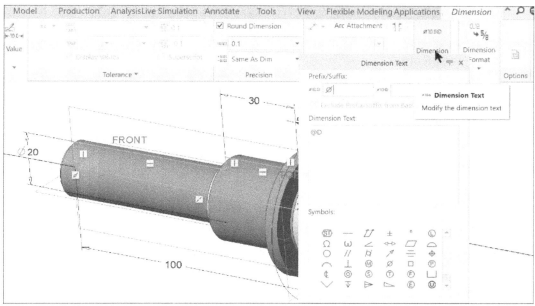

Figure 7.14(c) Dimension Text Tab

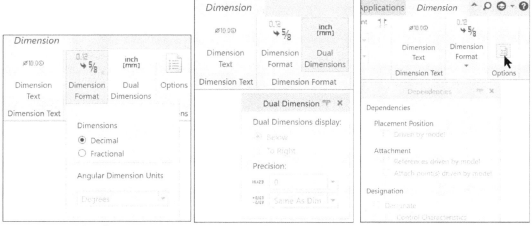

Figure 7.14(d-e-f) Dimension Format, Dual Dimensions, and Options

Model Player

The Model Player lets you observe how a part is built. You can:

- Move backward or forward through the feature-creation history of the model.
- Regenerate each feature in sequence, starting from the specified feature
- Display each feature as it is regenerated or rolled forward
- Update (regenerate all the features in) the entire display when you reach the desired feature
- Obtain information about the current feature (you can show dimensions, obtain regular feature information, investigate geometry errors, and enter Fix Model mode)

You can select one of the following:

- **Regenerate features** Regenerates each feature in sequence, starting from the specified feature
- **Display each feature** Displays each feature in the graphics window as it is being regenerated

Select one of the following commands:

- ⎣◀⎦ Go to the beginning of the model
- ⎣◀⎦ Step backward through the model one feature at-a-time
- ⎣▣⎦ Stop play
- ⎣▶⎦ Step forward through the model one feature at-a-time
- ⎣▶⎦ Go to the last feature in the model

 **Slider Bar** Drag the slider handle to the feature at which you want model playback to begin. The features are highlighted in the graphics window as you move through their position with the slider handle. The feature number and type are displayed in the selection panel [such as #4 (COORDINATE SYSTEM)], and the feature number is displayed in the **Feat** # box.

Select feature from screen or model tree lets you select a starting feature from the graphics window or the Model Tree. Opens the **SELECT FEAT** and **SELECT** menus. After you select a starting feature, its number and ID are displayed in the selection panel, and the feature number is displayed in the **Feat** # box.

Feat # 3   of 5 Let's you specify a starting feature by typing the feature number in the box. After you enter the feature number, the model immediately rolls or regenerates to that feature.

Use the following commands for information:

- **Show Dims** Displays the dimensions of the current feature
- **Feat Info** Provides regular feature information about the current feature in an Information window
- **Geom Check** Investigates the geometry error for the current feature
- **Fix Model** Activates Resolve mode by forcing the current feature to abort regeneration
- **Close** Closes the Model Player and enters Insert mode at the current feature
- **Finish** Closes the Model Player and returns to the last feature in the model

Click: **>** **Tool** tab **> Model Player >** ☑ Regenerate features ☑ Display each feature **>** |◄ **Go to the beginning of the model >** ▶ **>** ▶ **>** ▶ **>** ▶ **>** ▶ **>** Show Dims [Fig. 7.15] **>** ▶ **>** ▶| **> Finish**

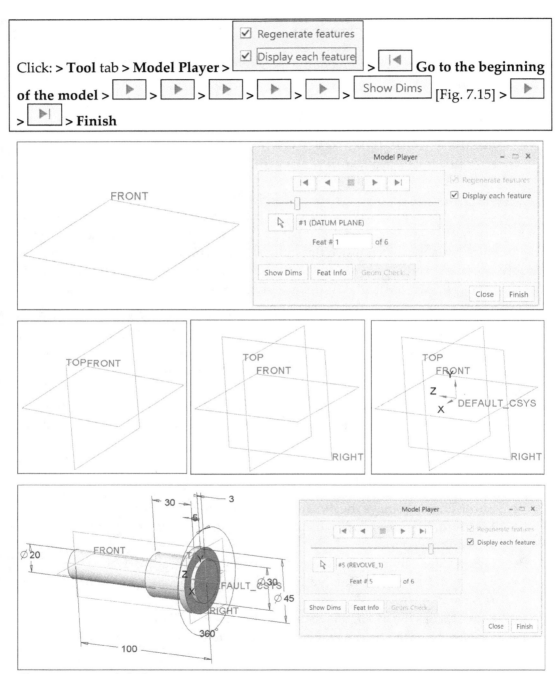

Figure 7.15 Model Player

Click: **Annotate** tab > select the features in the Model Tree [Fig. 7.16(a)] > **RMB** > 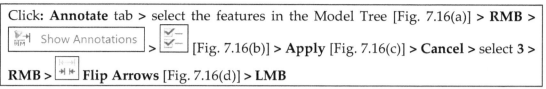 [Fig. 7.16(b)] > **Apply** [Fig. 7.16(c)] > **Cancel** > select **3** > **RMB** > **Flip Arrows** [Fig. 7.16(d)] > **LMB**

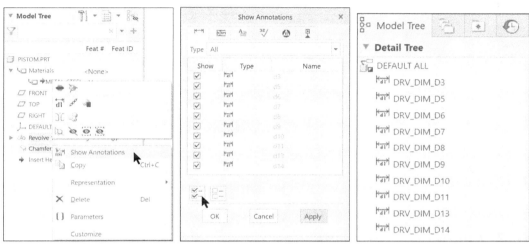

Figure 7.16(a) Show Annotations **Figure 7.16(b)** Select All **Figure 7.16(c)** Detail Tree

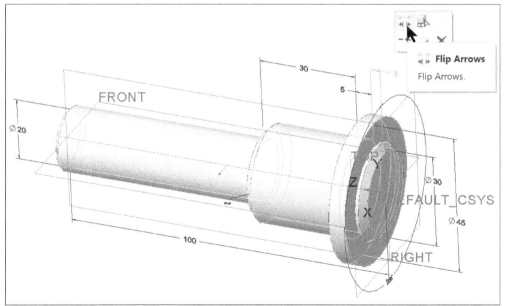

Figure 7.16(d) Repositioned Dimensions and Flip Arrow

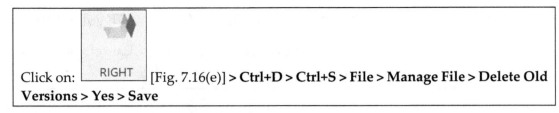

Click on: **RIGHT** [Fig. 7.16(e)] > **Ctrl+D > Ctrl+S > File > Manage File > Delete Old Versions > Yes > Save**

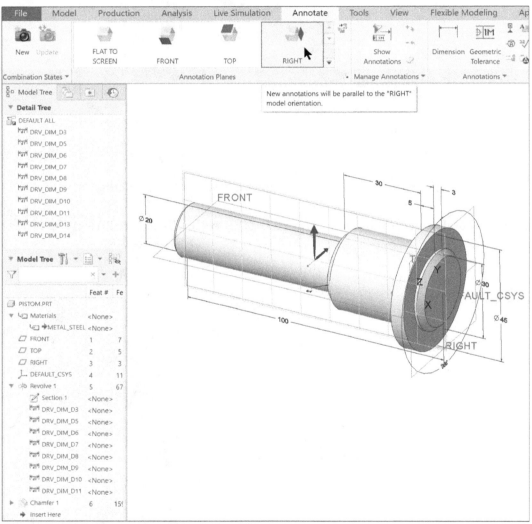

Figure 7.16(e) Annotation Orientation Plane

Printing and Plotting

From the **File** menu, you can print with the following options: scaling, clipping, displaying the plot on the screen, or sending the plot directly to the printer. Shaded images can also be printed from this menu. You can create plot files of the current object (sketch, part, assembly, drawing, or layout) and send them to the print queue of a plotter. If you are printing a non-shaded image, the Printer **Configuration** dialog box opens. The following applies for plotting/printing:

- Hidden lines appear as gray for a screen plot, but as dashed lines on paper.
- When Creo Parametric plots line fonts, it scales them to the size of a sheet. It does not scale the user-defined line fonts, which do not plot as defined.
- You can use the configuration file option *use_software_linefonts* to make sure that the plotter plots a user-defined font exactly as it appears.
- You can plot a cross section from Part or Assembly mode.

Click: **File > Print** [Fig. 7.17(a)] > **Page** [Fig. 7.17(b)] > **OK > Cancel**

Figure 7.17(a) Printer Configuration

Figure 7.17(b) Page tab

Expand the Model Tree [Fig. 7.18] > **File > Close > File > Manage Session > Erase Not Displayed > OK > File > Exit > Yes**

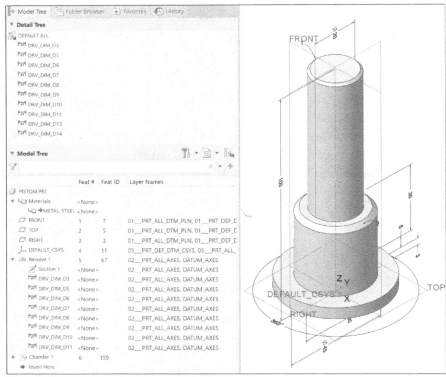

Figure 7.18 Completed Piston

Quiz

1. What is displayed in the Folder Browser?
2. What are Configuration Options used to control?
3. Understand and use the Navigation browser
4. How do you change Items and Columns displayed in the Model Tree?
5. What is the difference between the two types of sketched centerlines?
6. Name five Dimension Properties.
7. Why would you wish to reorder a feature?
8. What is the function of the Model Player?

This completes Chapter 7.

PART 3

Creating an assembly

Just as parts are created from related features, assemblies are created from related parts. The progressive combination of subassemblies, parts, and features into an assembly creates parent-child relationships based on the references used to assemble each component. Assemblies can be sectioned and exploded so as to view how the components fit together.

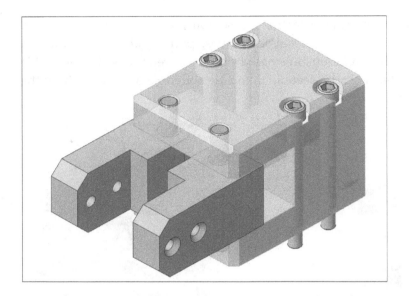

Assembly mode allows you to place together components and subassemblies to create an assembly. Assemblies can be modified, reoriented, documented, or analyzed. An assembly can be assembled into another assembly, thereby becoming a subassembly. *Bottom-up design* means that existing parts are assembled, one by one, until the assembly is complete. The assembly starts with a set of default datum planes and a coordinate system. The parts are constrained to the datum features of the assembly. The sequence of assembly will determine the parent-child relationships between components.

Objectives
- Perform placement of component parts
- Use analysis for mass properties and clearance checks
- Modify the dimensional values of component parts
- Using the 3D Dragger to position components while assembling
- Utilize a variety of constraint types
- Edit the existing assembly component constraints and position
- Create an assembly section
- Generate a BOM

Component Placement

The **3D Dragger** is a graphical tool for precision handling of assembly components. The *axes* are called **draggers**. Pull or rotate the draggers to make changes to the components position and orientation. The draggers enable movement in one or more *degrees of freedom* (DOFs). They support linear, planar, free, translation, and angular movements. You can pull a dragger along a 2D or 3D trajectory. When you move a geometric entity using a dragger, the relative distances from the start point of the entity appear in the graphics window as you pull the dragger. You can hold down the SHIFT key while pulling a dragger to snap the dragger to a geometric reference.

To assemble components, use: Assemble **Add a component to the assembly**. After selecting a component from the Open dialog box, the dashboard opens, and the component appears in the assembly window. Alternatively, you can select a component from a browser window and drag it into the graphics window. If there is an assembly in the window, Creo Parametric will begin to assemble the component into the current assembly. Using icons in the dashboard, you can specify the screen window in which the component is displayed while you position it. You can change window options at any time using: **Show component in a separate window while specifying constraints** or **Show component in the assembly window while specifying constraints**.

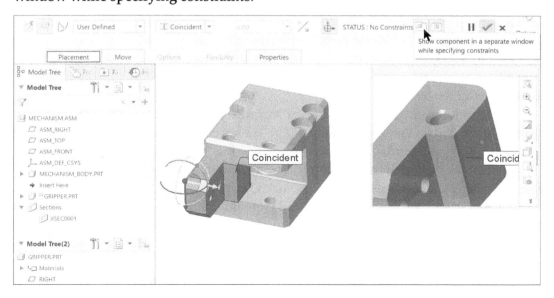

Chapter 8 STEPS

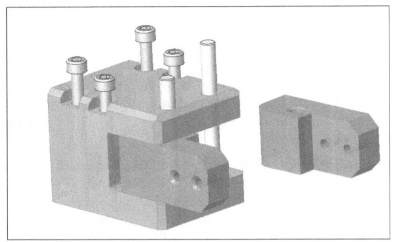

Figure 8.1 Mechanism

Mechanism Assembly

The parts required in this chapter were modeled previously except the **Socket Head Cap Screw** which will be downloaded from the company catalog.

Because you will be creating the Mechanism assembly [Fig. 8.1] using the *bottom-up design* approach, all the components must be available before any assembling starts. *Bottom-up design* means that existing parts are assembled, one by one, until the assembly is complete. The assembly starts with a set of default datum planes and a coordinate system. The parts are constrained to the datum features of the assembly. The sequence of assembly will determine the parent-child relationships between components.

Top-down design is the design of an assembly where one or more component parts are created in Assembly mode as the design unfolds. Some existing parts are available, such as standard components and a few modeled parts. The remaining design evolves during the assembly process. The main assembly will involve creating one part using the *top-down design* approach. Chapter 9 covers top-down-design

Regardless of the design method, the assembly default datum planes and coordinate system should be on their own separate *assembly layer*. Each part should also be placed on separate assembly layers; the part's datum features should already be on *part layers*.

*Unless instructed to do so, **do not use the library parts directly in the assembly**.*

Launch **Creo Parametric > Select Working Directory > OK >**

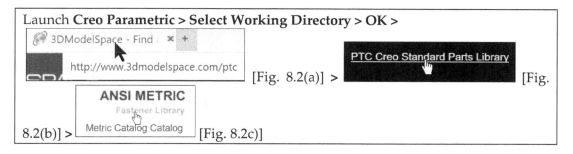 [Fig. 8.2(a)] > [Fig. 8.2(b)] > [Fig. 8.2c)]

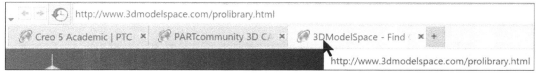

Figure 8.2(a) 3DModelSpace

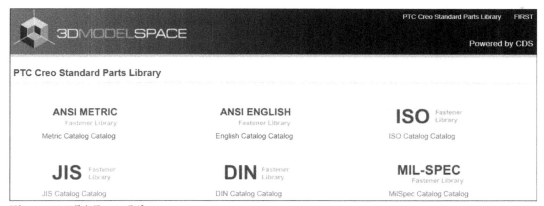

Figure 8.2(b) Parts Library

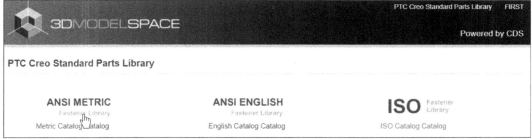

Figure 8.2(c) ANSI METRIC Fastener Library

Scroll to the bottom of the PTC Catalog Directory page and click:

I ACCEPT the Terms and Conditions Stated Above. [Fig. 8.2(d)] > Show All Categories [Fig. 8.2(e)]

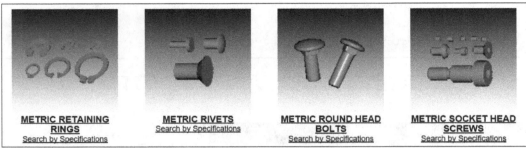

Figure 8.2(d) METRIC LIBRARY Metric Socket Head Cap Screws

Figure 8.2(e) METRIC LIBRARY All Categories

Select: **SOCKET HEAD CAP SCREWS > Nominal Diameter Thread Pitch > 12x1.45**
[Fig. 8.2(f)] **> Length > 120 > MSCS1014 > Choose Format > Pro/ENGINEER Wildfire 2.0 or later** [Fig. 8.2(g)] *(select the bottom option)*

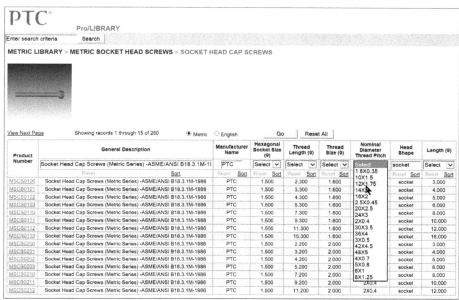

Figure 8.2(f) METRIC LIBRARY > METRIC TEE NUT BOLTS > T-NUTS

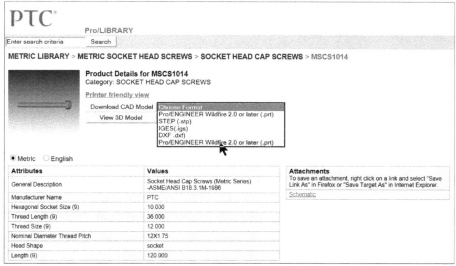

Figure 8.2(g) Download *(select the bottom option)*

Select: **Download CAD Model >** Drag this link into your Pro/ENGINEER or Creo session to open your model. drag and drop the link into the Graphics Window > double-click on **mscs1014 > Save >** off > double-click on the screw shaft > modify length to **130mm** [Fig. 8.2(h)] > change the model color: **View** tab > **Appearances > ptc-std-steel >** > in the Model Tree **MSCS1014 > MMB > File > Manage file > Rename > SOC_HD_CAP_SCR-12 > Rename in session** [Fig. 8.2(i)] > **OK > File > Save**

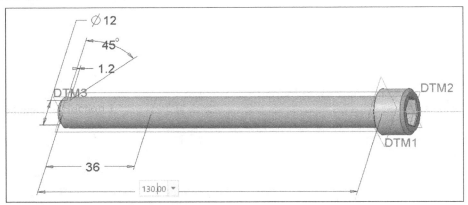

Figure 8.2(h) Modify Length to 130mm

ALTERNATE MODEL- *If your system cannot access the Standard Parts Library; in the embedded web Browser > type: www.cad-resources.com > Enter*

http://www.cad-resources.com/

Login | PT...   PARTcom...   Lamit and ...

> click on the appropriate book cover icon > drag and drop the link into the Graphics Window

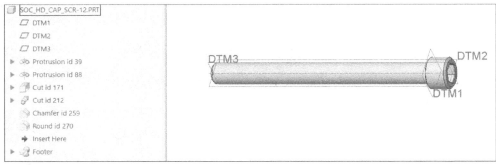

Figure 8.2(i) SOC_HD_CAP_SCR-12

Click: [▶] to expand the Model Tree features and Footer > **RMB** on Interfaces **INTFC001** > **Information** [Fig. 8.2(j)] > **Feature Information** [Fig. 8.2(k)] > [×] close the Browser > **Ctrl+D** > **Ctrl+S** > **File** > **Close**

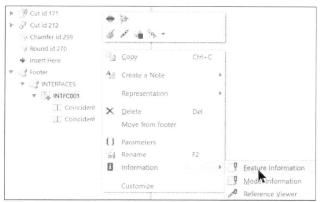

Figure 8.2(j) INTERFACES Feature Information

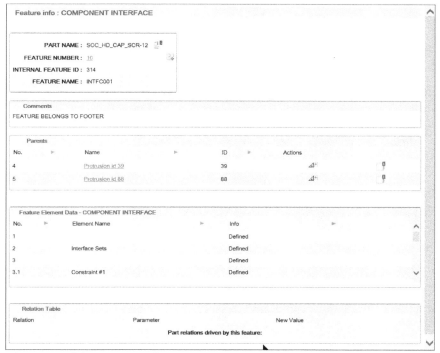

Figure 8.2(k) Feature information

Open the models for the Mechanism assembly > the **Gripper** [Fig. 8.3(a)], **Mechanism Body** [Fig. 8.3(b), and the **Soc_Hd_Cap_Scr-12** [Fig. 8.3(c)] > review the components and standard parts for unique *colors, layering, coordinate system naming,* and *set datum planes* > Close all windows. Components remain "in session".

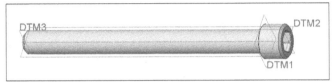

Figure 8.3(a) Soc_Hd_Cap_Scr-12

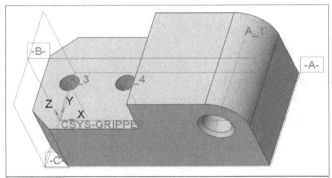

Figure 8.3(b) Gripper

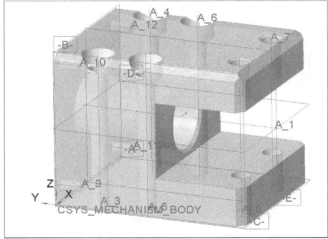

Figure 8.3(c) Mechanism body

You now have three components ready for assembly. *All parts must be in the same working directory used for the assembly.*

Click: ⬜ **Create a new model >** ◉ Assembly **> Sub-type** ◉ Design **> Name mechanism >** ⬜ Use default template [Fig. 8.4(a)] **> OK >** Template **start_assembly_mmks >** Parameters MODELED_BY *type **your name*** **> DESCRIPTION** *type* **Mechanism_Assembly** [Fig. 8.4(b)] **> OK > File > Prepare > Model Properties >** Units **change >** note that the units have already been set **> Include submodels** [Fig. 8.4(c)] **Close > Close**

Figure 8.4(a) New Dialog Box

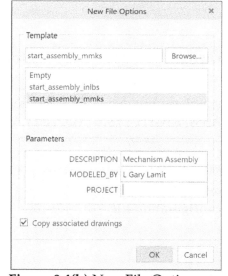

Figure 8.4(b) New File Options

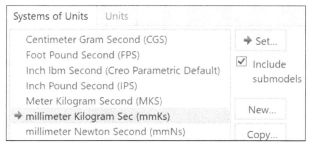

Figure 8.4(c) Systems of Units

Click: [image icon] **Settings** from the Navigator > [Tree Filters...] > check all Display options *on* [Fig. 8.4(d)] > **Apply > OK > Ctrl+S > OK**

Figure 8.4(d) Model Tree Items Dialog Box

Assembly datum planes and the coordinate system are created per the template provided by Creo Parametric. The datum planes will have the default names, **ASM_RIGHT**, **ASM_TOP**, and **ASM_FRONT**.

Change the coordinate system name: slowly double-click on **ASM_DEF_CSYS** in the Model Tree > *type the new name* **CSYS_MECHANISM** > **Enter** [Fig. 8.4(e)] > **LMB** to deselect > **File** > **Options** > **Configuration Editor** > **Import/Export** > **Import configuration file** > double-click on **Creo_textbook.pro** > **OK** > **No**

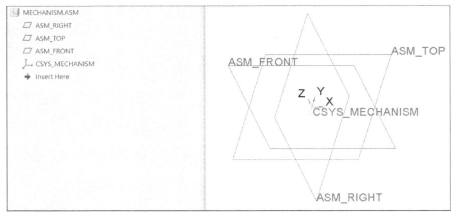

Figure 8.4(e) Sub-Assembly Datum Planes and Coordinate System

Regardless of the design methodology, the assembly datum planes and coordinate system should be on their own separate *assembly layer*. Each part should also be placed on separate assembly layers; the part's datum features should already be on *part layers*. Look over the default template for assembly layering.

Click: > **Layer Tree** > > **Expand All** [Fig. 8.4(f)] > **Model Tree**

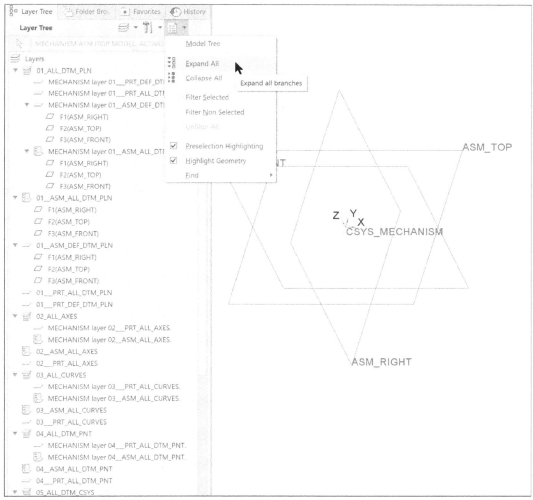

Figure 8.4(f) Default Template for Assembly Layering

The first component to be assembled to the subassembly is the Mechanism Body. The simplest and quickest method of adding a component to an assembly is to match the coordinate systems. The first component assembled is usually where this *constraint* is used, because after the first component is established, few if any of the remaining components are assembled to the assembly coordinate system (with the exception of *top-down design*) or, for that matter, other parts coordinate systems. All your models are in the same working directory before starting the assembly process.

Click: [icon] **Annotation Display** *off* > **Model** tab > [Assemble icon] > **mechanism_body.prt_> Preview** *on* > **Views** tab > **List** > **Show PopUp Viewer** [Fig. 8.5(a)] > **Open** > **LMB** to place anywhere on screen [Fig. 8.5(b)]

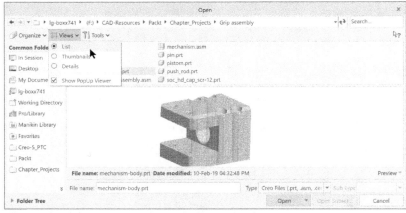

Figure 8.5(a) Previewed Mechanism Body

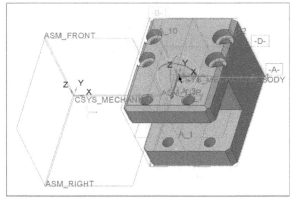

Figure 8.5(b) Placed Mechanism Body

When an assembly is complicated, or it is difficult to select constraining geometry, a separate window aids in the selection process. For simple assemblies working in the assembly window is more convenient. Since this is the first component being added to the assembly, a separate window is not needed.

In the Graphics Window, press: **RMB > Default Constraint** [Fig. 8.5(c)] (this option puts the component at the default position on the assembly model) **> MMB > Save > OK > File > Options > Model Display >** Default Model orientation: **Trimetric > Isometric > OK > No >** [icon] **> Expand All** [Fig. 8.5(d)]

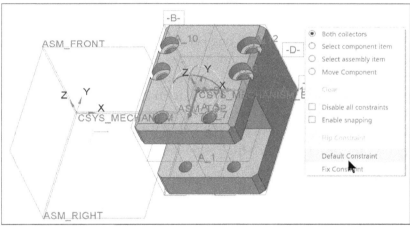

Figure 8.5(c) Default Constraint

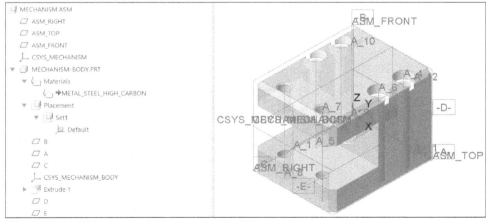

Figure 8.5(d) Expanded Placement Folder

The Mechanism Body has been assembled to the default location. This means to align the default Creo Parametric-created coordinate system of the component to the default Creo Parametric-created coordinate system of the assembly. Creo Parametric places the component at the assembly origin. By using the constraint, Coincident and selecting the assembly and then the component's coordinate systems would have accomplished the same thing, but with more picks.

Component placement is based on placement definition sets. These sets determine how and where the component relates to the assembly. The sets are either user-defined or predefined. A user-defined constraint set has zero or more constraints (a packaged component may have no constraints). Predefined constraint sets have a predefined number of constraints. Placement of a component in an assembly is determined by the constraints in all sets defined. A single set of constraints can define placement of a component. If constraints from one set conflict with constraints from another set, the placement status becomes invalid. The constraints must be redefined or removed until placement status becomes valid. Constraints can be added or deleted at will in a user-defined constraint set, there are no predefined constraints. Each type of predefined constraint set (also called a connection) has a predefined number of constraints. Constraint sets are displayed in the Placement folder of the Model Tree. Display hierarchy follows the order in which they were defined.

Click: [Assemble] > select **gripper.prt** > **Open** > [icon] > (**Select All**) *off* > **LMB** to temporarily place > **Placement** tab [Fig. 8.6(a)]

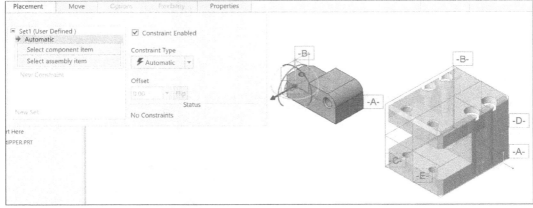

Figure 8.6(a) Gripper.prt Placed

Click: **Placement** tab *(close)* > pick on the hole surface of the GRIPPER [Fig. 8.6(b)] > pick on the hole surface of the MECHANIISM-BODY [Fig. 8.6(c)] (constraint becomes Coincident) > **Component Placement** tab *open*

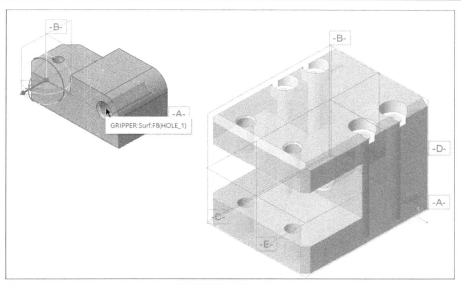

Figure 8.6(b) Select on the GRIPPER Hole Surface

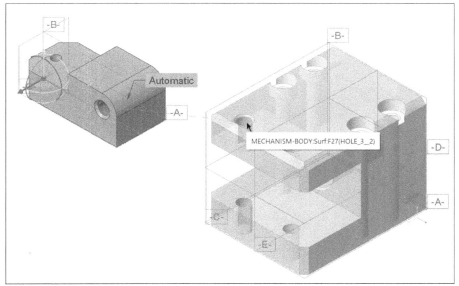

Figure 8.6(c) Select on the Mechanism-body Hole Surface

Click: ⊕ **Hide 3D Dragger** > **Placement** tab *(close)* > **RMB** > **New Constraint** > pick the Mechanism-body surface [Fig. 8.6(d)] > click **RMB** until correct surface is highlighted > **LMB** pick the Gripper.prt surface [Fig. 8.6(e)]

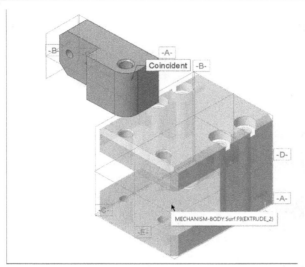

Figure 8.6(d) Select on the Small Circular Extrusion of the Mechanism-body

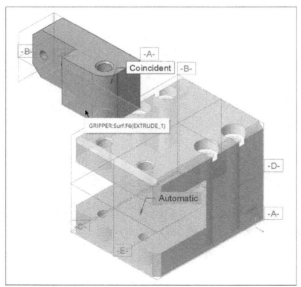

Figure 8.6(e) Select on the Underside Surface of the Gripper

292

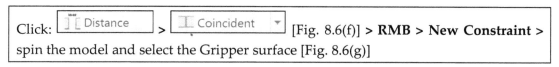

Click: [Distance] > [Coincident ▼] [Fig. 8.6(f)] > **RMB > New Constraint >**
spin the model and select the Gripper surface [Fig. 8.6(g)]

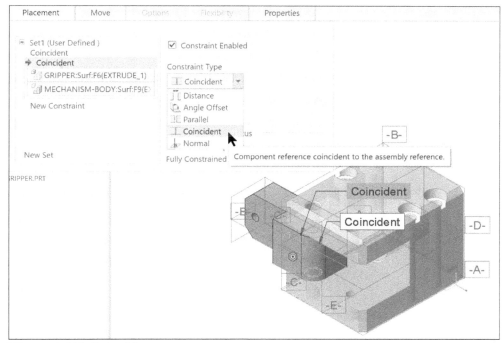

Figure 8.6(f) Coincident

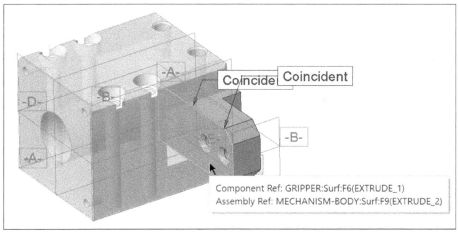

Figure 8.6(g) Second Constraint

Click: Constraint Type [Normal] > [Parallel] > pick the vertical surface
MECHANISM-BODY [Fig. 8.6(h)] > **MMB** [Fig. 8.6(i)] > **Ctrl+D** > **Save**

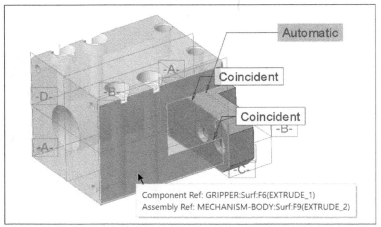

Figure 8.6(h) Coincident

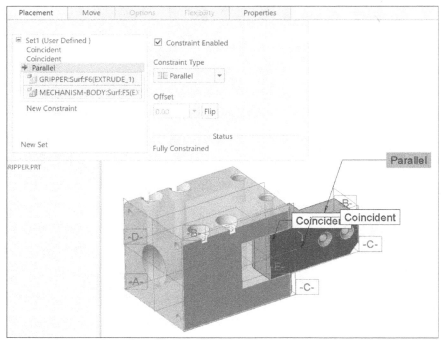

Figure 8.6(i) Fully Constrained Component

The Gripper is fully constrained. Next, we will convert one of the constraints to a *"Mechanism Pin"* [✗ Pin] constraint. The pin constraint controls the translation or rotation about the axis of a cylindrical surface in 3D models.

Click on **GRIPPER** in the Model Tree > [✎] **Edit Definition > Placement** tab > **Parallel > RMB > Delete >** *first* **Coincident** constraint > [☐ Constraint Enabled] [Fig. 8.6(j)] > **User Defined >** [✗ Pin] [Fig. 8.6(k)]

Figure 8.6(j) Constraint Disable

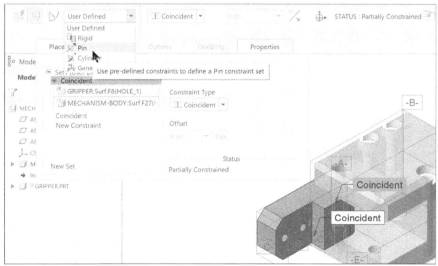

Figure 8.6(k) Convert constraint to "Pin" constraint

Click: [Fig. 8.6(l)] **MMB** > [Drag Components] > select the **Gripper** > move to rotate the component [Fig. 8.6(m)] > **MMB** to return to the original position > **MMB** > **MMB**

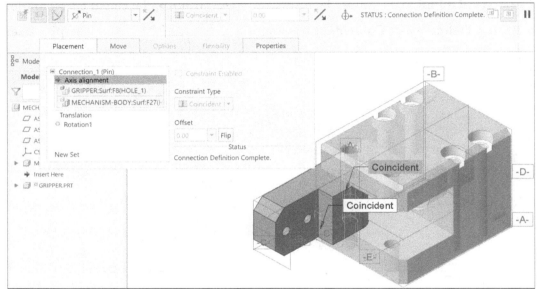

Figure 8.6(l) User defined

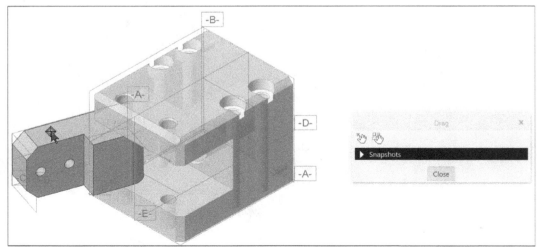

Figure 8.6(m) Pin connection

Select the **Gripper** in the Model Tree > **RMB** > **Mirror Component** [Fig. 8.6(n)] > **Preview** > **Reuse selected model** > select datum **E** [Fig. 8.6(o)] > **OK**

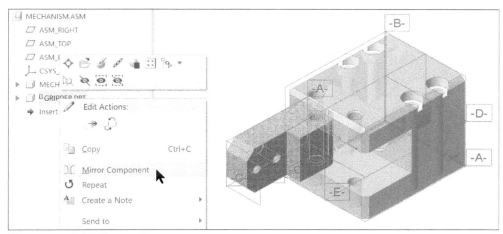

Figure 8.6(n) Mirror Component

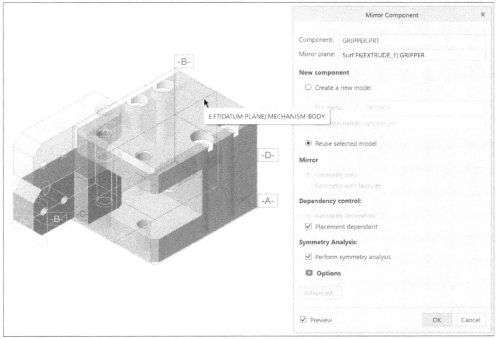

Figure 8.6(o) Mirror Plane

297

Select the new **Gripper** in the Model Tree > **RMB** > [🖰 **Edit Definition**] > **Confirm** > **Placement** tab > select the Mechanism-body hole and then the Gripper hole [Fig. 8.6(p)] > **New Constraint** > select the two surfaces as before [Fig. 8.6(q)]

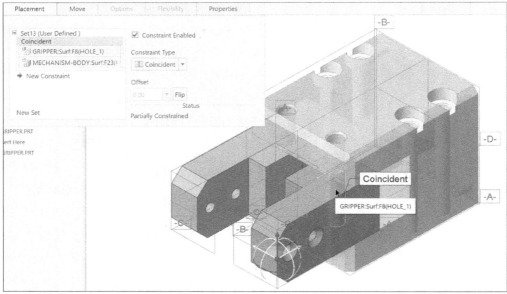

Figure 8.6(p) Edit Definition

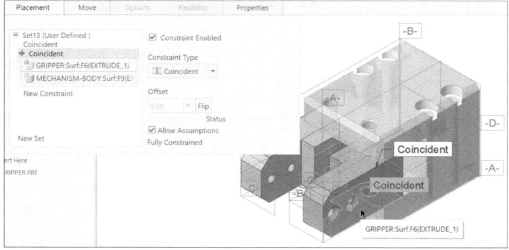

Figure 8.6(q) New Constraint

Select the *first* **Coincident** constraint > ☐ Constraint Enabled > **User Defined** > ✗ Pin [Fig. 8.6(r)] > **MMB** > 🖾 **Drag Components** > select the second **Gripper** > move to rotate the component [Fig. 8.6(s)] > **MMB > MMB > MMB > RMB > Regenerate**

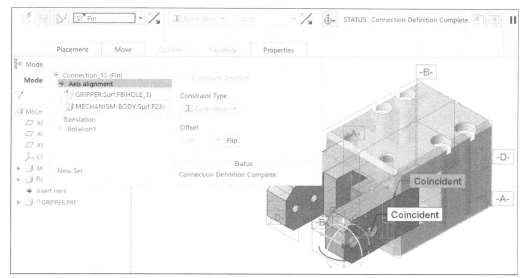

Figure 8.6(r) Pin

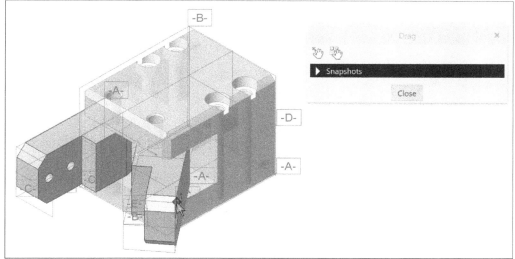

Figure 8.6(s) Drag Component

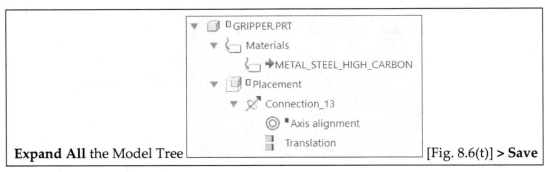

Expand All the Model Tree [Fig. 8.6(t)] **> Save**

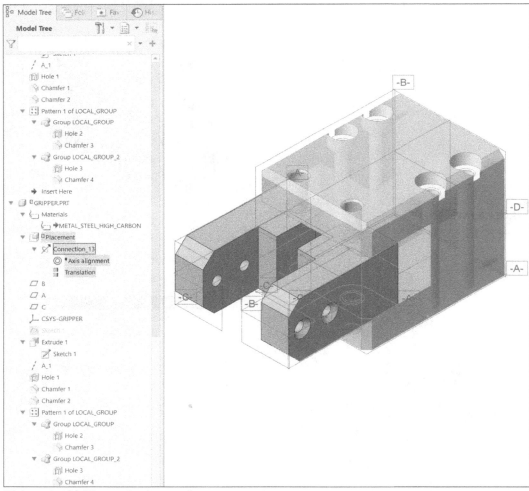

Figure 8.6(t) Placement

The next component to be assembled is the Pin. Click: **Assemble > pin.prt > Preview** *on* **> MMB** rotate the model in the Preview Window **> RMB** to see options [Fig 8.7(a)] **> No Hidden > RMB > Shaded > Open > LMB** pick a position > ⊕ *on* [Fig 8.7(b)]

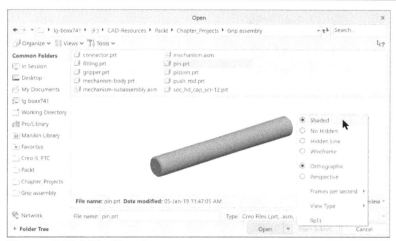

Figure 8.7(a) Pin Preview

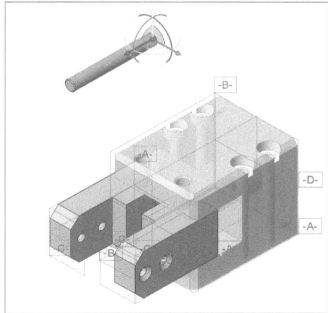

Figure 8.7(b) Placed Pin

Click: 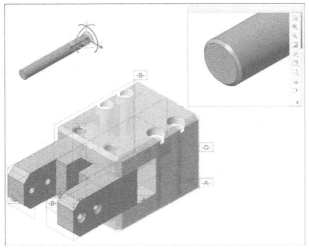 > roll **MMB** to zoom in on the Pin in the component window [Fig. 8.7(c)] > use the colored center ball and axes draggers to approximately reposition the component model [Fig. 8.7(d)]

Figure 8.7(c) Component in a Separate Window

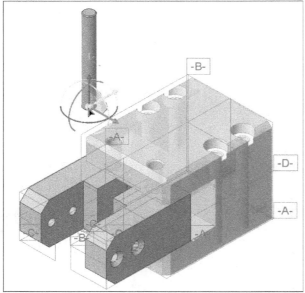

Figure 8.7(d) Reposition the Pin using the 3D Draggers

Pick the cylindrical surface of the hole of the Mechanism-body > pick the Pin's surface [Fig. 8.7(e)] > pick the end of the Pin in the component window > pick the lower surface of the Mechanism-body [Fig. 8.7(f)]

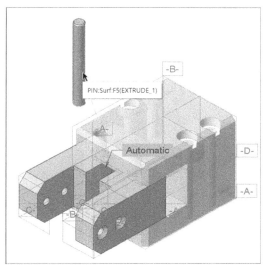

Figure 8.7(e) First Constraint

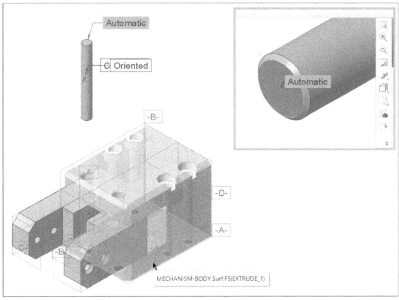

Figure 8.7(f) Second Constraint

Select **Coincident** [Fig. 8.7(g)] > 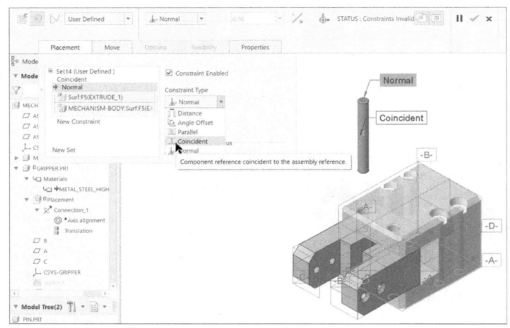 **Change orientation** [Fig. 8.7(h)] > **MMB**

Figure 8.7(g) Normal > Coincident

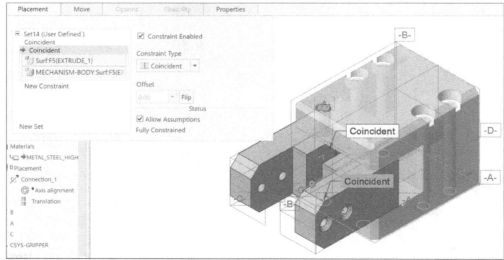

Figure 8.7(h) Coincident

Insert another Pin in the remaining hole [Fig. 8.8(a)] *(As an alternative, use Copy and Paste. This method requires fewer picks and therefore is faster.)* **> MMB** [Fig. 8.8(b)] **> Save**

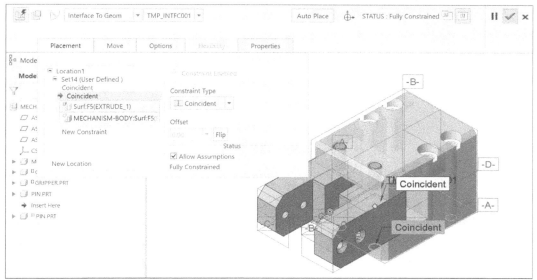

Figure 8.8(a) Assemble the second Pin

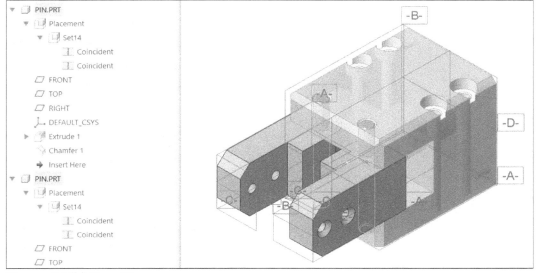

Figure 8.8(b) Two Pins

The next component to be assembled is the Socket Head Cap Screw. Click: **Assemble > soc_hd_cap_scr.12.prt > Open >** select the hole [Fig 8.9(a)] > select the bearing surface of the counterbored hole [Fig 8.9(b)]

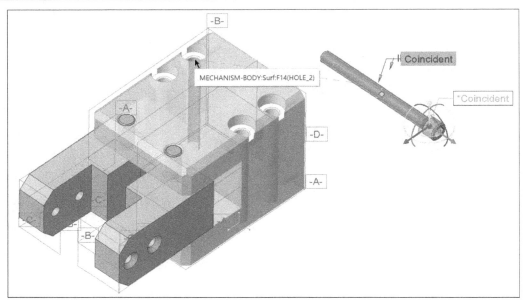

Figure 8.9(a) Socket Head Cap Screw Preview

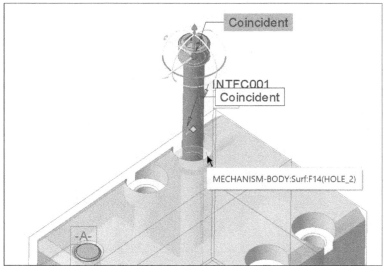

Figure 8.9(b) Placed Socket Head Cap Screw

Fully Constrained component [Fig 8.9(c)] **> MMB >** expand the **Model Tree** [Fig 8.9(d)]

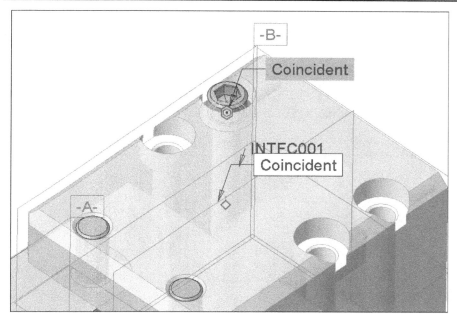

Figure 8.9(c) Fully Constrained

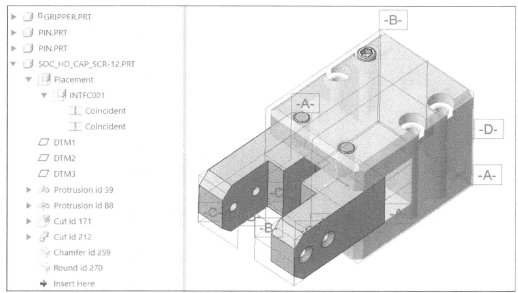

Figure 8.9(d) Socket Head Cap Screw

Component interfaces contain stored constraints or connections that are used to quickly place a component. After an interface is defined, it can be used whenever the component is placed in an assembly. The screw has its interface established so the assembly process will be quick since only the assembly selections need be made.

Select the **soc_hd_cap_scr-12 > Ctrl+C > Ctrl+V > LMB** to place > select the hole [Fig 8.10(a)] > select the bearing surface of the counterbored hole [Fig 8.10(b)] > **MMB** > repeat to assemble the remaining screws > **Save** *(If you used RMB >* ☑ Enable snapping *before copy and paste the pin would automatically select the hole)*

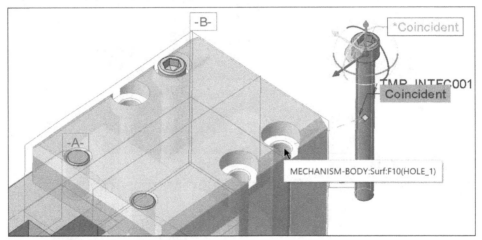

Figure 8.10(a) Select the Hole

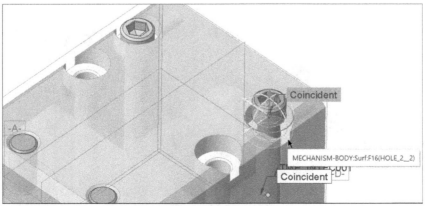

Figure 8.10(b) Select the Counterbore Bearing Surface

Click: ⬚ ▾ **Settings >** ⬚ Tree Columns... > use ⬚ >> ⬚ to add the columns names to be Displayed [Fig. 8.11(a)] > **Apply > OK >** resize the Model Tree and Model Tree column widths [Fig. 8.11(b)]

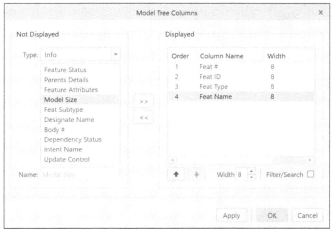

Figure 8.11(a) Model Tree Columns Dialog Box

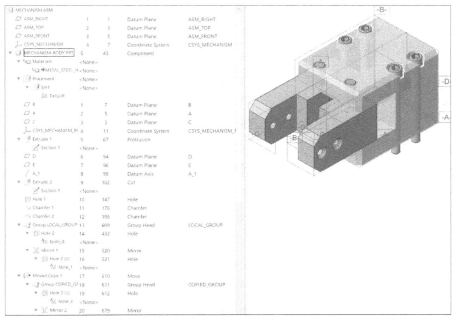

Figure 8.11(b) Model Tree with Adjusted Columns

Click: **Tools** tab > 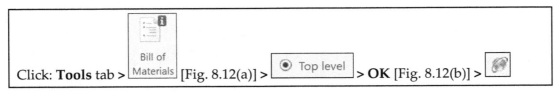 [Fig. 8.12(a)] > Top level > **OK** [Fig. 8.12(b)] >

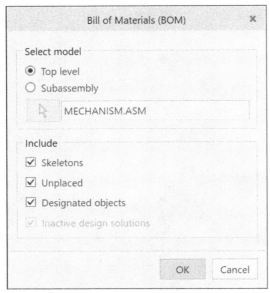

Figure 8.12(a) BOM Dialog Box

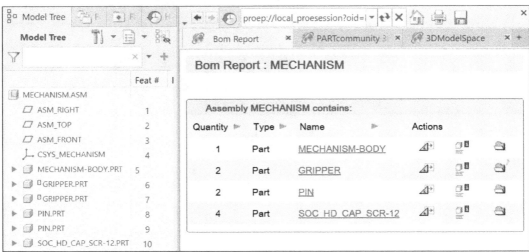

Figure 8.12(b) Bill of Materials (BOM)

Ctrl+D > Ctrl+S > View tab > 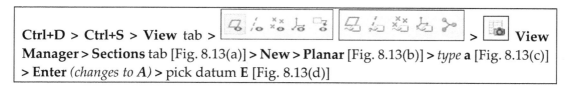 > 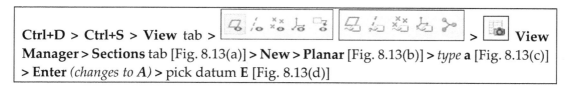 **View Manager > Sections** tab [Fig. 8.13(a)] **> New > Planar** [Fig. 8.13(b)] **>** *type* **a** [Fig. 8.13(c)] **> Enter** *(changes to A)* **>** pick datum **E** [Fig. 8.13(d)]

Figure 8.13(a) Sections   **Figure 8.13(b)** Planar   **Figure 8.13(c)** Section A

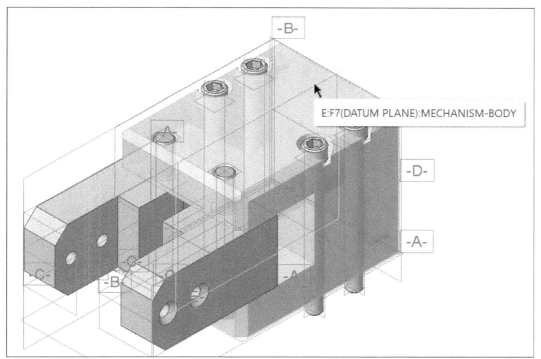

Figure 8.13(d) Select Assembly Datum Top

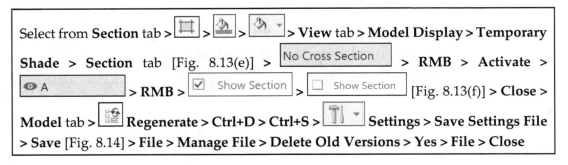

Select from **Section** tab > [icon] > [icon] > [icon] > **View** tab > **Model Display** > **Temporary Shade** > **Section** tab [Fig. 8.13(e)] > | No Cross Section | > **RMB** > **Activate** > | 👁 A | > **RMB** > | ☑ Show Section | > | ☐ Show Section | [Fig. 8.13(f)] > **Close** > **Model** tab > [icon] **Regenerate** > **Ctrl+D** > **Ctrl+S** > [icon] **Settings** > **Save Settings File** > **Save** [Fig. 8.14] > **File** > **Manage File** > **Delete Old Versions** > **Yes** > **File** > **Close**

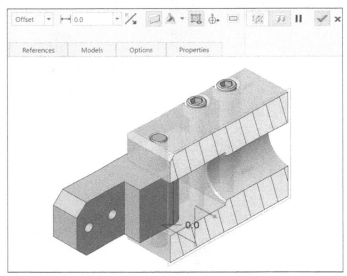

Figure 8.13(e) Show Section A Cross Hatching and New Color

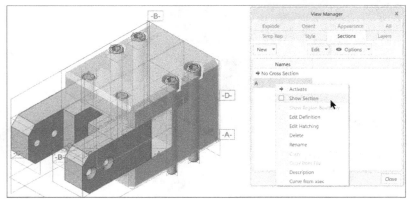

Figure 8.13(f) View Manager

312

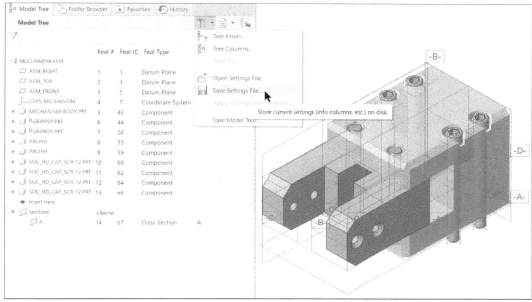

Figure 8.14 Save Tree Settings

Quiz

1. What is the difference between Top-down and Bottom-up design?
2. What is the Component Window used for when assembling?
3. What is a component's Placement Set?
4. What is a component's imbedded interface used for?
5. What does toggle off the Annotation Display accomplish?
6. What is the base component in an assembly?
7. What is the Top Level of an assembly when requesting a BOM?
8. What is a BOM?

This completes Chapter 8

CHAPTER 9: Top-down assembly design techniques

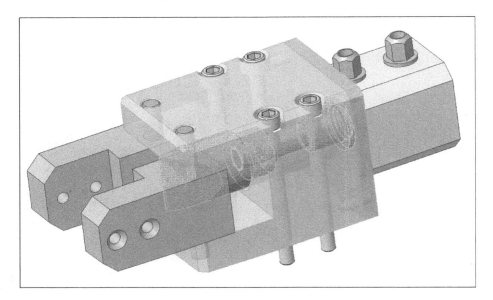

Top-down design is the design of an assembly where one or more component parts are created in Assembly mode as the design unfolds. Some existing sub-assemblies and components are available, such as standard components and a few modeled parts. The remaining design evolves during the assembly process. You can create different types of components: parts, subassemblies, skeleton models, and bulk items. The following methods allow component creation in the context of an assembly: create a component by copying another component or existing start part or start assembly, create a component with default datums, create an empty component, and create a mirror copy of an existing part or subassembly.

Objectives
1. Design a component in the assembly mode using Top-Down Design
2. Modeling a part in an active Assembly
3. Understand References and dependencies
4. Check for component interferences
5. Reference existing features for component modeling in Top-Down design
6. Drag component in an Assembly
7. Create BOM

Creating Components in the Assembly Mode

You can create different types of components: parts, subassemblies, skeleton models, and bulk items in the Assembly mode. You cannot reroute components created in the Assembly mode. The following methods allow component creation in the context of an assembly without requiring external dependencies on the assembly geometry:

- Create a component by copying a component, start part or start assembly
- Create a component with default datums
- Create an empty component
- Create the first feature of a new part; this feature is dependent on the assembly
- Create a component from an intersection of existing components
- Create a mirror copy of an existing part or subassembly
- Create Solid or Sheetmetal components
- Mirror Components

Feature references

Feature references are the dependencies between different features in a design. They are created in the context of a single part, or in the context of an assembly. Feature dependencies can be local references or external references. Local references only reference geometry of the model in which they were created. External dependencies reference geometry outside the model in which they were created.

For **external references**, the assembly in which the two components existed when the dependency was created is another important characteristic of the dependency.

If a feature is set as current, all models that are referenced by this feature or that are referencing this feature appear in the Parent and Children trees. You can expand these models to show the features that participate in dependencies with the current feature. If a component is set as current, all parents and children of its features appear.

Reference investigation

Reference investigation allows you to see the relationships and dependencies between features and models, enabling increased management of design intent. You can perform reference investigation through the Reference Viewer dialog box when working on individual parts or assemblies. Use **Tools >** **Reference Viewer** to access the Reference Viewer dialog box. By using filters in the Reference Viewer dialog box, you can customize the contents of the Reference Viewer dialog box to show only dependencies of interest. With the Reference Viewer you can:

- Identify the features in a model that have external or local references.
- Detect the features in a model that have a chain of dependencies from the feature to the referenced entity.
- Reroute or redefine a feature to break the dependency, if any of the external or local references are not required.
- Investigate regeneration failures by examining parent and child dependencies.
- Obtain information about the models that have external or local references to a specified model and about their relation references.
- Find references generated by relations and parameters.
- Identify circular references.
- Comprehend the relationships among various models, components, and features.
- Break dependencies between the specified model and its dependent model.

Bill of Materials

The Bill of Materials (BOM) lists all parts and part parameters in the current assembly or assembly drawing. It can be displayed in HTML or text format and is separated into two parts: breakdown and summary. The Breakdown section lists what is contained in the current assembly or part. The BOM HTML breakdown section lists quantity, type, name (hyperlink), and three actions (highlight, information and open) about each member or sub-member of your assembly:

- **Quantity** Lists the number of components or drawings
- **Type** Lists the type of the assembly component (part or sub-assembly)
- **Name** Lists the assembly component and is hyper-linked to that item. Selecting this hyperlink highlights the component in the graphics window
- **Actions** is divided into three areas:

  o **Highlight** Highlights the selected component in the assembly graphics window

  o **Information** Provides model information on the relevant component

  o **Open** Opens the component in another Creo Parametric window

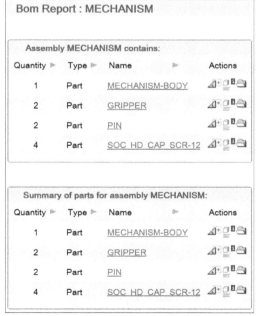

Chapter 9 STEPS

The Plate will be created using *top-down design*; where the Mechanism assembly is active, and the component is created within the assembly mode. Almost all of the Plate's geometry will be established by referencing edges from features in the mechanism-body.

Click: **Open** > double-click on **mechanism.asm** > **File** > **Options** > **Model Display** > **Isometric** > **Trimetric** > **OK** > **No** > spin the part > **View** tab > [toolbar icons] [toolbar icons] *off* > [icon] **Show** > **Show PopUp Viewer** > [icon] > **Open Settings File** > **tree.cfg** *(opens the Model Tree Columns settings that were saved)* > **Open** [Fig. 9.1]

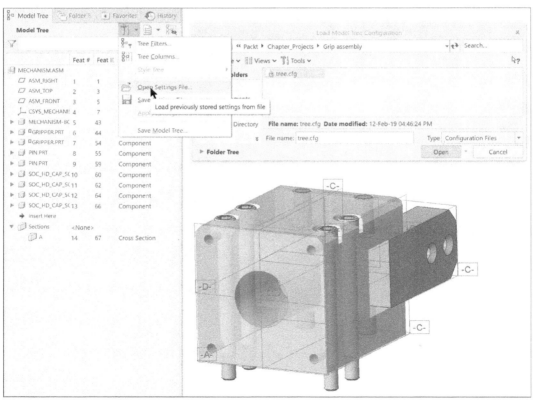

Figure 9.1 Mechanism Assembly

Click: **Model** tab > [⊞ **Create**] **Create a component in the active assembly** Component Create dialog box displays > Type **Part** > Sub-type **Soild** > Name **plate** [Fig. 9.2(a)] > **OK** Creation Options dialog box displays > **Create features** [Fig. 9.2(b)] > **OK** > [▶ ◈ PLATE.PRT   14] displays in the Model Tree, *the small symbol/icon* [⊞] *indicates that this component is now active* > expand and highlight the items in the Model Tree for the PLATE.PRT [Fig. 9.2(c)] > **LMB**

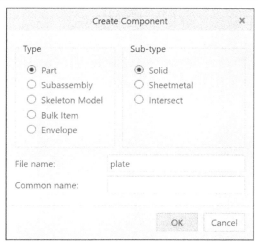

Figure 9.2(a) Create Component

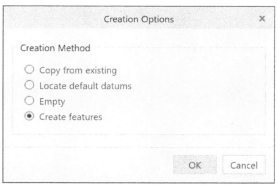

Figure 9.2(b) Creation Options

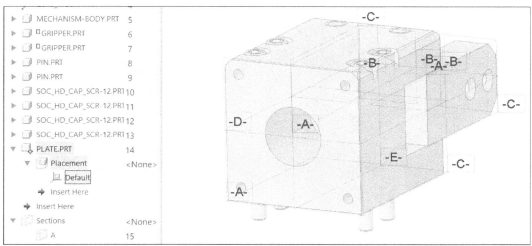

Figure 9.2(c) Model Tree showing featureless Plate part

319

Assembly Tools are now *unavailable* in the Model Ribbon. The current component is the Plate. *You are now effectively in Part mode,* except that you can see and reference assembly features and components.

Create the first feature, an extrusion, click: [Extrude] > depth value **12** > **Enter** > **Placement** tab > **Define** > Sketch Plane--- Plane: select the mechanism-body surface [Fig. 9.2(d)] > **Sketch** > **Close** References dialog box [Fig. 9.2(e)] > **Yes** > **Save** > **Yes**

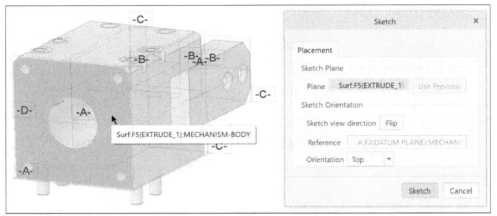

Figure 9.2(d) Sketch surface

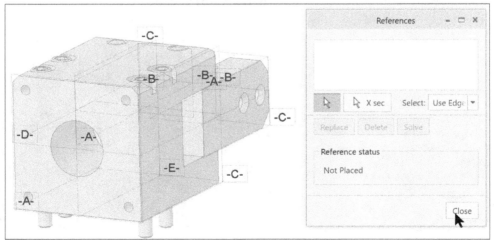

Figure 9.2(e) References

Click: 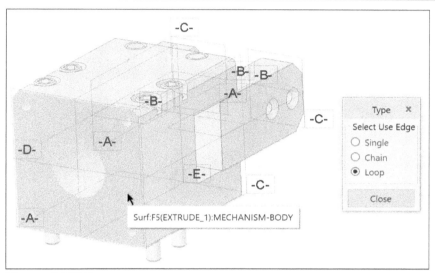 | Project | > **Loop** > select the mechanism's right vertical face [Fig. 9.2(f)] > **Next** > **Accept** the outer edge > **Next** > **Next** > **Next** > **Next** > **Next** > **Next** > **Accept** the large hole > repeat for each of the four small holes > from the **Graphics Toolbar** click ⎚ **Sketcher Display Filters** *all off* [Fig. 9.2(g)]

Figure 9.2(f) Loop

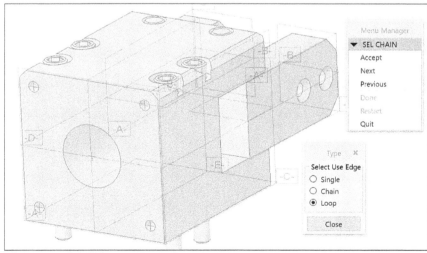

Figure 9.2(g) Edges selected

Click: **Close > RMB >** ☑ [Fig. 9.2(h)] **> MMB > LMB** [Fig. 9.2(i)]

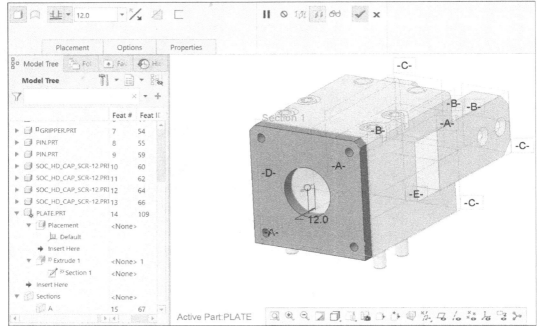

Figure 9.2(h) Plate Preview

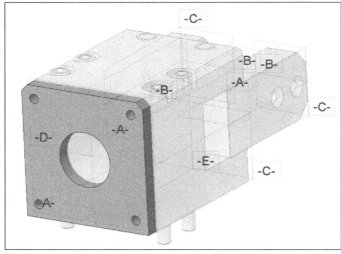

Figure 9.2(i) Plate Preview

In the Model Tree select **MECHANISM.ASM >** ◇ **Activate** the assembly Fig. 9.2(j)]
> select the **PLATE.PRT** in the Model Tree [Fig. 9.2(k)] **> LMB** in Graphics Window

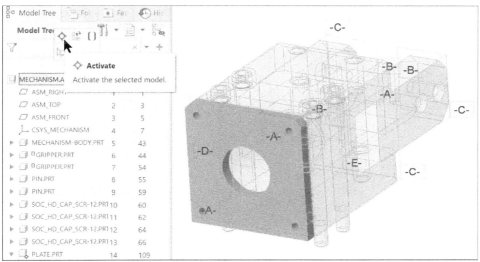

Figure 9.2(j) Activate the Assembly

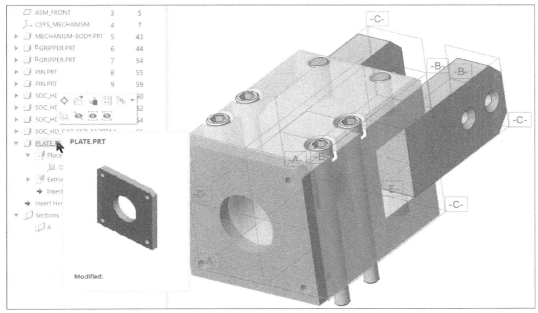

Figure 9.2(k) Plate Preview

323

Pick on the **PLATE.PRT** in the Model Tree > **RMB** > **Information** > **Reference Viewer**
>  (Extrude 1 *external references* displayed) > expand all [Fig. 9.3(a)] > **Close** > **Save**

Figure 9.3(a) Reference Viewer Extrude 1 external references

Select **PLATE.PRT** > ◇ **Activate** > **View** tab > **Appearances** > change the Plate's color [Fig. 9.3(b)] > **MECHANISM.PRT** > ◇ **Activate** [Fig. 9.3(c)] > **Save**

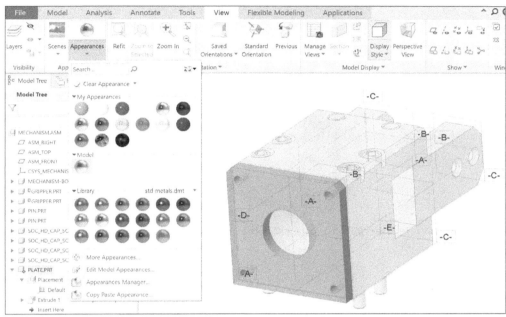

Figure 9.3(b) Change Color for Plate

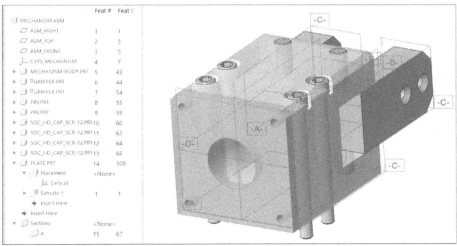

Figure 9.3(c) Competed Plate

Click: **Model** tab [Assemble icon] Assemble **Assemble > mechanism-subassembly.asm** [Fig. 9.4(a)] **> Open > LMB** to place [Fig. 9.4(b)]

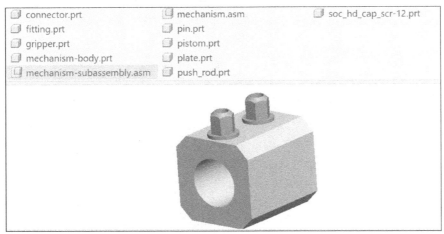

Figure 9.4(a) Preview mechanism-subassembly.asm

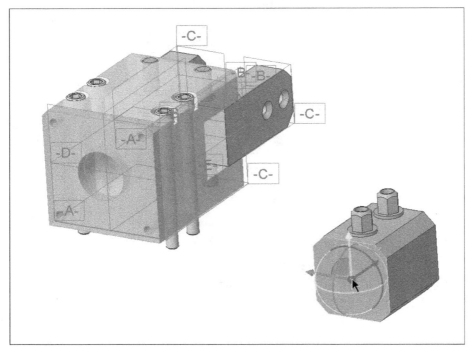

Figure 9.4(b) Placed Subassembly

Click: using the **3D Dragger** reposition the **mechanism-subassembly.asm >**
Placement tab > ⬚ **Component Window >** select the hole surface [Fig. 9.4(c)]

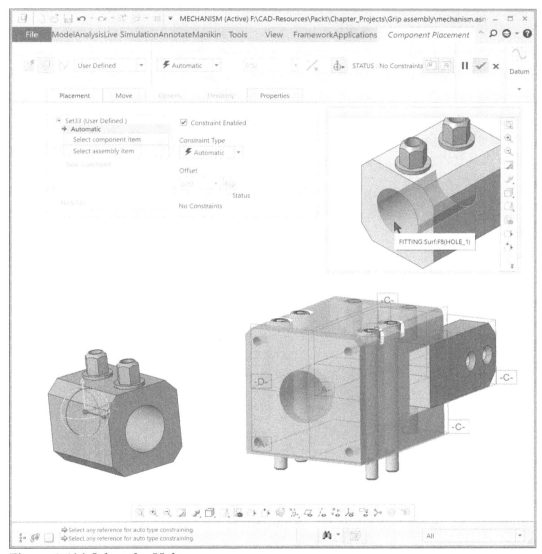

Figure 9.4(c) Select the Hole

Select the Plate's hole surface [Fig. 9.4(d)] **> RMB > New Constraint >** select the Fitting surface [Fig. 9.4(e)] **>** select the Plate's surface [Fig. 9.4(f)] **> Distance > Coincident**

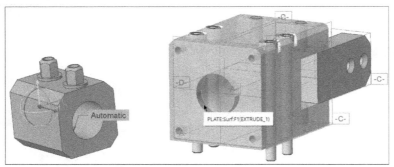

Figure 9.4(d) Placed Subassembly

Figure 9.4(e) Select the Fitting surface

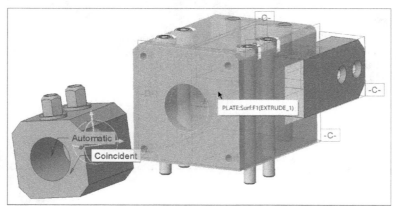

Figure 9.4(f) Select the Plate's surface

Click: **Placement** tab > **Allow Assumptions** *off* > **RMB** > **New Constraint** >
Component Window *closes* > using the **3D Dragger** rotate the sub-assembly [Fig.
9.4(g)] > **Automatic** > **Parallel** > select the top surface of the Fitting > select the Plate's
top surface [Fig. 9.4(h)] > **MMB** > **Save** [Fig. 9.4(i)]

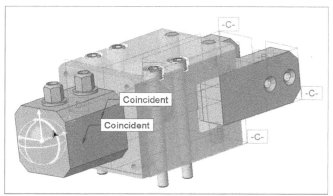

Figure 9.4(g) Rotate the Sub-Assembly using the 3D Dragger

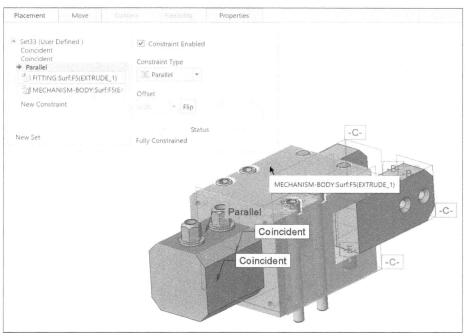

Figure 9.4(h) Select the Fitting and Mechanism-body upper surfaces

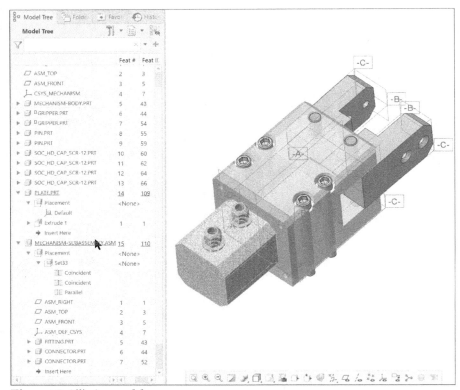

Figure 9.4(i) Assembly

Select the screws, pins and connectors in the **Model Tree > RMB > Hide** [Fig. 9.5(a)]

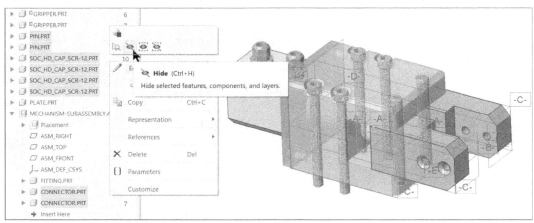

Figure 9.5(a) Assembly

330

Click: **Assemble > push_rod.prt >** drop the component **>** adjust its position using the 3D Dragger [Fig. 9.5(b)] **> Placement** tab **>** ⬚ Component Window **>** select the cylindrical surface of the Push_Rod [Fig. 9.5(c)]

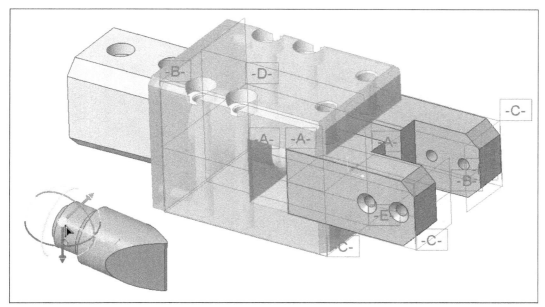

Figure 9.5(b) Placed Push_Rod

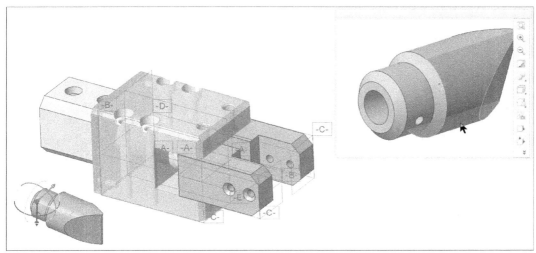

Figure 9.5(c) Select Push_Rod Surface

Select the large hole in the Mechanism-Body and the Push_Rod surface [Fig. 9.5(d)] > in the Model Tree select the **mechanism-body > RMB > Hide** [Fig. 9.5(e)]

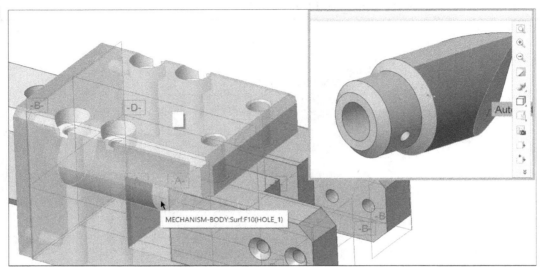

Figure 9.5(d) Select the hole

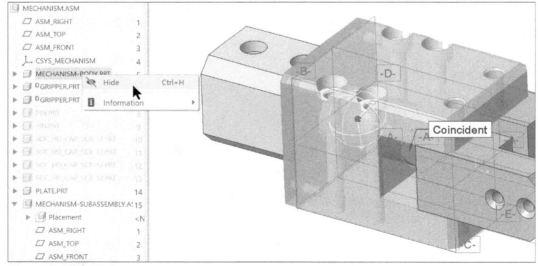

Figure 9.5(e) Hide

Click: **New Constraint** > select the Gripper surface [Fig. 9.5(f)] > select the Push_Rod surface [Fig. 9.5(g)] > becomes **Tangent** constraint

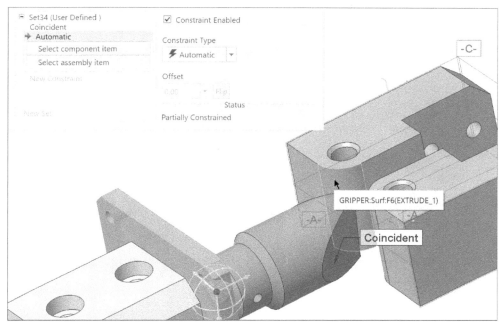

Figure 9.5(f) Select Gripper Surface

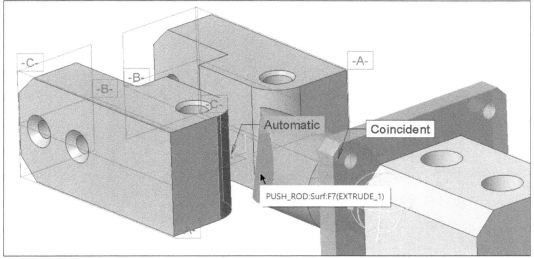

Figure 9.5(g) Select the Push_Rod Surface

Becomes **Tangent** constraint [Fig. 9.5(h)] **> New Constraint >** repeat for the opposite side [Fig. 9.5(i)] **> MMB >** ⬚ **Regenerate > Save**

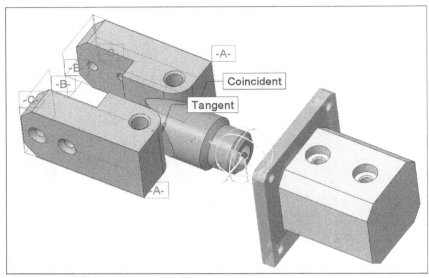

Figure 9.5(h) First Tangent Constraint

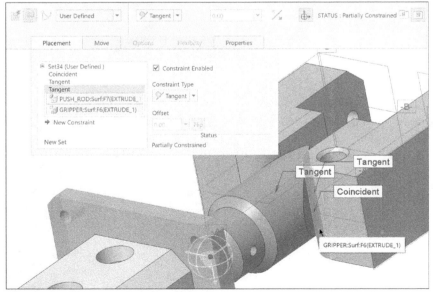

Figure 9.5(i) Second Tangent Constraint

The Push_Rod will be *Partially Constrained* because a "mechanism *pin* constraint" was previously created a for the Gripper.

Click: **Assemble > piston.prt >** place component > adjust position [Fig. 9.6(a)] > **Placement** tab > select the cylindrical surface of the Piston and the hole of the Push_Rod [Fig. 9.6(b)]

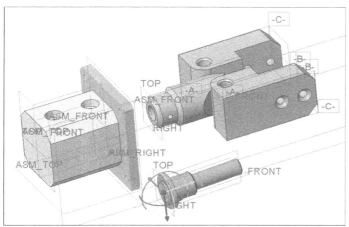

Figure 9.6(a) Placed Piston

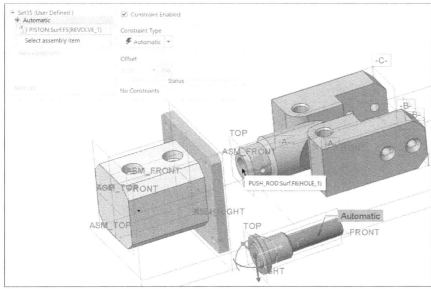

Figure 9.6(b) Select the Shaft and Hole

335

Select: ☑ Allow Assumptions > **New Constraint** > select the end of the Piston [Fig. 9.6(c)] > place the cursor near the end of the hole > click **RMB** until the hole's bottom highlights > **LMB** select the bottom of the Push_Rod hole *(Flip if needed)* [Fig. 9.6(d)]

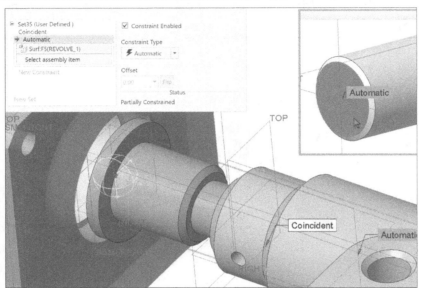

Figure 9.6(c) Select the end of the Piston

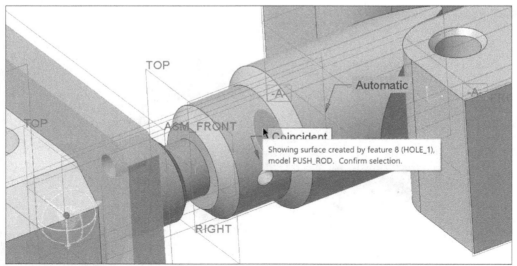

Figure 9.6(d) Select the bottom of the hole on the Push Rod

Click: [✓] [Fig. 9.6(e)] > select hidden parts in the Model Tree > [👁] **Show** [Fig. 9.6(f)]
> **Save** > **File** > **Manage File** > **Delete Old Versions** > **Yes**

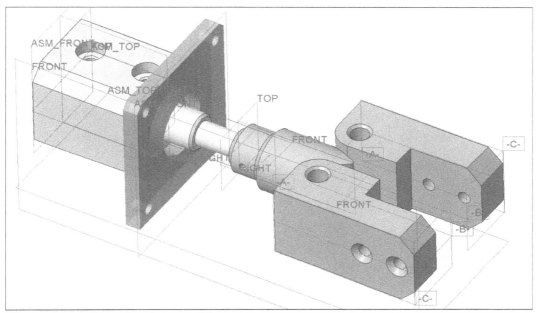

Figure 9.6(e) Completed Assembly

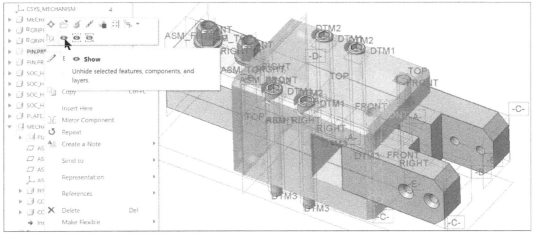

Figure 9.6(f) Show all Hidden Components

Perform a check on the assembly. Click: **Analysis** tab > 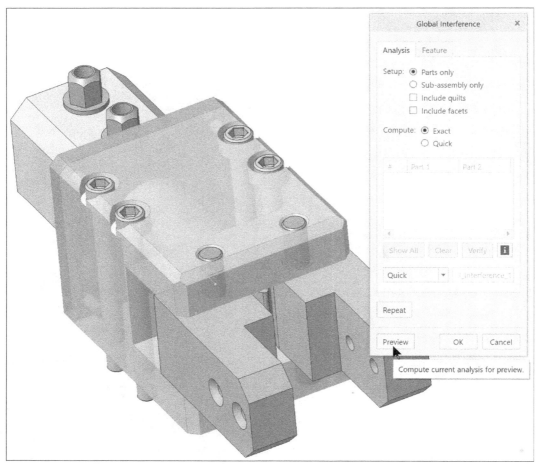 **Global Interference** > **View** tab > **Model Display > Temporary Shade >** Preview **Compute current analysis for preview** [Fig. 9.7] *(no interferences detected)* > **OK > LMB > Ctrl+S**

Figure 9.7 Global Interference Dialog Box (no interferences)

A bill of materials (BOM) can be seen by clicking: **Tools** tab > [Bill of Materials icon] > check all Include options [Fig. 9.8(a)] > **OK** [Fig. 9.8(b)] > [X icon] or [icon] to close the Browser > **Model** tab

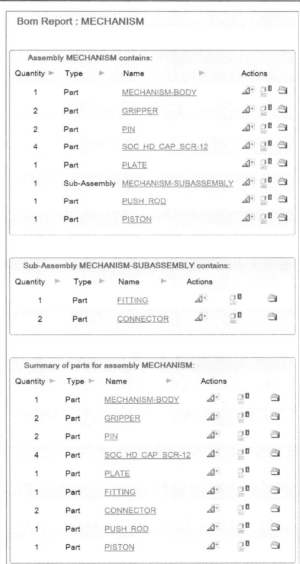

Figure 9.8(a) BOM   **Figure 9.8(b)** Assembly and Sub-Assembly

Click: **View** tab > **Orientation** group > [Orient Mode] > **RMB** > [Show Spin Center: Dynamic, Anchored, Delayed, ● Velocity] >

MMB > [icon] move cursor around screen (the speed of the model's movement will

depend on your graphics card) [Fig. 9.9] > try other options [Show Spin Center: Dynamic, Anchored, Delayed, ● Velocity] > **RMB**
> [Exit Orient Mode]

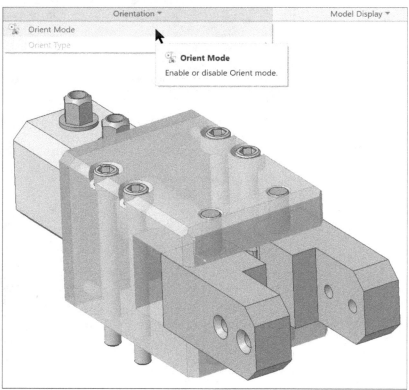

Figure 9.9 Orient Mode

Click: **Model** tab > 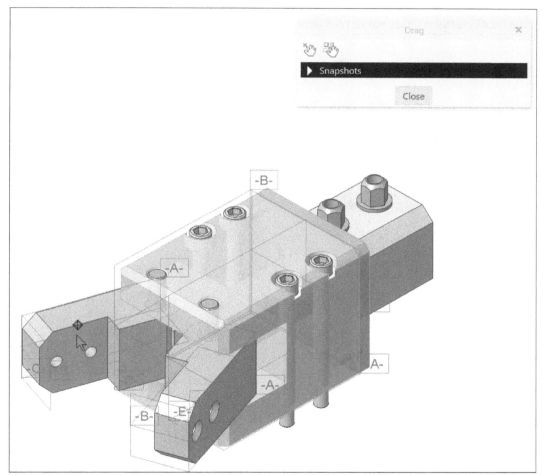 **Drag Components** > **LMB** > select the **Gripper** and move slightly [Fig. 9.10] > **MMB** > **OK** > **Close**

Figure 9.10 Drag Components

Click: **File > Manage File > Delete Old Versions > Yes > View** tab **> Model Display > Temporary Shade >** 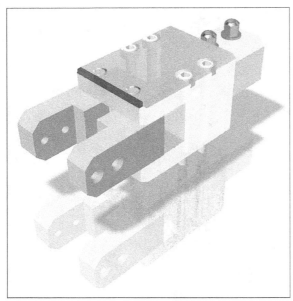 **Perspective View >** ⬚ **>** Shading With Reflections [Fig. 9.11] **> File > Save As >** Type ⬚ **> Zip File (*.zip) > OK >** upload to your course interface or attach to an email and send to your instructor or yourself **> File > Close**

Figure 9.11 Shading with Reflections

Quiz

1. What is a BOM?
2. What is an external reference?
3. What does allow assumptions do?
4. What does the placement tab display and allow access to?
5. Name five assembly constraints.
6. Explain the use of hiding components.
7. What is the use of analyzing global interference?
8. What is Orient mode?
9. What is Temporary Shade?

This completes Chapter 9

Assembly exploded views and style states

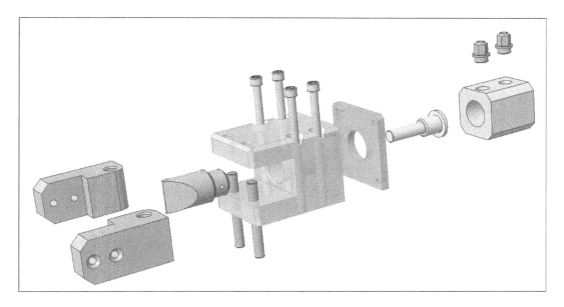

Pictorial illustrations such as exploded views are generated directly from the 3D model database. The model can be displayed and oriented in any position. Each component in the assembly can have a different display type: wireframe, hidden line, no hidden, shading, and transparent. You can select and orient the component to provide the required view orientation to display the component from underneath or from any side or position. Perspective projections are made with selections from menus. The assembly can be spun around, reoriented, and even clipped to show the interior features. You have the choice of displaying all components and subassemblies or any combination of components in the design.

Objectives
1. Create Exploded Views
2. Create Explode States
3. Utilize the View Manager to organize and control views states
4. Create unique component visibility settings (Style States)
5. Add a URL to a 3D Note
6. Create Perspective views of the model

Exploded views

Pictorial illustrations, such as exploded views, are generated directly from the 3D model database. The model can be displayed and oriented in any position. Each component in the assembly can have a different display type: wireframe, hidden line, no hidden, shading, and transparent. You can select and orient the component to provide the required view orientation to display the component from underneath or from any side or position. Perspective projections are made with selections from menus. The assembly can be spun around, reoriented, and even clipped to show the interior features. You have the choice of displaying all components and subassemblies or any combination of components in the design.

Using the **Explode State** option in the **View Manager**, you can automatically create an exploded view of an assembly. Exploding an assembly affects only the display of the assembly; it does not alter true design distances between components. Explode states are created to define the exploded positions of all components. For each explode state, you can toggle the explode status of components, change the explode locations of components, and create and modify explode offset lines to show how explode components align when they are in their exploded positions. The Explode State Explode Position functionality is similar to the Package/Move functionality.

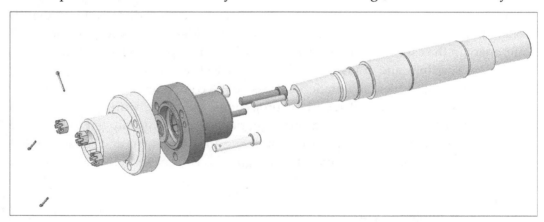

You can define multiple explode states for each assembly and then explode the assembly using any of these explode states at any time. You can also set an explode state for each drawing view of an assembly. Creo Parametric gives each component a default explode position determined by the placement constraints. By default, the reference component of the explode is the parent assembly (top-level assembly or subassembly).

344

To explode components, you use a drag-and-drop user interface similar to the Package/Move functionality. You select the motion reference and one or more components, and then drag the outlines to the desired positions. The component outlines drag along with the mouse cursor. You control the move options using a Preferences setting. Two types of explode instructions can be added to a set of components. The children components follow the parent component being exploded or they do not follow the parent component. Each explode instruction consists of a set of components, explode direction references, and dimensions that define the exploded position from the final (installed) position with respect to the explode direction references. When using the explode functionality, keep in mind the following:

- You can select parts or entire subassemblies from the Model Tree or main window.
- If you explode a subassembly, in the context of a higher-level assembly, you can specify the explode state to use for each subassembly.
- You do not lose component explode information when you turn the status off. Creo Parametric retains the information so that the component has the same explode position if you turn the status back on.
- All assemblies have a default explode state called "Default Explode", which is the default explode state created from the component placement instructions.
- Multiple occurrences of the same subassembly can have different explode characteristics at a higher-level assembly.

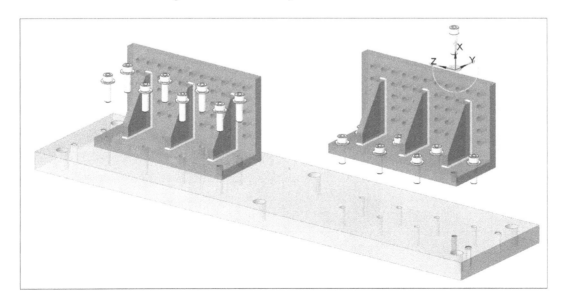

Component display

Style, also accessed through the View Manager, manages the display styles of an assembly. **Simp Rep**, **Sections**, **Layers**, **Orient**, **Explode**, and **All** are on separate tabs from this dialog. **Wireframe**, **Hidden line**, **No hidden**, **Shaded**, or **Transparent** display styles can be assigned to each component. The components will be displayed according to their assigned display styles in the current style state (that is, blanked, shaded, drawn in hidden line color, and so on). The current setting, in the View tab > Display Style, controls the display of unassigned components.

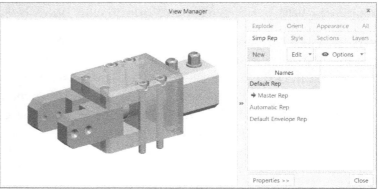

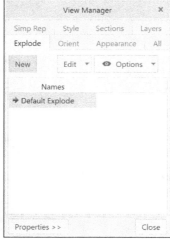

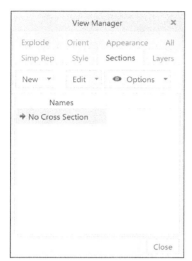  

Components appear in the currently assigned style state. The current setting is indicated in the display style column in the Model Tree window. Component display or style states can be modified without using the View Manager. You can select desired models from the graphics window, Model Tree, or search tool, and then use the View tab > Display Style commands to assign a display style (wireframe, hidden, no hidden, shaded and transparent) to the selected models. The Style representation is temporarily changed. These temporary changes can then be stored to a new style state or updated to an existing style state. You can also define default style states. If the default style state is updated to reflect changes different from that of the master style state, then that default style state will be reflected when the model is retrieved.

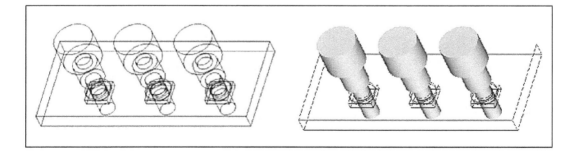

URLs and Model Notes

Model notes are text strings that you can attach to objects. You can include model notes in Annotation features. This way, you can define a library of company-specific annotation, and then place it in a model. You can attach any number of notes to any object in your model. You can use model notes to:

- Tell other members of your workgroup how to review or use a model
- Explain how you approached or solved a design problem
- Explain changes that you have made to the features of a model over time

You can create the following types of notes:

- Note not attached to any reference
- Note placed on the selected reference
- Note with a leader
- Note with leader normal to the annotation plane
- Note with leader tangent to the annotation plane

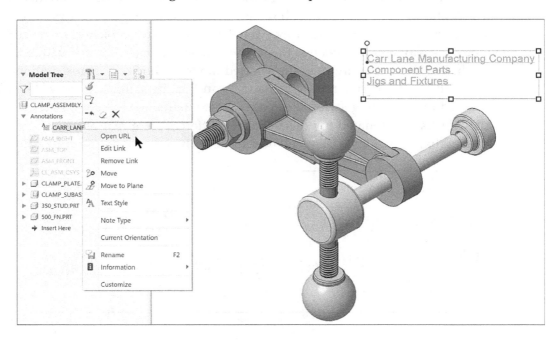

Chapter 10 STEPS

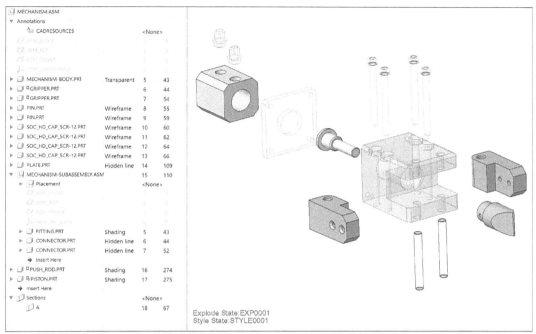

MECHANISM.ASM				
▽ Annotations				
CADRESOURCES		<None>		
MECHANISM-BODY.PRT	Transparent	5	43	
GRIPPER.PRT		6	44	
GRIPPER.PRT		7	54	
PIN.PRT	Wireframe	8	55	
PIN.PRT	Wireframe	9	59	
SOC_HD_CAP_SCR-12.PRT	Wireframe	10	60	
SOC_HD_CAP_SCR-12.PRT	Wireframe	11	62	
SOC_HD_CAP_SCR-12.PRT	Wireframe	12	64	
SOC_HD_CAP_SCR-12.PRT	Wireframe	13	66	
PLATE.PRT	Hidden line	14	109	
▽ MECHANISM-SUBASSEMBLY.ASM		15	110	
▷ Placement		<None>		
FITTING.PRT	Shading	5	43	
CONNECTOR.PRT	Hidden line	6	44	
CONNECTOR.PRT	Hidden line	7	52	
➔ Insert Here				
PUSH_ROD.PRT	Shading	16	274	
PISTON.PRT	Shading	17	275	
➔ Insert Here				
▽ Sections		<None>		
A		18	67	

Explode State:EXP0001
Style State:STYLE0001

Figure 10.1 Explode State and Style State Mechanism

In this chapter, you will use the previously created assembly [Fig. 10.1] to establish and save new views, exploded views, and views with component style states that differ from one another. The View Manager Dialog box will be employed to control and organize a variety of different states.

You will also be required to move and rotate components of the assembly before cosmetically displaying the assembly in an exploded state. A 3D Note with a URL will be added to the model as an information feature.

Launch **Creo Parametric > File > Manage Session > Select Working Directory >** select the directory where the **mechanism.asm** was saved **> OK > File > Open > mechanism.asm > Open > File > Options > Model Display > Trimetric > Isometric > OK > No >** [icon] **Settings > Tree Filters >** toggle all *on* **> OK >** Filters: Geometry *(bottom right side of screen) >* [Annotation] **>** press **Ctrl** and window-in hole notes in the Graphics Window **> RMB >** [Hide] **> View** tab **>** [icons] **> Layers** from the Ribbon **>** pick on [Layers] **> RMB > Hide >** [icon] **Layers** *(toggles to Model Tree)* [Fig. 10.2(a)]

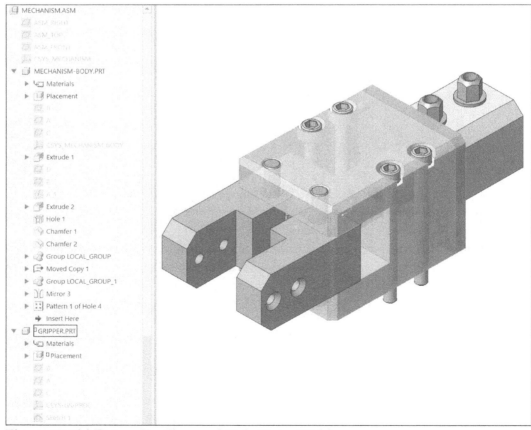

Figure 10.2(a) Datum Features and Hole Notes Hidden

Click **Annotate** tab > **Flat to Screen** [Fig. 10.2(b)] > **RMB** (on FLAT TO SCREEN) > **Set** > [A≣ ▼] **Unattached Note** (Annotations Group) > pick a position for the note *(you may use your own company or school names)* > [win_font ▼ | 8.000000] >

type **CAD-Resources Product Design Company** > **Enter** >

type **Manufacturing and Design** > **Enter** >

type **Mechanism** > move and resize [Fig. 10.2(c)]

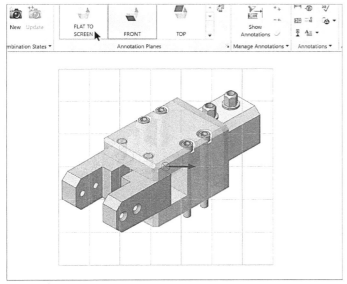

Figure 10.2(b) FLAT TO SCREEN

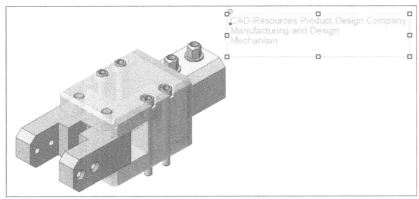

Figure 10.2(c) Unattached Note

Press: **RMB** [Fig. 10.2(d)] **Add Link > www.cad-resources.com** [Fig. 10.2(e)] **>
ScreenTip >** Screen tip text: *type* **CAD-Resources** [Fig. 10.2(f)] **> OK > OK > RMB >
Text Style > Height** [Fig. 10.2(g)] **> 7 > Enter > Apply > OK >** In the Model Tree
▼ Annotations **>** A≡ Note_0 **> RMB > Rename >** *type* **CADRESOURCES > Enter**

Figure 10.2(d) Add Link

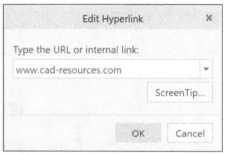

Figure 10.2(e) Edit Hyperlink Dialog Box

Figure 10.2(f) Set Hyperlink ScreenTip

Figure 10.2(g) Text Style Dialog Box

Click: **LMB** to deselect > place your pointer over the screen note [Fig. 10.2(h)] **Ctrl+LMB** > edit the address if needed > 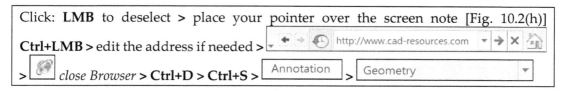 *close Browser* > **Ctrl+D** > **Ctrl+S** > Annotation > Geometry

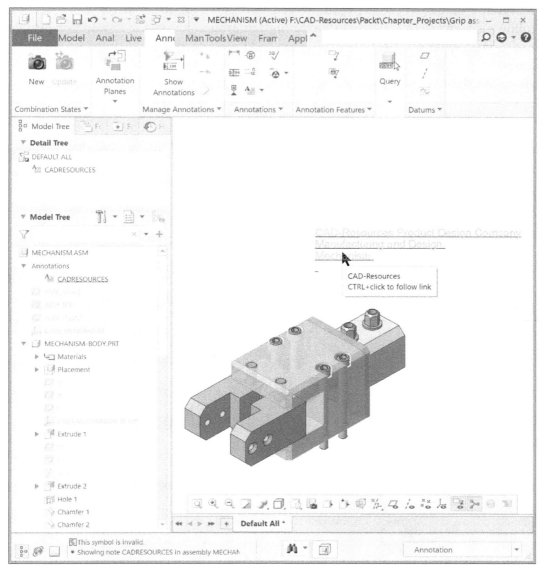

Figure 10.2(h) Note Displayed

Views: Perspective, Saved and Exploded

You will now create a variety of cosmetically altered view states. Cosmetic changes to the assembly do not affect the model itself, only the way it is displayed on the screen. One type of view that can be created is the perspective view.

Perspective creates a single-vanishing-point perspective view of a shaded or wireframe model. These views allow you to observe an object as the view location follows a curve, axis, cable, or edge through or around an object. To add perspective to a model view, you select a viewing path and then control the viewing position along the path in either direction. You can also rotate the perspective view in any direction, zoom the view in or out, and change the view angle at any point along the path.

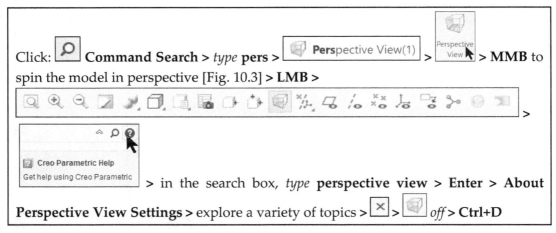

Click: **Command Search** > *type* **pers** > **Pers**pective View(1) > **Perspective View** > **MMB** to spin the model in perspective [Fig. 10.3] > **LMB** > > in the search box, *type* **perspective view** > **Enter** > **About Perspective View Settings** > explore a variety of topics > ⊠ > *off* > **Ctrl+D**

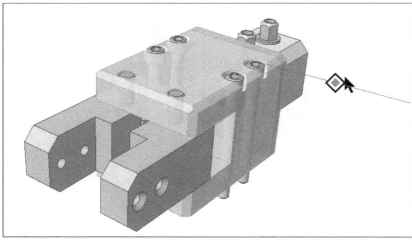

Figure 10.3 Perspective View

Saved Views

Create a saved view and explode state to be used later on an assembly drawing. When using the View Manager to set display and explode states, it is a good idea to create one or more saved views to be used later for exploding. The default trimetric and isometric views do not adequately represent the assembly in its functional position.

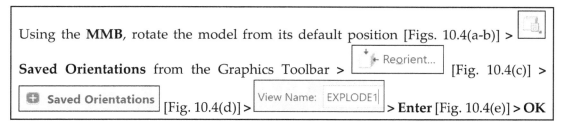

Using the **MMB**, rotate the model from its default position [Figs. 10.4(a-b)] >

Saved Orientations from the Graphics Toolbar > Reorient... [Fig. 10.4(c)] >

Saved Orientations [Fig. 10.4(d)] > View Name: EXPLODE1 > **Enter** [Fig. 10.4(e)] > **OK**

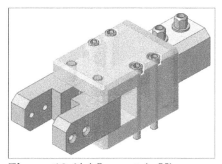

Figure 10.4(a) Isometric View

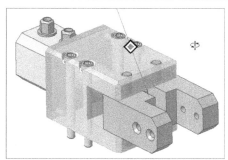

Figure 10.4(b) Reoriented View

Figure 10.4(c) View

Figure 10.4(d) Saved

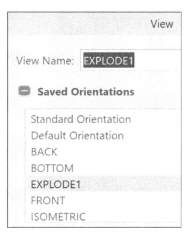

Figure 10.4(e) EXPLODE1

Default exploded views

When you create an *exploded view*, Creo Parametric moves apart the components of an assembly to a set default distance. The default position is seldom the most desirable.

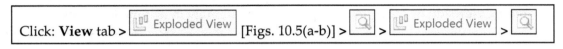

Click: **View** tab > [□□ Exploded View] [Figs. 10.5(a-b)] > [Q] > [□□ Exploded View] > [Q]

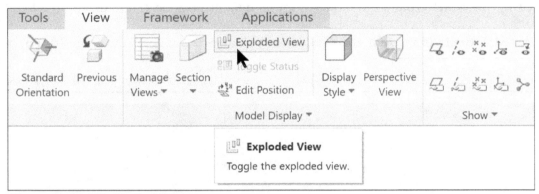

Figure 10.5(a) Exploded View

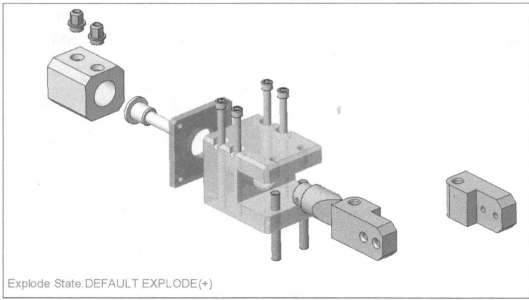

Explode State:DEFAULT EXPLODE(+)

Figure 10.5(b) Default Exploded View (yours will look different)

Place the pointer inside the Graphics Toolbar > **RMB** > **Location** > **Show in Status Bar** [Fig. 10.6(a)] > press **LMB** on the bottom edge of the Graphics Window (⊞) > move the pointer to change the height of the message area [Fig. 10.6(b)] > **MMB** to slightly rotate the model

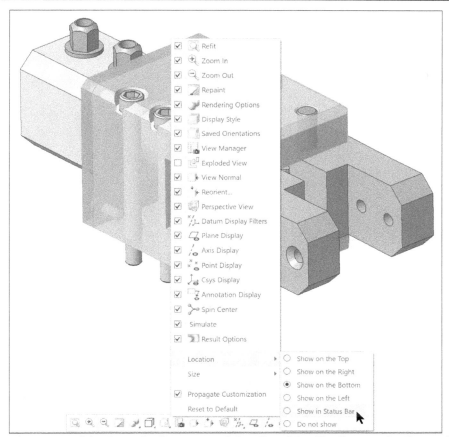

Figure 10.6(a) Move the Location of the Graphics Toolbar to the Status Bar

Figure 10.6(b) Resized Message Log and Status Bar with Integrated Graphics Toolbar

Click: **View** tab > **View Manager** > **Simp Rep** tab > **Master Rep** > **Options** > **Activate** > **Orient** tab > **Explode1(+)** > **RMB** > **Save** [Fig. 10.7(a)] > **OK** [Fig. 10.7(b)] > **Explode** tab > **New** > **Enter** to accept the default name: **Exp0001** [Fig. 10.7(c)] > **Properties >>** (bottom left of the View Manager dialog box) >  **Edit position** [Fig. 10.7(d)] > **References** tab [Fig. 10.7(e)]

Figure 10.7(a) View Manager Orient Tab

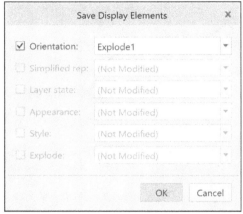

Figure 10.7(b) Save Display Elements

Figure 10.7(c) Exp0001

Figure 10.7(d) Edit Position

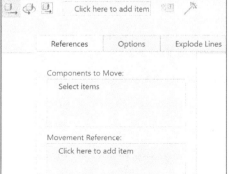

Figure 10.7(e) References tab

Click: **Options** tab > ☑ Move with Children [Fig. 10.7(f)] > **References** tab > Components to Move: select the top of the FITTING [Fig. 10.7(g)]

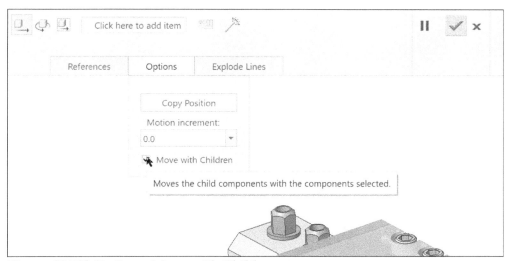

Figure 10.7(f) Options: Move with Children

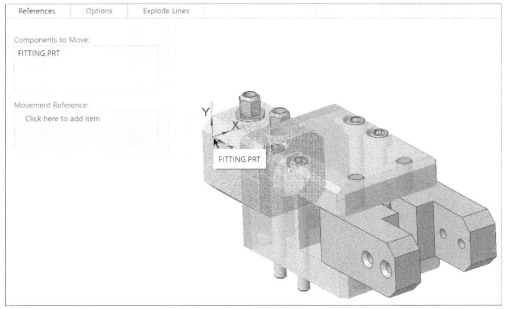

Figure 10.7(g) References tab, Components to Move

Using the **LMB**, select and hold the **Z axis** of the temporary coordinate system [Fig. 10.7(h)] > drag the components to a new position > **LMB** [Fig. 10.7(i)]

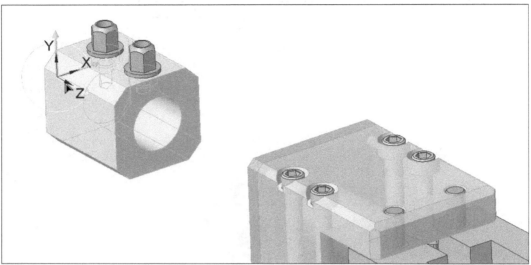

Figure 10.7(h) Press and hold the LMB on the Z Axis

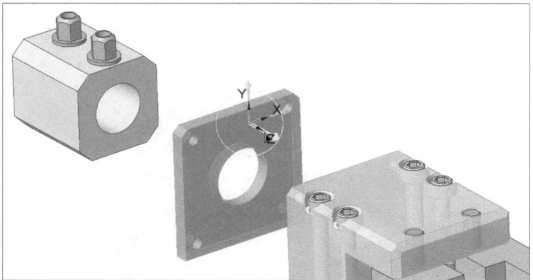

Figure 10.7(i) Move the components to a new position

Click: **Options** tab > ☐ Move with Children > **References** tab > select the **GRIPPER** [Fig. 10.7(j)] > drag to a new position > repeat [Fig. 10.7(k]

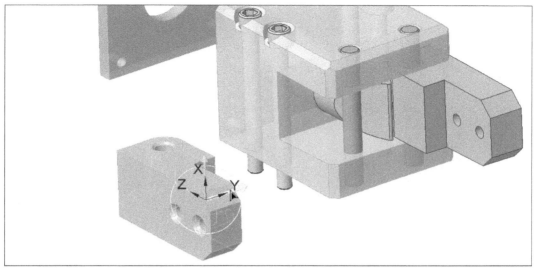

Figure 10.7(j) Drag Component by the Axis

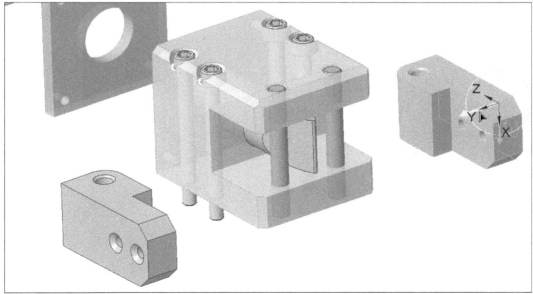

Figure 10.7(k) Moving second Gripper

Select the remaining components using the Options that work best [Fig. 10.7(l)] > you can use Undo or 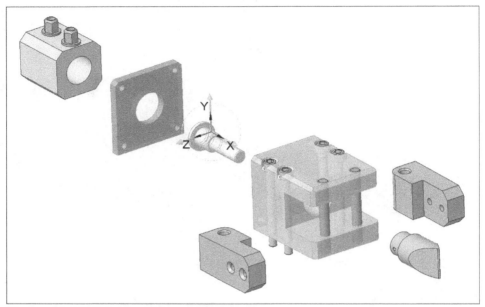 Toggle to redo a position change [Fig. 10.7(m)]

Figure 10.7(l) Select and move the Piston

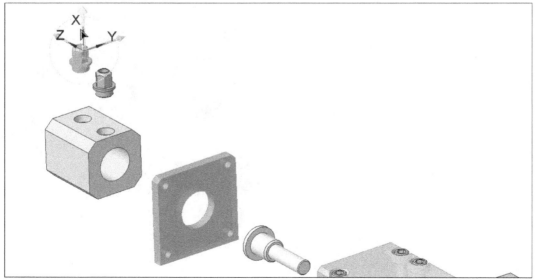

Figure 10.7(m) Drag the Connectors

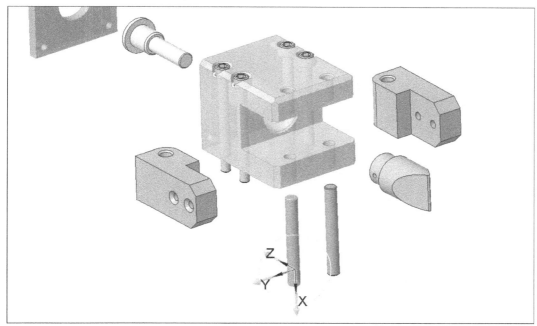

Figure 10.7(n) Select the CLAMP_SWIVEL

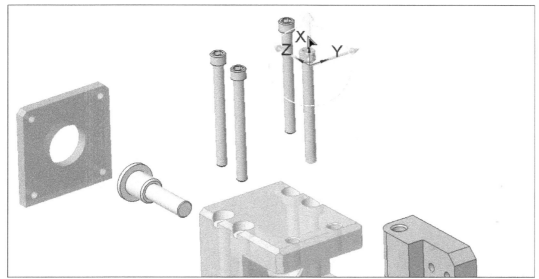

Figure 10.7(o) Drag the CLAMP_SWIVEL

Select the **MECHANSIM_BODY** [Fig. 10.7(p)] > [✓] > [🔍] [Fig. 10.7(q)]

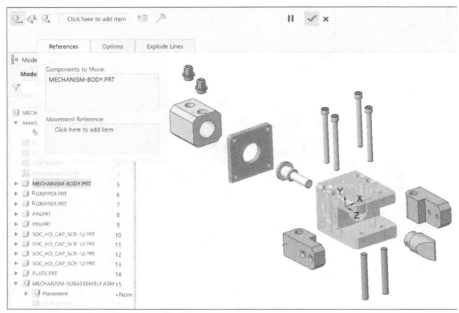

Figure 10.7(p) Move the CLAMP_FOOT

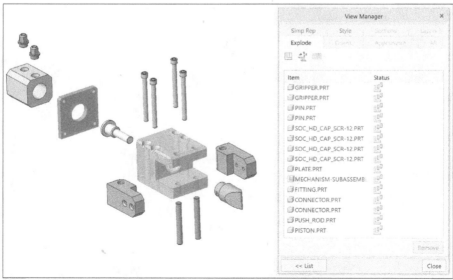

Figure 10.7(q) View Manager Explode tab

Click: **<< List > Exp0001(+) > RMB > Save** [Fig. 10.7(r)] **> OK** [Fig. 10.7(s)] **> Orient** tab **> Explode1(+) > Edit > Save > OK > Close > Save >** Conflicts **OK > RMB > Regenerate > Save** *(if not saved the states will not be available next time the view is requested)*

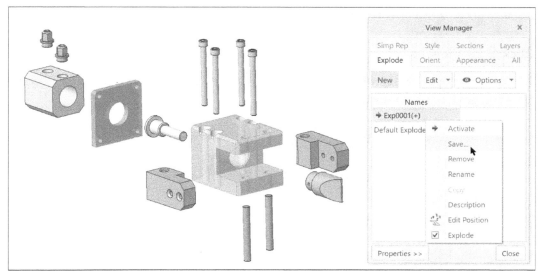

Figure 10.7(r) Save the Explode State *(you must save!)*

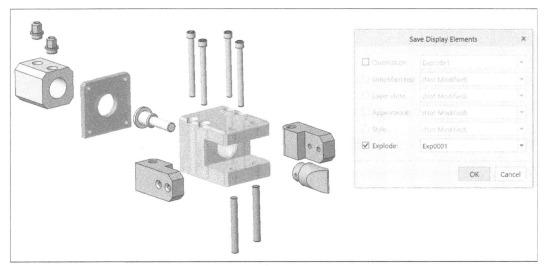

Figure 10.7(s) Save Display Elements Dialog Box

View Style

The components of an assembly (whether exploded or not) can be displayed individually with **Wireframe, Hidden Line, No Hidden, Shading,** or **Transparent**. **Style** is used to manage the display of an assembly's components. The components are displayed according to their assigned display style in the current style state.

Click:  **View Manager** Open the View Manager **> Style** tab **> New > Enter** [Fig. 10.8(a)] to accept the default name: Style0001 **> Show** tab **>** ⦿ Wireframe **>** select the pins and screws **> Preview** [Fig. 10.8(b)]

Figure 10.8(a) Style State Style0001

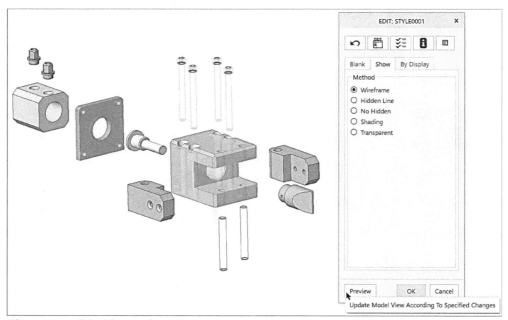

Figure 10.8(b) Edit Dialog Box, Show Tab, Wireframe

Click: [⊙ Hidden Line] > press **Ctrl** key > select the **PLATE** and **CONNECTORS** > **Preview** [Fig. 10.8(c)]

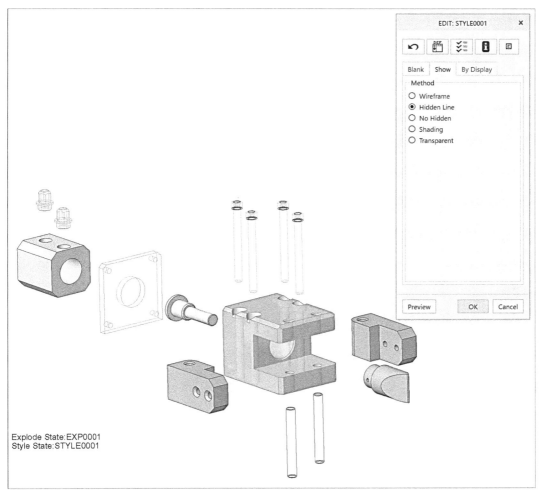

Figure 10.8(c) Edit Dialog Box, Show Tab, Hidden Line

367

Click: ⊙ No Hidden > press **Ctrl** > select both **PUSH_ROD** and **PISTON** > **Preview** [Fig. 10.8(d)] > ⊙ Shading > select **FITTING** > **Preview**

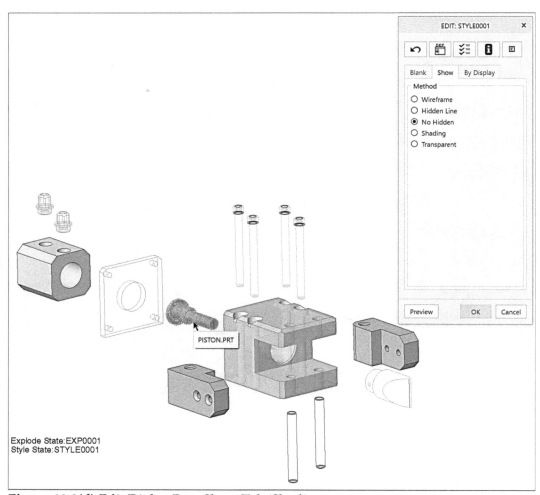

Figure 10.8(d) Edit Dialog Box, Show Tab, Shading

Click: [⊙ Transparent] > select **MECHANISM_BODY > Preview** [Fig. 10.8(e)] > change the **PISTON** and **PUSH_ROD** to **Shading > OK**

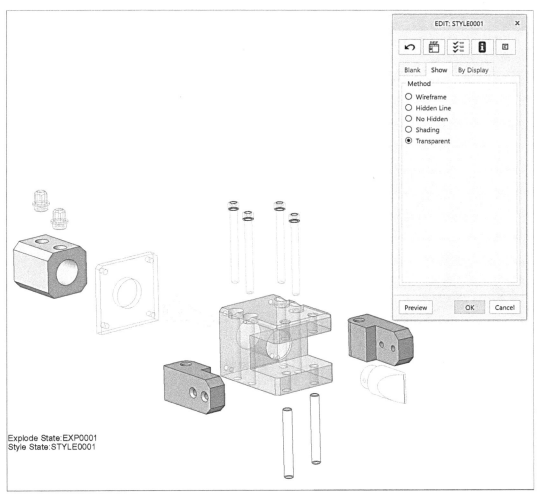

Figure 10.8(e) Style State

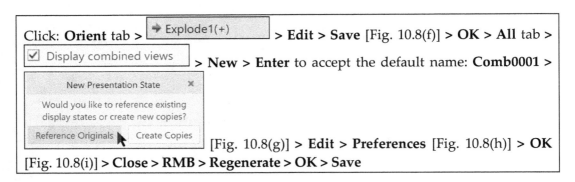

Click: **Orient** tab > Explode1(+) > **Edit** > **Save** [Fig. 10.8(f)] > **OK** > **All** tab > ✓ Display combined views > **New** > **Enter** to accept the default name: **Comb0001** >

New Presentation State

Would you like to reference existing display states or create new copies?

Reference Originals | Create Copies

[Fig. 10.8(g)] > **Edit** > **Preferences** [Fig. 10.8(h)] > **OK** [Fig. 10.8(i)] > **Close** > **RMB** > **Regenerate** > **OK** > **Save**

Figure 10.8(f) Orient Tab

Figure 10.8(g) All Tab

Figure 10.8(h) Preferences

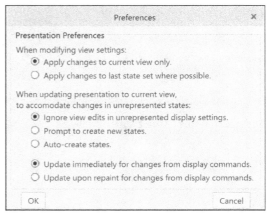

Figure 10.8(i) All Edit Preferences

Model Tree

You can display component style states and explode states in the Model Tree.

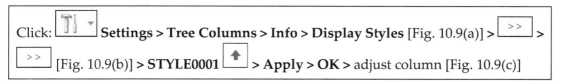

Click: [T] ▼ **Settings > Tree Columns > Info > Display Styles** [Fig. 10.9(a)] > `> >` >
`> >` [Fig. 10.9(b)] > **STYLE0001** [↑] > **Apply > OK >** adjust column [Fig. 10.9(c)]

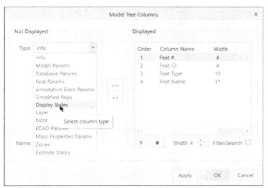

Figure 10.9(a) Model Tree Columns

Figure 10.9(b) Adding Display Style

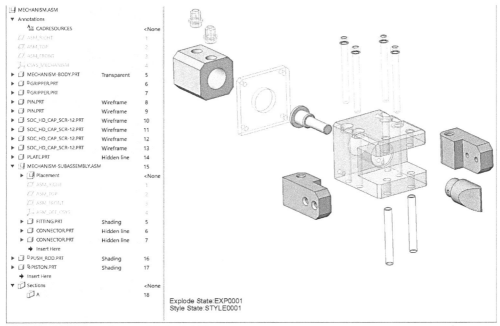

Figure 10.9(c) Adjusted Model Tree

Click: 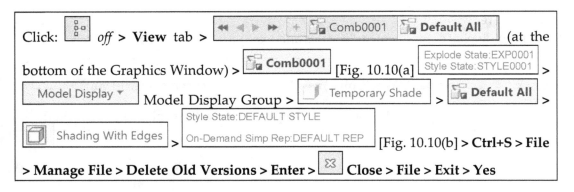 *off* > **View** tab > Comb0001 Default All (at the bottom of the Graphics Window) > Comb0001 [Fig. 10.10(a)] Explode State:EXP0001 Style State:STYLE0001 >

Model Display ▼ Model Display Group > Temporary Shade > Default All >

Shading With Edges > Style State:DEFAULT STYLE On-Demand Simp Rep:DEFAULT REP [Fig. 10.10(b)] > **Ctrl+S** > **File** > **Manage File** > **Delete Old Versions** > **Enter** > ☒ **Close** > **File** > **Exit** > **Yes**

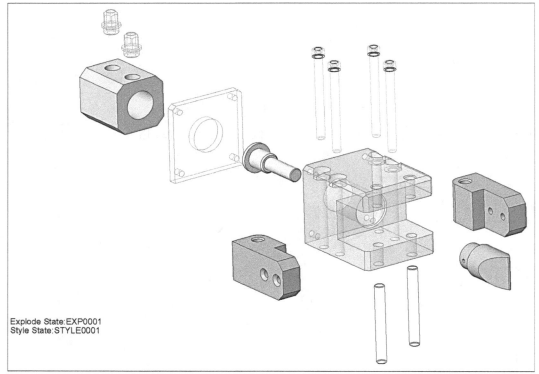

Explode State:EXP0001
Style State:STYLE0001

Figure 10.10(a) Comb0001

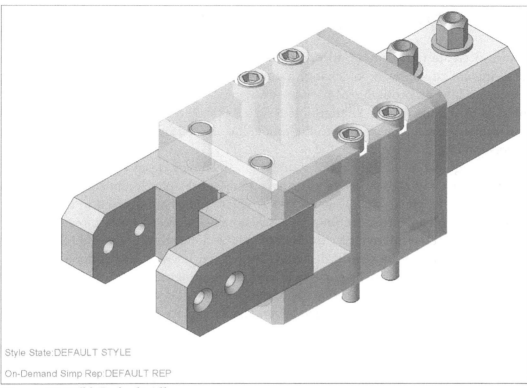

Style State:DEFAULT STYLE

On-Demand Simp Rep:DEFAULT REP

Figure 10.10(b) Default All

Quiz

1. Name three uses of Exploded Views.
2. What is the Default Exploded State used for?
3. What is the View Manager used for?
4. What are Style States?
5. How do you add a URL to a Note?
6. What is an Annotation Plane?
7. What types of View Styles are available?
8. Why do you need to save view states?

This completes Chapter 10.

PART 4: Documenting components and assemblies

You can create drawings of all parametric design models. All model views in the drawing are *associative:* if you change a dimensional value in one view, other drawing views update accordingly. Moreover, drawings are associated with their parent models. Any dimensional changes made to a drawing are automatically reflected in the model. Any changes made to the model are also automatically reflected in their corresponding drawings.

Engineering designs require drawings to convey design and manufacturing information. Drawings consist of a Format and views of a part (or assembly). Standard views, sectional views, detail views, and auxiliary views are utilized to describe the object's features and sizes. Sectional views, also called sections, are employed to clarify and dimension the internal construction of an object. Sections are needed for interior features that cannot be clearly described by hidden lines in conventional views. A wide variety of views can be generated from the parametric model. Among the most common are projection views. Once a model has been added to the drawing, you can place views of the model on a sheet. When a view is placed, you can determine how much of the model to show in a view, whether the view is of a single surface or shows cross sections, and how the view is scaled. You can then display the associative dimensions passed from the 3D model or add reference dimensions as necessary. Basic view types include general, projection, auxiliary, and detailed.

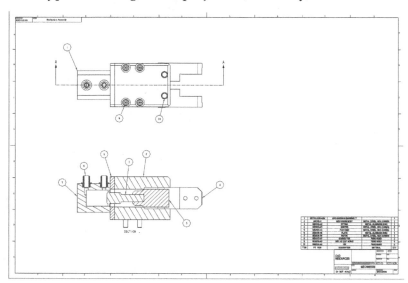

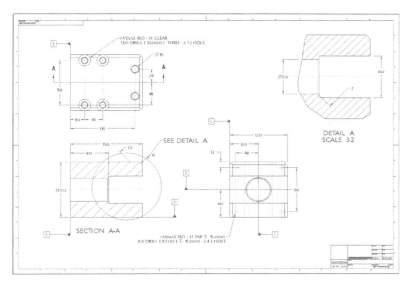

Designers and drafters use drawings to convey design and manufacturing information. Drawings consist of a **Format** and views of a part (or assembly). *Standard views, sectional views, detail views,* and *auxiliary views* are utilized to describe the object's features and sizes. **Sectional views**, also called **sections**, are employed to clarify and dimension the internal construction of an object. Sections are needed for interior features that cannot be clearly described by hidden lines in conventional views. **Auxiliary views** are used to show the *true shape/size* of a feature or the relationship of features that are not parallel to any of the principal planes of projection.

Objectives
1. Understand Formats and Drawing Templates
2. Establish a Drawing Options file to use when detailing
3. Identify the need for views to clarify interior features of a part
4. Create Cross Sections using datum planes
5. Produce Projection and Detail Views
6. Setup and save Drawing Properties files
7. Understand Model Annotations
8. Alter drawing text using Text Style options
9. Become comfortable with dimensioning and detailing capabilities
10. Use multiple drawing sheets

Drawing formats, views and title blocks

Formats are user-defined drawing sheet layouts. A drawing can be created with an empty format and have a standard size format added as needed. Formats can be added to any number of drawings. The format can also be modified or replaced in a Creo Parametric drawing at any time. **Views** created by Creo Parametric are identical to views constructed manually by a designer on paper. The same rules of projection apply; the only difference is that you choose commands in Creo Parametric to create the views as needed. **Title Blocks** are standard or sketched line entities that can contain parameters (object name, tolerances, scale, and so on) that will show when the format is added to the drawing.

Formats

Formats consist of draft entities, not model entities. There are two types of formats: standard and sketched. You can select from a list of **Standard Formats** or create a new size by entering values for length and width. **Sketched Formats** created in Sketcher mode may be parametrically modified, enabling you to create nonstandard-size formats or families of formats. Formats can be altered to include note text, symbols, tables, and drafting geometry, including drafting cross sections and filled areas.

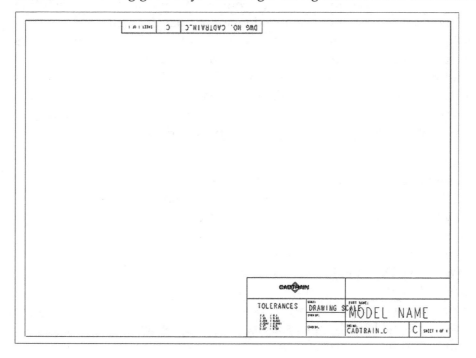

With Creo Parametric, you can do the following in Format mode:

- Create draft geometry and notes
- Move, mirror, copy, group, translate, and intersect geometry
- Use and modify the draft grid
- Enter user attributes
- Create drawing tables
- Use interface tools to create plot, DXF, SET, and IGES files
- Import IGES, DXF, and SET files into the format
- Create user-defined line styles
- Create, use, and modify symbols
- Include drafting cross sections in a format

Whether you use a standard format or a sketched format, the format is added to a drawing that is created for a set of specified views of a parametric 3D model.

When you place a format on your drawing, the system automatically writes the appropriate notes based on information in the model you use.

Formats

If you want to use an existing template, select a listed template, or select a template from the appropriate directory. If you want to use the existing format, using Browse will open Creo Parametric's System Formats folder. Select from the list of standard formats or navigate to a directory with user or company created formats.

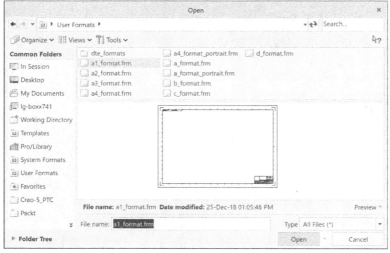

If you want to create your own variable size format, enter values for width and length. The main grid spacing and format text units depend on the units selected for a variable size format. The New Drawing dialog box also provides options for the orientation of the format sheet:

- **Portrait** Uses the larger of the dimensions of the sheet size for the format's height; uses the smaller for the format's width
- **Landscape** Uses the larger of the dimensions of the sheet size for the format's width; uses the smaller for the format's height
- **Variable** Select the unit type, Inches or Millimeters, and then enter specific values for the Width and Height of the format

A0	841 X 1189	mm	**A**	8.5 X 11	in.
A1	594 X 841	mm	**B**	11 X 17	in.
A2	420 X 594	mm	**C**	17 X 22	in.
A3	297 X 420	mm	**D**	22 X 34	in.
A4	210 X 297	mm	**E**	34 X 44	in.
			F	28 X 40	in.

Navigation Panel

The Navigation area contains the Drawing Tree and the Model Tree. The Drawing Tree updates dynamically to reflect drawing objects relevant to the currently active tab. For example, when the Annotate tab is active, the annotations on the current sheet are listed in the Drawing Tree. In the navigation area, you can toggle between the Drawing Tree and the Layer Tree. Similarly, you can toggle between the Model Tree and the Layer Tree. However, you cannot display the Layer Tree simultaneously in both the Drawing Tree area as well as the Model Tree area.

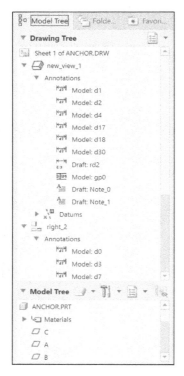  

The **Drawing sheet** tabs are located below the graphics window. You can create multiple drawing sheets and move items from one sheet to another. You can move or copy, add, rename, or delete a sheet.

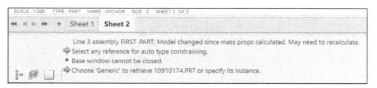

380

Drawing templates

Drawing templates may be referenced when creating a new drawing. Templates can automatically create the views, set the desired view display, create snap lines, and show model dimensions. Drawing templates contain three basic types of information for creating new drawings. The first type is basic information that makes up a drawing but is not dependent on the drawing model, such as notes, symbols, and so forth. This information is copied from the template into the new drawing. The second type is instructions used to configure drawing views and the actions that are performed on their views. The instructions are used to build a new drawing object. The third type is a parametric note. Parametric notes are notes that update to new drawing model parameters and dimension values. The notes are re-parsed or updated when the template is instantiated. Use the templates to: Define the layout of views, Set view display, Place notes, Place symbols, Define tables, Create snap lines, and Show dimensions

Template View

You can also create customized drawing templates for the different types of drawings that you construct. Creating a template allows you to establish portions of drawings automatically, using the customizable template. The **Template View Instructions** dialog box is accessed through **Tools** tab > **Template** > **Layout tab** > **Template View,** when in the Drawing mode.

You can use the following options in the **Template View Instructions** dialog box to customize your drawing templates:

- **View Name** Set the name of the drawing view used as the view symbol label
- **View Orientation** Create a General view or a Projection view
- **Model "Saved View"** Name Orient the view based on a name view in the model
- **Place View** Places the view after you have set the appropriate options and values
- **Edit View** Symbol Edit the view symbol using the Symbol Instance dialog box
- **Replace View** Symbol Allow you to replace the view symbol using the Symbol Instance dialog box

View Options	View Values
View States—Specify the type of view. By default, the **View States** check box is selected and the view state is displayed when the **Template View Instructions** dialog box opens. The value of **Orientation** is FRONT, by default. If you select **Combination State**, the **Orientation**, **Simplified Rep**, **Explode** and **Cross Section** boxes display the text Defined by Combination State. The **Arrow Placement View** and **Show X-Hatching** check boxes also become available for selection after you specify the Combination State.	Combination State, Orientation, Simplified Rep, Explode, Cross Section, Arrow Placement View
Scale—Type a new value or use default value.	View Scale
Process Step—Set the process step for the view. You can specify the step number and set the view of the tool by checking the **Tool View** check box under **Process Step**.	Step Number, Tool View
Model Display—Set the view display for the drawing.	Follow Environment, Wireframe, Hidden Line, No Hidden, Shading

Tan Edge Display—Set the tangent edge display.	Tan Solid, No Disp Tan, Tan Ctrln, Tan Phantom, Tan Dimmed, Tan Default
Snap Lines—Set the number, spacing, and offset.	Number, Incremental Spacing, Initial Offset
Dimensions—Show dimensions on the view.	Create Snap Lines, Incremental Spacing, Initial Offset
Balloons—Show balloons on the view.	

Views

A wide variety of views can be derived from the parametric model. Among the most common are projection views. Creo Parametric creates projection views by looking to the left of, to the right of, above, and below the picked view location to determine the orientation of a projection view. When conflicting view orientations are found, you are prompted to select the view that will be the parent view. A view will then be constructed from the selected view.

At the time when they are created, projection, auxiliary, detailed, and revolved views have the same representation and explosion offsets, if any, as their parent views. From that time onward, each view can be simplified, be restored, and have its explosion distance modified without affecting the parent view. The only exception to this is detailed views, which will always be displayed with the same explosion distances and geometry as their parent views.

Once a model has been added to the drawing, you can place views of the model on a sheet. When a view is placed, you can determine how much of the model to show in a view, whether the view is of a single surface or shows cross sections, and how the view is scaled. You can then show the associative dimensions passed from the 3D model, or add reference dimensions as necessary. Basic view types used by Creo Parametric include general, projection, auxiliary, and detailed:

- **General** Creates a view with no particular orientation or relationship to other views in the drawing. The model must first be oriented to the desired view orientation established.

- **Projection** Creates a view that is developed from another view by projecting the geometry along a horizontal or vertical direction of viewing (orthographic projection). The projection type is specified by you in the drawing setup file and can be based on third-angle (default) or first-angle rules.
- **Auxiliary** Creates a view that is developed from another view by projecting the geometry at right angles to a selected surface or along an axis. The surface selected from the parent view must be perpendicular to the plane of the screen.
- **Detailed** Details a portion of the model appearing in another view. Its orientation is the same as that of the view it is created from, but its scale may be different so that the portion of the model being detailed can be better visualized.
- **Revolved** A revolved view is a cross section of an existing view, revolved 90 degrees around a cutting plane projection. You can use a cross section created in the 3D model as the cutting plane, or you can create one on the fly while placing the view. The revolved view differs from a cross-sectional view in that it includes a line noting the axis of revolution for the view.

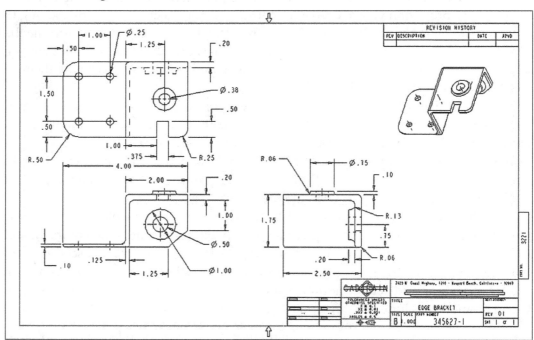

The view options that determine how much of the model is visible in the view are:

- **Full View** Shows the model in its entirety.
- **Half View** Removes a portion of the model from the view on one side of a cutting plane.
- **Broken View** Removes a portion of the model from between two selected points and closes the remaining two portions together within a specified distance.
- **Partial View** Displays a portion of the model in a view within a closed boundary. The geometry appearing within the boundary is displayed; the geometry outside of it is removed.

Options determine whether the view is of a single surface or has a cross section are:

- **Section** Displays an existing cross section of the view if the view orientation is such that the cross-sectional plane is parallel to the screen.
- **No Xsec** Indicates that no cross section is to be displayed.
- **Of Surface** Displays a selected surface of a model in the view. The single-surface view can be of any view type except detailed.

The options that determine whether the view is scaled are:

- **Scale** Allows you to create a view with an individual scale shown under the view. When a view is being created, Creo Parametric will prompt you for the scale value. This value can be modified later. General and detailed views can be scaled.
- **No Scale** A view will be scaled automatically using a pre-defined scale value.
- **Perspective** Creates a perspective general view.

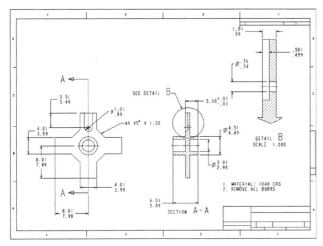

385

Chapter 11 STEPS

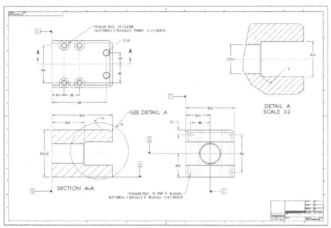

Figure 11.1 Mechanism_Body Drawing,

Mechanism Body Drawing
You will be creating a multiple sheet detail drawing of the Mechanism_Body [Fig. 11.1]. Views will be displayed according to visibility requirements per standards.

Launch **Creo Parametric > Select Working Directory >** select the directory where the **mechanism_body.prt** is saved **> OK >** [☐] **> [◉ ⌐ Drawing] >** Name **mechanism_body > [☐ Use default template]** [Fig. 11.2(a)] *(if "Use default template" is checked; the Front, Top, and Right drawing views are created)* **> OK > A0** Fig. 11.2(b)] Default Model **Browse >** pick **mechanism_body.prt > Preview** *on* [Fig. 11.2(c)] **> Open**

Figure 11.2(a) New

Figure 11.2(b) New Drawing

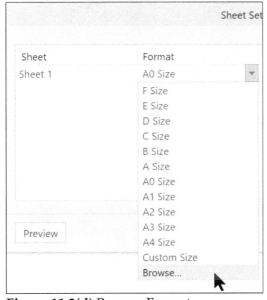

Figure 11.2(c) mechanism_body.prt

Select: **OK** [Fig. 11.2(d)] > **RMB** > **Sheet Setup** > **A0 Size** [Fig. 11.2(e)] > ⬇ > **Browse** > **a1_format.frm** > **Preview** > **Open** > **OK** > **Save** > **Enter**

Figure 11.2(d) Browse Formats   **Figure 11.2(e)** Open a1_format.frm

Click: **File > Prepare > Drawing Properties** > Sort: ▾ > **Alphabetical** > Detail Options **change** [Fig. 11.2(f)] > make changes to create a new **.dtl** file

Option:	*allow_3d_dimensions*	Value:	*yes*	>	**Add/Change**
Option:	*arrow_style*	Value:	*filled*	>	**Add/Change**
Option:	*gtol_datums*	Value:	*std_iso*	>	**Add/Change**
Option:	*text_height*	Value:	*.25*	>	**Add/Change**

Click: **Apply >** 🖫 **Save a copy of the currently displayed configuration file** to your Working directory > *type* **draw_options > OK > Close > Close > Save**

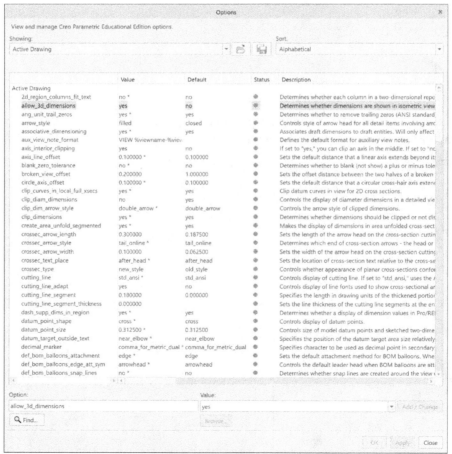

Figure 11.2(f) Drawing Options Dialog Box

388

Click: 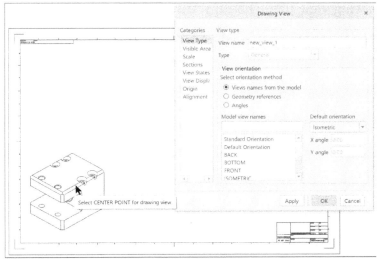 (to close the Navigator so that you can see a larger drawing) > **Ctrl+5** >

Layout tab > **RMB** > [⊟ General View] > **No Combined State** > **OK** > pick a position for the view [Fig. 11.3(a)] > Model view names **LEFT** > **Apply** > **OK** > **LMB** to deselect the view [Fig. 11.3(b)]

Figure 11.3(a) Select a Position

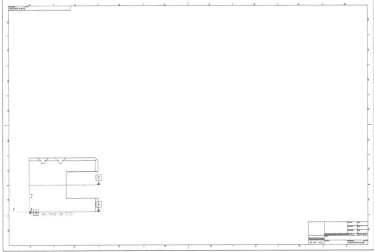

Figure 11.3(b) Front Drawing View

Click: [×/×.] **Datum Display Filters** > [☐ (Select All)] > with the new view selected > from Ribbon [Projection View] > [Select CENTER POINT for drawing view.] pick a position for the Right Side drawing view [Fig. 11.3(c)] > **LMB** to deselect > pick on the first view > press **RMB** > [Projection View] > [Select CENTER POINT for drawing view.] pick a position for the "Top" drawing view [Fig. 11.3(d)] **RMB** > [Lock View Movement] *off* > pick on a view, [✛] and reposition as needed > **LMB** > [🔍] [Fig. 11.3(e)]

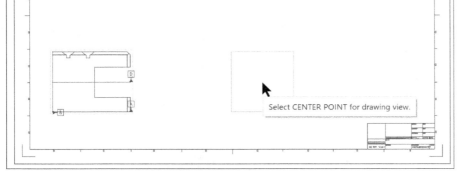

Figure 11.3(c) Add Right Side Projected Drawing View

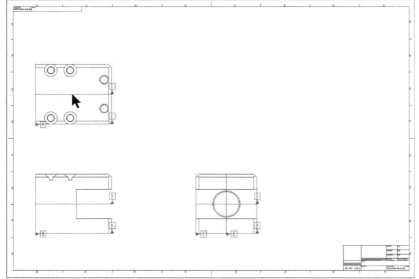

Figure 11.3(d) Add Top Projected Drawing View

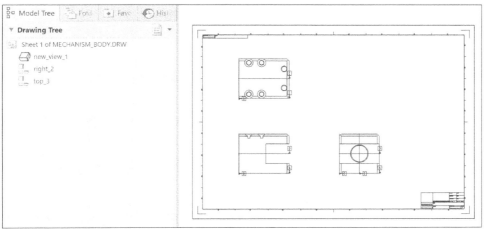

Figure 11.3(e) Repositioned Views

Next, change the Front drawing view into a sectional view. Double-click on the Front drawing view as the view *(or select the view > RMB >* ![icon] *Properties) >* Categories Sections > ⦿ 2D cross-section > ➕ **Add cross-section to view** [Fig. 11.4(a)]

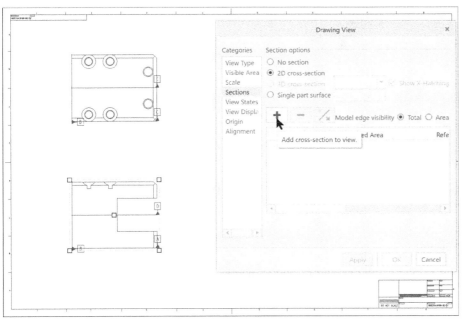

Figure 11.4(a) Select the Front Drawing View

Click: *Planar* > *Single* > **Done** > *type* **A** > **Enter** > select datum **E** [Fig. 11.4(b)] > **Apply** [Fig. 11.4(c)] > **Cancel** > **LMB** > double click on the section lining [Fig. 11.4(d)] > **Spacing** from the Menu Manager > **Half** or **Double** as needed > **Done** *(your crosshatching may look different)*

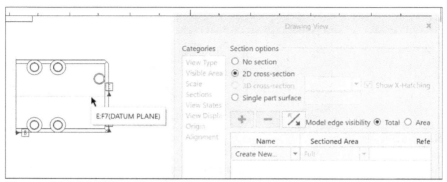

Figure 11.4(b) Select Datum E

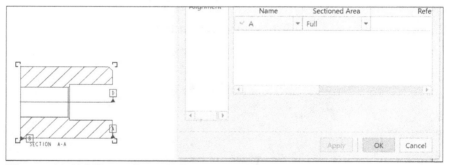

Figure 11.4(c) Front Section Drawing View

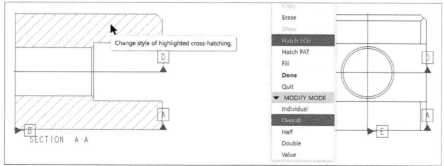

Figure 11.4(d) Double-click on the Section Lining

Show all dimensions and axes (centerlines), click: **Annotate** tab > window in to capture

Front and Top drawing views > [Show Model Annotations] > [⊢⊣] **Dimensions** tab > [☑—☑—] [Fig. 11.5(a)]

> **Apply** > [image] **Datums** tab > [☑—☑—] [Fig. 11.5(b)] > **Apply** > **Cancel**

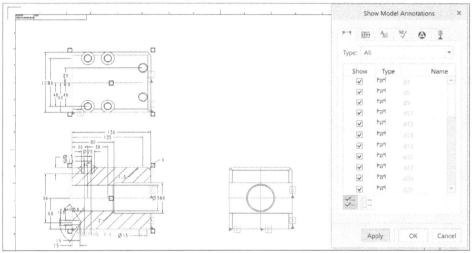

Figure 11.5(a) Dimensions Displayed

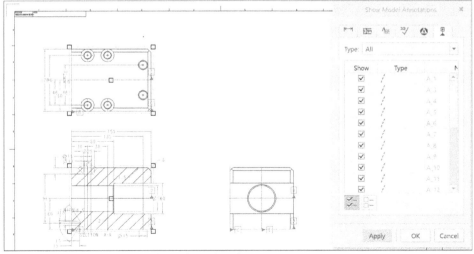

Figure 11.5(b) Axes displayed in the three views

Capture all dimensions by enclosing them in a selection box > **RMB** > **Cleanup Dimensions** [Fig. 11.5(c)] > ☐ Create snap lines > Increment: .5 > **Enter** > **Apply** [Fig. 11.5(d)] > **Close** > **LMB**

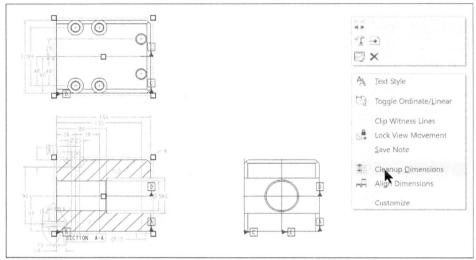

Figure 11.5(c) Press RMB > Cleanup Dimensions

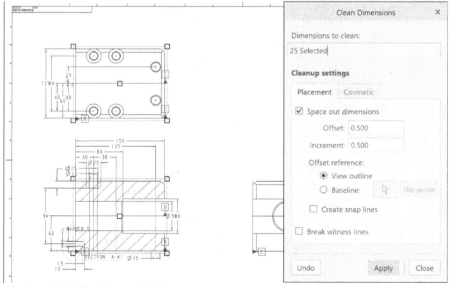

Figure 11.5(d) Cleaned Dimensions

Select the hole **50** dimension > 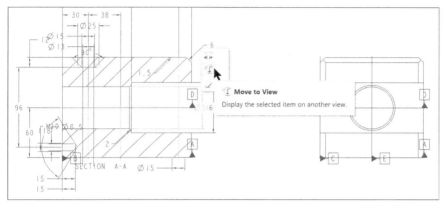 [Fig. 11.6(a)] > pick on the Right Side drawing view > pick on and reposition the **50** [Fig. 11.6(b)] > move **120** dimension to the Right Side drawing view [Fig. 11.6(c)]

Figure 11.6(a) Select the 50mm Diameter Dimension

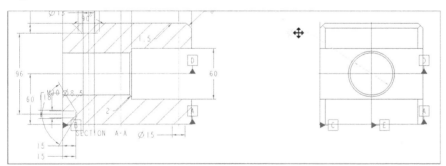

Figure 11.6(b) Diameter Dimension Moved to Right Side Drawing View

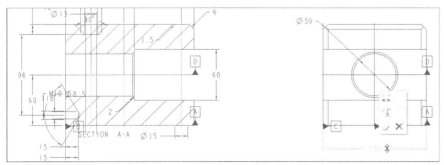

Figure 11.6(c) 120mm Dimension moved to the Right Side Drawing View

Select **Annotate** tab **>** window- in the three views **>** **Notes** tab **>** **Show Model Annotations >** 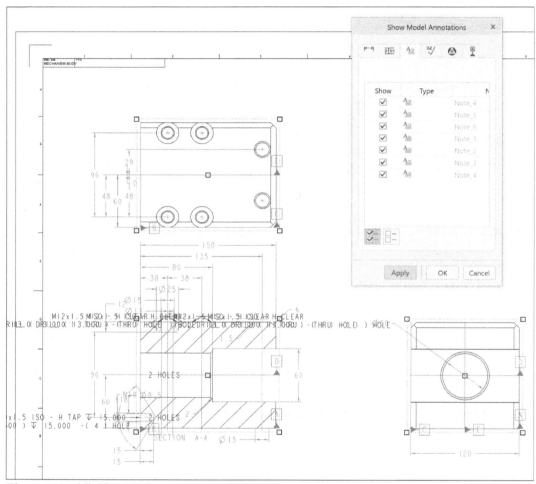 [Fig. 11.6(d)] **> Apply > Cancel**

Figure 11.6(d) Show Notes

Double-click on the Right Side drawing view > Display style **Hidden** > Tangent edges display style **Dimmed** [Fig. 11.6(e)] > **Apply** > **OK** [Fig. 11.6(f)]

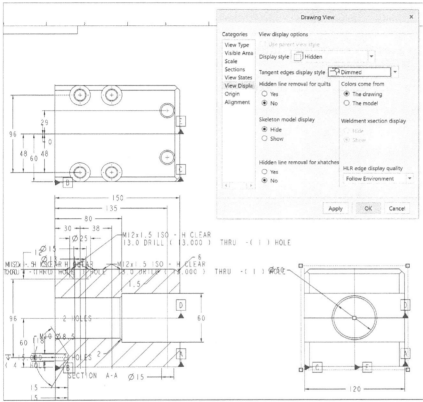

Figure 11.6(e) Edited View

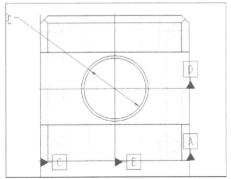

Figure 11.6(f) Hidden Lines Display

397

Pick **Layout** tab > select the **Front** view > **RMB** > **Add Arrows** [Fig. 11.6(g)] > pick on the **TOP** View [Fig. 11.6(h)] > Erase redundant notes, reposition dimensions, move dimension text, clip extension lines, trim centerlines, or flip arrows and text where appropriate. Use filters [General ▼] to help in selections. Reposition, move, clip, or erase axes. To reposition datums activate the **Annotate** tab > select and move footed datums [B ◄] > erase extras and move as required

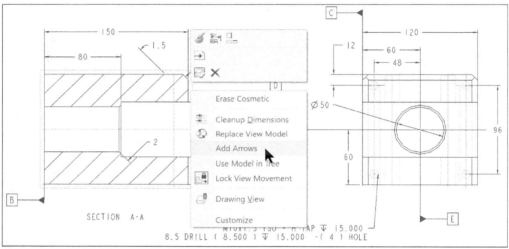

Figure 11.6(g) Add Arrows

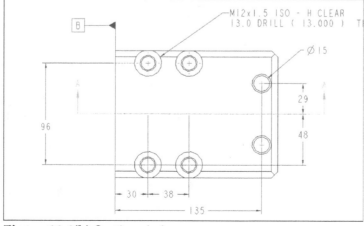

Figure 11.6(h) Section A Arrows

Select **Layout** tab > **Text Style** from the Ribbon > window-in a region containing all dimensions and notes > **OK** > Text Style dialog opens > **font** > **filled** [Fig. 11.6(i)] > **Apply** > **OK** [Fig. 11.6(j)] > **MMB**

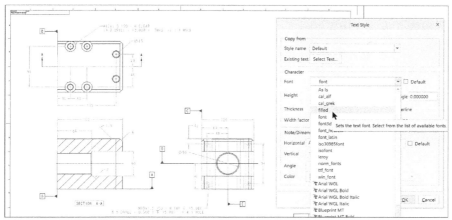

Figure 11.6(i) filled Font

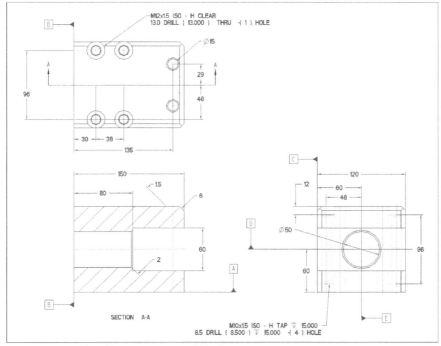

Figure 11.6(j) All Text is now filled

Add a reference dimension select: **Annotate** tab > Annotations ▾ group in Ribbon > Reference Dimension > press and hold the **Ctrl** key > pick the bottom edge of the part [Fig. 11.7(a)] > pick the top edge of the part > **MMB** to place the reference dimension [Fig. 11.7(b)] > **LMB > MMB >** change the reference dimensions font to filled

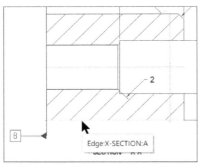

Figure 11.7(a) Edge Selection

Figure 11.7(b) Placing Reference Dimension

Select the Note > **Attachment > Change Ref** [Fig. 11.7(c)] > pick a new position on the edge of the hole for the arrows point > **MMB** > reposition as necessary [Fig. 11.7(d)] > **MMB > LMB > Save**

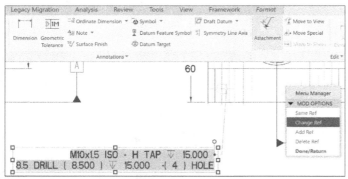

Figure 11.7(c) Change Reference

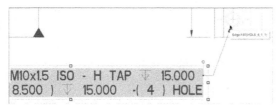

Figure 11.7(d) Select Edge

To increase the functionality of the drawing, you will need to master a number of capabilities. Partial views, detail views, multiple sheets, and modifying section lining (crosshatch lines) are just a few of the many options available in Drawing Mode.

Select **Layout** tab > [Detailed View] > [Select center point for detail on an existing view.] pick the top edge of the hole, an **X** will display at the selected position [Fig. 11.8(a)] > [Sketch a spline, without intersecting other splines, to define an outline.] *each **LMB** pick adds a point to the spline* [Fig. 11.8(b)] > **MMB** *to end (and close) the spline* [Fig. 11.8(c)] > [🔍]

Note: you do not have to "close" the spline sketch – just get near the start of the spline and clicking the MMB will close the spline for you.

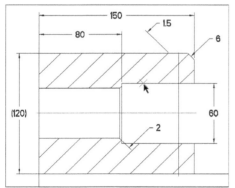
Figure 11.8(a) Select Center for Detail View

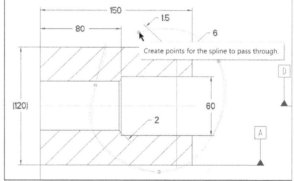
Figure 11.8(b) Sketch a Spline

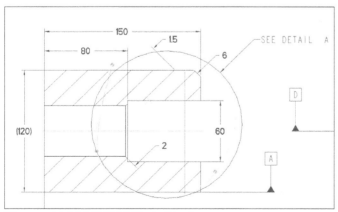
Figure 11.8(c) DETAIL A Circle

401

⟹ Select CENTER POINT for drawing view. pick in the upper right corner of the drawing sheet to place the view [Fig. 11.8(d)] > **MMB** > double-click on the **Detail View** > Categories **Scale** > **1.500** > **Enter** > **OK** > **LMB** > **Annotate** tab > click on the **Datum A** > ⟨ **Erase** ⟩ [Fig. 11.8(e)] > **LMB** > **Ctrl+S**

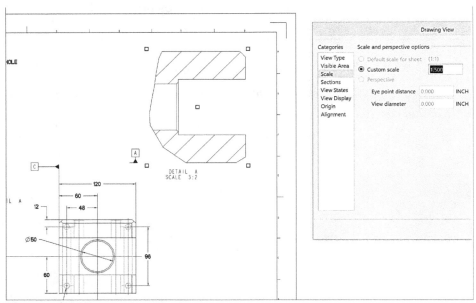

Figure 11.8(d) Detail View A

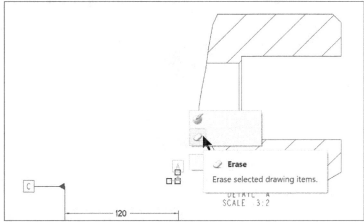

Figure 11.8(e) Detail A

Add an axis to the hole in view DETAIL A. **Click >** 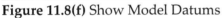 **>**
[Fig. 11.8(f)] **>** pick on the hole (feature) or DETAIL A [Fig. 11.8(g)] **> Show** [Fig.
11.8(h)] **> Cancel >** **> Ctrl+S**

Figure 11.8(f) Show Model Datums

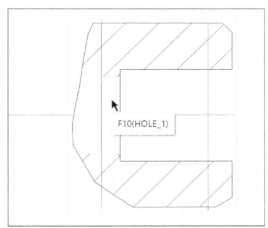

Figure 11.8(g) Select the Hole

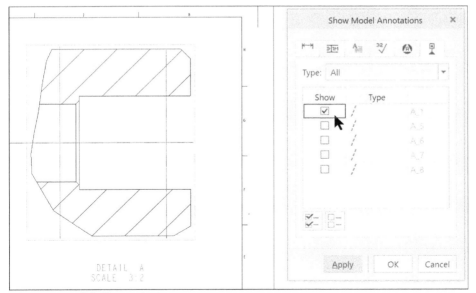

Figure 11.8(h) Show Axis

In **DETAIL A** adjust the axis > double-click on **DETAIL A 1.500** > **Format** tab opens > **filled** > **.375** Change the text height [Fig. 11.8(i)] > **Enter** > move the note [Fig. 11.8(j)] > repeat for the **SECTION A-A** and **SEE DETAIL A** notes > **Ctrl+S** [Fig. 11.8(k)]

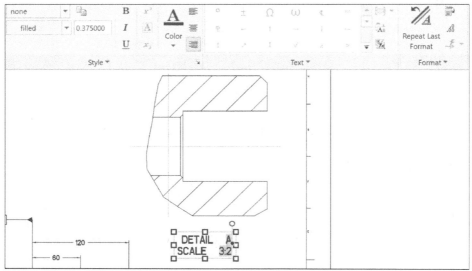

Figure 11.8(i) Select the Text items and change their Height

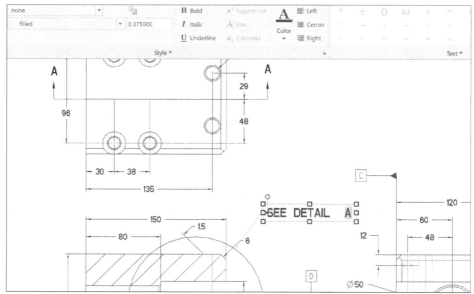

Figure 11.8(j) Text Format Ribbon

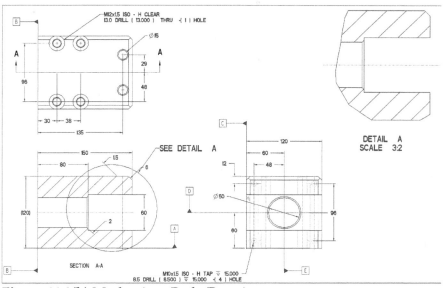

Figure 11.8(k) Mechanism_Body Drawing

Change the height of the section identification lettering to **.375** > **Annotate** tab > check your filter [General ▼] > pick on "**A**" > press **RMB** > [AA Text Style] [Fig. 11.8(l)] > next to Height [☐ Default] (uncheck) > [Height .375] > **Enter** > **Apply** > **OK** > **LMB** to deselect > **Apply** > **OK** > **LMB** to deselect > **Ctrl+S**

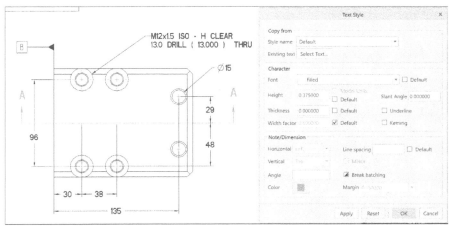

Figure 11.8(l) Text Style of the Section Identification Lettering

The Arrows for the cutting plane and dimensions are too small. These are controlled by Drawing Options, click: **File > Prepare > Drawing Properties** [Fig. 11.9(a)] > Detail Options **change** > Sort: **Alphabetical** > *draw_arrow_length* *.25* > **Enter** > *draw_arrow_width* *.10* > **Enter** > *crossec_arrow_length* *.375* > **Enter** > *crossec_arrow_width .125* > **Enter** [Fig. 11.9(b)] > **Add/Change** > *arrow_style* > *filled* > **Enter** > **Apply** > **Close** > **Close** > **Save** [Fig. 11.9(c)]

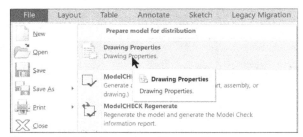

Figure 11.9(a) Drawing Properties

	Value	Default	Status	Description
▼ These options control cross sections and their arrows				
clip_curves_in_local_full_xsecs	yes *	yes	●	Clip datum curves in view for 2D cross sections.
crossec_arrow_length	.375	0.187500	●	Sets the length of the arrow head on the cross-section cutt
crossec_arrow_style	tail_online *	tail_online	●	Determines which end of cross-section arrows - the head o
crossec_arrow_width	.125	0.062500	●	Sets the width of the arrow head on the cross-section cutti
crossec_text_place	after_head *	after_head	●	Sets the location of cross-section text relative to the cross-
crossec_type	new_style *	old_style	●	Controls whether appearance of planar cross-sections conf
cutting_line	std_ansi *	std_ansi	●	Controls display of cutting line. If set to "std_ansi," uses the

Figure 11.9(b) Cross Section Drawing Options

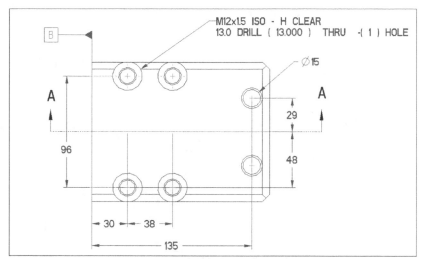

Figure 11.9(c) Section Arrows Length and Width Changed

Select **2mm** and **60mm** dimensions in the **FRONT** view, and the **50mm** diameter in the **RIGHT** side view > ⎡ Move to View ⎦ [Fig. 11.10(a)] > select **DETAIL A** > reposition as needed > clip extension lines *(for the whole drawing)* [Figs. 11.10(b-c)] > **LMB** > change the section lining in **DETAIL A** > **Layout** tab > double-click on the **Xhatching** in view **DETAIL A** [Fig. 11.11(a)] > **Det Indep** > **Spacing** > **Half** [Fig. 11.11(b)] > **Done**

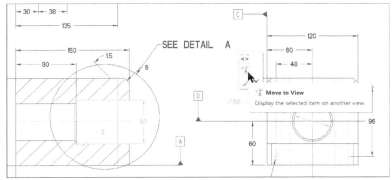

Figure 11.10(a) Select the 2mm, 50mm and 60mm Dimensions

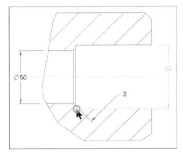

Figure 11.10(b) Clip the Extension Lines

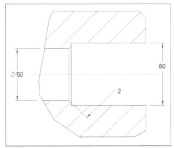

Figure 11.10(c) Completed DETAIL View

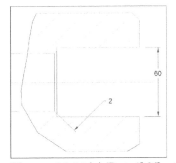

Figure 11.11(a) Detail Xhatching

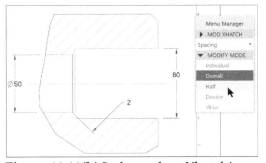

Figure 11.11(b) Independent Xhatching

Change the text style. Click: **Annotate** tab > Annotation ▼ filter > enclose all text and dimensions with a selection box [Fig. 11.12(a)] > **RMB > Text Style** [Fig. 11.12(b)] > ☐ Default > ▼ **Blueprint MT Bold** [Fig. 11.12(c)] > **Apply** [Fig. 11.12(d)] > **OK > LMB > Save** [Fig. 11.12(e)]

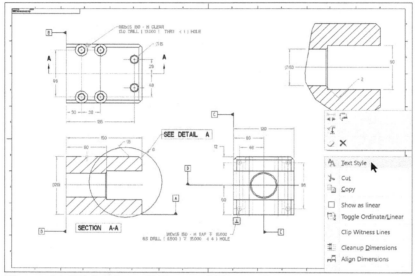

Figure 11.12(a) Select all Text and Dimensions

Figure 11.12(b) Text Style

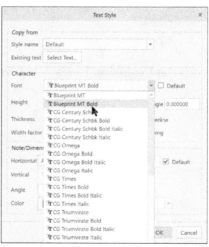

Figure 11.12(c) Character- Font- Blueprint MT

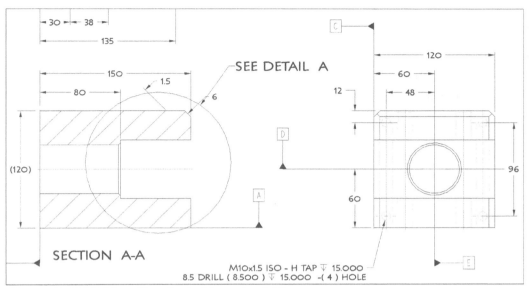

Figure 11.12(d) New Text Style Blueprint MT

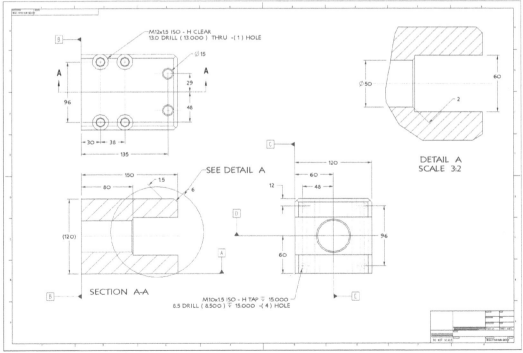

Figure 11.12(e) Completed First Sheet

Create a *second sheet* with an isometric view of the Mechanism_Body. Click: **Layout** tab

> New Sheet > filter General ▼ > **RMB** > Sheet Setup >

A1_FORMAT > Browse [Fig. 11.13(a)] > System Formats **a3_format.frm** [Fig. 11.13(b)]
> Open > OK > Remove All > Yes >

SCALE : 1:1	TYPE : PART	NAME : MECHANISM-BODY	SIZE : A3	SHEET 2 OF 2
◄◄ ◄ ► ►► + Sheet 1 **Sheet 2**				

>

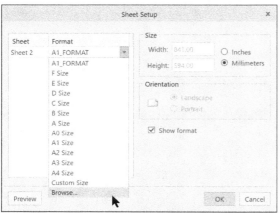

Figure 11.13(a) Sheet Setup Dialog Box

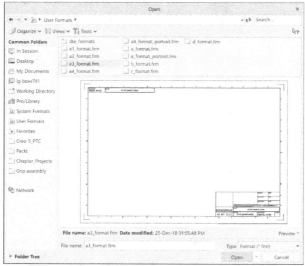

Figure 11.13(b) a3_format.frm

Click: 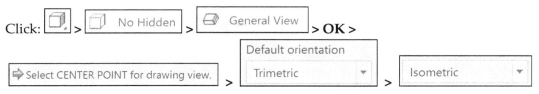 **> OK >**

Select CENTER POINT for drawing view. > Default orientation: Trimetric > Isometric

[Fig. 11.13(c)] **> OK > LMB** [Fig. 11.13(d)]

Figure 11.13(c) Drawing View

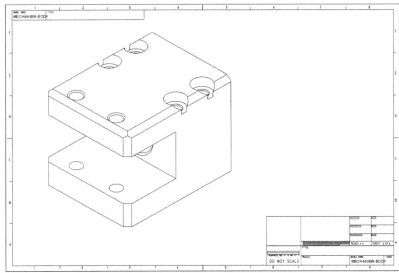

Figure 11.13(d) Isometric View

411

Double-click on the pictorial view > **View Display** > 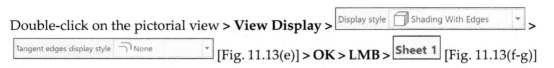 >

Tangent edges display style [None] [Fig. 11.13(e)] > **OK** > **LMB** > Sheet 1 [Fig. 11.13(f-g)]

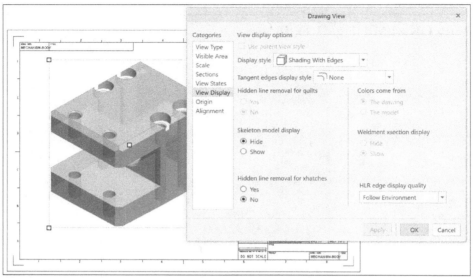

Figure 11.13(e) Drawing View Dialog Box

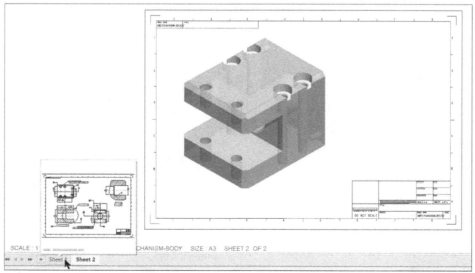

Figure 11.13(f) Drawing Sheet 1 Preview

412

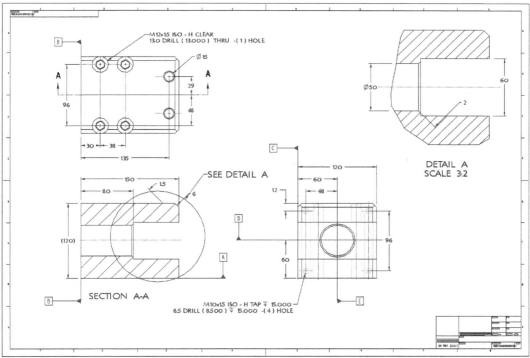

Figure 11.13(g) Completed Drawing

Quiz

1. Name five things that drawing can contain.
2. How do you display dimension, notes, and centerlines?
3. What is a Drawing Format?
4. What are some of the items displayed in the Drawing Tree?
5. View Display allows for what changes to a drawing view?
6. How do you trim extension lines?
7. What are Drawing Options used for?
8. Identify the need for views to clarify interior features of a part?
9. How do you create a section?
10. What is the difference between Projection and Detail Views?
11. What are Model Annotations?
12. Name three items you can change and control with Text Style options.

This completes Chapter 11.

CHAPTER 12: Assembly drawing setup and formatting

Creo Parametric incorporates a great deal of functionality into drawings of assemblies. You can assign parameters to parts in the assembly that can be displayed on a *parts list* in an assembly drawing. Creo Parametric can also generate the item balloons for each component on standard orthographic views or on an exploded view. In addition, a variety of specialized capabilities allow you to alter the way individual components are displayed in views and in sections. The format for an assembly is usually different from the format used for detail drawings.

The most significant difference is the presence of a Parts List. A parts list is a *Drawing Table object* that is formatted to represent a bill of materials in a drawing. By defining *parameters* in the parts in your assembly that agree with the specific format of the parts list, you make it possible for Creo Parametric to add pertinent data to the assembly drawing's parts list automatically as components are added to the assembly. After the parts list and parameters have been added, Creo Parametric can balloon the assembly drawing automatically.

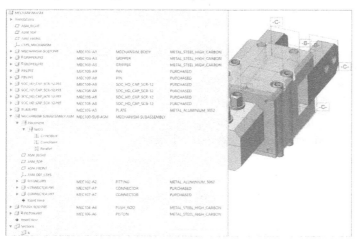

Objectives

- Create an Assembly Drawing Format
- Add Notes and Parametric Notes to a Drawing Format's Title Block
- Add Parameters to parts
- Create a Table to generate a parts list automatically
- Understand the function of .dtl files
- Create Repeat regions

414

Chapter 12 STEPS

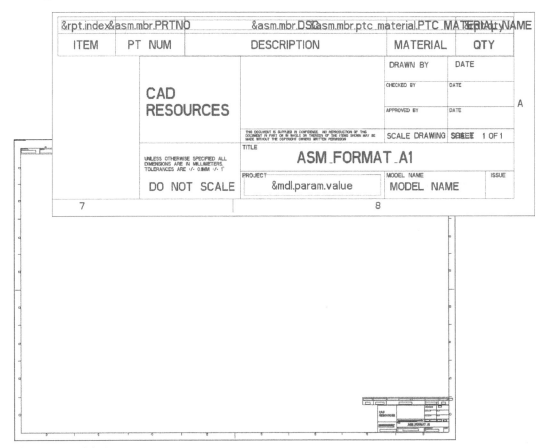

Figure 12.1(a) Format

The format [Fig. 12.1(a)] for an assembly drawing is usually different from the format used for detail drawings. The most significant difference is the presence of a parts list. You will create a standard "A1" size format and place a standard parts list on it.

A parts list is a *Drawing Table object* that is formatted to represent a bill of material (BOM) in a drawing. By defining parameters in the parts in your assembly that agree with the specific format of the parts list, you make it possible for Creo Parametric to add pertinent data to the assembly drawing parts list automatically, as components are added to the assembly.

Launch **Creo Parametric > Select Working Directory >** select the directory where the **mechanism.asm** was saved **> OK > Ctrl+O >** Common Folders **User Formats > a1_format.frm > Open > File > Save As > Save a Copy >** *type a unique name for your format:* New Name **asm_format_a1 > OK > File > Close > File > Open >** double-click on **asm_format_a1.frm**

The **format** will have a **.dtl file** associated with it, and the **drawing** will have a unique **.dtl file** associated with it. *They are separate .dtl files.* When you activate a drawing and then add a format, the. dtl for the format controls the font, etc. for the format only. The drawing .dtl file that controls items on the drawing needs to be established separately in the Drawing mode.

Click: **File > Prepare > Detail Options > change** (Options dialog box opens) > *text_height 4* **> Enter > Enter >** *arrow_style filled* **> Apply >** *draw_arrow_length 4* **> Apply >** *draw_arrow_width 1* **> Apply > Apply >** Sort: **As Set** [Fig. 12.1(b)] > **Save a copy of the currently displayed configuration file >** File name: **asm_a1_properties.dtl > OK > Close > Close > Ctrl+S > OK**

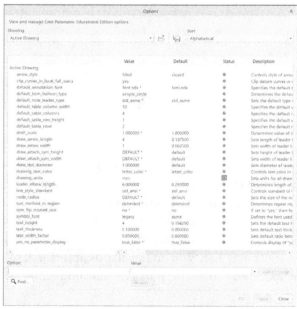

Figure 12.1(b) Options

416

Zoom into the title block region > **Annotate** tab > 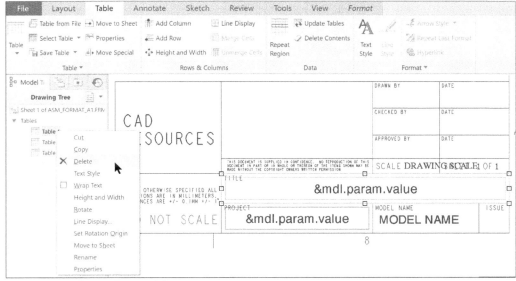 **A≡ Note** > **Unattached Note** > tool pick a point for the note in the title block [Fig. 12.2(a)] > **B** **Bold** in Ribbon > *type* **CAD** > **Enter** > **RESOURCES** > ⊕ move as needed > **LMB** > **Table** tab > select **Table 1** in Model Tree [Fig. 12.2(b)] > **RMB** > **Delete**

Figure 12.2(a) Select Location for Note

Figure 12.2(b) Delete Table 1

Select > **Annotate** tab > [A≡ Note] > [**B**] > pick position [Fig. 12.2(c)] > *type* **&dwg_name** [Fig. 12.2(d)] > **LMB** outside of text field box > **LMB** [Fig. 12.2(e)] > **SAVE**

The note changes to the drawing name of the active object ASM_FORMAT_A1. It will change to the drawing name when used as a format on your drawings.

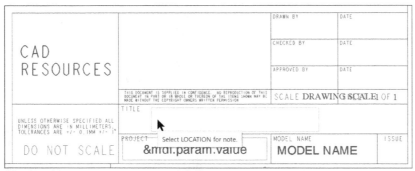

Figure 12.2(c) Select Location for Note in TITLE area

Figure 12.2(d) Parametric Note: &dwg_name

Figure 12.2(e) Title

The parts list table can now be created and saved with this format. You can add and replace formats and keep the table associated with the drawing. Next, start the parts list by creating a table.

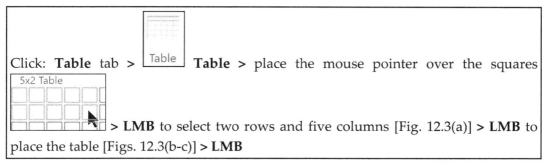

Click: **Table** tab > Table **Table** > place the mouse pointer over the squares > **LMB** to select two rows and five columns [Fig. 12.3(a)] > **LMB** to place the table [Figs. 12.3(b-c)] > **LMB**

Figure 12.3(a) Inserting 5x2 Table

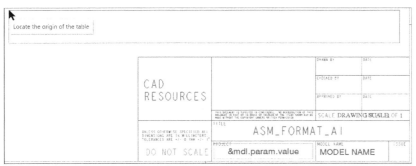

Figure 12.3(b) Locate the origin of the Table

Figure 12.3(c) Table temporarily placed

Select the top left cell > **RMB** > **Height and Width** [Fig. 12.3(d)] > change the column's width to **20** [Fig. 12.3(e)] > **Preview** > **OK** > change the second column's width to **24** > third **70** > fourth **24** > fifth **20** [Fig. 12.3(f)] > **LMB** to deselect

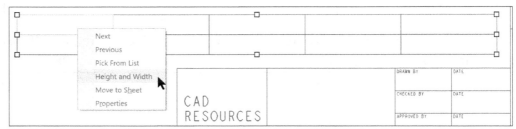

Figure 12.3(d) Highlight Column

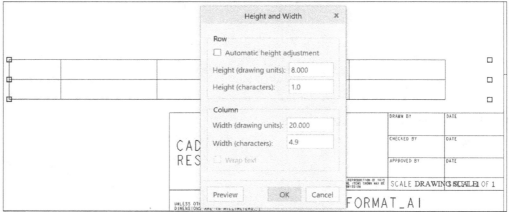

Figure 12.3(e) Height and Width

Figure 12.3(f) Placed Table

Position the pointer over the top row (left side edge) until it highlights

Row:Table **> RMB > Properties > Automatic height adjustment** (uncheck) > column's height **6** [Fig. 12.3(g)] **> OK >** the pointer over the top corner [Fig. 12.3(h)] > move the table [Fig. 12.3(i)] **> LMB > LMB** [Fig. 12.3(j)] **> Save > File > Manage File > Delete Old Versions > Yes**

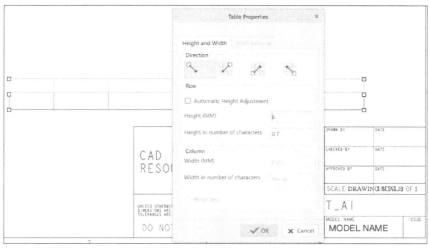

Figure 12.3(g) First Row Height is 6

Figure 12.3(h) Place the Pointer on the Upper Left Corner of the Table

Figure 12.3(i) Move the Pointer to Position the Table

421

Click: **Table** tab > [Repeat Region icon] > **Add** > **Simple** > pick in the left block > pick in the right block [Fig. 12.4(a)] > **Attributes** > select the Repeat Region just created > **No Duplicates** > **Recursive** > **Done/Return** > **Done** [Fig. 12.4(b)]

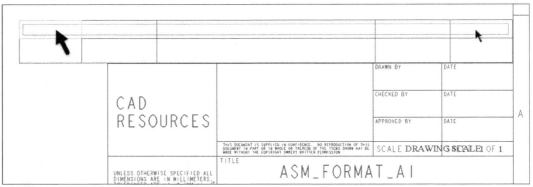

Figure 12.4(a) Create a Repeat Region

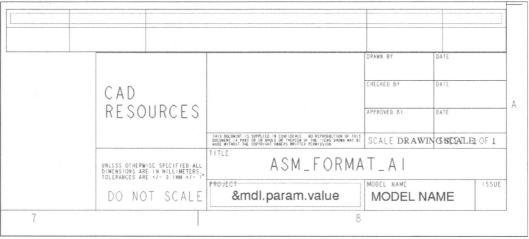

Figure 12.4(b) Repeat Region

Insert column headings using plain text, double-click on the first block of the second row [Fig. 12.5(a)] > *type* **ITEM** [Fig. 12.5(b)] (the text is case sensitive) > **LMB** to deselect

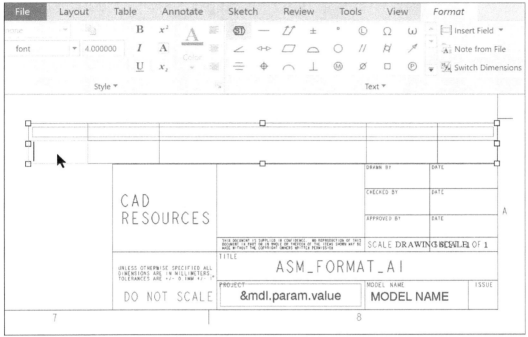

Figure 12.5(a) Select the First Block

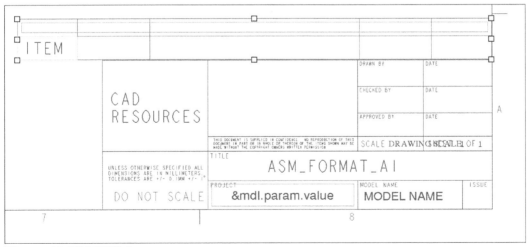

Figure 12.5(b) ITEM

The Repeat Region now needs to have some of its headings correspond to the parameters that will be created in each component model.

Double-click on the second block > *type* **PT NUM** [Fig. 12.5(c)] > double-click on the third block > **Ctrl+B** > **DESCRIPTION** > double-click on the fourth block > **MATERIAL** > double-click on the fifth block > *type* **QTY** > **LMB** > **LMB** [Fig. 12.5(d)]

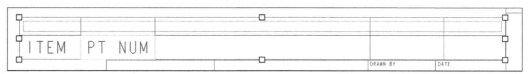

Figure 12.5(c) PT NUM

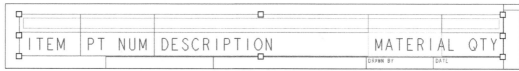

Figure 12.5(d) ITEM, PT NUM, DESCRIPTION, MATERIAL, QTY

With the **Ctrl** key pressed, select all five text cells > release the **Ctrl** key > press **RMB** > **Text Style** Text Style dialog box opens [Fig. 12.5(e)] > Font **filled** > Note/Dimension-Horizontal **Center** > Vertical **Middle** > **Apply** [Figs. 12.5(f-g)] > **OK** > **LMB** > **Ctrl+S**

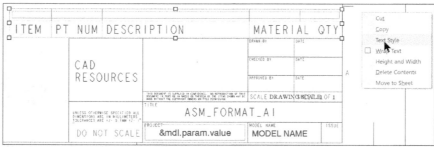

Figure 12.5(e) Press RMB > Text Style

Figure 12.5(f) Text Style Preview

Figure 12.5(g) Text Style Dialog Box

Insert parametric text (Report Symbols) into the table cells. Double-click on the first table cell of the Repeat Region (the table cell ABOVE the text ITEM) **> rpt…** from the Report Symbol dialog box [Fig. 12.6(a)] **> index** [Figs. 12.6(b-c)]

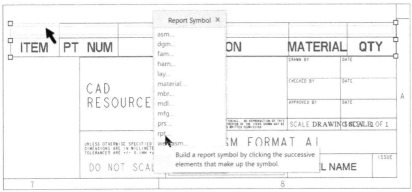

Figure 12.6(a) Report Symbol Dialog Box, click rpt…

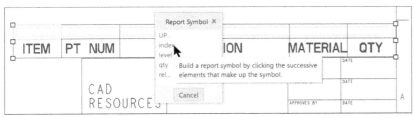

Figure 12.6(b) Click index

Figure 12.6(c) &rpt.index

Double-click on the fifth table cell of Repeat Region **> rpt...** [Fig. 12.6(d)] **> qty** [Figs. 12.6(e-f)]

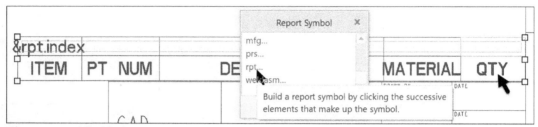

Figure 12.6(d) Click rpt...

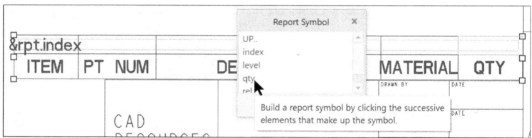

Figure 12.6(e) Click qty

Figure 12.6(f) &rpt.qty

Double-click on the third (middle) table cell of the Repeat Region **> asm…** [Fig. 12.6(g)] **> mbr…** [Fig. 12.6(h)] **> User Defined** [Fig. 12.6(i)] > Enter symbol text: *type* **DSC >** **Enter** [Fig. 12.6(j)]

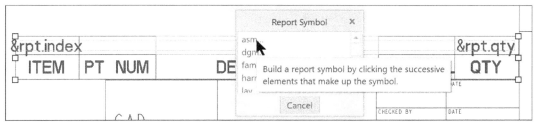

Figure 12.6(g) Click asm…

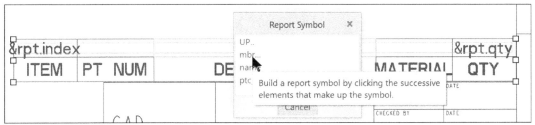

Figure 12.6(h) Click mbr…

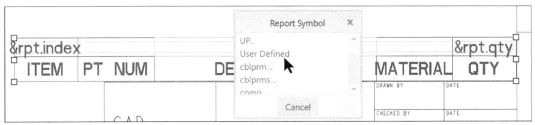

Figure 12.6(i) Click User Defined

| &rpt.index | | | &asm.mbr.DSC | | &rpt.qty |
| ITEM | PT NUM | | DESCRIPTION | MATERIAL | QTY |

Figure 12.6(j) &asm.mbr.DSC

Double-click on the fourth table cell of the Repeat Region > **asm...** > **mbr...** > **ptc_material...** > **PTC_MATERIAL_NAME** [Fig. 12.6(k)] > double-click on the second table cell of the Repeat Region > **asm...** > **mbr...** > **User Defined** > **PRTNO** > **Enter** > **LMB** > window in the title block and table > **RMB** > **Text Style** > Font **filled** > Note/Dimension- Horzontal **Center** > Vertical **Middle** > Height **3** > **Apply** [Fig. 12.6(l)]

> **OK** > **LMB** > [🔄 Update Tables] > **Save** > **File** > **Close**

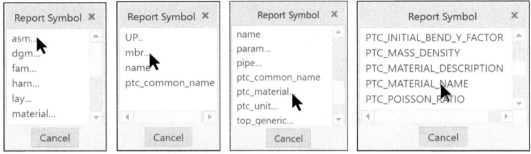

Figure 12.6(k) asm... > mbr... > ptc_material... > PTC_MATERIAL_NAME

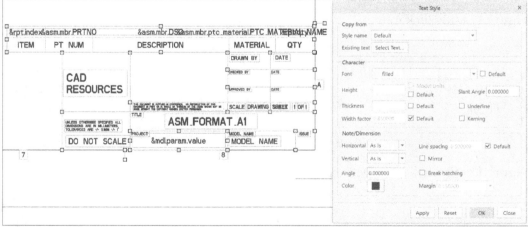

Figure 12.6(l) &asm.mbr.PRTNO

Adding parts-list (BOM) data

When you save your standard assembly format, the Drawing Table that represents your standard parts list is now included. You must be aware of the titles of the parameters under which the data is stored, so that you can add them properly to your components. As you add components to an assembly, Creo Parametric reads the parameters from them and updates the parts list. You can also see the same effect by adding these parameters after the drawing has been created. Creo Parametric also provides the capability of displaying Item Balloons on the first view that was placed on the drawing. To improve their appearance, you can move these balloons to other views and alter the locations where they attach.

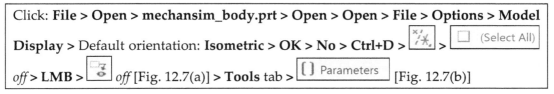

Click: **File > Open > mechansim_body.prt > Open > Open > File > Options > Model Display** > Default orientation: **Isometric > OK > No > Ctrl+D >** [icon] **>** [ ] (Select All) *off* **> LMB >** [icon] *off* [Fig. 12.7(a)] **> Tools** tab **>** [ ] Parameters [Fig. 12.7(b)]

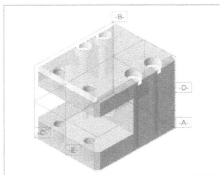

Figure 12.7(a) Mechansim_body

Figure 12.7(b) Parameters Dialog Box

429

Click: **Parameters** from Parameters dialog box > **Add Parameter** [Fig. 12.7(c)] > Name field should be highlighted [Fig. 12.7(d)], *type* **PRTNO** [Fig. 12.6(e)] > Designate ☑ > click in Type field [Fig. 12.7(f)] > ▼ [Fig. 12.7(g)] > **String**

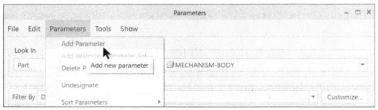

Figure 12.7(c) Add Parameter

Name	Type	Value	Designate	Access	Source
DESCRIPTION	String		☑	🔒Full	User-Defined
PROJECT	String		☑	🔒Full	User-Defined
MODELED_BY	String		☑	🔒Full	User-Defined
PTC_MATERIAL_NAME	String	METAL_STEEL_HIGH_CARBON	☐	🔒Full	User-Defined
PARAMETER_1	Real Nu	0.000000	☐	🔒Full	User-Defined

Figure 12.7(d) Adding Parameters

Name	Type	Value	Designate	Access	Source
DESCRIPTION	String		☑	🔒Full	User-Defined
PROJECT	String		☑	🔒Full	User-Defined
MODELED_BY	String		☑	🔒Full	User-Defined
PTC_MATERIAL_NAME	String	METAL_STEEL_HIGH_CARBON	☑	🔒Full	User-Defined
PRTNO	Real Number	0.000000	☑	🔒Full	User-Defined

Figure 12.7(e) Name PRTNO

MODELED_BY	String		☑	🔒Full	User-Defin
PTC_MATERIAL_NAME	String	METAL_STEEL_HIGH_CARBON	☑	🔒Full	User-Defin
PRTNO	Real Number	0.000000	☑	🔒Full	User-Defin

Figure 12.7(f) Click in Type Field- Real Number

Name	Type	Value	Designate	Access	Source
DESCRIPTION	String		☑	🔒Full	User-Defin
PROJECT	String		☑	🔒Full	User-Defin
MODELED_BY	String		☑	🔒Full	User-Defin
PTC_MATERIAL_NAME	String	METAL_STEEL_HIGH_CARBON	☑	🔒Full	User-Defin
PRTNO	Real Number	0.000000	☑	🔒Full	User-Defin
	Integer				
	Real Number				
	String				
	Yes No	Main		Properties...	
	Note	String			

Figure 12.7(g) String

Click in Value field > *type* **MEC101-A1** [Fig. 12.7(h)] > 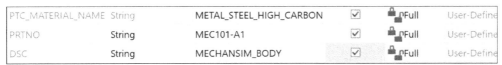 **Add new Parameter** [Fig. 12.7(i)] > **DSC** > ⬇ > **String** > click in Value field > **MECHANSIM_BODY** [Fig. 12.7(j)] > Designate ☑ *all* [Fig. 12.7(k)] > **OK > File > Save > Enter > File > Close**

| PTC_MATERIAL_NAME | String | METAL_STEEL_HIGH_CARBON | ☑ | 🔒ₚFull | User-Define |
| PRTNO | String | MEC101-A1 | ☑ | 🔒ₚFull | User-Define |

Figure 12.7(h) Value MEC101-A1 (text is case sensitive)

MODELED_BY	String		☑	🔒ₚFull	User-Define
PTC_MATERIAL_NAME	String	METAL_STEEL_HIGH_CARBON	☑	🔒ₚFull	User-Define
PRTNO	String	MEC101-A1	☑	🔒ₚFull	User-Define
PARAMETER_1	Real Number	0.000000	☐	🔒ₚFull	User-Define

Figure 12.7(i) Add New Parameter

PTC_MATERIAL_NAME	String	METAL_STEEL_HIGH_CARBON	☑	🔒ₚFull	User-Define
PRTNO	String	MEC101-A1	☑	🔒ₚFull	User-Define
DSC	String	MECHANSIM_BODY	☑	🔒ₚFull	User-Define

Figure 12.7(j) Add Description

Figure 12.7(k) Parameters

Click: **Ctrl+O > fitting.prt > Open > File > Prepare > Model Properties >** Materials **change > metal_aluminium_5052 > Assign > OK > Close > Tools** tab **> Parameters > Parameters > Add Parameter >** complete the parameters [Fig. 12.8(a)] **> OK > File > Save > Enter > File > Close**

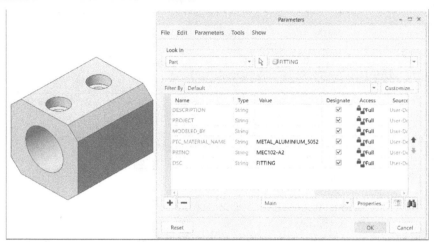

Figure 12.8(a) Fitting Parameters

Click: **File > Open > gripper.prt > Open > Tools** tab **> Parameters > Parameters > Add Parameter >** complete the parameters as shown [Fig. 12.8(b)] **> OK > File > Save > Enter > File > Close**

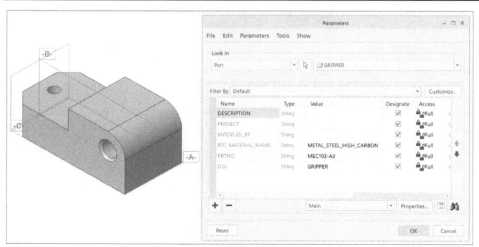

Figure 12.8(b) Gripper Parameters

Click: **File > Open > push_rod.prt > Open > Tools** tab **> Parameters > Parameters >
Add Parameter >** complete the parameters as shown [Fig. 12.8(c)] **> OK > File > Save
> Enter > File > Close**

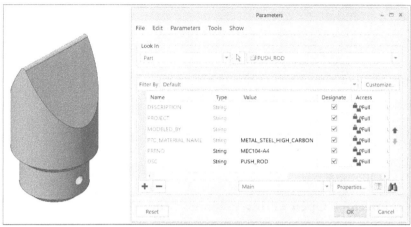

Figure 12.8(c) Push_Rod Parameters

Click: **File > Open > plate.prt > Open > File > Prepare > Model Properties >** Material
change > metal_aluminium_5052 > Assign > OK > Close > Tools tab **> Parameters >
Parameters > Add Parameter >** complete the missing and new parameters [Fig.
12.8(d)] **> OK > File > Save > OK > File > Close File > Save > Enter**

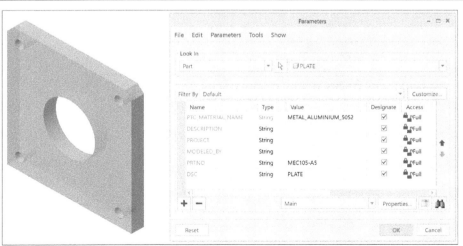

Figure 12.8(d) Plate Parameters

Click: **File > Open > piston.prt > Open > Tools** tab **> Parameters > Parameters > Add Parameter >** complete the parameters [Fig. 12.8(e)] **> OK > File > Save > File > Close**

Figure 12.8(e) Piston Parameters

Click: **File > Open > connector > Open > File > Prepare > Model Properties >** Material **change >** 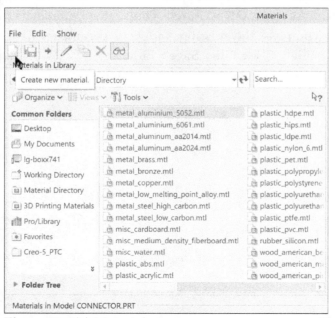 **Create new material** [Fig. 12.9(a)] > Name field **PURCHASED** [Fig. 12.9(b)] > Description: **CONNECTOR > Save to Library**

Figure 12.9(a) Materials   **Figure 12.9(b)** Material Definition

Navigate to the correct directory, click: **OK** > navigate to the correct directory (you should be able to click on **Working Directory**) > **purchased.mtl** > **OK** > **OK** > **Close** > **Tools** tab > ⌨ Model Information [Fig. 12.9(c)] > 🐚 *close*

Figure 12.9(c) Model Info, MATERIAL FILENAME: PURCHASED

Click: **Tools** tab > **Parameters** > add the Parameters > Designate ☑ [Figs. 12.9(d)] > **OK** > **Ctrl+S** > **OK** > **File** > **Close** (set Parameters for the other two standard parts and change to unique colors)

Figure 12.9(d) Connector

Press: **Ctrl+O** > SOC_HD_CAP_SCR-12 [Fig. 12.9(e)] > **Open** > **File** > **Prepare** > **Model Properties** > Material **change** > navigate to the correct directory where you saved the *purchased.mtl* material > double-click on **purchased.mtl** > **OK** > **Close** > **Tools** tab > **Parameters** > check Parameters > **Model Information** > ✗ > **OK** > **Save** > **File** > **Close**

Figure 12.9(e) SOC_HD_CAP_SCR-12

Press: **Ctrl+O > pin.prt** [Fig. 12.9(f)] **> Open > File > Prepare > Model Properties >** **Material change > Working Directory > purchased.mtl > OK > Close > Tools** tab **> Parameters >** check Parameters **> OK > Ctrl+S > OK > File > Close**

Figure 12.9(f) Pin

Click: **File > Open > mechanism.asm > Open >** 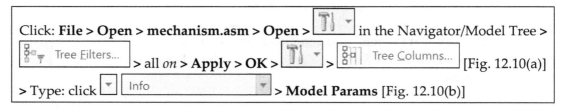 in the Navigator/Model Tree > Tree Filters... **> all** *on* **> Apply > OK >** > Tree Columns... [Fig. 12.10(a)] **> Type:** click Info **> Model Params** [Fig. 12.10(b)]

Figure 12.10(a) Tree Columns

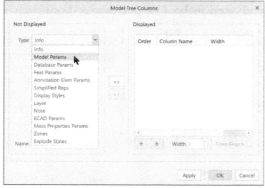

Figure 12.10(b) Model Params

Double-click in the Name field > *type* **PRTNO** > **Enter** [Fig. 12.10(c)] > double-click in the Name field > *type* **DSC** > **Enter** [Fig. 12.10(d)] > **PTC_MATERIAL_NAME** > ⌐>>⌐ [Fig. 12.10(e)] > **Apply** > **OK** [Fig. 12.10(f)] > **Regenerate** > **Save** (if something is incorrect or missing open the part model and edit)

Figure 12.10(c) Type in the Name field: PRTNO

Figure 12.10(d) PRTNO and DSC

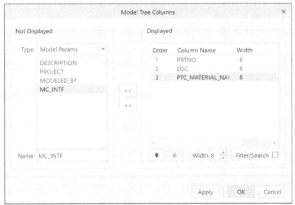

Figure 12.10(e) PTC_MATERIAL_NAME

437

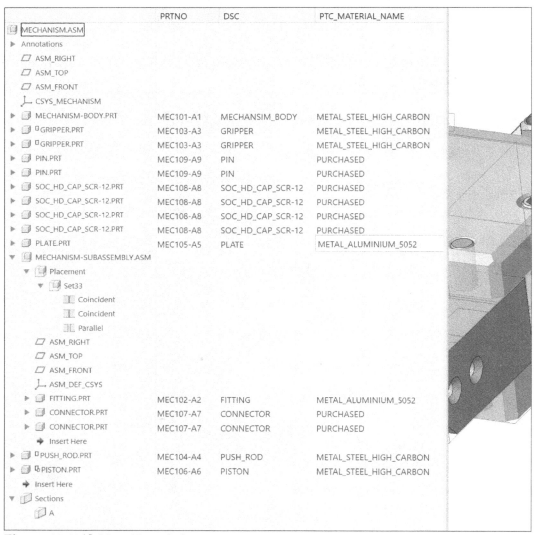

	PRTNO	DSC	PTC_MATERIAL_NAME
MECHANISM.ASM			
▶ Annotations			
⬭ ASM_RIGHT			
⬭ ASM_TOP			
⬭ ASM_FRONT			
⌙ CSYS_MECHANISM			
▶ MECHANISM-BODY.PRT	MEC101-A1	MECHANSIM_BODY	METAL_STEEL_HIGH_CARBON
▶ GRIPPER.PRT	MEC103-A3	GRIPPER	METAL_STEEL_HIGH_CARBON
▶ GRIPPER.PRT	MEC103-A3	GRIPPER	METAL_STEEL_HIGH_CARBON
▶ PIN.PRT	MEC109-A9	PIN	PURCHASED
▶ PIN.PRT	MEC109-A9	PIN	PURCHASED
▶ SOC_HD_CAP_SCR-12.PRT	MEC108-A8	SOC_HD_CAP_SCR-12	PURCHASED
▶ SOC_HD_CAP_SCR-12.PRT	MEC108-A8	SOC_HD_CAP_SCR-12	PURCHASED
▶ SOC_HD_CAP_SCR-12.PRT	MEC108-A8	SOC_HD_CAP_SCR-12	PURCHASED
▶ SOC_HD_CAP_SCR-12.PRT	MEC108-A8	SOC_HD_CAP_SCR-12	PURCHASED
▶ PLATE.PRT	MEC105-A5	PLATE	METAL_ALUMINIUM_5052
▼ MECHANISM-SUBASSEMBLY.ASM			
▼ Placement			
▼ Set33			
⫾⫾ Coincident			
⫾⫾ Coincident			
⫾⫾ Parallel			
⬭ ASM_RIGHT			
⬭ ASM_TOP			
⬭ ASM_FRONT			
⌙ ASM_DEF_CSYS			
▶ FITTING.PRT	MEC102-A2	FITTING	METAL_ALUMINIUM_5052
▶ CONNECTOR.PRT	MEC107-A7	CONNECTOR	PURCHASED
▶ CONNECTOR.PRT	MEC107-A7	CONNECTOR	PURCHASED
➜ Insert Here			
▶ PUSH_ROD.PRT	MEC104-A4	PUSH_ROD	METAL_STEEL_HIGH_CARBON
▶ PISTON.PRT	MEC106-A6	PISTON	METAL_STEEL_HIGH_CARBON
➜ Insert Here			
▼ Sections			
A			

Figure 12.10(f) New Tree Columns

438

Resize the Model Tree and Model Tree columns. From the Model Tree, pick on **MECHANISM-SUBASSEMBLY.ASM** > click in the **PRTNO** field [Fig. 12.11(a)] > Type: click [Real Number ▼] > **String** > click in the Value field, *type* **MEC100-SUB-ASM** > [☑ Designated] > click in the Description field, *type* **part number** [Fig. 12.11(b)] > **OK** > click in the **DSC** field > Type: [Real Number ▼] > **String** > click in the Value field, *type* **MECHANISM-SUBASSEMBLY.ASM** > [☑ Designated] > click in the Description field, *type* **SUB-ASSEMBLY** > **OK** > **LMB** in the Graphics Window to deselect > **Ctrl+S** > regenerate models if warned > **Model** tab > [Regenerate] [Fig. 12.11(c)] > **File** > **Close**

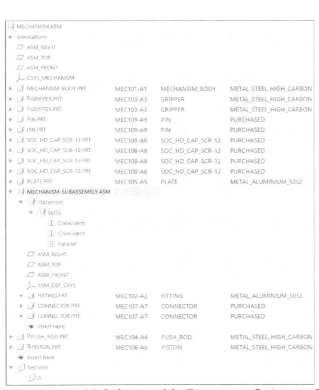

Figure 12.11(a) Subassembly Parameter String   **Figure 12.11(b)** MEC100-SUB-ASM

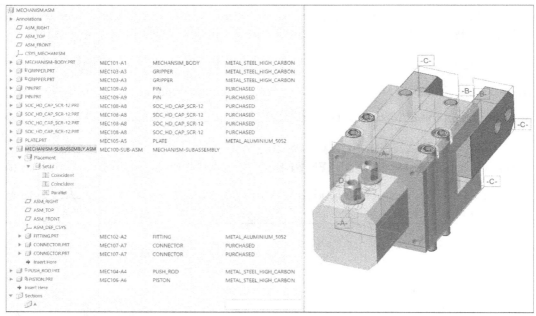

Figure 12.11(c) Mechanism

Quiz

1. What is the difference between part and assembly drawing formats?
2. Name three parameters that can be added to a component model.
3. Why is a parametric BOM Table important to an assembly drawing?
4. What is a .dtl file?
5. How do you add parameters to a component?
6. What is a Repeat region?
7. What is a Purchased item, and what does it take the place of?
8. What are Report Symbols?

This completes Chapter 12.

Assembly drawing and BOM with ballooning

Creo Parametric incorporates a great deal of functionality into drawings of assemblies. You can assign parameters to parts in the assembly that can be displayed on a parts list in an assembly drawing. The format for an assembly is usually different from the format used for detail drawings. The most significant difference is the presence of a Parts List. A parts list is a Drawing Table formatted to represent a bill of materials in a drawing. By defining parameters in the parts in your assembly that agree with the specific format of the parts list, you make it possible for Creo Parametric to add pertinent data to the assembly drawing's parts list automatically as components are added to the assembly. After the parts list and parameters have been added, Creo Parametric can balloon the assembly drawing automatically.

Objectives
1. Create an Assembly Drawing
2. Generate a Parts List from a Bill of Materials (BOM)
3. Balloon an assembly drawing
4. Create a section assembly view and change component visibility
5. Create an exploded view for the drawing

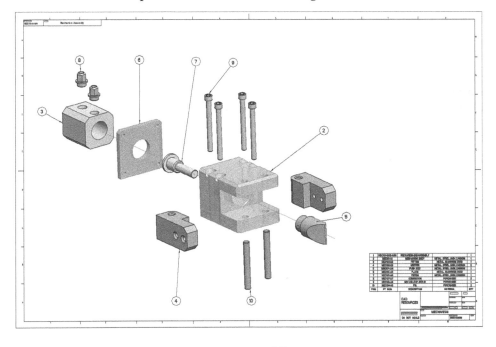

Chapter 13 STEPS

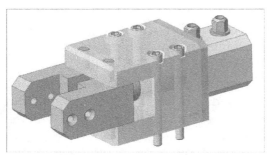

Figure 13.1(a) Mechanism

Mechanism Assembly Drawing

The format for an assembly drawing is different from the format used for detail drawings. The most significant difference is the presence of a parts list.

A parts list is a *Drawing Table object* that is formatted to represent a bill of material (BOM) in a drawing. By defining parameters in the parts in your assembly that agree with the specific format of the parts list, you make it possible for Creo Parametric to add pertinent data to the assembly drawing parts list automatically, as components are added to the assembly. The parameters (and their values) have been established for each part. The assembly format with related parameters in a parts list table has been created and saved in your (format) directory. You can now create a drawing of the assembly, where the parts list will be generated automatically, and the assembly ballooned.

In this chapter you will create an assembly drawing of the Mechanism [Fig. 13.1(a)]. In Chapter Four a drawing of the subassembly was created [Fig. 13.1(b)].

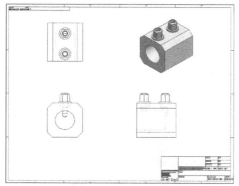

Figure 13.1(b) Mechanism Subassembly drawing

Click: **Open > mechanism.asm > Open > File > Close** *(the assembly will remain "in session")* **> Ctrl+N >** ⊙ 🖳 Drawing **>** Name **MECHANISM >** ☐ Use default template [Fig. 13.2(a)] **> OK >** ⊙ Empty with format **>** Format **Browse >** Common Folders **Working Directory >** select **asm_format_a1.frm** [Fig. 13.2(b)] **> Open** [Fig. 13.2(c)] **> OK >** ✗⁄⁄ **>** ☐ (Select All)

Figure 13.2(a) New Drawing

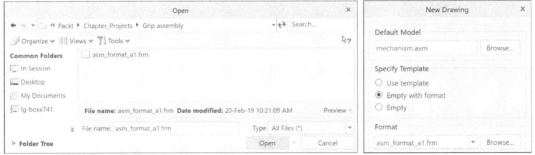

Figure 13.2(b) asm_format_a1.frm   **Figure 13.2(c)** New Drawing Dialog Box

Select **Table** tab > zoom in on the title block > window-in to select the table [Fig. 13.3(a)] > move table above the title block > **File** > **Prepare** > **Drawing Properties** > Detail Options **change** > ⬚ **Open a configuration file** > 🗋 asm_a1_properties.dtl > **Open** > **Apply** > **Close** > **Close** > pick on the corner of the table > move as needed [Fig. 13.3(b)] > **LMB** > **Ctrl+S**

Figure 13.3(a) BOM and Title Block

ITEM	PT NUM	DESCRIPTION	MATERIAL	QTY
1	MEC100-SUB-ASM	MECHANISM-SUBASSEMBLY		1
	Portion:ID2(DETAIL ENTITY)	MECHANSIM BODY	METAL STEEL HIGH CARBON	
3	MEC102-A2	FITTING	METAL ALUMINIUM 5052	
4	MEC103-A3	GRIPPER	METAL STEEL HIGH CARBON	
5	MEC104-A4	PUSH ROD	METAL STEEL HIGH CARBON	
6	MEC105-A5	PLATE	METAL ALUMINIUM 5052	
7	MEC106-A6	PISTON	METAL STEEL HIGH CARBON	
8	MEC107-A7	CONNECTOR	PURCHASED	2
9	MEC108-A8	SOC HD CAP SCR-12	PURCHASED	4
10	MEC109-A9	PIN	PURCHASED	2

CAD RESOURCES

DRAWN BY	DATE
CHECKED BY	DATE
APPROVED BY	DATE

THIS DOCUMENT IS SUPPLIED IN CONFIDENCE. NO REPRODUCTION OF THIS DOCUMENT IN PART OR IN WHOLE OR THEREOF OF THE ITEMS SHOWN MAY BE MADE WITHOUT THE COPYRIGHT OWNERS WRITTEN PERMISSION

SCALE 1:1   SHEET 1 OF 1

TITLE   **MECHANISM**

UNLESS OTHERWISE SPECIFIED ALL DIMENSIONS ARE IN MILLIMETERS, TOLERANCES ARE +/- 0.5MM +/- 1°

DO NOT SCALE

PROJECT   MODEL NAME   MECHANISM   ISSUE

7   8

Figure 13.3(b) Reposition the BOM

444

Select the second column [Fig. 13.3(c)] > **Width** [Fig. 13.3(d)] > **40** > **Enter** > **Preview** [Fig. 13.3(e)] > **OK** > change the MATERIAL column to **60** and the ITEM and QTY columns to **14** > **OK** > reposition the table as needed [Fig. 13.3(f)] > **LMB** > 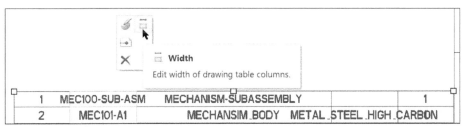 **Refit** [Fig. 13.3(g)] > **Ctrl+S** > **OK**

1	MEC100-SUB-ASM	MECHANISM-SUBASSEMBLY		1
2	MEC101 Cell:Table	MECHANSIM BODY	METAL STEEL HIGH CARBON	
3	MEC102-A2	FITTING	METAL ALUMINIUM 5052	

Figure 13.3(c) Select the Cell

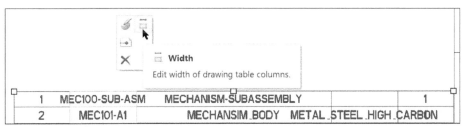

| 1 | MEC100-SUB-ASM | MECHANISM-SUBASSEMBLY | | 1 |
| 2 | MEC101-A1 | MECHANSIM BODY | METAL STEEL HIGH CARBON | |

Figure 13.3(d) Width

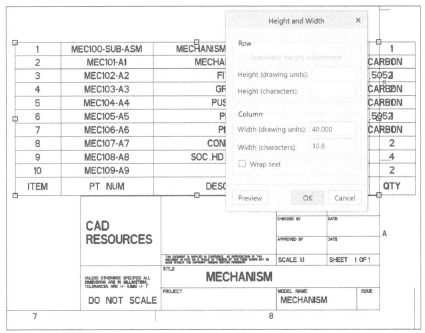

Figure 13.3(e) New Width

445

ITEM	PT NUM	DESCRIPTION	MATERIAL	QTY
1	MEC100-SUB-ASM	MECHANISM-SUBASSEMBLY		1
2	MEC101-A1	MECHANSIM BODY	METAL STEEL HIGH CARBON	1
3	MEC102-A2	FITTING	METAL ALUMINIUM 5052	1
4	MEC103-A3	GRIPPER	METAL STEEL HIGH CARBON	2
5	MEC104-A4	PUSH ROD	METAL STEEL HIGH CARBON	1
6	MEC105-A5	PLATE	METAL ALUMINIUM 5052	1
7	MEC106-A6	PISTON	METAL STEEL HIGH CARBON	1
8	MEC107-A7	CONNECTOR	PURCHASED	2
9	MEC108-A8	SOC HD CAP SCR-12	PURCHASED	4
10	MEC109-A9	PIN	PURCHASED	2

CAD RESOURCES

DRAWN BY		DATE	
CHECKED BY		DATE	
APPROVED BY		DATE	
THIS DOCUMENT IS SUPPLIED IN CONFIDENCE. NO REPRODUCTION OF THIS DOCUMENT IN PART OR IN WHOLE (IS THEREIN OF THE TERMS SHOWN) MAY BE MADE WITHOUT THE COPYRIGHT OWNERS WRITTEN PERMISSION		SCALE 1:1	SHEET 1 OF 1

UNLESS OTHERWISE SPECIFIED ALL DIMENSIONS ARE IN MILLIMETERS. TOLERANCES ARE +/- 0.5MM +/- 1°

DO NOT SCALE

TITLE **MECHANISM**

| PROJECT | MODEL NAME **MECHANISM** | ISSUE |

Figure 13.3(f) BOM Table

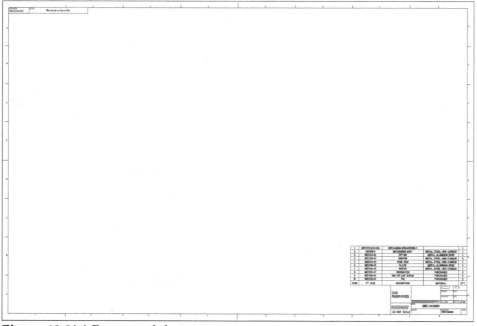

Figure 13.3(g) Formatted drawing

Click: **Layout** tab > in the Graphics Window, press **RMB** > [⬜ General View] > **No Combined State** [Fig. 13.4(a)] > **OK** > [⇒ Select CENTER POINT for drawing view.] *(pick approximately where you want a Front drawing view)* > Model view names **LEFT** [Fig. 13.4(b)] > **Apply** > Default Orientation **Isometric** > **View Display** > Display style **No Hidden** > Tangent edges **Dimmed** > **Apply** [Fig. 13.4(c)] > **Cancel** > with the view selected > **RMB** > [🔒 Lock View Movement] *off* > move view to be positioned as a "Front Drawing View" (*Drawing views* are different from *Model views*.)

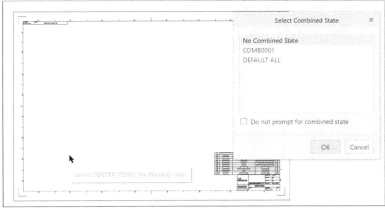

Figure 13.4(a) No Combined State

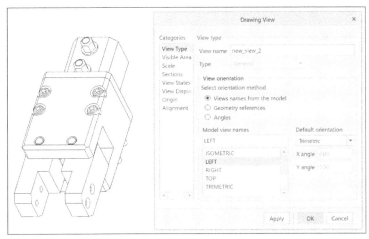

Figure 13.4(b) Drawing View Dialog Box

447

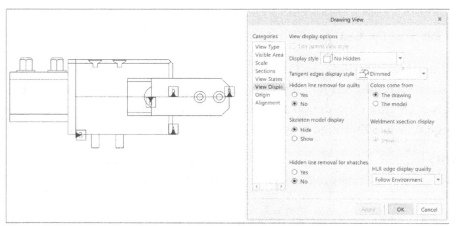

Figure 13.4(c) Front Drawing View Display Selections

With the Front drawing view selected > double-click on **SCALE** >

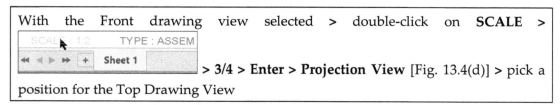

> 3/4 > **Enter** > **Projection View** [Fig. 13.4(d)] > pick a position for the Top Drawing View

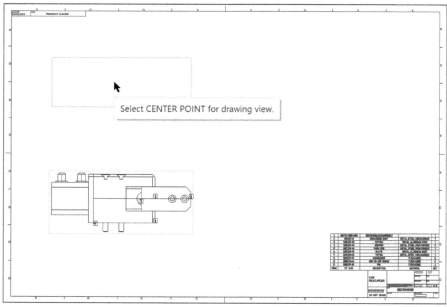

Figure 13.4(d) Projection View

Double-click on the Front View *or select view* > *RMB* > *Properties* [Fig. 13.5(a)] > Categories **Sections** > ⊙ 2D cross-section > ✓ A [Fig. 13.5(b)] > **Apply** > **OK**

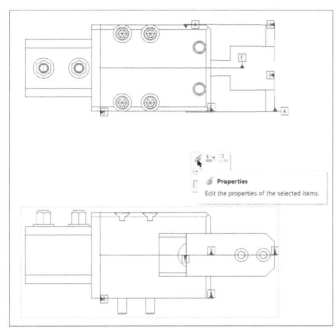

Figure 13.5(a) View Properties

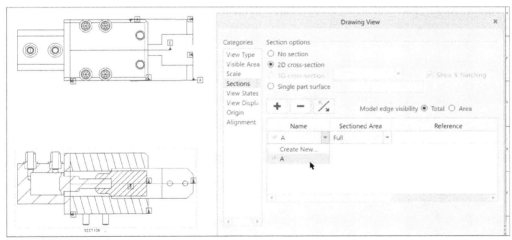

Figure 13.5(b) SECTION A-A

Click: **View** tab > 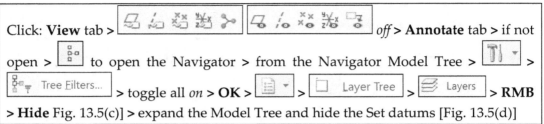 *off* > **Annotate** tab > if not open > ⧉ to open the Navigator > from the Navigator Model Tree > 🔽 > ▤ Tree Filters... > toggle all *on* > **OK** > ▤ ▾ > ☐ Layer Tree > ▤ Layers > **RMB** > **Hide** Fig. 13.5(c)] > expand the Model Tree and hide the Set datums [Fig. 13.5(d)]

Figure 13.5(c) Hide Layers

Figure 13.5(d) Hide all Datum Features

Click: **File** > **Prepare** > **Drawing Properties** > **Detail Options** > **change** > *draw_arrow_length 6* > **Enter** > *draw_arrow_width 2* > **Enter** > *max_balloon_radius 8* > **Enter** *min_balloon_radius 8* > **Enter** > *crossec_arrow_length 8* > **Enter** > *crossec _arrow_width 4* > **Enter** > *def_view_text_height 6* > **Enter** > **Apply** > Sort: **As Set** > 🔲 **Save a copy** > File name: **asm_a1_properties.dtl** > **OK** > **Close** > **Close** > **Ctrl+S** > **OK** > **Layout** tab > select the Front Drawing View [Fig. 13.6(a)] > **RMB** > **Add Arrows** > select the Top Drawing View [Fig. 13.6(b)] > **LMB** > **Save**

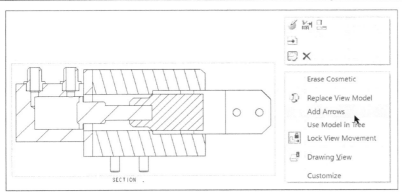

Figure 13.6(a) Add Arrows

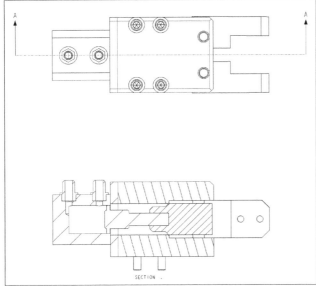

Figure 13.6(b) Section A-A

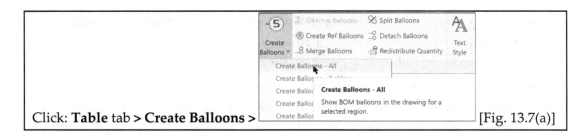

Click: **Table** tab **> Create Balloons >**   [Fig. 13.7(a)]

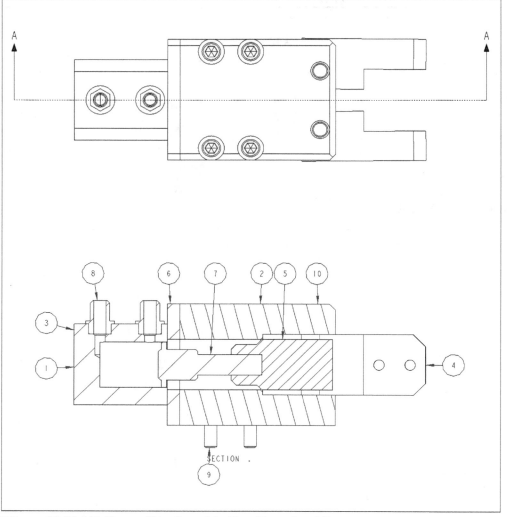

Figure 13.7(a) Balloons Displayed in Top Drawing View

452

While pressing the **Ctrl** key, pick on balloons 1, 9, and 10 > **RMB** > **Move Item to View** > pick on the Top Drawing view [Fig. 13.7(b)] > pick a balloon to move > reposition the balloon > **RMB** > **Edit Attachment** > **On Entity** > pick on an edge to reposition the arrow > **MMB** [Fig. 13.7(c)] > **LMB**

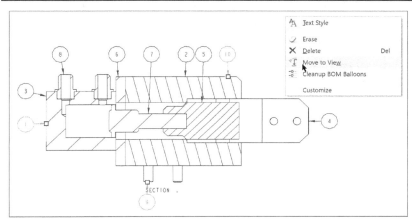

Figure 13.7(b) RMB > Move Item to View

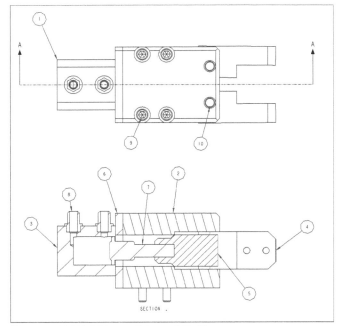

Figure 13.7(c) Repositioned Balloons

Most companies (and as per drafting standards) require that rounded purchased items, such as nuts, bolts, studs, springs, and die pins be excluded from sectioning even when the section cutting plane passes through them.

Click: **Layout** tab > double-click on the crosshatching in the Front Drawing view [Fig. 13.8] (the Pate is now active) > **Spacing** > **Half** > **Half** > **Next** (Push_Rod is now active) > **Next** (Piston is now active) > **Spacing** > **Half** > **Angle 120** > **Next** (Fitting is now active) > **Spacing** > **Half** > **Angle 150** > **Next** (Connector is now active) > **Fill** > **Next** (Connector is now active) > **Fill** > **Next** (Mechanism-body is now active) **Angle 120** > **Next** > **Done** > **LMB** > **Ctrl+S**

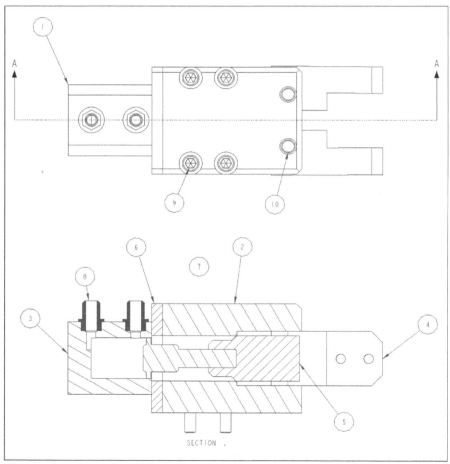

Figure 13.8 Sectioned View

454

Exploded Mechanism Drawing

The process required to place an exploded view on a drawing is like adding assembly orthographic views. The BOM will display all components on this sheet.

Click: **Layout** tab > **New Sheet** > 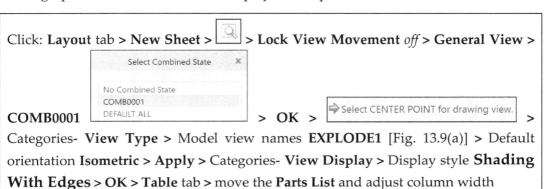 > **Lock View Movement** *off* > **General View** >

COMB0001 > **OK** >

Categories- **View Type** > Model view names **EXPLODE1** [Fig. 13.9(a)] > Default orientation **Isometric** > **Apply** > Categories- **View Display** > Display style **Shading With Edges** > **OK** > **Table** tab > move the **Parts List** and adjust column width

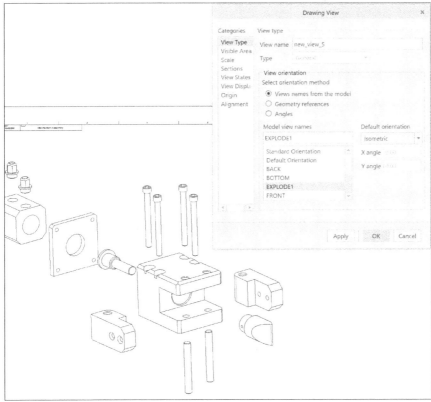

Figure 13.9(a) Drawing View options

455

Select **Layout** tab > select the view > **Annotation** tab > [🔲] **Show Model Annotations**
> [🔲] > select the large hole in the **Fitting** >

Show	Type	Name
☑	/	A_1

[Fig. 13.9(b)]
> **Apply** > **Cancel** > click on the centerline and drag (axis) to extend both ends > **LMB**
[Fig. 13.9(c)] > **Save**

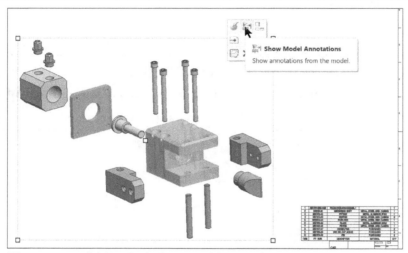

Figure 13.19(b) Exploded Assembly Drawing

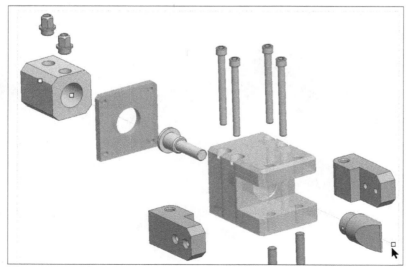

Figure 13.9(c) Drag the Axis

456

Click: **Table** tab > **Create Balloons** > | Create Balloons - All | > | ⇨ Select a region. | pick in the
BOM field > delete **Balloon 1** > modify **Text Style** to **6** height and **filled** on Balloons >
reposition the balloons and attachment points > **Layout** tab > double-click on balloon
5 > **Cancel** > | ⚡ Arrow Style ▾ | > | ─○ Dot | > pick on the **Push_Rod** [Fig. 13.10] > **LMB**
[Fig. 13.11(a)]

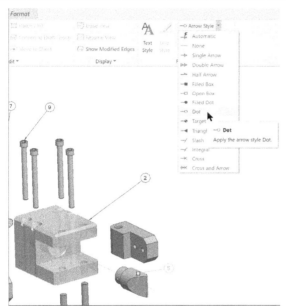

Figure 13.10 Exploded View

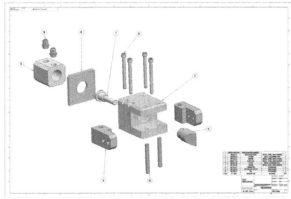

Figure 13.11(a) Completed Drawing, Sheet 2

Click: **Layout** tab [Fig. 13.11(b)] > Sheet 1 > **Ctrl+S > File > Save**

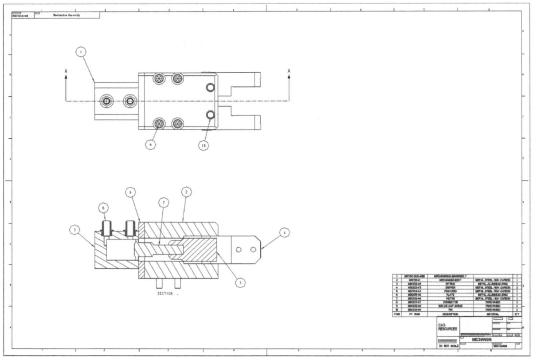

Figure 11.11(b) Completed Drawing, Sheet 1

Quiz

1. Name five things that part's list could contain.
2. How do you display dimension, notes, and centerlines?
3. What is a Repeat region?
4. What are some of the items that can be modified using Text Style?
5. View Display allows for what changes to a drawing view?
6. How do you edit a Balloon's text, leader, and arrow style?
7. How do you navigate between sheets?

This completes Chapter 13

PART 5: Advanced capabilities

In this Part you will utilize commends and techniques introduced in the first four Parts of the book. New and more advanced procedures will be used to complete the projects.

In Part 5 the Chapters step-by-step commands have been simplified since it is assumed that many of the capabilities have been previously mastered. Chapters 18-20 are "video lecture chapters". Using knowledge obtained from the book and instructions provided in the lecture you will complete these assembly assignments.

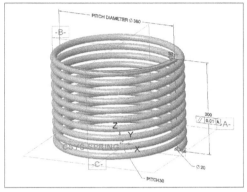

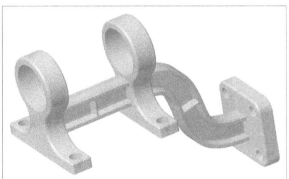

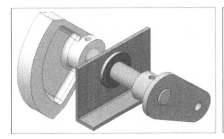
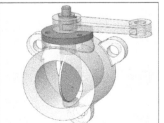

CHAPTER 14: Rib, Draft, Insert, Shell, Suppress, and Render

The Draft feature adds a draft angle between surfaces. A wide range of parts incorporate drafts into their design. Casting, injection mold, and die parts normally have drafted surfaces. Suppressing features by using the Suppress command temporarily removes them from regeneration. Suppressed features can be "unsuppressed" at any time. Text can be included in a sketch for extruded extrusions and cuts, trimming surfaces, and cosmetic features. To decrease regeneration time of the model, text can be suppressed after it has been created. Text can also be drafted. Trajectory ribs are most often used to strengthen plastic parts that include a base and a shell or other hollow area between pocket surfaces. The rib has a top and a bottom. The bottom is the end that intersects the part surface.

Objectives
1. Create Draft/Taper geometry
2. Shell a part
3. Suppress and Resume a set of suppressed features
4. Create a swept cut
5. Create Text features on parts
6. Create Trajectory Ribs
7. Create a section
8. Use Insert mode to add new features at any point in the modeling sequence
9. Render the mode

Shells

The Shell Tool enables you to remove a surface or surfaces from the solid, then hollows out the inside of the solid, leaving a shell of a specified wall thickness. If you flip the thickness side by entering a negative value, dragging a handle, or using the **Change thickness direction** icon, the shell thickness is added to the outside of the part. If you do not select a surface to remove, a "closed" shell is created, with the whole inside of the part hollowed out and no access to the inside. In this case, you can add the necessary cuts or holes to achieve the proper geometry at a later time.

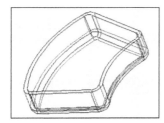 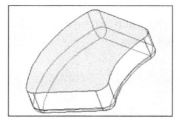 

When defining a shell, you can also select surfaces where you want to assign a different thickness. You can specify independent thickness values for each such surface. However, you cannot enter negative thickness values, or flip the thickness side, for these surfaces. The thickness side is determined by the default thickness of the shell. When Creo Parametric makes the shell, all the features that were added to the solid before you started the Shell Tool are hollowed out. Therefore, the order of feature creation is very important when you use the Shell Tool. To access the Shell Tool, click icon in the **Model** tab **Engineering Group**. The **Thickness** box lets you change the value for the default shell thickness. You can type the new value, or select a recently used value from the drop-down list.

In the graphics window, you can use the shortcut menu (press **RMB**) to access the following options:

- **Removed Surfaces** Activates the collector of surfaces. You can select any number of surfaces
- **Non-Default Thickness** Activates the collector of surfaces with a different thickness
- **Exclude Surfaces** Activates the collector of excluded surfaces
- **Clear** Remove all references from the collector that is currently active
- **Flip** Change the shell side direction

461

The Shell Dashboard displays the following slide-up/down panels (tabs):

- **References** Contains the collector of references used in the Shell feature
- **Options Contains the collector of Excluded surfaces**
- **Properties** Contains the feature name and an icon to access feature information

The **References** slide-up/down panel (tab) contains the following elements:

- The **Removed surfaces** collector lets you select the surfaces to be removed. If you do not select any surfaces, a "closed" shell is created.
- The **Non-default thickness** collector lets you select surfaces where you want to assign a different thickness. For each surface included in this collector, you can specify an individual thickness value.

The **Properties** panel (tab) contains the Name text box

Name | SHELL_ID_200, where you can type a custom name for the shell feature, to replace the default name. It also contains the icon that you can click to display information about this feature in the Browser.

Text Extrusions

When you are modeling, **Text** can be included in a sketch for extruded extrusions and cuts, trimming surfaces, and cosmetic features. The characters that are in an extruded feature use the font **font3d** as the default. Other fonts are available.

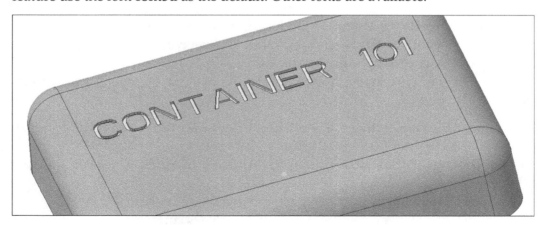

Reordering features

You can move features forward or backward in the feature creation (regeneration) order list, thus changing the order in which features are regenerated. You can reorder features in the Model Tree by dragging one or more features to a new location in the feature list. If you try to move a child feature to a higher position than its parent feature, the parent feature moves with the child feature in context, so that the parent/child relationship is maintained.

You can reorder multiple features in one operation, as long as these features appear in *consecutive* order. Feature reorder *cannot* occur under the following conditions:

- **Parents** Cannot be moved so that their regeneration occurs after the regeneration of their children
- **Children** Cannot be moved so that their regeneration occurs before the regeneration of their parents

You can select the features to be reordered by choosing an option:

- **Select** Select features to reorder by picking on the screen or from the Model Tree
- **Layer** Select all features from a layer by selecting the layer
- **Range** Specify the range of features by entering the regeneration numbers of the starting and ending features

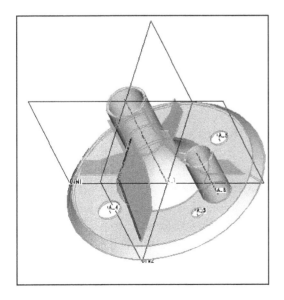
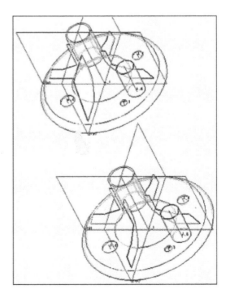

Inserting Features

Normally, Creo Parametric adds a new feature after the last existing feature in the part, including suppressed features. Insert Mode allows you to add new features at any point in the feature sequence, except before the base feature or after the last feature. You can also insert features using the Model Tree. There is an arrow-shaped icon on the Model Tree that indicates where features will be inserted upon creation. By default, it is always at the end of the Model Tree. You may drag the location of the *arrow* higher or lower in the tree to insert features at a different point. When the *arrow* is dropped at a new location, the model is rolled backward or forward in response to the insertion *arrow* being moved higher or lower in the tree.

Suppressing and resuming features

Suppressing a feature is similar to removing the feature from regeneration temporarily. You can "unsuppress" (**Resume**) suppressed features at any time. Features on a part can be suppressed to simplify the part model and decrease regeneration time. For example, while you work on one end of a shaft, it may be desirable to suppress features on the other end of the shaft. Similarly, while working on a complex assembly, you can suppress some of the features and components for which the detail is not essential to the current assembly process.

Unlike other features, the base feature cannot be suppressed. If you are not satisfied with your base feature, you can redefine the section of the feature, or you can delete it and start over again. Select feature(s) to suppress by: selecting it, picking on it from the Model Tree, specifying a *range*, entering its *feature number* or *identifier*, or using *layers*.

You can use **Suppress** and **Resume** to simplify the part before inserting features such as text extrusions. In addition, you may wish to suppress the text extrusion if there is other work to be done on the part. Text extrusions take time to regenerate and increase the file size considerably. Suppressing features by using the **Suppress** command temporarily removes them from regeneration. Suppressed features can be "unsuppressed" (**Resume**) at any time. It is sometimes convenient to suppress text extrusions and rounds to speed up regeneration of the model. Suppressing removes the item from regeneration and requires you to resume the item later. **Hide** is another option. Creo Parametric allows you to hide and unhide some types of model entities. When you hide an item, Creo Parametric removes the item from the graphics window. The hidden item remains in the Model Tree list, and its icon dims to reveal its hidden status. When you unhide an item, its icon returns to normal display (undimmed) and the item is redisplayed in the graphics window. The hidden status of items is saved with the model. Unlike the suppression of items, hidden items are regenerated. **Text** can be included in a sketch for extruded extrusions and cuts, trimming surfaces, and cosmetic features. To decrease regeneration time of the model, text can be suppressed after it has been created. Text can also be drafted.

Drafts

The **Draft** feature adds a draft angle between surfaces. A wide range of parts incorporate drafts into their design. Casting, injection mold, and die parts normally have drafted surfaces. When creating an **Extrude** feature a **Taper** can be imbedded, eliminating the need to use a separate Draft feature. When creating a **Trajectory Rib** the rib **Drafts** can be integrated into the feature.

The **Draft Tool** adds a draft angle between two individual surfaces or to a series of selected planar surfaces. During draft creation, remember the following:

- You can draft only the surfaces that are formed by tabulated cylinders or planes.
- The draft direction must be normal to the neutral plane if a draft surface is cylindrical.
- You cannot draft surfaces with fillets around the edge boundary. However, you can draft the surfaces first, and then fillet the edges.

The following table lists the terminology used in drafts.

TERM	DEFINITION
Draft surfaces	Model surfaces selected for drafting.
Draft Hinges	Draft surfaces are pivoted about the intersection of the neutral plane with the draft surfaces.
Pull direction	Direction that is used to measure the draft angle. It is defined as normal to the reference plane.
Draft angle	Angle between the draft direction and the resulting drafted surfaces. If the draft surfaces are split, you can define two independent angles for each portion of the draft.
Direction of rotation	Direction that defines how draft surfaces are rotated with respect to the neutral plane or neutral curve.
Split areas	Areas of the draft surfaces to which you can apply different draft angles. Split object is also a choice.

Chapter 14 STEPS

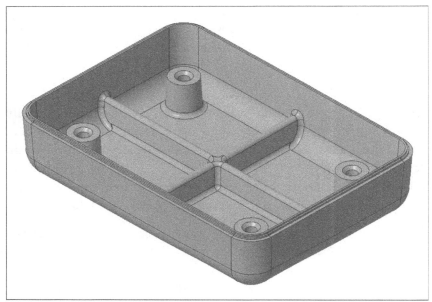

Figure 14.1(a) Container

Container

The Container is a plastic injection-molded part [Fig. 14.1(a)]. A variety of drafts and tapers will be used in the design of this part. A *raised text extrusion* will be modeled on the outside of the Container.

Select Working Directory > OK > Ctrl+N > Name **Container > OK > File > Options > Configuration Editor > Import/Export > Import configuration file >** select your previously created and saved file (**Creo_texbook.pro**) **> Open > OK > No > File > Prepare > Model Properties >** Units **change >** Units Manager **millimeter Newton > Set > Interpret > Close >** Material **change >** double-click on **➡PLASTIC_POLYURETHANE_MOLDED >** convert the units **Yes > OK > Close >** rename the coordinate system to **CSYS_CONTAINER > Enter > Ctrl+S > Enter > File > Options > Customize Ribbon > Import > Import customization file >** select your previously saved **.ui** file (creo_parametric_customization.ui) **> Import > Open > Import for all modes > Import > OK > LMB**

Make the first extrusion a **350mm** (width) **X 250mm** (height) **X 80mm** (depth) using a **Center Rectangle** sketch feature. Sketch on datum **TOP** [Figs. 14.1(b-c)]. Incorporate the draft angle using a Taper instead of adding a separate draft feature.

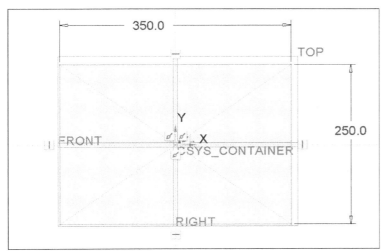

Figure 14.1(b) Sketch on the TOP Datum

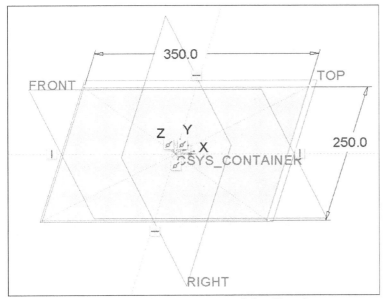

Figure 14.1(c) Standard Orientation of the Sketch

467

RMB > 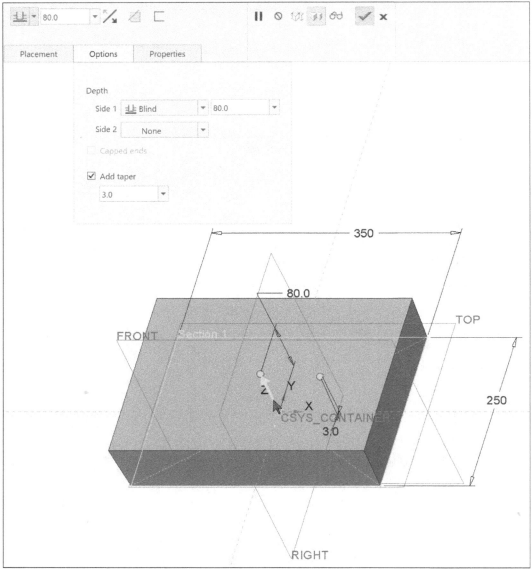 to compete the sketch **> Options** tab > ☑ Add taper **> 3 > Enter** [Fig. 14.1(d)] **> MMB > Ctrl+S > LMB**

Placement | Options | Properties

Depth
Side 1 ⊥ Blind ▾ 80.0 ▾
Side 2   None ▾

☐ Capped ends

☑ Add taper
3.0 ▾

Figure 14.1(d) Adding a 3-degree Taper

Add a **30mm** round [Fig. 14.2(a)] **> MMB > Ctrl+D** [Fig. 14.2(b)] **> LMB > Save**

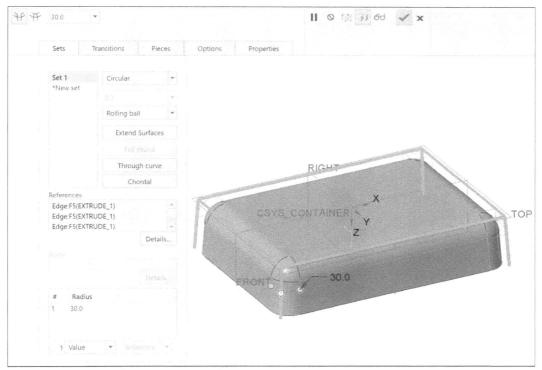

Figure 14.2(a) Add a 30mm Round

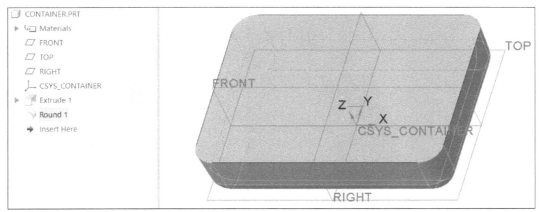

Figure 14.2(b) Completed Round

Shell > Thickness **8mm** > **Enter** > select the face to be removed [Fig. 14.3(a)] > **References** tab > pick in the **Non-default thickness** field > **10mm** > **Enter** > select the surface to be **10mm** [Fig. 14.3(b)] > **MMB** > **LMB** > **Save**

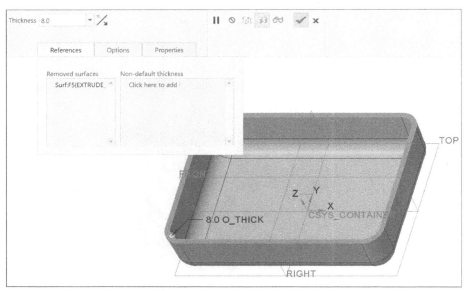

Figure 14.3(a) Select the Surface to Remove

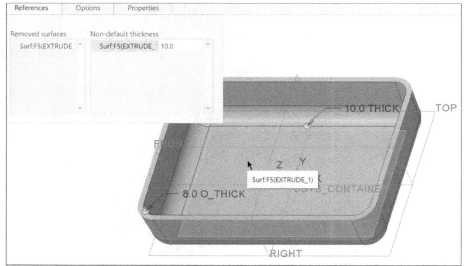

Figure 14.3(b) Non-default thickness selection

470

Create the circular boss. **Extrude > Placement** tab > **Define** > select the shell surface [Fig. 14.4(a)] > **Sketch >** 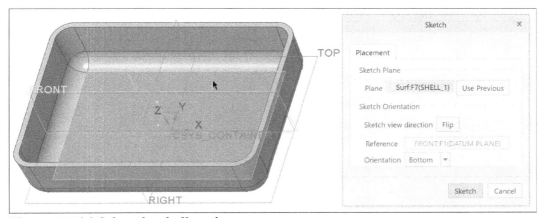 **> Circle > 40 > Enter >** modify placement dimension values [Fig. 14.4(b)] > **Ctrl+D > RMB >** ☑ [Fig. 14.4(c)]

Figure 14.4(a) Select the shell surface

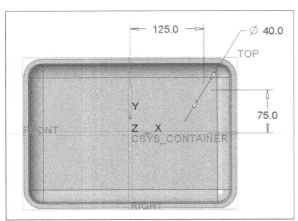

Figure 14.4(b) Design Dimensions

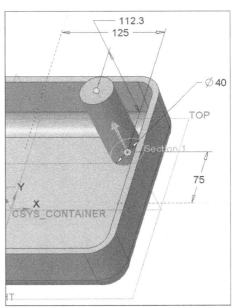

Figure 14.4(c) Extrusion Preview

Datum *(right side of Ribbon)* > ▭ Plane > select datum **TOP** > Translation **50** [Fig. 14.4(d)] > **OK** *(DTM1 will be used to control the height of the boss)* > ▶ **Resumes** > place the pointer over the depth handle [Fig. 14.4(e)] > **RMB** > **To Selected** [Fig. 14.4(f)]

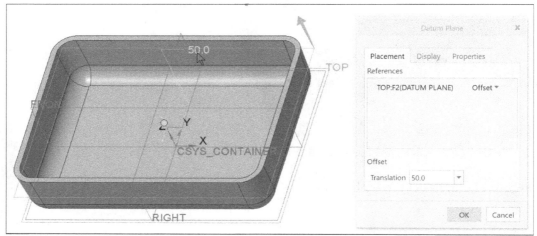

Figure 14.4(d) Creating an Internal Datum Plane

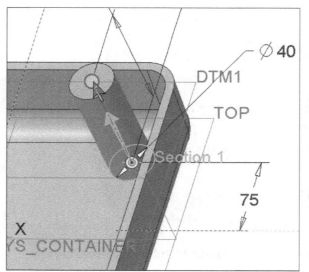

Figure 14.4(e) Place Pointer on Drag Handle

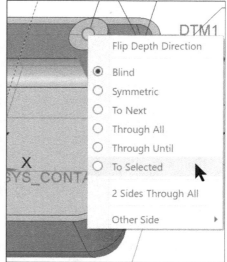

Figure 14.4(f) To Selected

472

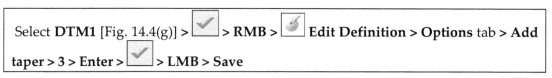

Select **DTM1** [Fig. 14.4(g)] > [✓] > **RMB** > [🖊] **Edit Definition > Options** tab > **Add taper > 3 > Enter >** [✓] **> LMB > Save**

Figure 14.4(g) Select DTM1 to establish the Depth

Create a **5mm** round [Fig. 14.5].

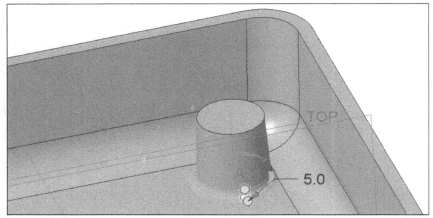

Figure 14.5 Round

Create a **M14x1.25** coaxial hole on the upper surface of the boss [Fig. 14.6(a)]

Figure 14.6(a) Coaxial Hole

Ctrl+ select **A_1** and the upper surface of the boss > **Shape** tab [Fig. 14.6(b)] > **MMB**

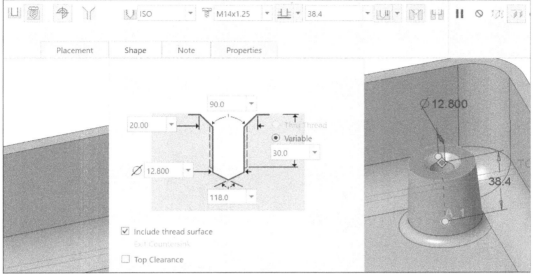

Figure 14.6(b) Hole Depth to Selected Surface

Group the boss, hole and round. Select features > [🐾 **Group**] [Fig. 14.7] > change Group name > **BOSS** > **Enter** > **LMB** > **Ctrl+S**

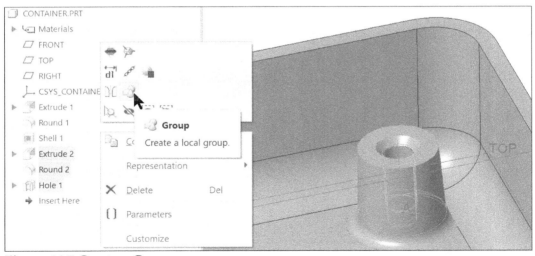

Figure 14.7 Create a Group

From the Model Tree, select: Group **BOSS** > ⬚ **Mirror** > select datum **RIGHT** [Fig. 14.8(a)] > ✓ > with the **Ctrl** key pressed, select Group **BOSS** and **Mirror 1** from the Model Tree > ⬚ **Mirror** > select datum **FRONT** [Fig. 14.8(b)] > ✓ > **Save**

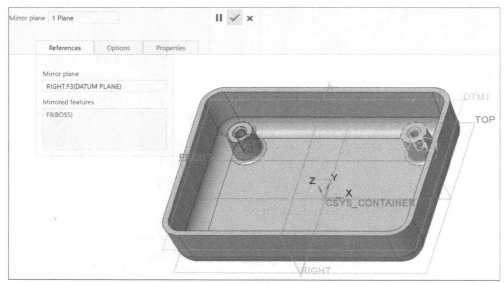

Figure 14.8(a) Group Copied and Mirrored about Datum RIGHT

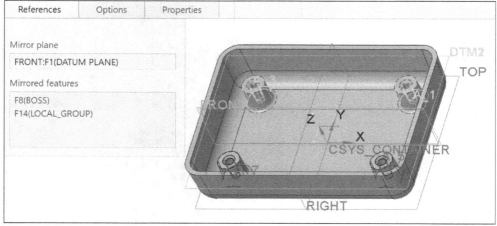

Figure 14.8(b) Previewed Groups Copied and Mirrored about Datum FRONT

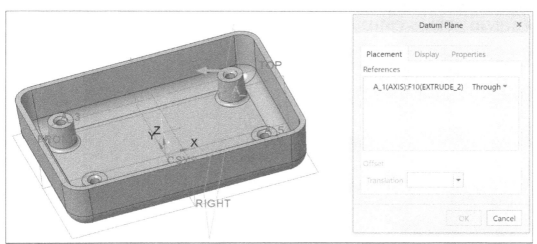

Figure 14.9(a) Select Axis A_1 *(your id's may be different)*

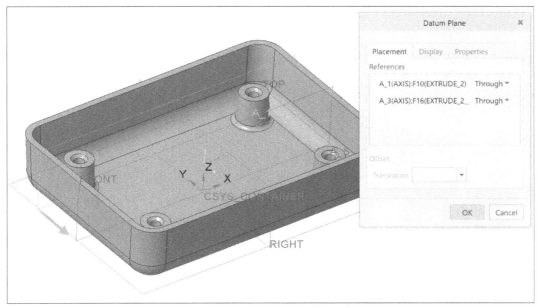

Figure 14.9(b) Select Axis A_3 *(your id's may be different)*

Create a cross section through the part. With the new datum selected, click: **View** tab > 📷 **View Manager** > **Sections** > **New** > **Planar** > **A** > **Enter** > set options [Fig. 14.10(a)] > **MMB** > **RMB** > ☐ Show Section [Fig. 14.10(b)] > **No Cross Section** > **RMB** > **Activate** > **Close** > **Ctrl+D** > **Ctrl+S**

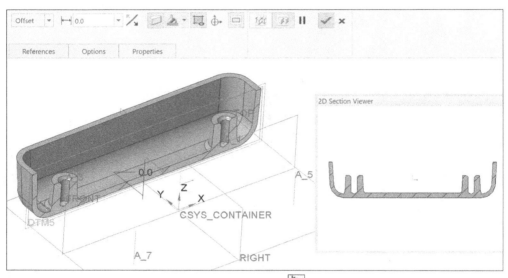

Figure 14.10(a) Active Section A and Rotated 🗎 2D Section Viewer

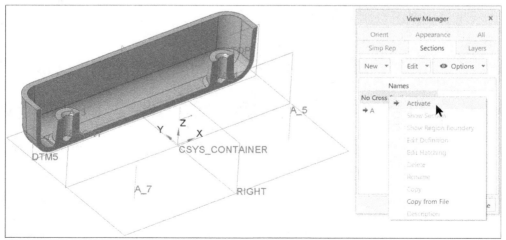

Figure 14.10(b) Activate No Cross Section

Suppressing and resuming features using Layers

You can suppress features on a part to simplify the part model and decrease regeneration time. For example, while you work on one end of a shaft, it may be desirable to suppress features on the other end of the shaft. Similarly, while working on a complex assembly, you can suppress some of the features and components for which the detail is not essential to the current assembly process. Suppress features to do the following:

- Concentrate on the current working area by suppressing other areas
- Speed up a modification process because there is less to update
- Speed up the display process because there is less to display
- Temporarily remove features to try different design iterations

Unlike other features, the base feature cannot be suppressed.

Click on **Group BOSS** in the Model Tree > press and hold the **Shift** key > click **DTM2** in the Model Tree (the last feature in the Model Tree before *Insert Here*) [Fig. 14.11(a)]

> **RMB** > Suppress [Fig. 14.11(b)] > **OK** [Fig. 14.11(c)] > **LMB**

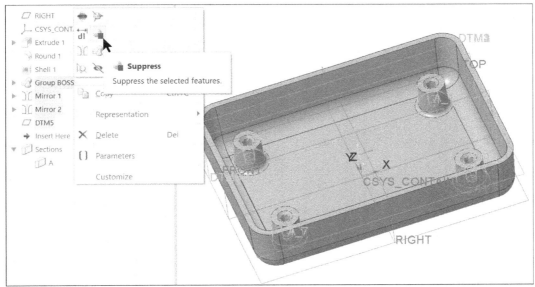

Figure 14.11(a) Select the Features in the Model Tree to be Suppressed

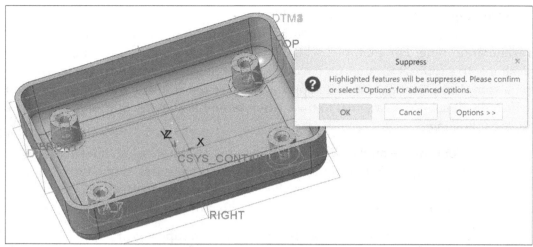

Figure 14.11(b) Suppress Highlighted Features

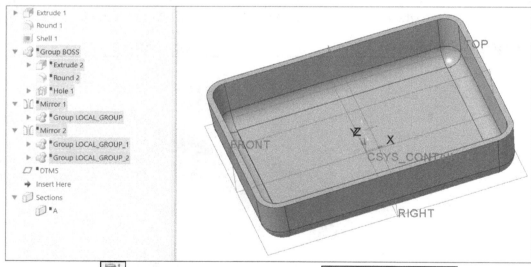

Figure 14.11(c) ⊞ Tree Filters checked to display ☑ Suppressed objects)

The regeneration time for your model will now be shorter. Next, add the text extrusion.

| Extrude | > **Placement** tab > **Define** > select the *bottom surface of the Container* [Fig. 14.12(a)] > ⊡ > A Text > select *start point* of a line to determine text starting position [Fig. 14.12(b)] > select *second point* of a line to determine text height and orientation [Fig. 14.12(c)] |

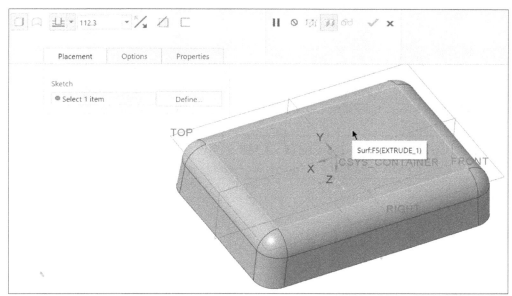

Figure 14.12(a) Sketching Plane

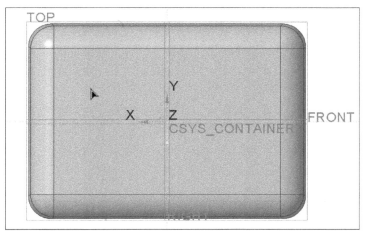

Figure 14.12(b) Pick First Point to Determine the Starting Point of the Lettering

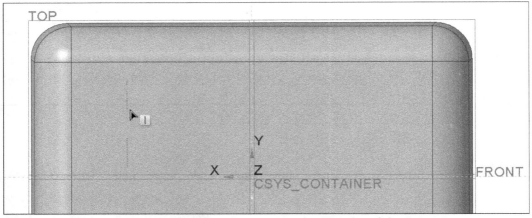

Figure 14.12(c) Pick Second Point to Determine the Height of the Lettering

Ctrl+1 Ctrl+2 Ctrl+3 Ctrl+5 Ctrl+6 Ctrl+4 > LMB > type **CONTAINER 101** in Text line
field [Fig. 14.12(d)] **> OK > MMB >** window-in (select) to capture all dimensions

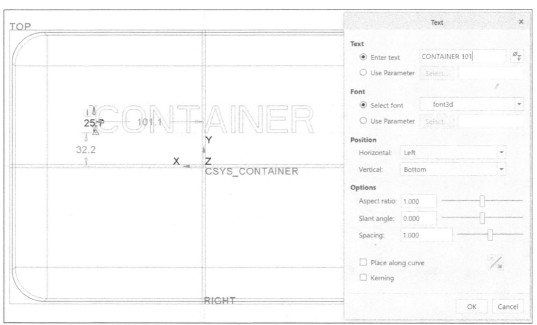

Figure 14.12(d) Type the Text "CONTAINER 101"

Modify the dimensions [Fig. 14.12(e)] > **OK** > **LMB** > **RMB** > [✓] > **Ctrl+2** [Fig. 14.12(f)]

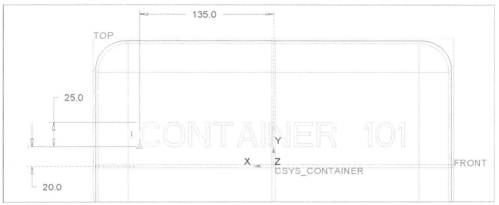

Figure 14.12(e) Modified Dimensions

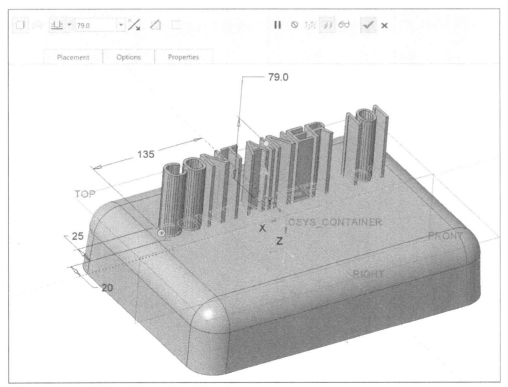

Figure 14.12(f) Text Extrusion Preview

RMB > Remove Material > 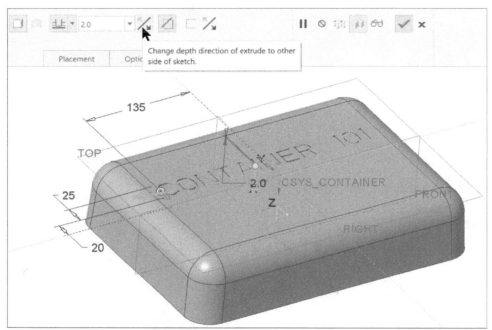 Change Depth Direction > 2 > Enter [Fig. 14.12(g)] > **> Ctrl+S > LMB >** make the text "bottom surface" a different color [Fig. 14.12(h)]

Figure 14.12(g) Dynamic Preview

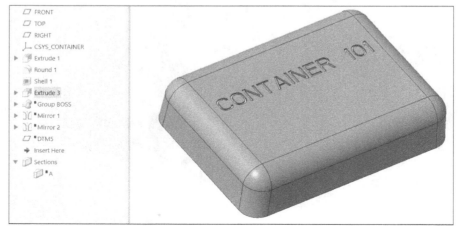

Figure 14.12(h) Completed Text Extrusion

Model tab > **Ctrl+D** > **Operations** group > **Resume** > **Resume All** [Fig. 14.13(a)] > **Ctrl+S** [Fig. 14.13(b > **LMB**

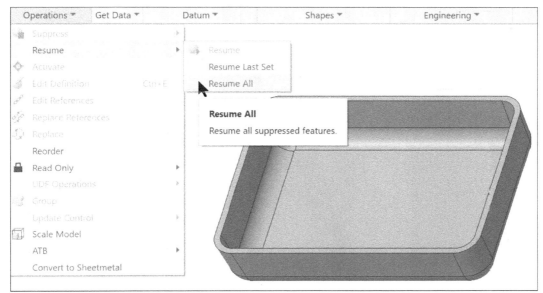

Figure 14.13(a) Resume All

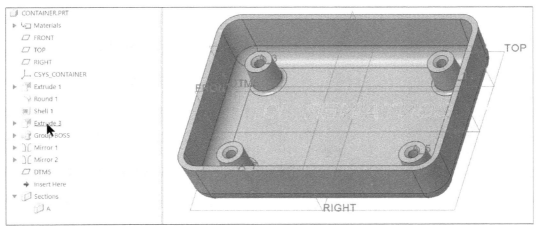

Figure 14.13(b) Suppressed Features Resumed

Next, roll back the model and insert the rib and the lip cut.

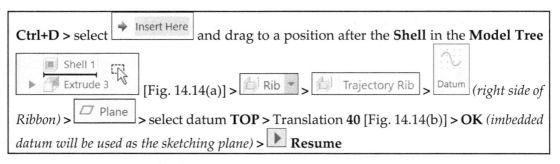

Ctrl+D > select [Insert Here] and drag to a position after the **Shell** in the **Model Tree**

[Fig. 14.14(a)] > Rib > Trajectory Rib > Datum *(right side of Ribbon)* > Plane > select datum **TOP** > Translation **40** [Fig. 14.14(b)] > **OK** *(imbedded datum will be used as the sketching plane)* > ▶ **Resume**

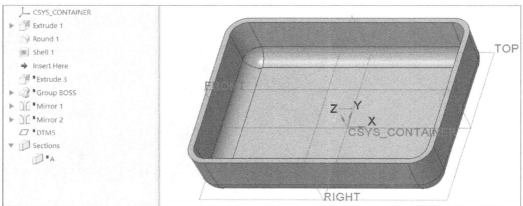

Figure 14.14(a) Features after Insert Here are now suppressed

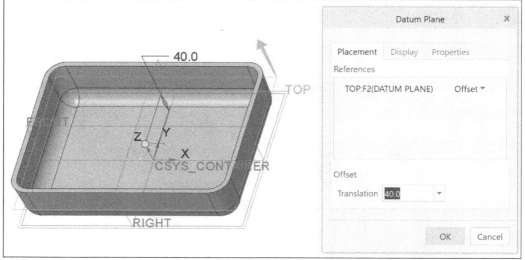

Figure 14.14(b) Datum plane for sketching

486

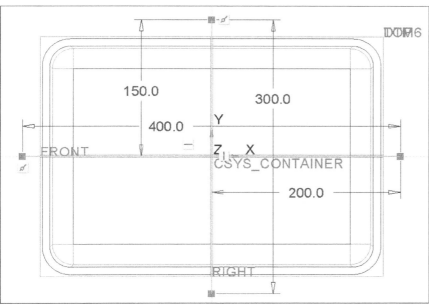

Figure 14.14(c) Sketch horizontal and vertical lines

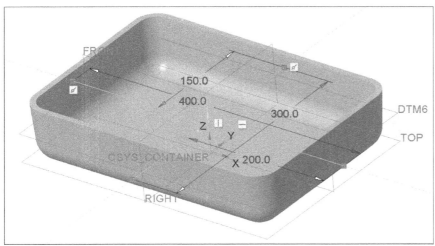

Figure 14.14(d) Completed sketch

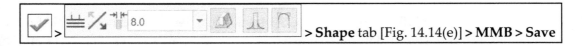

> **Shape** tab [Fig. 14.14(e)] > **MMB** > **Save**

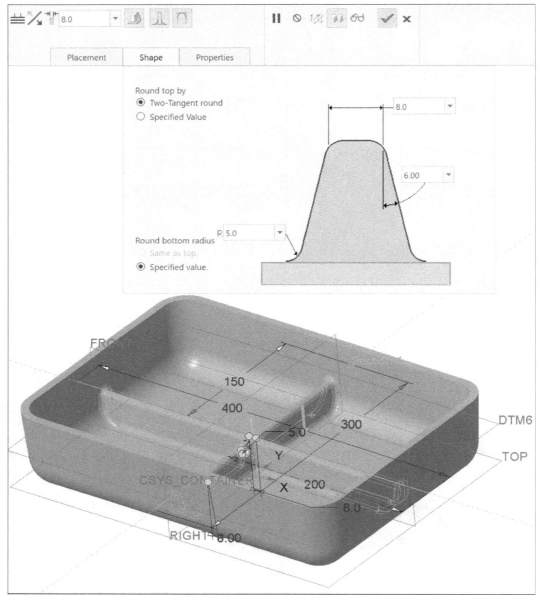

Figure 14.14(e) Rib preview

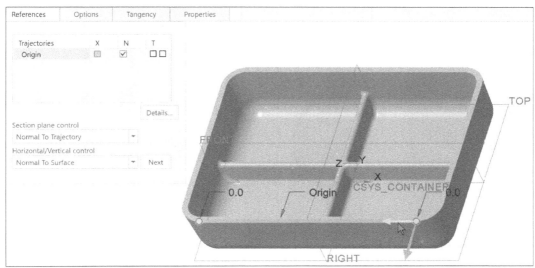

Figure 14.15(a) Trajectory **Origin**

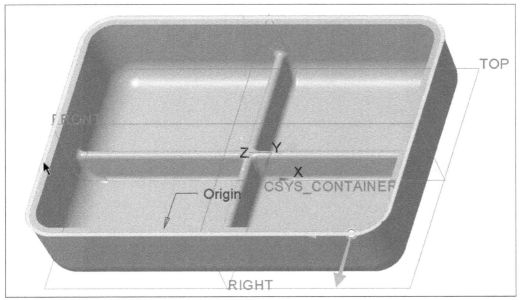

Figure 14.15(b) Trajectory Tangent Loop

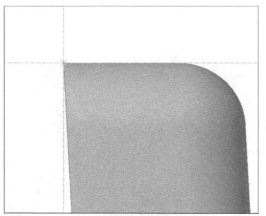 **Create or edit sweep section** > 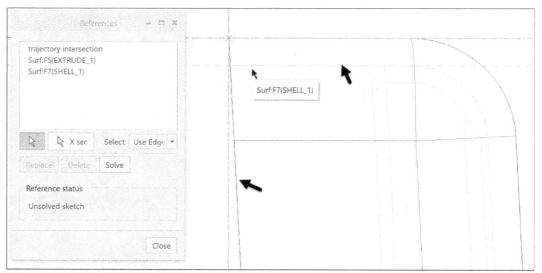 [Fig. 14.15(c)] > **Ctrl+5** [Fig. 14.15(d)] > **RMB** > **References** > pick the top edge > pick the Shell edge [Fig. 14.15(e)] > **Solve** > **Close**

Figure 14.15(c) Sketch View

Figure 14.15(d) Hidden Line Display

Figure 14.15(e) Add two References

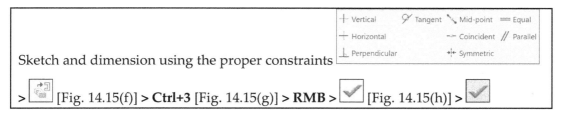
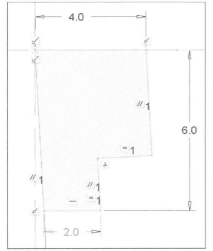

Figure 14.15(f) Section Sketch

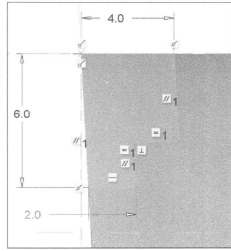

Figure 14.15(g) Hidden Line Display

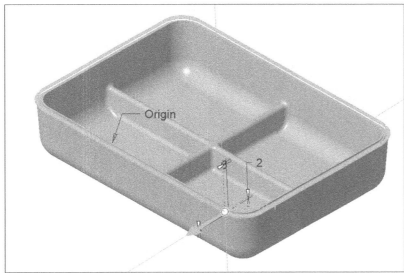

Figure 14.15(h) Swept Cut Preview

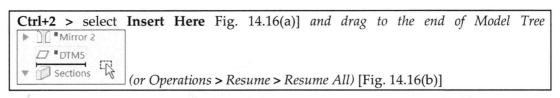

Ctrl+2 > select **Insert Here** Fig. 14.16(a)] *and drag to the end of Model Tree* *(or Operations > Resume > Resume All)* [Fig. 14.16(b)]

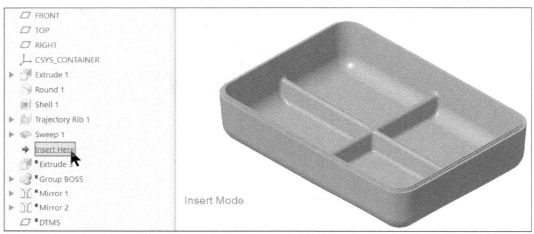

Figure 14.16(a) Insert Mode

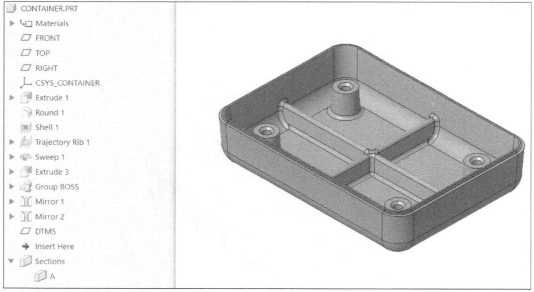

Figure 14.16(b) Completed Container

Select **Section A** in the Model Tree > **Activate Cross-Section** [Fig. 14.17(a)] > section
displays [Fig. 14.17(b)] > **RMB** > ⟨☒ **Deactivate**⟩ section > **Ctrl+D** > **Save**

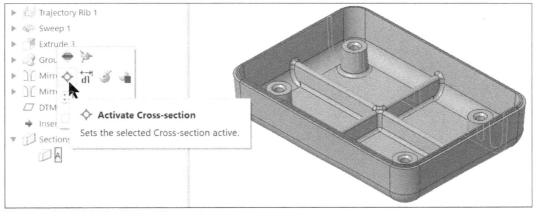

Figure 14.17(a) Activate Cross-Section

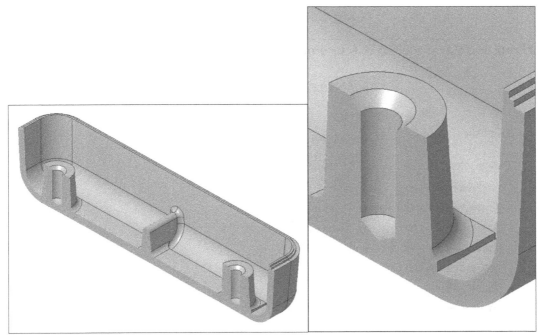

Figure 14.17(b) Section A

493

File > Prepare > ModelCHECK Geometry Check [Fig. 14.18(a)] **> OK >** [x] [Fig. 14.18(b)] **> Ctrl+D > Ctrl+S**

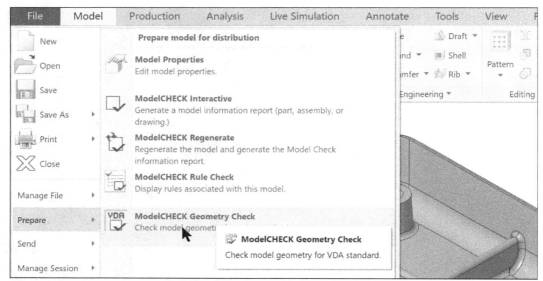

Figure 14.18(a) ModelCHECK Geometry Check

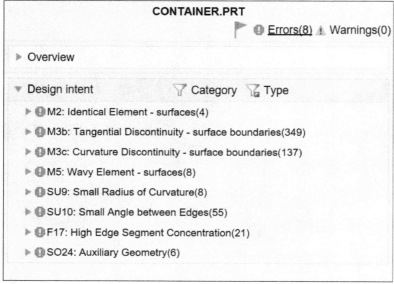

Figure 14.18(b) ModelCHECK

Applications tab > **Render Studio** > **Real-Time** > **Real-Time Settings** > **Custom** > try a variety of settings > **OK** [Fig. 14.19(a)] > **Scenes** > **Edit Scene** > **Lights** tab > ⬚ **Add new spotlight** ✓ Show Light > Name ⬚ **Color for lighting** [Fig. 14.19(b)] > adjust slide bars in the Color Editor > change model color as desired

Figure 14.19(a) Render Studio

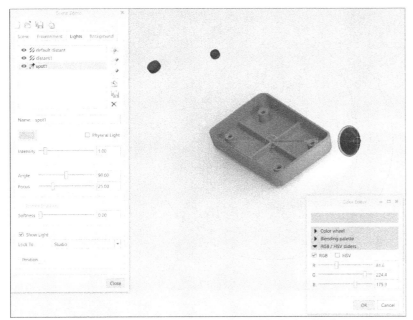

Figure 14.19(b) Adjust the Spot Light RGB Color Values

Scene > double-click on  **indoor_room_scene > Save scene with model** [Fig. 14.19(c)] **> Close**

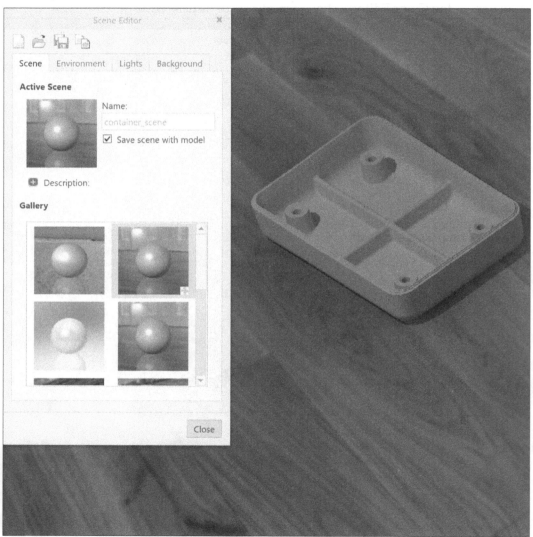

Figure 14.19(c) New Scene

Analysis tab >  **Mass Properties** > **Quick** > **Saved** > **Preview** [Fig. 14.20] > **OK** > **File** > **Save As** > **Save a Copy** > New Name **Container_one_off** > **OK** > **File** > **Save As** > **Save a Copy** > Type ⬚ > **Zip File (*.zip)** > New Name **container_one_off.prt.zip** > **OK** > **upload** the zip file to your course interface or attach to an email

Figure 14.20 Mass Properties

Quiz
1. Name four uses for rendered illustrations
2. What is a Trajectory Rib?
3. Is there a difference between a Draft and a Taper?
4. What is Suppress used for when designing?
5. Can a Shell feature have multiple thicknesses?
6. How do you create a feature at an earlier stage in the design history?

This completes Chapter 14.

CHAPTER 15: Blends, Shell, Group and Patterns

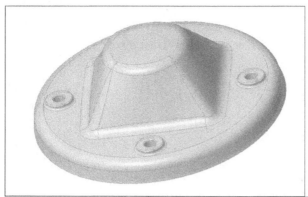

A blended feature consists of a series of at least two planar sections that are joined together at their edges with transitional surfaces to form a continuous feature. A blend will be created as a parallel blend. The component will be shelled to a consistent thickness. You will group features before patterning. Appearances and Cross Sections will be covered in more depth in this chapter.

Objectives
1. Create a Blend feature
2. Apply the Shell Tool with shell thickness variations
3. Create a Feature Pattern
4. Use Group to gather features into one unit
5. Alter and save new Appearances
6. Create a Section of the component

Blends

A blended feature consists of a series of at least two planar sections that are joined together at their edges with transitional surfaces to form a continuous feature. A Blend can be created as a **Parallel Blend** as used here, or you can construct a **Swept Blend**.

Blends are created between the corresponding sections. The illustration below shows a parallel blend for which the *section* consists of several *subsections*. Each segment in the subsection is matched with a segment in the following subsection; to create the transitional surfaces; Creo Parametric connects the *starting points* of the subsections and continues to connect the vertices of the subsections in a clockwise manner. By changing the starting point of a blend subsection, you can create blended surfaces that twist between the subsections. The default starting point is the first point sketched in the subsection.

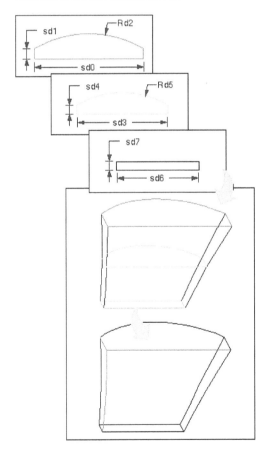

Blends use one of the following transitional surface options:

- **Straight** Create a straight blend by connecting vertices of different subsections with straight lines. Edges of the sections are connected with ruled surfaces.
- **Smooth** Create a smooth blend by connecting vertices of different subsections with smooth curves. Edges of sections are connected with ruled (spline) surfaces.
- **Parallel** All blend sections lie on parallel planes in one section sketch.
- **Rotational** The blend sections are rotated.
- **Select Section** Select section entities.
- **Sketch Section** Sketch section entities.

Blend Type	Section --Smooth --Straight
Parallel--All blend sections lie on parallel planes in one section sketch.	Subsection 1 Subsection 2 Subsection 3
Rotational--Blend sections are rotated about the Y-axis, up to a maximum of 120 degrees. Each section is sketched individually and aligned using the coordinate system of the section.	Section 1 and 3 Section 2

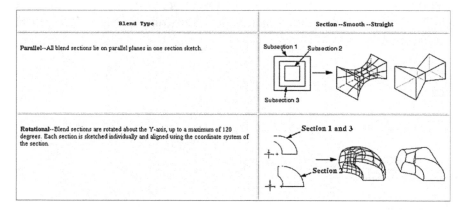

A **parallel blend** is created from a single section that contains multiple sketches called *subsections*. A first or last subsection can be defined as a point resulting in a blend vertex. The starting point for each subsection must be selected as per the design requirements including the starting points

Subsection 1
Subsection 2
Subsection 3

Each subsection contains four segments.

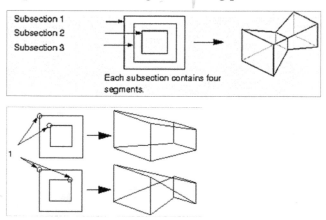

Chapter 15 STEPS

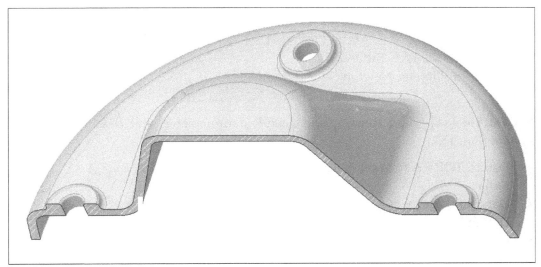

Figure 15.1(a) Cap Section

The Cap [Fig. 15.1(a)] is a part created with a Parallel Blend. The blend sections are a circle and a square (four lines). Because *the sections of a blend must have equal number of segments*, the "circle" is four equal arcs. The component is shelled to one thickness [Fig. 15.1(b)].

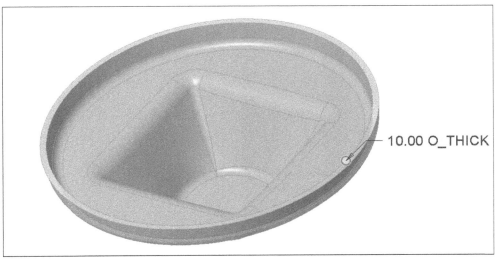

10.00 O_THICK

Figure 15.1(b) Cap Shell

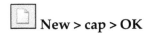 **New > cap > OK**

Model Properties:
- **Material** = METAL_BRONZE
- **Units** = millimeter Newton Second (mmNs)

Set Datum $\boxed{\text{-A-}}$ and **Rename** the default datum planes and default coordinate system [Fig. 15.2]:

- Datum TOP = **A** *(select A in the Model Tree >* $\boxed{\text{📋}}$ *Properties > Name: A >* $\boxed{\text{-A-}}$ *> Enter)*
- Datum FRONT = **B**
- Datum RIGHT = **C**
- Coordinate System = **CSYS_CAP**

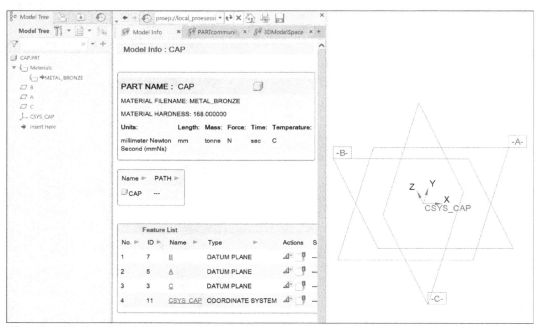

Figure 15.2 Cap Model Properties

502

Model the circular extrusion Ø**550mm** by **50mm** thick, with a **-10** degree taper. Sketch the first extrusion on datum **A (TOP)** and centered on **B (FRONT)** and **C (RIGHT)** [Fig. 15.3] > **MMB** > **Save**

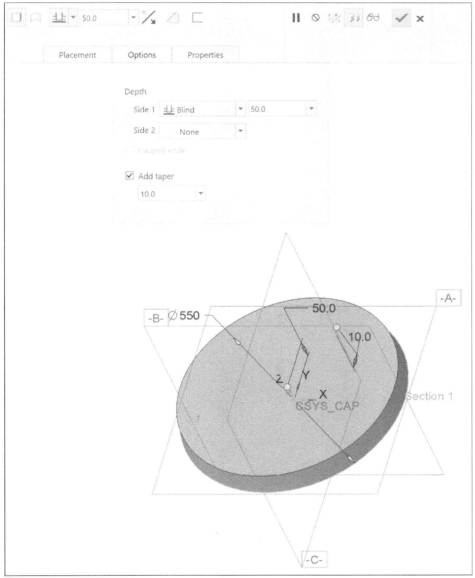

Figure 15.3 First Extrusion

Model tab > **Shapes** Group > **Blend** > **Sections** tab > **Define** > select the top of the extrusion as the sketching plane [Fig. 15.4(a)] > **Sketch** > **Ctrl+4** > **Center Rectangle** > sketch a **290mm** square [Fig. 15.4(b)] > **RMB** >

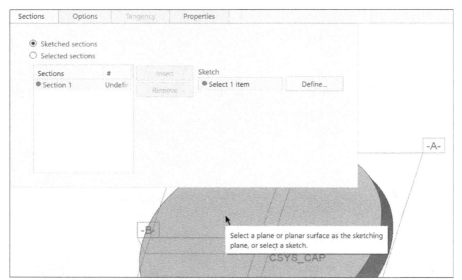

Figure 15.4(a) Select the Sketching Plane

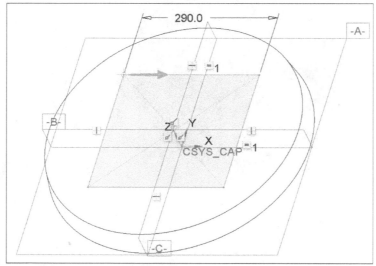

Figure 15.4(b) Square Sketch

Insert (Section 2) > Offset from Section 1 **128 > Sketch** [Fig. 15.4(c)] > 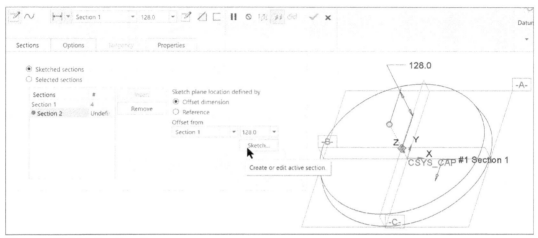 **Sketch View > RMB > Centerline >** draw two centerlines through the origin and corners of the square [Fig. 15.4(d)]

Figure 15.4(c) Section 2

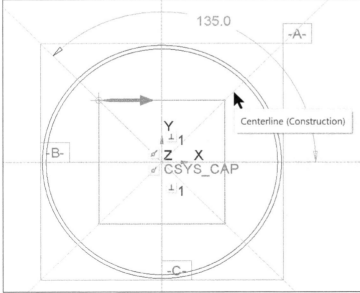

Figure 15.4(d) Construction Centerlines

Sketch four equal center end points arcs [Figs. 15.4(e-g)] > click on end of the arrow start point > **MMB > RMB >** pick the arrow start end > **RMB > Start Point > R 90** [Fig. 15.3(h)] > **RMB >** ✓ > **Ctrl+D > Ctrl+2** [Fig. 15.4(i)] > **MMB > Save**

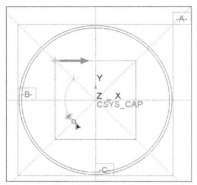

Figure 15.4(e) First Arc

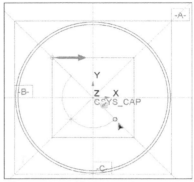

Figure 15.4(f) Second Arc

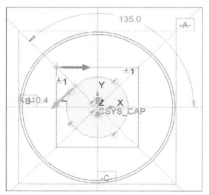

Figure 15.4(g) Third and Fourth Arc

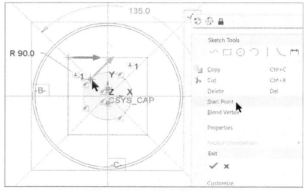

Figure 15.4(h) R 90 and Start Point

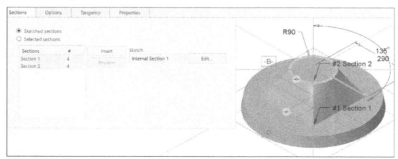

Figure 15.4(i) Blend Preview

Add **R25** rounds [Fig. 15.5] > shell the part with a **10mm** thickness [Fig. 15.6]

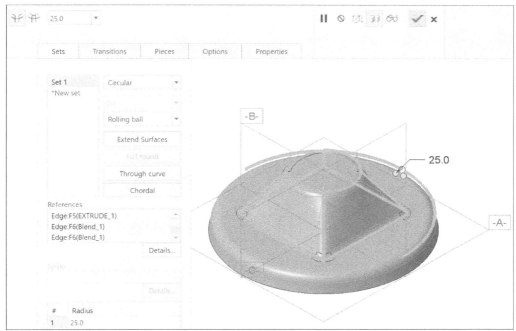

Figure 15.5 Rounds Preview

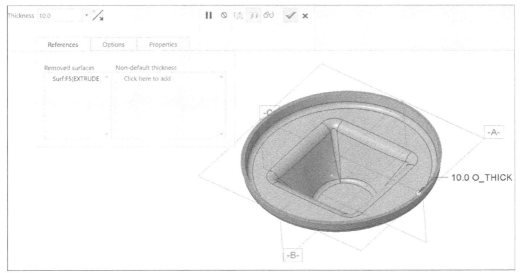

Figure 15.6 Shell Preview

Extrude > select the sketch surface [Fig. 15.7(a)] **> Ctrl+4 >** sketch a **420mm** diameter circle > select the circle > **Construction** [Fig. 15.7(b)]

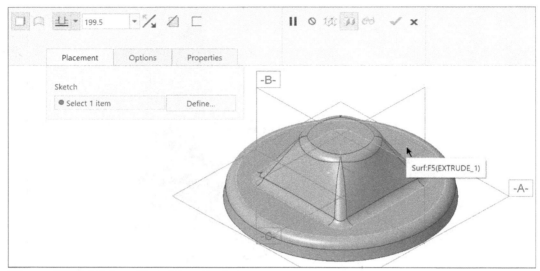

Figure 15.7(a) Select Sketching Surface

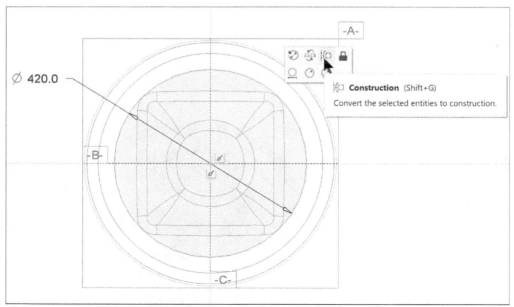

Figure 15.7(b) Change the circle into Construction Circle

Add a **60mm** diameter circle at the intersection of the construction circle and datum **C**

[Fig. 15.8(a)] > **RMB** > ✔ > **Ctrl+2** > **Ctrl+D** > **10** height [Fig. 15.8(b)] > **MMB**

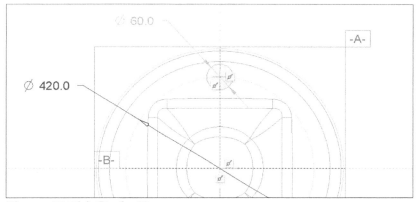

Figure 15.8(a) Circle 60mm

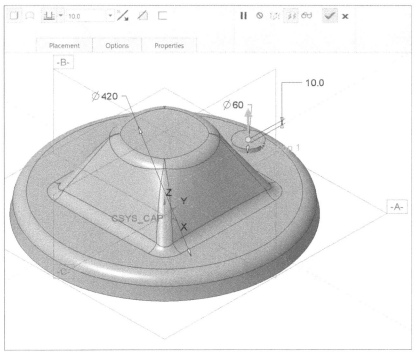

Figure 15.8(b) Boss 60mm x 10mm

Add a **25mm** diameter through all hole on the boss extrusion using the axis for location and the bosses top as the placement surface [Fig. 15.9] > add a **5mm** radius to the boss edge [Fig. 15.10] > **Save**

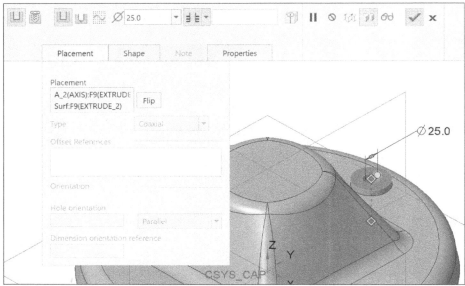

Figure 15.9 Hole

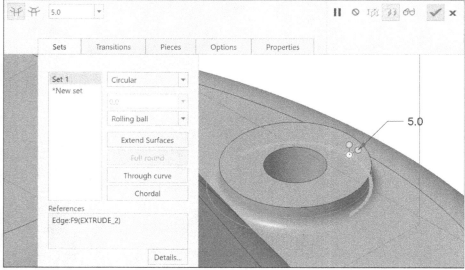

Figure 15.10 Radius

Add two **2mm** chamfers [Fig. 15.11] **>** change model color **> Group** the boss, hole, round, and chamfer [Fig. 15.12] **> Save**

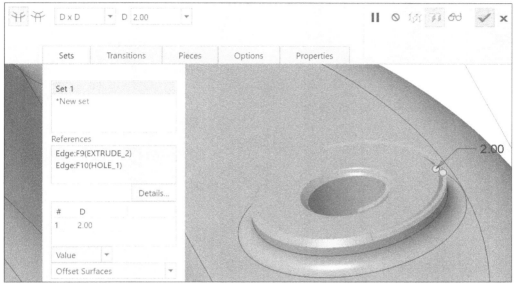

Figure 15.11 Hole

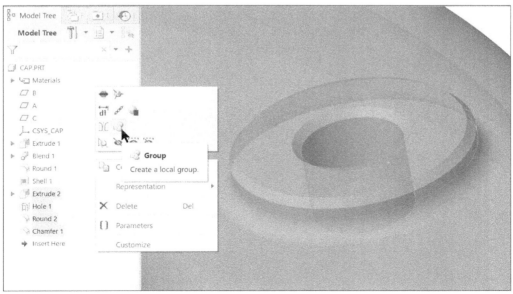

Figure 15.12 Group

With the Group selected > 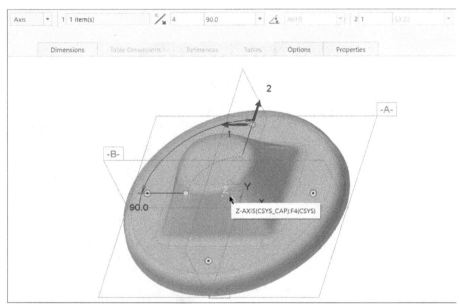 **Pattern** > Dimension ▼ > Axis ▼ > select the **Z axis** of the coordinate system [Fig. 15.13(a)] > complete the pattern with the options and references > **MMB** [Fig. 15.13(b)]

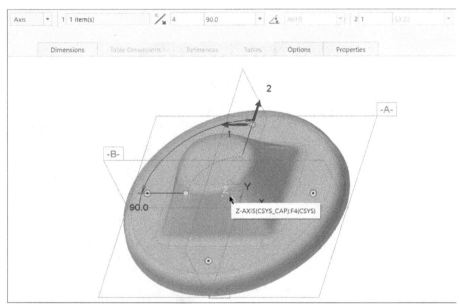

Figure 15.13(a) Patterning the Group

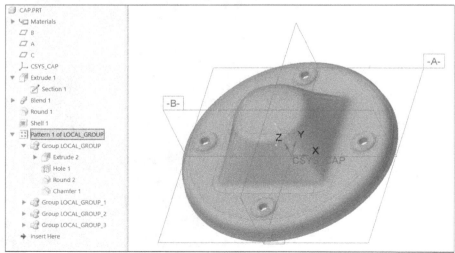

Figure 15.13(b) Completed Group Pattern

View tab > **Appearences** > **PTC_STD_BRASS** > select **CAP** in Model Tree > **MMB** > **Appearences** > **PTC_STD_BRASS** > **RMB** > **Edit** [Fig. 15.14(a)] > Class **Metal** > **Generic** > adjust the color > change **Highlight** color > **OK** > Transparency **20** [Fig. 15.14(b)] > **Close**

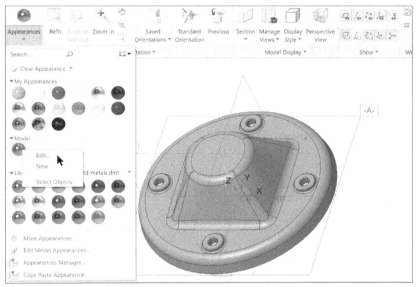

Figure 15.14(a) Appearances

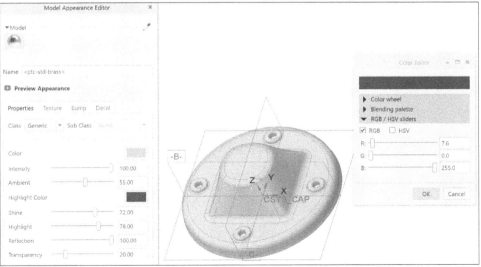

Figure 15.14(b) Model Appearance Editor and Color Editor

View tab > **Appearences** > **Appearance Manager** > [icon] > **Names and Thumbnails** >

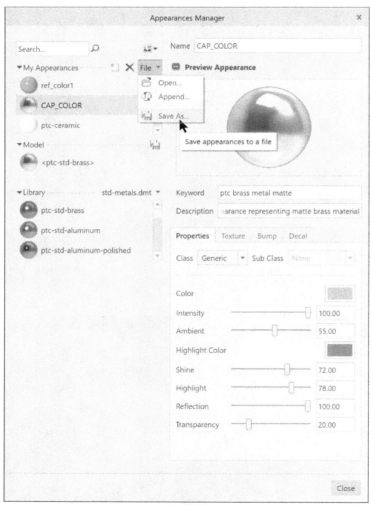

RMB [graphic] > Name **CAP_COLOR** > adjust colors and settings as desired > **File** > **Save As** [Fig. 15.14(c)] > **CAP_COLOR** > **OK** > **Close** > **Appearances** > **CAP_COLOR** > pick **CAP** in the Model Tree > **MMB**

Figure 15.14(c) Appearances Manager

View tab > ⬛📷 **View Manager > Sections > New > Planar > A > Enter >** set options [Fig. 15.15(a)] **>** drag the Axis out and rotate the section [Fig. 15.15(b)] **> Undo > Undo > MMB > Close**

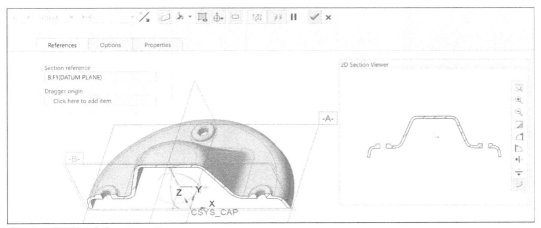

Figure 15.15(a) Section A

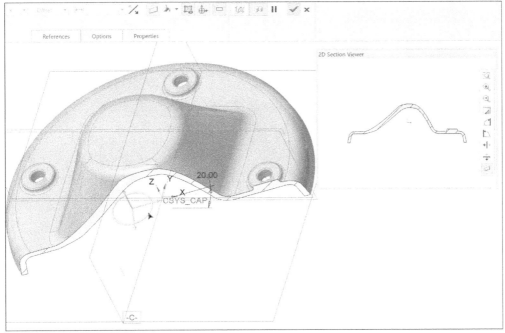

Figure 15.15(b) Modified Cutting Plane

RMB on section **A** in the Model Tree **> RMB > Edit Hatching** [Fig. 15.15(c)] **> Use a solid fill > Use hatch from the library > Plastic >** Angle: **180 >** Scale: **Half the size >** Color: yellow [Fig. 15.15(d)] **> OK > Ctrl+D > Save > RMB** on section **A** in the Model Tree **> RMB >** ☐ Show Section **> RMB > Deactivate > LMB > Ctrl+D > Ctrl+S**

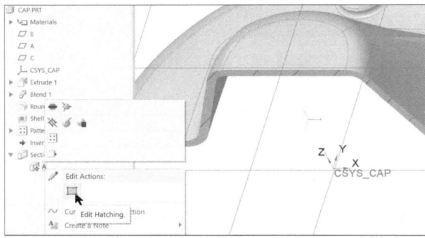

Figure 15.15(c) Edit Hatching

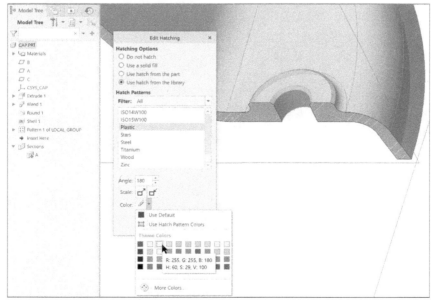

Figure 15.15(d) Edit Hatching Dialog Box

Perspective > **Ctrl+1** [Fig. 15.16] > **Ctrl+S > OK > File > Manage File > Delete Old Versions > Enter > File > Save As >** Type ⬚ > **Zip File (*.zip) > OK >** upload the zip file to your course interface or attach to an email > **File > Close > File > Exit >Yes**

Figure 15.16 Completed Cap

Quiz

1. What type of Blend features are available?
2. What are Blend Sections?
3. Why group features?
4. What is the difference between a Straight and a Smooth Blend?
5. What options accompany Section lining?
6. How do you create and save new Appearances?

This completes Chapter 15.

CHAPTER 16: Helical Sweep, Family Table and Model Based Definition

A helical sweep is created by sweeping a section along a helical trajectory. The trajectory is defined by both the profile of the surface of revolution (which defines the distance from the section origin of the helical feature to its axis of revolution) and the pitch (the distance between coils). The trajectory and the surface of revolution are construction tools and do not appear in the resulting geometry. Annotation features are data features that you can use to manage the model annotation including surface finish, geometric tolerances, notes, and so on. Model notes are pieces of text, which can contain links (URL's), which you can attach to objects. Model notes increase the amount of information that you can attach to any entity in your model.

Understanding the functionality of Family Tables and what circumstances should promote its proper use. When you create a Family Table, Creo Parametric allows you to *select dimensions,* which can vary between instances. You can also *select features* to add to the Family Table.

Objectives

1. Create a base feature for the spring using a Helical Sweep
2. Add 3D Notes to annotate the model
3. Create a Family Table for multiple instances and design variations
4. Use 3D detail to document the project without drawings
5. Understand and master model-based definition
6. Embed URL's into notes
7. Insert dimensions, surface finishes, geometric tolerances on a "3D Drawing"
8. Convert Legacy Datum Annotations

Helical sweeps

The Helical Sweep command is available for both solids and surfaces. Options include:

- **Keep constant section** The pitch is constant
- **Vary section** The pitch is variable and defined by a graph
- **Thru axis of revolution** The section lies in a plane that passes through the axis of revolution
- **Normal To trajectory** The section is oriented normal to the trajectory
- **Normal to projection** The section is oriented normal to the projection
- **Use right handed rule** The trajectory is defined by the right-hand rule
- **Use left handed rule** The trajectory is defined by the left-hand rule

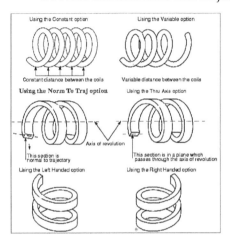

Model Notes and Annotation Features

Model notes are text strings, which can be placed flat to the screen (view plane) in model space. Note(s) can be attached to any entity in your model. When you attach a note to an entity, that entity is considered the parent of the note. Annotation features can also be notes, and can include symbols, surface finish, geometric tolerance, set datum tags, ordinate baseline, and driven dimensions.

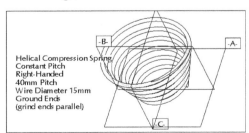

Family tables

Family tables are used to create part families from generic models by tabulating dimensions or the presence of certain features or parts. A family table might be used, for example, to catalog a series of couplings with varying width and diameter.

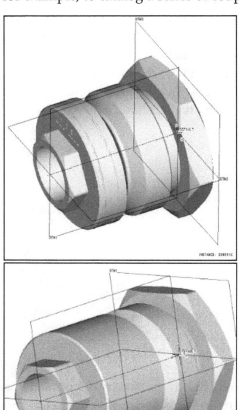

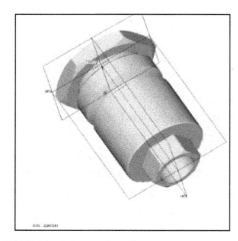

Type	Instance Name	Common Name	d30	d46	F1068 [CUT]	F829 [SLOT]	F872 [SLOT]	F2620 COPIED_G...
	COUPLING-FITTI...		2.06	0.3130	Y	Y	Y	Y
	CPLA		3.00	0.5000	N	N	N	N
	CPLB		3.25	0.6250	N	Y	N	N
	CPLC		3.50	0.7500	Y	N	Y	Y

Chapter 16 STEPS

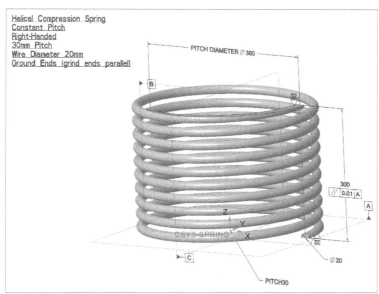

Figure 16.1 Helical Compression Spring with ground ends

Helical Compression Spring

Springs [Fig. 16.1] and other helical features (threads) are created with the Helical Sweep command. A helical sweep is created by sweeping a *section* along a *trajectory* that lies in the *surface of revolution:* The trajectory is defined by the *profile* of the surface of revolution and the distance between coils. The component is a *constant-pitch right-handed helical spring with ground ends, a pitch of 30mm, and a wire diameter of 20mm.*

New > Part > Name **helical_spring**

- Material = **METAL_STEEL_HIGH_CARBON**
- Units = **millimeter Newton Second (mmNs)**

Set Datum [-A-] and **Rename** the default datum planes and coordinate system:

- Datum TOP = **A**
- Datum FRONT = **B**
- Datum RIGHT = **C**
- Coordinate System = **CSYS-SPRING**

521

Sweep ▼ > ▼ > **Helical Sweep** **Helical Sweep > References** tab > **Define** [Fig. 16.2(a)] > select datum **B** > **Sketch** > ⬚ > **RMB** > ⬚ **Create axis of revolution** > create the axis vertical and through the origin > **MMB** > **RMB** > ⬚ **Line Chain** > starting on the edge of datum A create the vertical line > **MMB** > **MMB** [Fig. 16.2(b)]

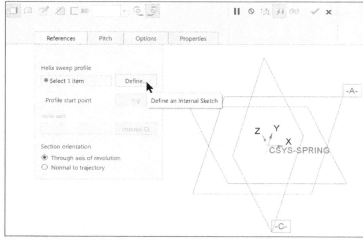

Figures 16.2(a) Helical Sweep Tool

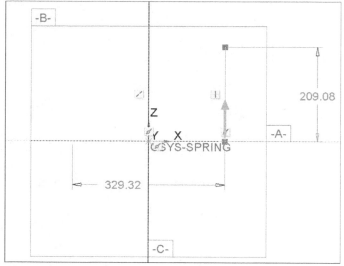

Figure 16.2(b) Helix Sweep Profile Sketch. Note the Start Arrow Direction

Modify the values [Fig. 16.2(c)] **> Ctrl+D** [Fig. 16.2(d)] **> RMB >**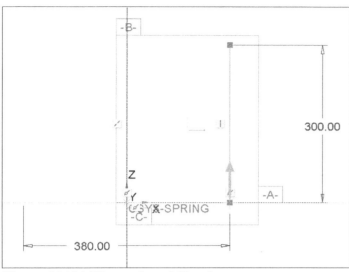

Figure 16.2(c) Dimensioned Sketch

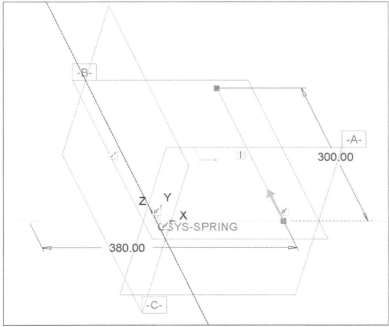

Figure 16.2(d) Trimetric View

References tab > pitch value **30** > **Enter** [Fig. 16.2(e)] > 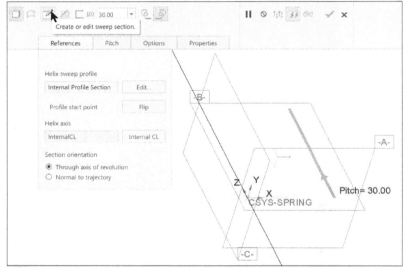 **Create or edit sweep section** from the Dashboard > Center and Point Fig. 16.2(f)] > modify to **20** diameter [Fig. 16.2(g)] > **RMB** >

Figure 16.2(e) Pitch 30

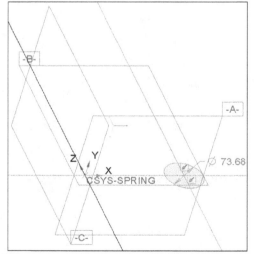

Figure 16.2(f) Sketch a Circle

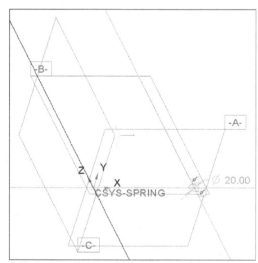

Figure 16.2(g) Wire Diameter 20mm

Pitch tab [Fig. 16.2(h)] > **MMB** [Fig. 16.2(i)] > *(try varriations of profile and pitch)* [Fig. 16.2(j)] > **Undo**

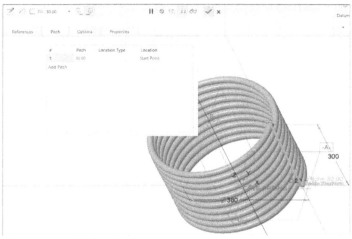

Figure 16.2(h) Helix Preview

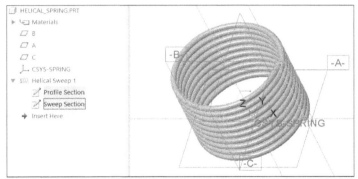

Figure 16.2(i) Completed Helical Sweep

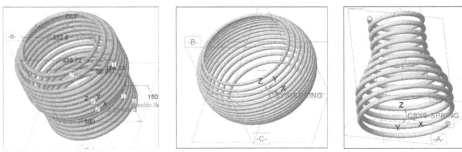

Figure 16.2(j) Pitch and Profile variations

Create the *ground ends*: **Model** tab > ⬜ Extrude > ⬜ ▾ > ⬜ **Extrude on both sides** > ◪ **Remove Material** > **RMB** > **Define Internal Sketch** > pick datum **C** > Reference-pick datum **A** > Orientation- **Bottom** [Fig. 16.3(a)] > **Sketch** > ⬚ > ⌵⌵ **Line Chain** > draw a horizontal line > modify the dimension [Fig. 16.3(b)] > **RMB** > ✓

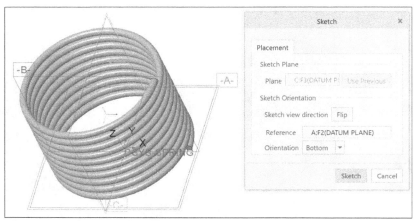

Figure 16.3(a) Cut Sketch Orientation

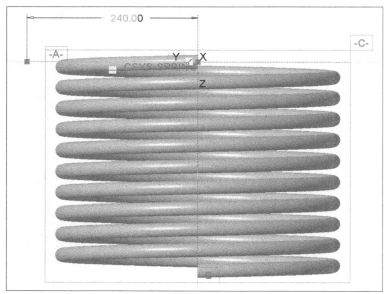

Figure 16.3(b) Ground Ends (any length will work greater than the coil radius)

In the Graphics Window, **RMB > Flip Material Side** *(or click on the arrow)* **>** drag a depth handle to include the full spring [Fig. 16.3(c)] > ☑ [Fig. 16.3(d)] > **LMB**

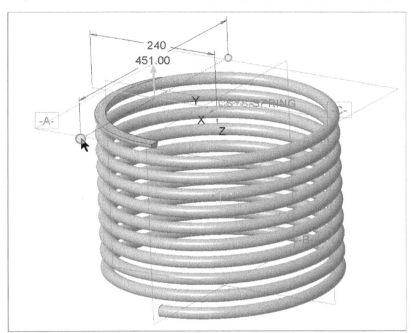

Figure 16.3(c) Depth Handles

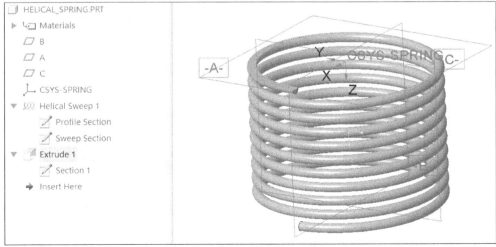

Figure 16.3(d) Completed Cut for Ground End

Model tab > ⬛ Extrude > ⬛ ▼ > ⬛ **Extrude on both sides** > ◻ **Remove Material** > **RMB > Define Internal Sketch > Use Previous** > ⬛ > sketch a line from the center of the wire to beyond the spring coil (240mm) > **RMB > Dimension** > select the line and datum **A > MMB** to place the dimension > **Dim>Ref** [Fig. 16.4(a)] > **RMB** > ☑ > **Ctrl+D** > click on the arrow [Figs. 16.4(b-c)] > **MMB > Ctrl+S**

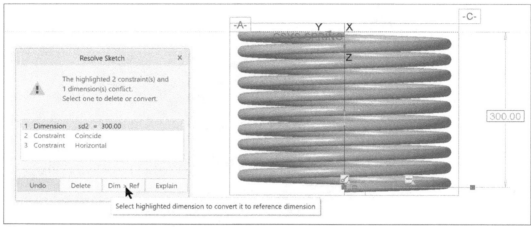

Figure 16.4(a) Creating Reference Dimension

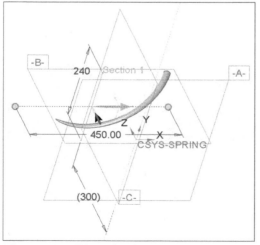

Figure 16.4(b) Pick on Arrow to Flip

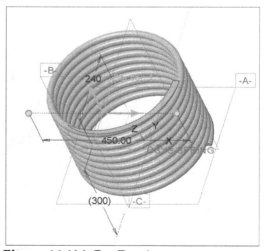

Figure 16.4(c) Cut Preview

528

Family Tables

Family Tables are used any time a part or assembly has several unique iterations developed from the original model. The iterations must be considered as separate models, not just iterations of the original model.

You will be creating a Family Table from the generic model. The (base) model is the **Generic**. Each variation is referred to as an **Instance**. When you create a Family Table, Creo Parametric allows you to *select dimensions,* which can vary between instances. You can also *select features* to add to the Family Table. Features can vary by being suppressed or resumed in an instance. When you are finished selecting items (e.g., dimensions, features, and parameters), the Family Table is automatically generated.

When adding features to the table; enter an **N** to suppress the feature, or a **Y** to resume the feature. Each instance must have a unique name.

Family tables are spreadsheets, consisting of columns and rows. *Rows* contain instances and their corresponding values; *columns* are used for items. The column headings include the *instance name* and the names of all of the *dimensions, parameters, features, members,* and *groups* that were selected to be in the table. The Family Table dialog box is used to create and modify family tables. Family tables include:

- The base object (generic object or *generic*) on which all members of the family are founded.
- Dimensions, parameters, feature numbers, user-defined feature names, and assembly member names that are selected to be table-driven (*items*).
  Dimensions are listed by name (for example, **d67**) with the associated symbol name (if any) on the line below it (for example, depth).
  Parameters are listed by name (dim symbol).
  Features are listed by feature number with the associated feature type (for example, [cut]) or feature name on the line below it. The generic model is the first row in the table. Only modifying the actual part, suppressing, or resuming features can change the table entries belonging to the generic; *you cannot change the generic model by editing its row entries in the family table.*
- Names of all family members (*instances*) created in the table and the corresponding values for each of the table-driven items

Tools tab > 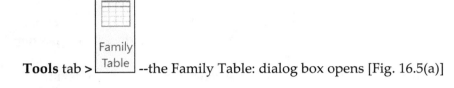 --the Family Table: dialog box opens [Fig. 16.5(a)]

Figure 16.5(a) Family Table Dialog Box

Ctrl+4 > 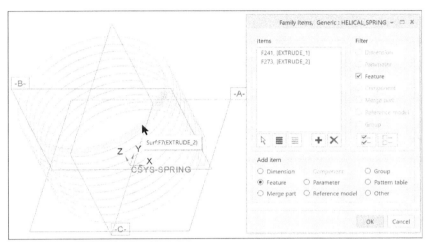 **Add/delete the table columns >** ⊙ Feature from the Add Item options > select the cuts from the model or the Model Tree [Fig. 16.5(b)] *(the order in which the items are listed will determine the default order in which they will appear in the table – default column order)* > ⊙ Dimension > select the model > **All** > select **380 DIA** and **20 Wire DIA** and **PITCH 30** [Fig. 16.5(c)]

Figure 16.5(b) Adding Features

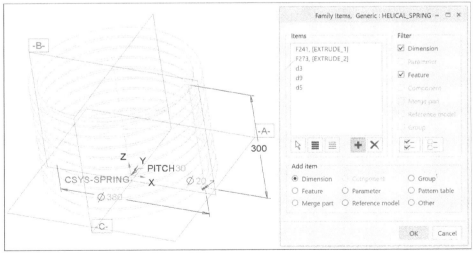

Figure 16.5(c) Add 380, 20 and 30

OK [Fig. 16.5(d)] > ⊞ **Insert a new instance at the selected row** > adjust column widths > pick on the first instance **HELICAL_SPRING_INST** > *type* **HELICAL_SPRING_101 > Enter** *(adds a new instance)* > **HELICAL_SPRING_102 > Enter > HELICAL_SPRING_103 >** change Common Names [Fig. 16.5(e)] > pick in the cell of each cut and change to **N** [Fig. 16.5(f)] > modify cell dimensions [Fig. 16.5(g)]

Family Table :HELICAL_SPRING								
File Edit Insert Tools								
Look In: HELICAL_SPRING								
Type	Instance File Name	Common Name	F241 [EXTRUDE_1]	F273 [EXTRUDE_2]	d3	d9	d5	
	HELICAL_SPRING	helical_spring.prt	Y	Y	380.000000	20.000000	30.000000	

Figure 16.5(d) New Family Table

Type	Instance File Name	Common Name	F241 [EXTRUDE_1]	F273 [EXTRUDE_2]	d3	d9	d5
	HELICAL_SPRING	helical_spring.prt	Y	Y	380.000000	20.000000	30.000000
	HELICAL_SPRING_101	SPR-101	*	*	*	*	*
	HELICAL_SPRING-102	SPR-102	*	*	*	*	*
	HELICAL_SPRING_103	SPR-103	*	*	*	*	*

Figure 16.5(e) Add Instances and change Instance File Name and Common Names

Type	Instance File Name	Common Name	F241 [EXTRUDE_1]	F273 [EXTRUDE_2]	d3	d9	d5
	HELICAL_SPRING	helical_spring.prt	Y	Y	380.00	20.00	30.00
	HELICAL_SPRING_101	SPR-101	N	N	*	*	*
	HELICAL_SPRING-102	SPR-102	*	Y	*	*	*
	HELICAL_SPRING_103	SPR-103	*	N	*	*	*

Figure 16.5(f) HELICAL_SPRING_101 Extrude cuts not used (N)

Look In: HELICAL_SPRING							
Type	Instance File Name	Common Name	F241 [EXTRUDE_1]	F273 [EXTRUDE_2]	d3	d9	d5
	HELICAL_SPRING	helical_spring.prt	Y	Y	380.00	20.00	30.00
	HELICAL_SPRING_101	SPR-101	N	N	*	*	28.00
	HELICAL_SPRING-102	SPR-102	*	*	400.00	22.00	*
	HELICAL_SPRING_103	SPR-103	*	*	410.00	24.00	*

Figure 16.5(g) Dimension Variations

 **Excel** [Fig. 16.5(h)] > Close **Excel** >  **Verify instances of the family** [Fig. 16.5(i)] > **VERIFY** [Fig. 16.5(j)] > **CLOSE** [Fig. 16.5(k)] > **OK** > **Ctrl+D** > **Ctrl+R** > **Ctrl+2** > **Save**

Figure 16.5(h) Excel

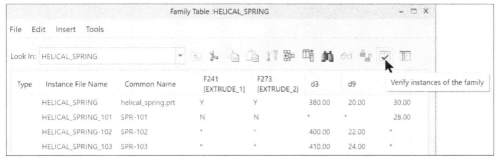

Figure 16.5(i) Verify Instances of the Family

Figure 16.5(j) Verify

Figure 16.5(k) Verification Status

Click: **Tools** tab > **Family Table** > **HELICAL_SPRING_101** > [Open] [Fig. 16.5(l)]

> **File** > **Close** > **Family Table** > **HELICAL_SPRING_103** > [Open] [Fig. 16.5(m)]
> **File** > **Close**

(Note that you can make Family Tables within new Instances)

Figure 16.5(l) HELICAL_SPRING_101 No Cuts

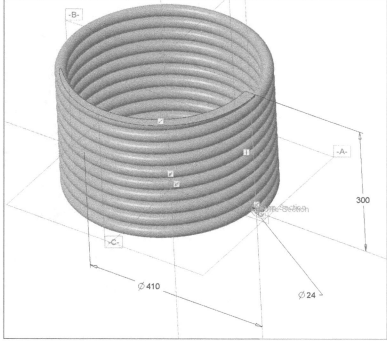

Figure 16.5(m) HELICAL_SPRING_103

Annotations

When you attach a note to an entity, that entity is considered the "parent" of the note. Deleting the parent deletes all of the notes of the parent. You can attach model notes anywhere in the model; they do not have to be attached to a parent. Here we will add a note to the part and describe the spring.

Annotate tab > [FLAT TO SCREEN] > **RMB** on the command button > **Set** > [A≡] > [A≡ Unattached Note] [Fig. 16.6(a)] > select a place on the screen to place the note > type the following note [Fig. 16.6(b)]:

Helical Compression Spring
Constant Pitch
Right-Handed
30mm Pitch
Wire Diameter 20mm
Ground Ends (grind ends parallel)

Figure 16.6(a) Unattached Note

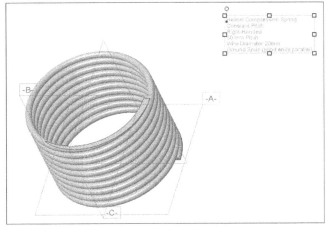

Figure 16.6(b) Note

Drag 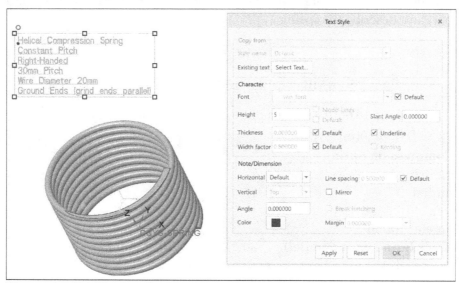 > move as needed > **RMB > Text Style** [Fig. 16.6(c)] > ☐ Default > Height **10** (or as needed) > **Enter** > Font **filled** > **Apply** [Fig. 16.6(d)] > **OK > LMB > Ctrl+S**

Figure 16.6(c) Placing the Note

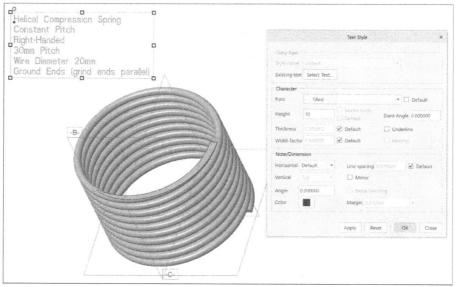

Figure 16.6(d) Completed Note

You can toggle model annotations on and off using ⬜ **Turn on or off 3D annotations and annotation elements** > toggle the annotations *off* and *on* > display the note in the Model Tree by clicking: ⬜ > ⬜ Tree Filters... > toggle all *on* [Fig. 16.6(e)] > **Apply** > **OK** > select ⬜ Note_0 from Model Tree or Drawing Tree > **RMB** > ⬜

⬜ **Properties**

Edit Properties > **OK** [Fig. 16.6(f)]

Display	Feature types
☑ Features	General Cabling Piping
☑ Placement folder	
☑ Materials	☑ ▱ Datum plane
☑ Annotations	☑ ⁄ Datum axis
☑ Section	☑ Curve
Toggle display of annotations	☑ Datum point
☐ NC owner	☑ ⌞ Coordinate system
☐ Mold/cast owner	☑ Round
☑ Suppressed objects	☑ Auto round member
☑ Incomplete objects	☑ Cosmetic
☑ Excluded objects	
☑ Blanked objects	
☑ Envelope components	
☑ Copied references	
☑ Weld solids	

Figure 16.6(e) Displaying Annotations) in Drawing Tree

Note ✕

Name

Note_2   ID: 2

Parent

Part   ▼

⬚ ☝ HELICAL_SPRING.PRT

Text

Helical Compression Spring
Constant Pitch
Right-Handed
30mm Pitch
Wire Diameter 20mm
Ground Ends (grind ends parallel)

Insert ▼   Style...   Symbols...

Placement

Unplace   Move Text...

Mod Attach...   Move...

URL

Hyperlink...

OK   Cancel

Figure 16.6(f) Note

Note **> RMB > Rename > SPRING > Enter > RMB > Add Link** [Fig. 16.7(a)] **>** www.thespringstore.com [Fig. 16.7(b)] **>** ScreenTip... **> SPRING STORE** [Fig. 16.6(c)] **> OK > OK > LMB** [Fig. 16.7(d)] **>** place your pointer over the note to see the Screen Tip [Fig. 16.7(e)] **> Ctrl+S**

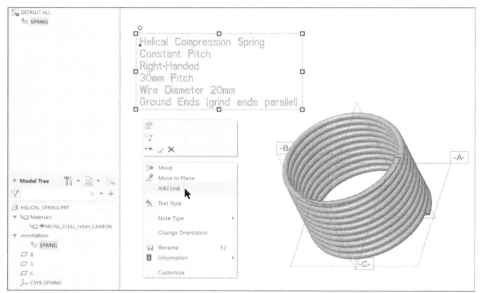

Figure 16.7(a) Add Link

Figure 16.7(b) Hyperlink

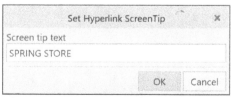

Figure 16.7(c) Screen Tip

Figure 16.7(d) Note

Figure 16.7(e) Screen Tip Displayed

$\boxed{\text{A} \equiv \text{SPRING}}$ **> RMB > Open URL** [Fig. 16.6(f)] *(URL opens in the browser window)* [Fig. 16.7(g)] **> Custom Springs >** $\boxed{}$ **close > LMB > Ctrl+D > Ctrl+S > File > Manage File > Delete Old Versions > Enter**

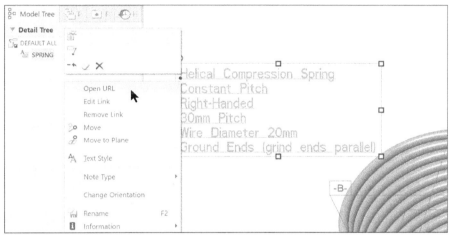

Figure 16.7(f) Open URL

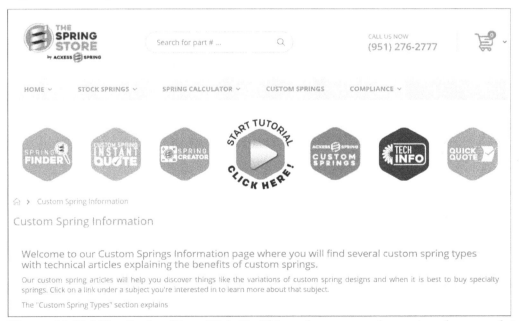

Figure 16.67g) The Spring Store Website (this webpage may have since been updated)

Model Based Definition

Creo Parametric enables designers to implement **MBD** and increase efficiency in product development by reducing dependency on 2D drawings. Creo permits designers to reduce the errors that result from incorrect, incomplete, or misinterpreted information by guiding and educating designers in the proper application of Geometric Dimensioning and Tolerance (GD&T) information. Creo also validates that the GD&T is captured in the 3D CAD model and is compliant with standards.

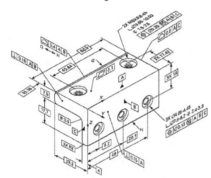

3D Notes can also be added to an entity using **Annotation Features**. Annotation features are data features that you can use to manage the model annotation and propagate model information to other models, or to manufacturing processes. The Annotation Feature Tool options correspond to the **ASME Y14.41 Digital Product Definition Data Practices.**

Figure 16.7 Digital Product Definition, ASME Y14.41

An Annotation feature consists of one or more Annotation Elements. Each Annotation Element (AE) can contain one annotation item, along with associated references and parameters. You can include the following types of annotations in an Annotation Element: Note, Symbol, Surface Finish, Geometric Tolerance, Set Datum Tag, Ordinate Baseline, Driven Dimension, Ordinate Driven Dimension, Reference Dimension, Ordinate Reference Dimension, and Existing Annotation.

Digital product definition data practices

"ASME Y14.41 establishes requirements for preparing, organizing and interpreting 3-dimensional digital product images [Fig. 16.7]. Digital Product Definition Data Practices, which represents an extension of the Y14.2 standard for 2-dimensional drawings, reflects the growing need for a uniform method of documenting the data created in today's computer-aided design (CAD) environments. ASME Y14.41 sets forth the requirements for tolerances, dimensional data, and other annotations. ASME Y14.41 advances the capabilities of Y14.2, Dimensioning and Tolerancing, the standard pertaining to 2-D engineering drawings".

In the following steps you will create a single-view 3D definition of the model for manufacturing, instead of a traditional multi-view drawing.

File > Options > Model Display > Isometric > OK > No > Annotate tab > select the Helical Sweep feature > **RMB > Show Annotations** [Fig. 16.8(a)] > [⊢→] tab > [☑] > **OK** from the Show Annotations dialog box > **Apply** > rotate model to see the dimensions [Fig. 16.8(b)] > **Cancel > LMB**

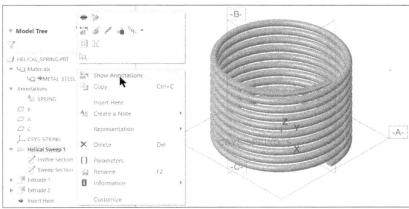

Figure 16.8(a) Show Annotations

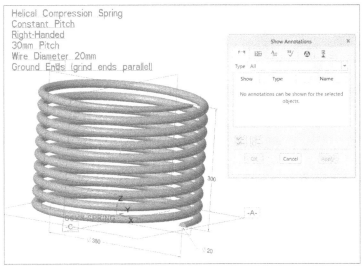

Figure 16.8(b) Displayed Dimensions

541

Select a dimension [Fig. 16.8(c)] > move the dimension as desired > continue moving the annotations so that the 3D view displays all dimensions appropriately [Fig. 16.8(d)] > **Ctrl+S**

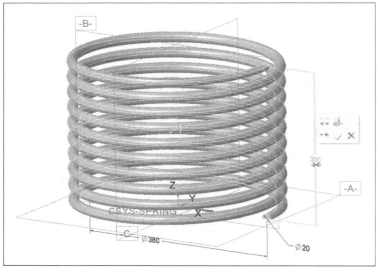

Figure 16.8(c) Move Dimensions as needed

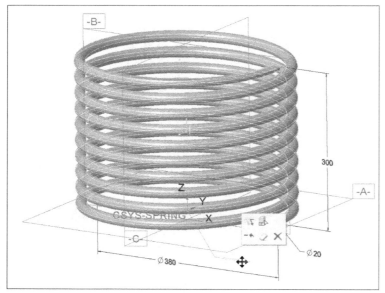

Figure 16.8(d) Current Orientation

Select **FRONT** in Ribbon > **RMB** > **Set** > **PITCH 30** > **RMB** > **Change Orientation**

⦿ Named Model Orientation > ▾ > **FRONT** [Fig. 16.8(e)] > **Flip** > **OK** > [Fig. 16.8(f)] >

RMB > **Move to Plane** > select datum **B** > **RMB** > ⤶ **Flip Text** > **LMB** > select the 3D
note > **RMB** > **Text Style** > Height **8** > **Apply** > **OK** > **Ctrl+R** > **Save**

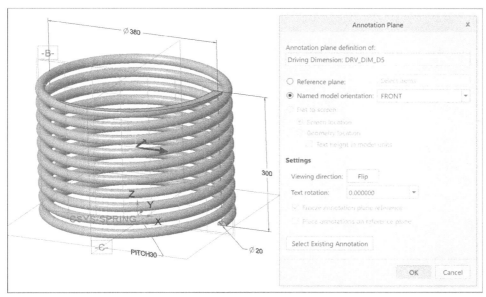

Figure 16.8(e) Annotation Plane

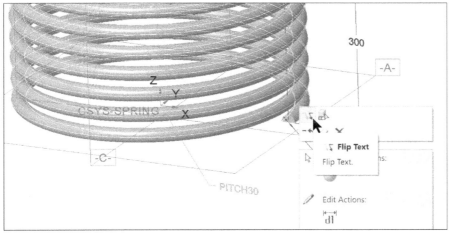

Figure 16.8(f) Flip Text

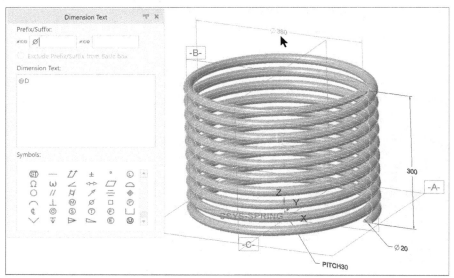 **Open the View Manager > Orient** tab **> New > Annotations > Enter > Close > Annotate** tab **>** select the **380** dimension [Fig. 16.9(a)] **> Display Text >** *type* **PITCH DIAMETER** [Fig. 16.9(b)] **> LMB > Ctrl+S** [Fig. 16.9(c)]

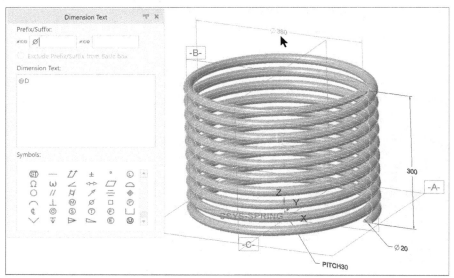

Figure 16.9(a) Dimension Text

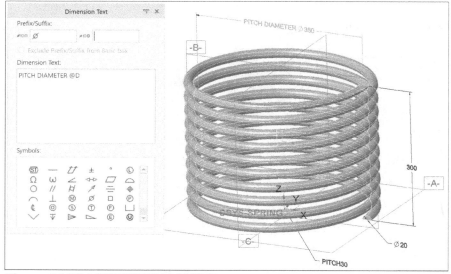

Figure 16.9(b) PITCH DIAMETER

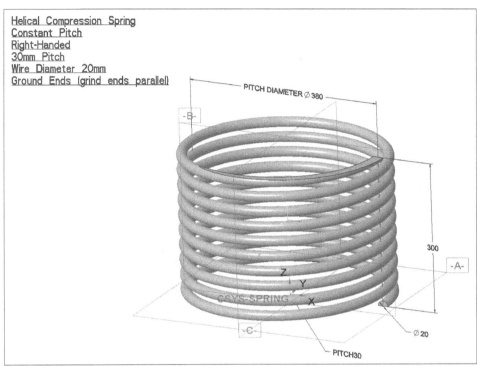

Helical Compression Spring
Constant Pitch
Right-Handed
30mm Pitch
Wire Diameter 20mm
Ground Ends (grind ends parallel)

PITCH DIAMETER ⌀ 380

-B-

300

-A-

CSYS SPRING

-C-

⌀ 20

PITCH30

Figure 16.9(c) Annotated Part

Annotation Feature > Specify a geometric tolerance [Fig. 16.10(a)]

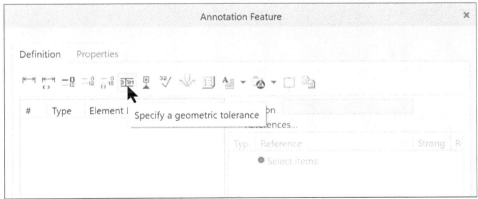

Annotation Feature

Definition   Properties

Type   Element   Specify a geometric tolerance

Typ   Reference   Strong   R

Select items

Figure 16.10(a) Annotation Feature Dialog Box, Geometric Tolerance

Select the **300mm** dimension [Fig. 16.10(b)] > **LMB > MMB** [Fig. 16.10(c)] > **LMB >**

Filters | Geometry ▼ | > | Annotation ▼ | > select the GTOL

annotation | 300 ... AE_GTOL0 (ANNOTATION ELEMENT):F340 (ANNOTATION_1) Model :HELICAL_SPRING | > | Geometric Characteristic ▼ | > // **Parallelism** [Fig. 16.10(d)]

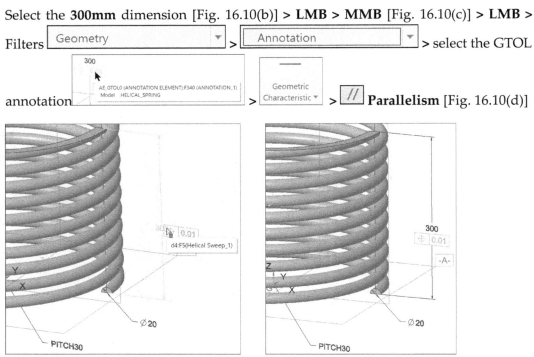

Figure 16.10(b) Geometric Tolerance   **Figure 16.10(c)** Placed Geometric Tolerance

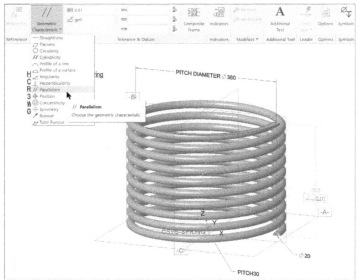

Figure 16.10(d) Parallelism

Type **A** as the Primary Datum Reference [Fig. 16.10(e)] **> LMB**

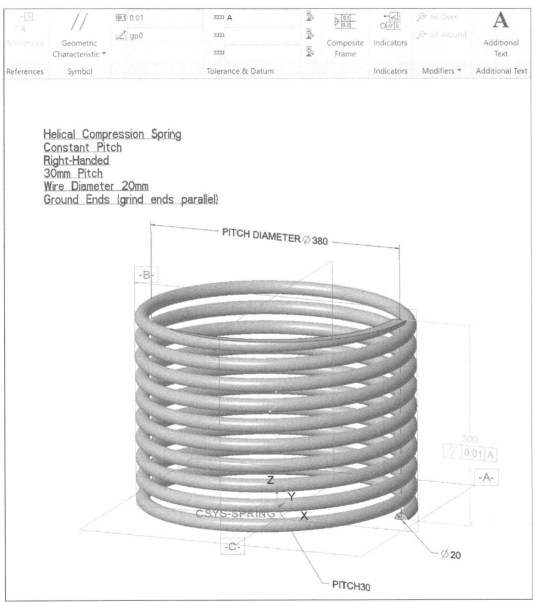

Figure 16.10(e) Datum A Primary Datum Reference

Click: 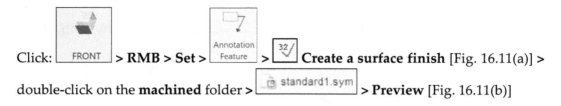 **FRONT** > **RMB** > **Set** > **Annotation Feature** > **Create a surface finish** [Fig. 16.11(a)] > double-click on the **machined** folder > **standard1.sym** > **Preview** [Fig. 16.11(b)]

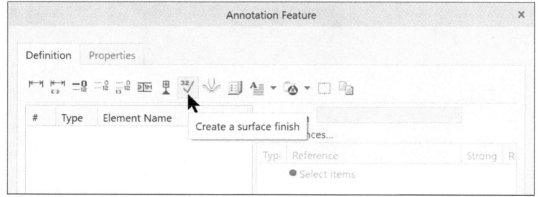

Figure 16.11(a) Create a Surface Finish

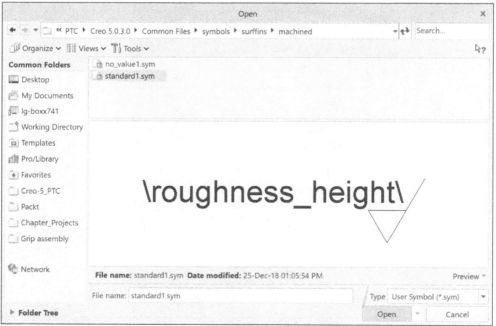

Figure 16.11(b) Preview of Surface Symbol standard1.sym

Click: **Open** [Fig. 16.11(c)] and the Surface Finish dialog box opens with its References collector active > select the ground surface [Fig. 16.11(d)]

Figure 16.11(c) Surface Finish Dialog Box

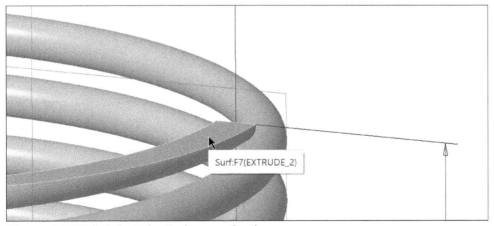

Figure 16.11(d) Select the Reference Surface

Click inside the Placement collector for Attachment references [Fig. 16.11(e)] > select the symbol position on the cut surface [Figs. 16.11(f-g)] > **MMB**

Figure 16.11(e) Placement Collector

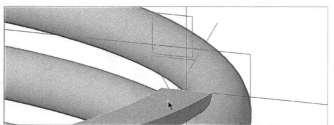

Figure 16.11(f) Select the Surface Finish Symbol Position

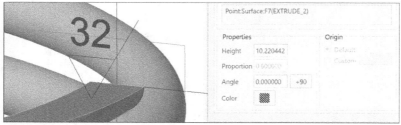

Figure 16.11(g) Completed Symbol Placement

Click: **Variable Text** tab > **32** [Fig. 16.11(h)] > **MMB** > **OK** [Fig. 16.11(i)]

Figure 16.11(h) Variable Text- roughness_height 32

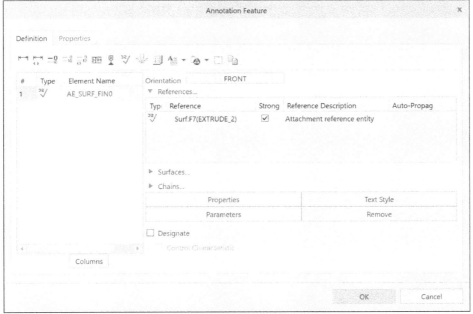

Figure 16.11(i) Annotation Feature

Click: ⌈32/⌉ tab [Fig. 16.11(j)] **>** repeat the process to create an annotation feature finish symbol on the opposite end of the spring [Fig. 16.11(k)] **> MMB > OK** Annotation Feature dialog box **> OK > LMB**

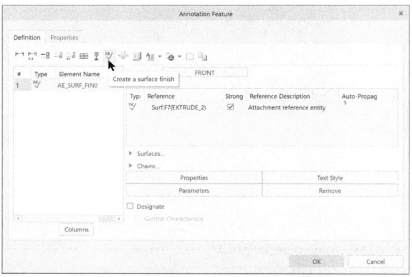

Figure 16.11(j) Annotation Feature Dialog Box

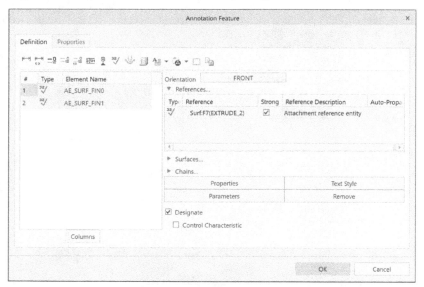

Figure 16.11(k) Second Surface Finish Annotation

Ctrl+4 > **View** tab > **View Manager** > **Orient** > click on **Annotations** > **RMB** > **Activate** > **Edit** > **Save** > **OK** > **Close** > **Ctrl+2** > **Ctrl+S** > **File** > **Manage File** > **Delete Old Versions** > **Yes** > **File** > **Close** > **Open** > **In Session** > **helical_spring** > **Open** > Select Instance **The generic** [Fig. 16.12] > **Open** > **Annotate** tab > **Command Locater** > *type* **Legacy** > **Legacy** [Fig. 16.13(a)]

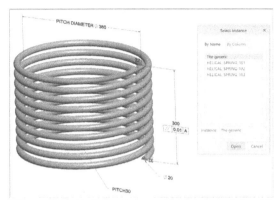

Figure 16.12 Opening an Instance of the Component's Family Table

Impact of ASME and ISO Standards on Datums

Creo Parametric 3.0 and earlier uses the older versions of standards: ASME Y14.5, ISO 1101, and ISO 5459. In Creo Parametric 3.0 and earlier, you can place datums on axis systems or on nonreal geometry surfaces, and reference them from the GTOL frame. Creo Parametric 4.0 and later uses more recent versions of these standards. As a result, you can only place datums on real geometry surfaces or on other annotations, as stacked annotations. You cannot reference legacy set datums from GTOLs. GTOLs support only set datum tag annotations and semantic datum feature symbol annotations. Normally, you need to reestablish the connections between GTOLs that previously referenced set datums. Here, we will convert but not change references because it is a helical shape where only the two cut surfaces are actually geometry able to be referenced.

Figure 16.13(a) Legacy Datum Annotation Conversion

`Convert All Set Datums` [Fig. 16.13(b)] > **Close** (datum symbols change to footed symbols [Fig. 16.13(c)] > **Yes** *(for the feature references we have kept the same references)* [Fig. 16.13(d)]

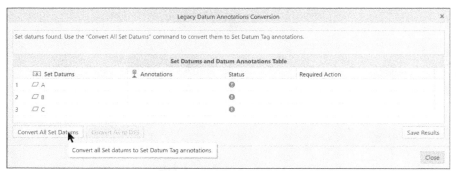

Figure 16.13(b) Legacy Datum Annotations Conversion

Figure 16.13(c) Set Datums and Datum Annotation Table

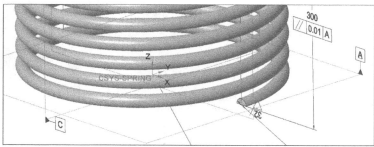

Figure 16.13(d) Footed Datum Symbols for Set Datums

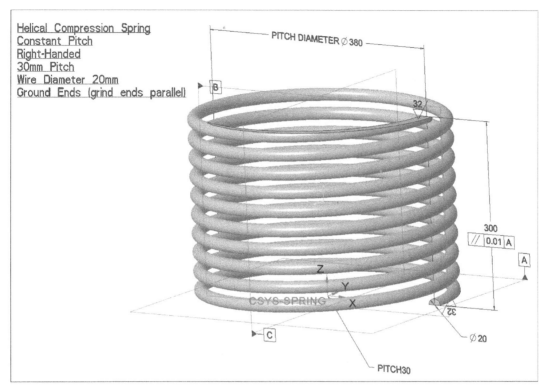

[Fig. 16.14] **> Ctrl+S > File > Close**

Figure 16.14 Spring

Quiz
1. What two items need to be defined when creating a helical sweep?
2. What is Model Based Definition?
3. What is a 3D Drawing?
4. How and why do Family Tables reduce modeling?
5. What elements can be incorporated into an Annotation Feature?
6. What is an Annotation Feature and how is it different from a 3D Note?
7. Why is Legacy Datum Annotations Conversion?

This completes Chapter 16.

Sweep, Trajectory Rib, Pattern, and Mirror

Adding geometry can be quickly accomplished by using Copy, Paste, and Paste Special in 3D. These commands are like keyboard commands for documents. A rib is a protrusion designed to create a thin fin or web that is attached to a part. Because of the way ribs are attached to the parent geometry, profile ribs are sketched as open sections. While creating the sweep you will use the sketcher Palette to introduce standard geometric shapes. Trajectory Ribs are incorporated in the design.

Objectives
1. Use Copy, Paste, and Paste Special commands
2. Use shapes from Palette when sketching
3. Create a swept feature
4. Sketch a Trajectory for a sweep
5. Sketch and locate a Sweep section
6. Create Trajectory Ribs
7. Use Patterns and Mirror to replicate geometry
8. Use Render Studio

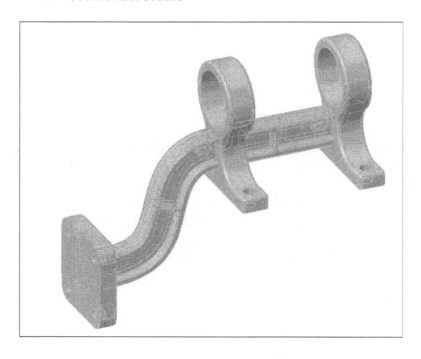

Sweeps

A Sweep is created by sketching or selecting a *trajectory* and then sketching a *section* to follow along it. The Pipe Bracket uses a sweep in its design. A *constant-section sweep* use either trajectory geometry sketched at the time of feature creation or a trajectory made up of selected datum curves or edges. The trajectory must have adjacent reference surfaces or be planar. When defining a sweep, Creo Parametric checks the specified trajectory for validity and establishes normal surfaces.

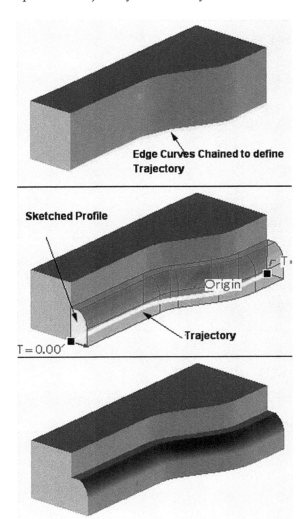

Chapter 17 STEPS

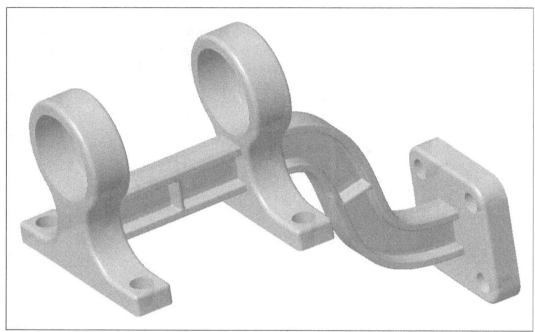

Figure 17.1 Pipe_bracket

The Pipe Bracket [Fig. 17.1] requires the use of the Sweep command. The I-shaped section is swept along the sketched *trajectory*.

Ctrl+N > Name **pipe_bracket**

- **Material** = METAL_ALUMINIUM_6061
- **Units = millimeter Newton Second**

- Coordinate System = **CSYS-PIPE_BRACKET**

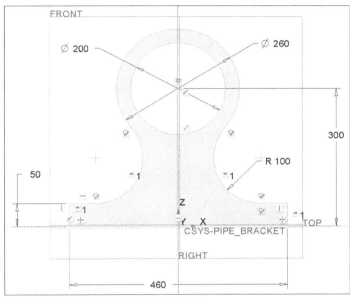

Figure 17.2(a) Section

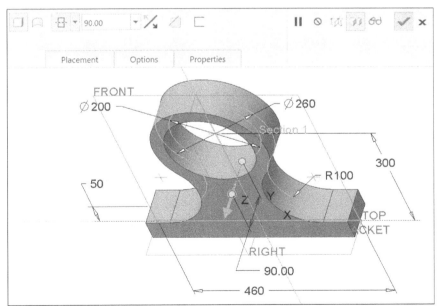

Figure 17.2(b) Extrude both sides of sketching plane

Hole > Create Standard Hole > Create clearance hole > No Tapping > Placement tab **> M30x1.5 > Drill to intersect all surfaces > Adds counterbore**

> select the placement surface **>** drag the location handles to datum **RIGHT** (Offset **185**) [Fig. 17.3(a)] and datum **FRONT** (Offset **Align**) [Fig. 17.3(b)] **> MMB**

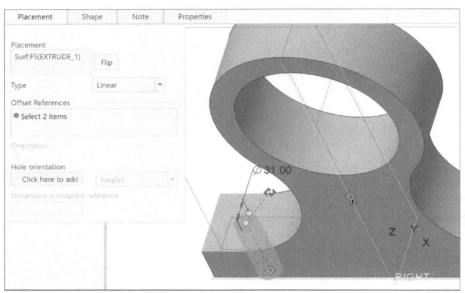

Figure 17.3(a) Select the Placement Surface

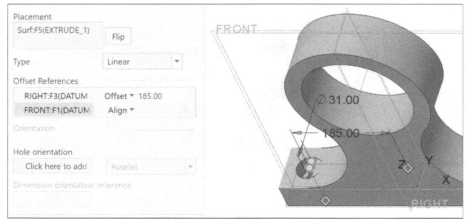

Figure 17.3(b) Drag Handles to Datum RIGHT and FRONT

The hole is partially covered [Fig. 17.3(c)] > double-click on the extrude feature > modify **R100** to **R90** [Fig. 17.3(d)] > **Enter** [Fig. 17.3(e)] > **LMB** > **LMB** > **Save**

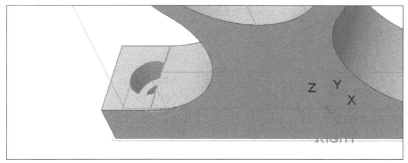

Figure 17.3(c) Hole does not go through round

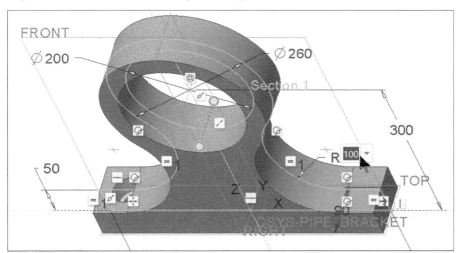

Figure 17.3(d) Modify R100

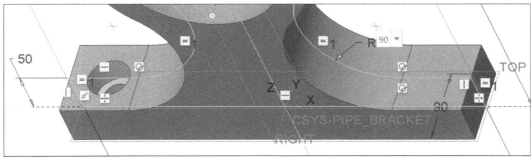

Figure 17.3(e) New value is R90

561

Select **Hole 1** in the Model Tree > **Edit Definition** Fig. 17.3(f)] > **Shape** Tab > **Medium Fit** [Fig. 17.3(g)] > **MMB** > select **Hole 1** > [dl] **Edit Dimensions** > modify counterbore diameter to **50mm** [Fig. 17.3(h)] > **Enter** > **LMB** > **LMB**

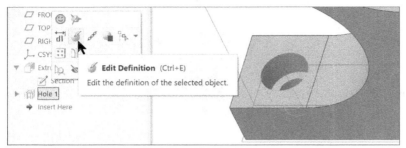

Figure 17.3(f) Edit Definition

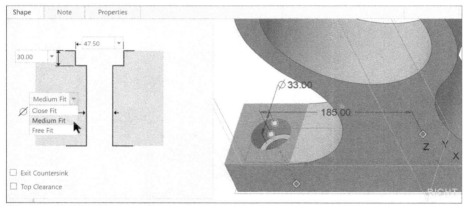

Figure 17.3(g) Shape tab

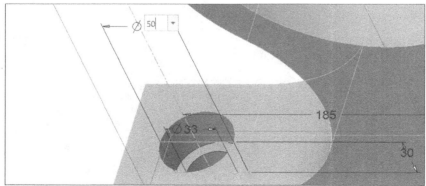

Figure 17.3(h) Modify Diameter

Select **Hole 1** > ⊔⊏ **Mirror** > **Sets** tab > select datum **RIGHT** > [Fig. 17.3(i)] > **MMB** > **Round** > select the edges [Fig. 17.4] > **10** > **Enter** > **MMB** > **LMB** > **Save**

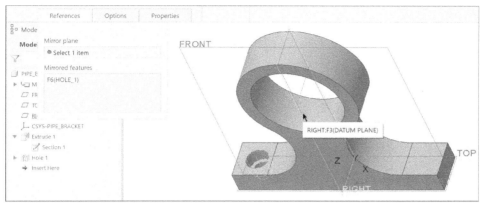

Figure 17.3(i) Mirror Plane

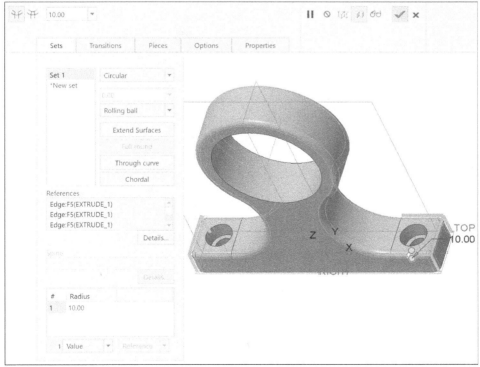

Figure 17.4 Rounds

Group [Fig. 17.5(a)] > **RMB** > **Copy** [Fig. 17.5(b)] > **Paste Special** [Fig. 17.5(c)]

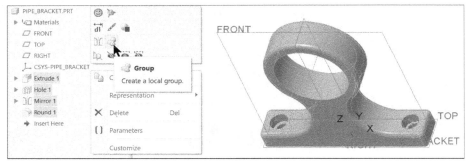

Figure 17.5(a) Group

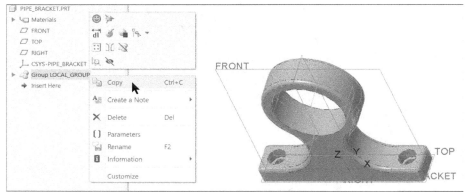

Figure 17.5(b) Copy

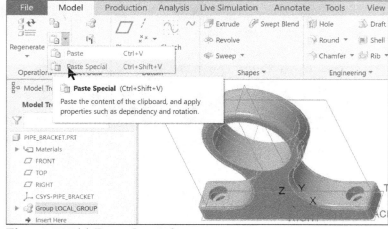

Figure 17.5(c) Paste Special

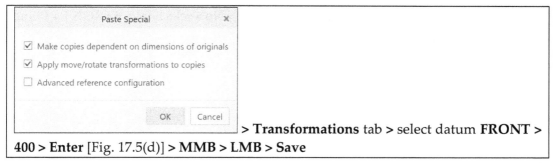 > **Transformations** tab > select datum **FRONT** >
400 > Enter [Fig. 17.5(d)] > **MMB > LMB > Save**

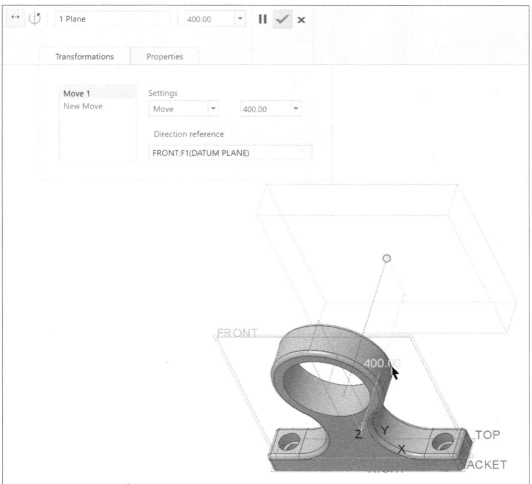

Figure 17.5(d) Paste Special

File > Options > Model Display > Isometric > OK > No > select datum **FRONT** > **Plane** [Fig. 17.6(a)] **800** [Fig. 17.6(b)] > **OK** > **Save**

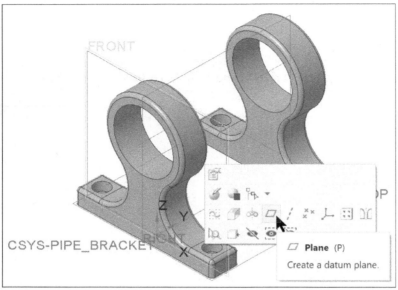

Figure 17.6(a) Create Plane

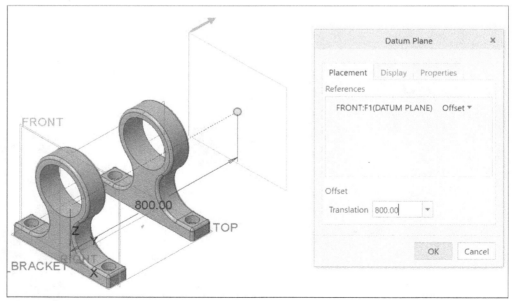

Figure 17.6(b) Offset Datum Plane

With new datum still selected > **Extrude** > 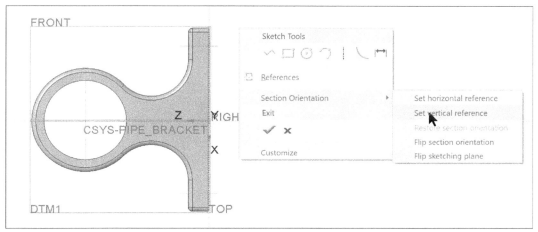 **Sketch View** > *(if necessary)* **RMB** > **Section Orientation** > **Set vertical reference** [Fig. 17.6(c)] > select datum **RIGHT** > **RMB** > **Centerline** > create a vertical centerline through the origin [Fig. 17.6(d)]

Figure 17.6(c) Set vertical reference

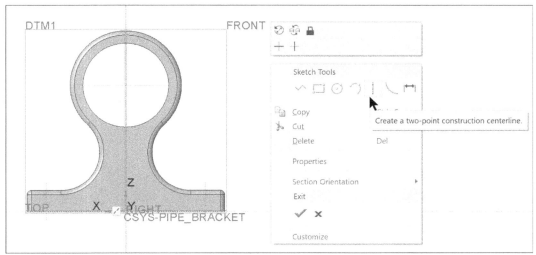

Figure 17.6(d) Select Datum RIGHT

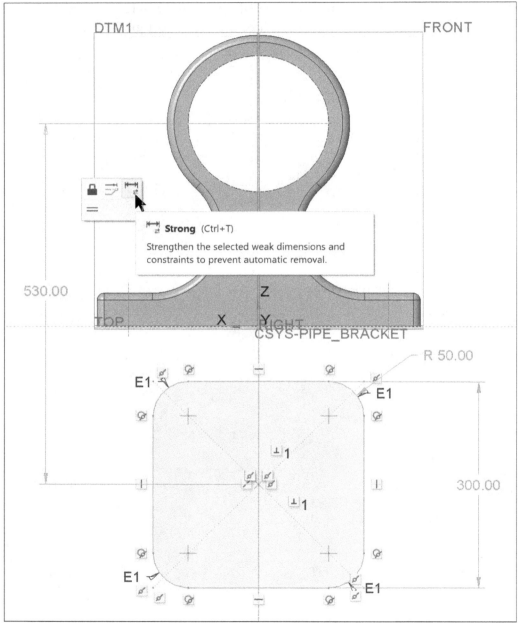

Figure 17.6(e) Section with Strong Dimensions

Spin model > **60** depth > ☑ OK Fig. 17.6(f)] > **MMB > LMB > Save**

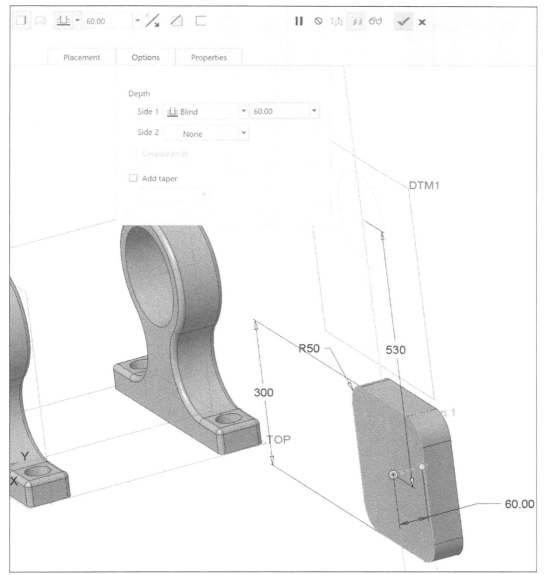

Figure 17.6(f) Extrude Preview

Double-click on **DTM1** Fig. 17.6(g)] **> 900 > LMB > LMB >** select **Extrude 2 > Edit definition >** click on arrow twice [Fig. 17.6(h)] **> MMB**

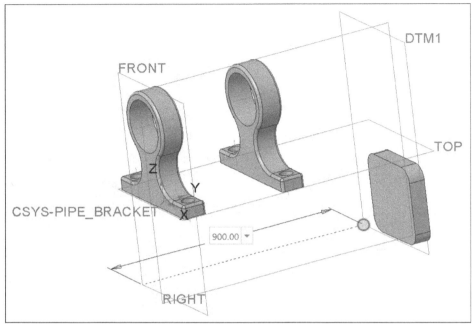

Figure 17.6(g) Modify

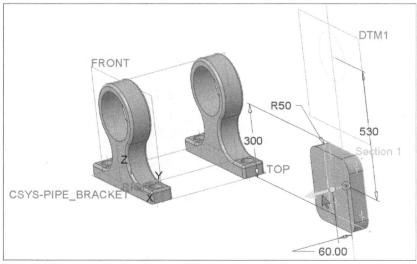

Figure 17.6(h) Click on Arrow twice

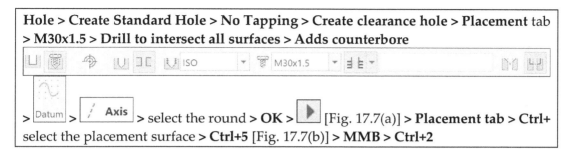

> **Hole > Create Standard Hole > No Tapping > Create clearance hole > Placement** tab **> M30x1.5 > Drill to intersect all surfaces > Adds counterbore**

> Datum > Axis > select the round > OK > ▶ [Fig. 17.7(a)] **> Placement tab > Ctrl+** select the placement surface **> Ctrl+5** [Fig. 17.7(b)] **> MMB > Ctrl+2**

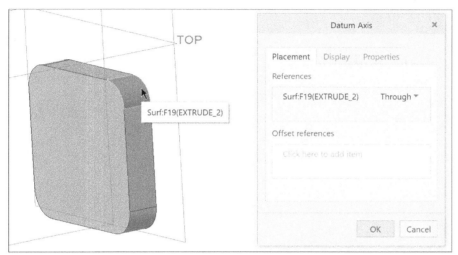

Figure 17.7(a) Select round

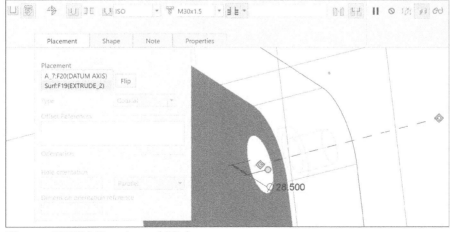

Figure 17.7(b) Previewed Hole

571

With hole selected: **RMB > Pattern > Dimension > Direction >** select the right side [Fig. 17.7(c)] **> -200 > Enter > RMB > Direction 2 reference >** select the top surface **> -200** Fig. 17.7(d)] **> Enter > MMB > LMB > Save**

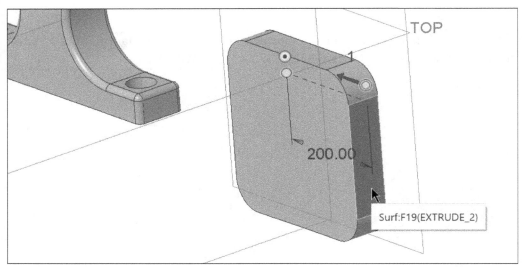

Figure 17.7(c) Direction 1 reference

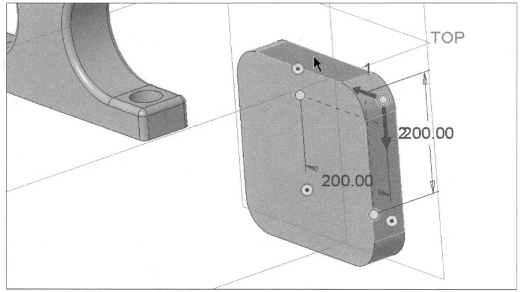

Figure 17.7(d) Direction 2 reference

Add a **10mm** round [Fig. 17.8(a)] > **MMB** > **Ctrl+D** > change color [Fig. 17.8(b)] > **Save**

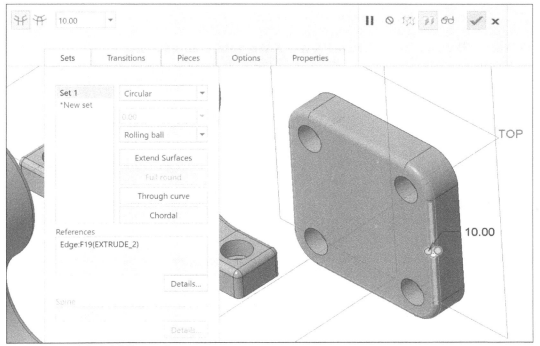

Figure 17.8(a) Add Round

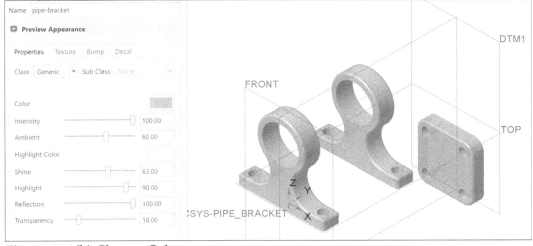

Figure 17.8(b) Change Color

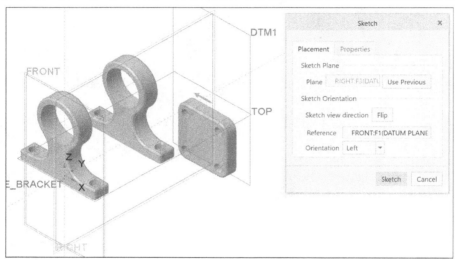

Figure 17.9(a) Sweep Trajectory Sketching Plane

Figure 17.9(b) Delete and add References

574

Line Chain > draw a horizontal line between the two references [Fig. 17.9(c)] > **MMB** > **More** Group > [⌒ Spline] > sketch the four-point spline > **MMB** [Fig. 17.9(d)]

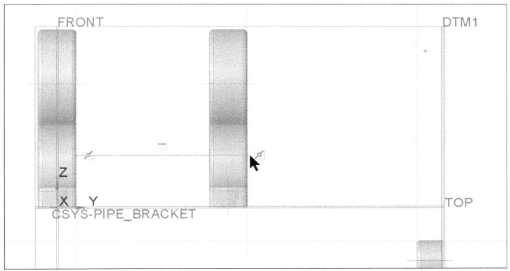

Figure 17.9(c) Draw Horizontal Line between the two References

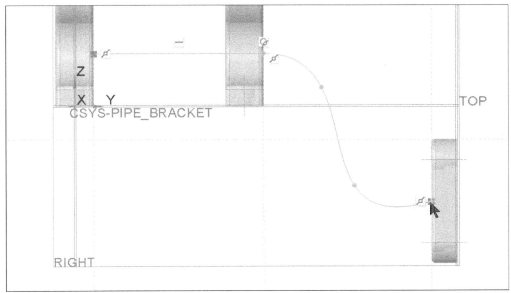

Figure 17.9(d) Spline

Centerline > draw a centerline through the point [Fig. 17.9(e)] **> MMB > LMB >**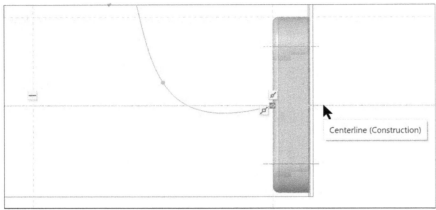
Tangent > select the centerline and the spline [Fig. 17.9(f)] **>** if necessary, repeat to

make the upper spline is tangent to the first sketched horizontal line

Figure 17.9(e) Construction Centerline

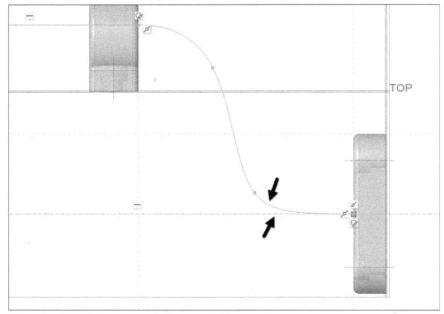

Figure 17.9(f) Tangent Spline and Centerline

Double-click on the spline (Spline tab opens) > pick on a point and slide to a new position [Fig. 17.9(g)] > place pointer on spline > **RMB** > **Add Point** [Fig. 17.9(h)]

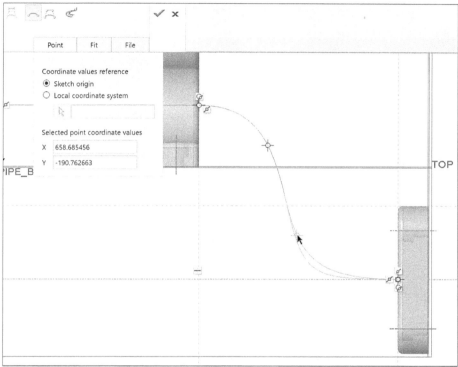

Figure 17.9(g) Spine tab

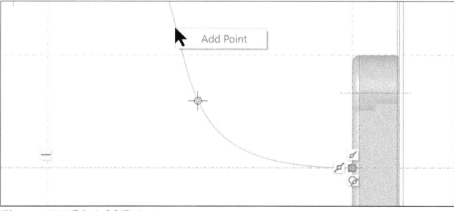

Figure 17.9(h) Add Point

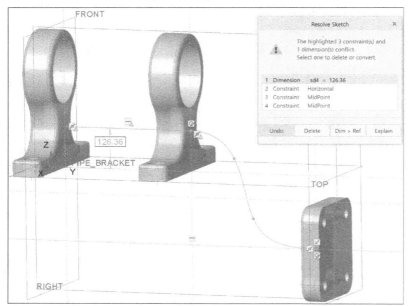

> add reference dimension [Fig. 17.9(i)] > **Dim>Ref > RMB >** ☑ > ▶ [Fig. 17.9(j)]

Figure 17.9(i) Add Dimension

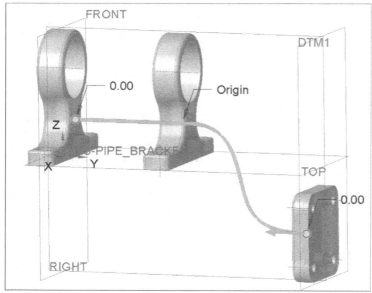

Figure 17.9(j) Trajectory

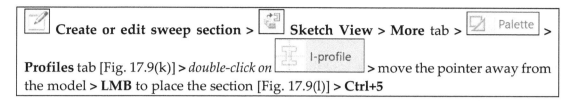

Create or edit sweep section > **Sketch View > More** tab > Palette >
Profiles tab [Fig. 17.9(k)] > *double-click on* I-profile > move the pointer away from
the model > **LMB** to place the section [Fig. 17.9(l)] > **Ctrl+5**

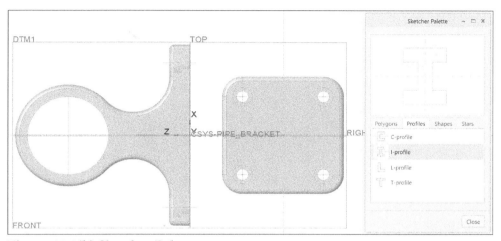

Figure 17.9(k) Sketcher Palette

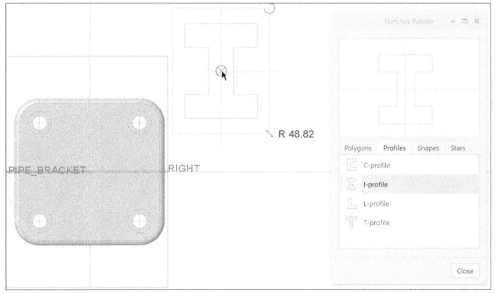

Figure 17.9(l) Place the Section

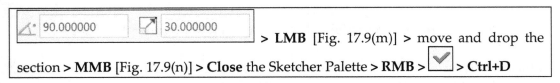

> **LMB** [Fig. 17.9(m)] > move and drop the section > **MMB** [Fig. 17.9(n)] > **Close** the Sketcher Palette > **RMB** > > **Ctrl+D**

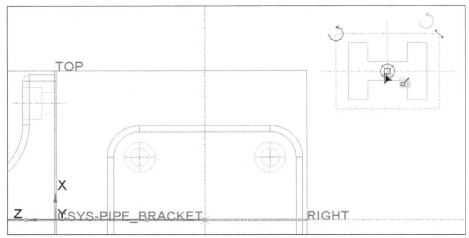

Figure 17.9(m) Move the Section

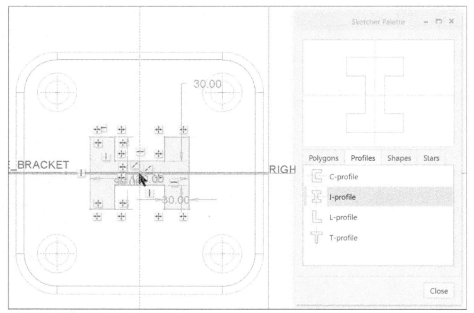

Figure 17.9(n) Drop the Section

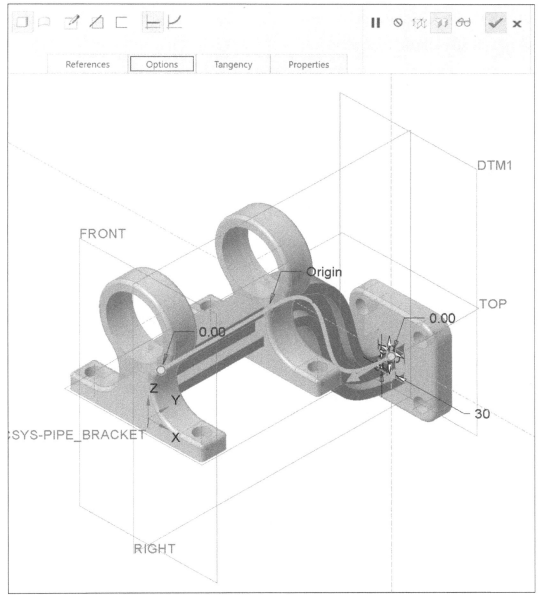

Figure 17.9(o) Sweep Preview

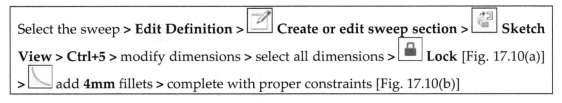

Select the sweep > **Edit Definition** > 🖉 **Create or edit sweep section** > 📲 **Sketch View** > **Ctrl+5** > modify dimensions > select all dimensions > 🔒 **Lock** [Fig. 17.10(a)] > ◣ add **4mm** fillets > complete with proper constraints [Fig. 17.10(b)]

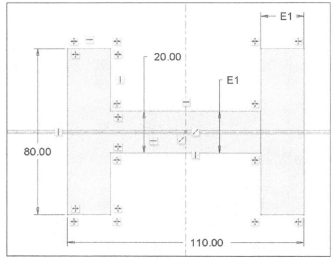

Figure 17.10(a) Sweep Section

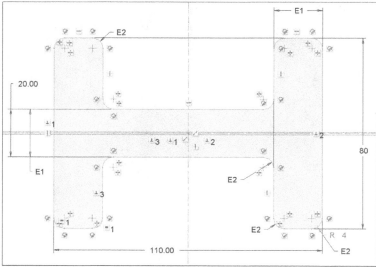

Figure 17.10(b) Completed Section

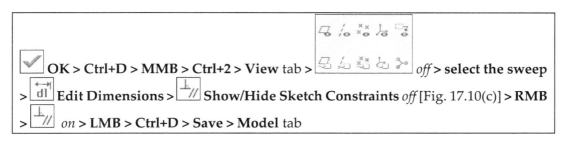

OK > Ctrl+D > MMB > Ctrl+2 > View tab > *off* **> select the sweep** > Edit Dimensions > Show/Hide Sketch Constraints *off* [Fig. 17.10(c)] **> RMB** > *on* **> LMB > Ctrl+D > Save > Model** tab

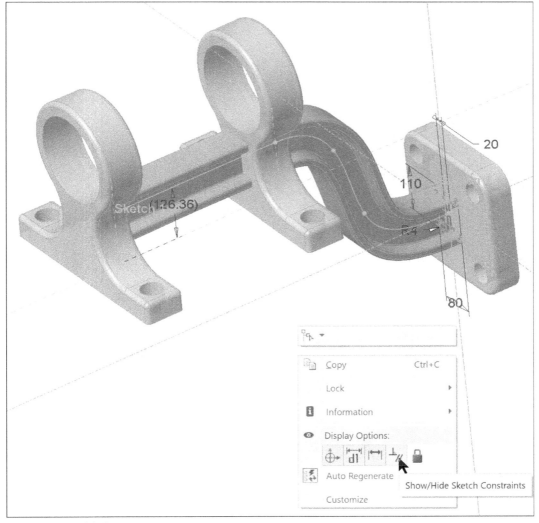

Figure 17.10(c) Sweep

Rib ▼ > **Trajectory Rib** > **RMB** > **Define Internal Sketch** > select the sweep surface [Fig. 17.11(a)] > **Sketch** > **RMB** > **References** > select the top and bottom of the sweep and faces of first extrusions [Fig. 17.11(b)] > **Solve** > **Close**

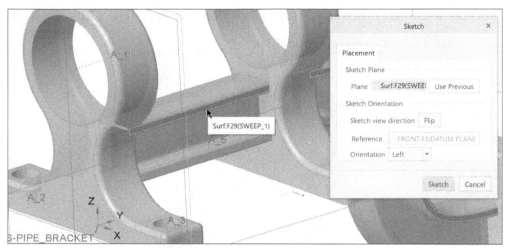

Figure 17.11(a) Sketch Plane

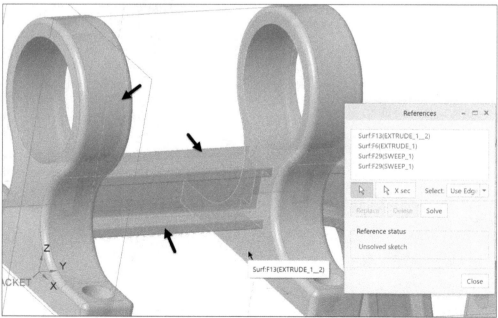

Figure 17.11(b) References

584

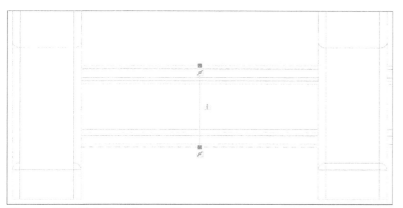

Figure 17.11(c) Sketch one line

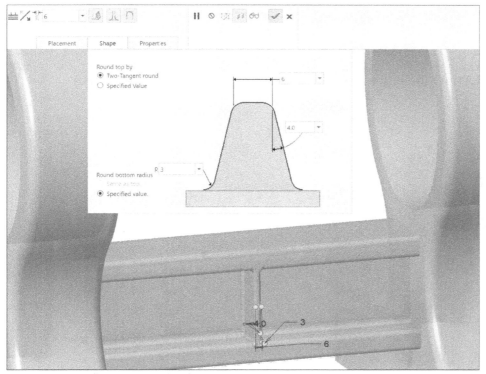

Figure 17.11(d) Previewed Rib

RMB > Define Internal Sketch > Sketch View > add references and one line [Fig. 17.11(e)] > ✓ **OK >** spin model > **Ctrl+3** Fig. 17.11(f)]

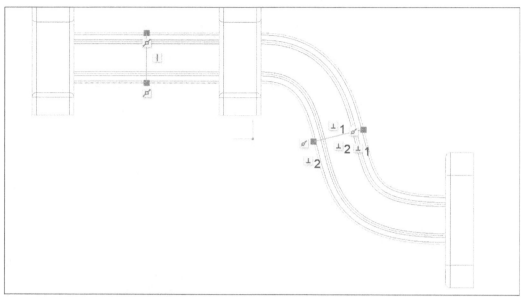

Figure 17.11(e) Rib Section (you may try more complex ribbing as desired)

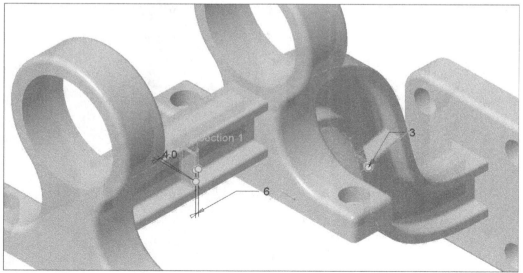

Figure 17.11(f) Ribs

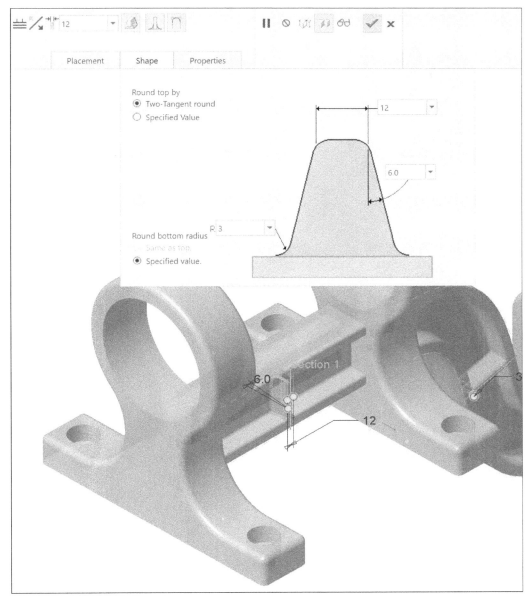

Figure 17.11(g) Rib Preview

587

With the rib selected > 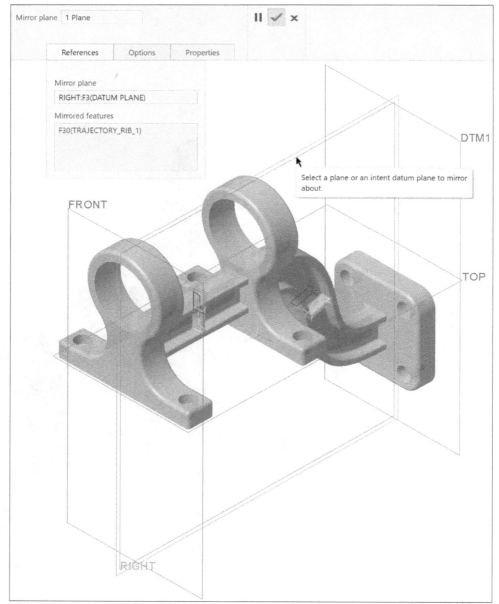 **Mirror** [Fig. 17.11(h)] > **References** tab > select **RIGHT** > **MMB** > **LMB** > **Save**

Figure 17.11(h) Mirrored Rib

Set datums as shown [Fig. 17.12(a)]

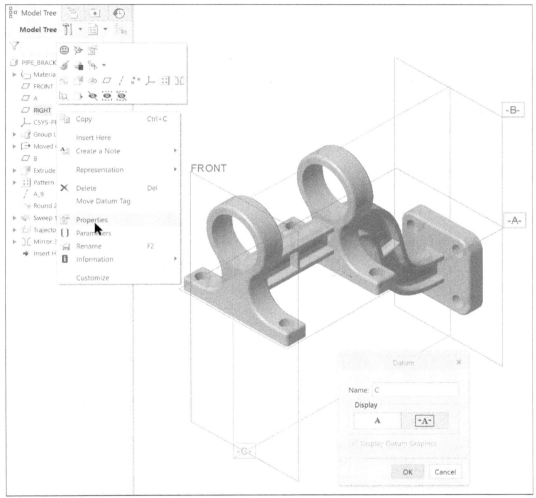

Figure 17.12(a) Set Datums

Ctrl+5 > Annotate tab **> Annotations >** `Legacy Datum Annotations Conversion` **>** `Convert All Set Datums` [Fig. 17.12(b)] **> Change Reference** [Fig. 17.12(c)] **>** click **RMB** to filter to and select bottom of first extrusion (formally datum A) [Fig. 17.12(d)]

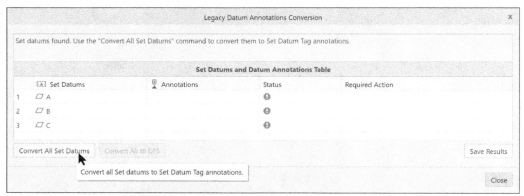

Figure 17.12(b) Legacy Datum Annotations Conversion

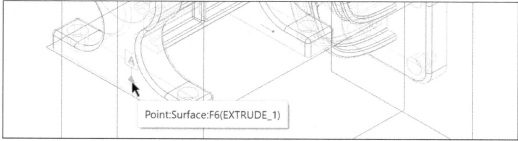

Figure 17.12(c) Set Datums and Datum Annotation Table

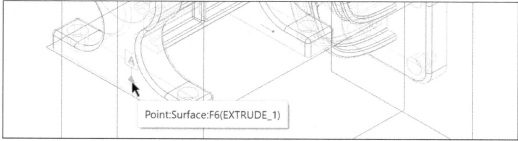

Figure 17.12(d) Select surface for Datum

MMB to place footed symbol for Datum **A** [Fig. 17.12(e)] > 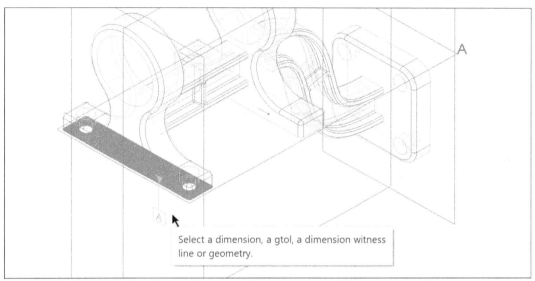 *on* > hide the holes notes in the Model Tree [Fig. 17.12(f)]

Figure 17.12(e) Datum A

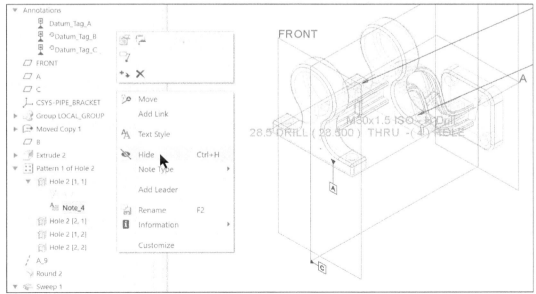

Figure 17.12(f) Hide Notes

Change Reference [Fig. 17.12(g)] > select the end of the extrusion (formally datum B) [Fig. 17.12(h)] > **MMB** [Figs. 17.12(i-j)] *(you will reorient the symbol later)*

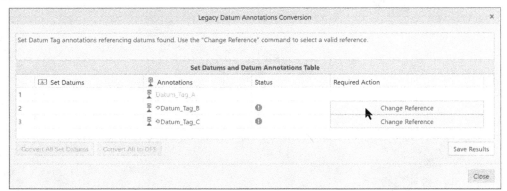

Figure 17.12(g) Legacy Datum Annotations Conversion

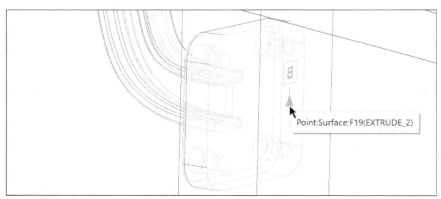

Figure 17.12(h) Select Surface

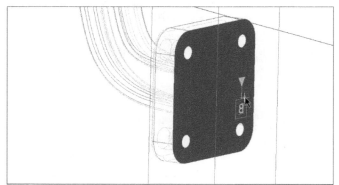

Figure 17.12(i) Place the symbol

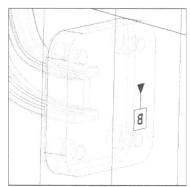

Figure 17.12(j) B Datum

Change Reference [Fig. 17.12(k)] **>** select the side of the extrusion [Fig. 17.12(l)] **> MMB** [Fig. 17.12(m)] **> Close**

Figure 17.12(k) Legacy Datum Annotations Conversion

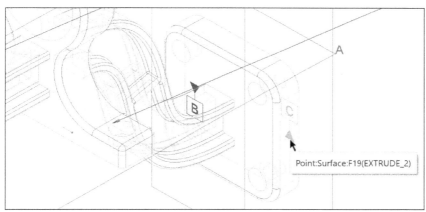

Figure 17.12(l) Select Surface

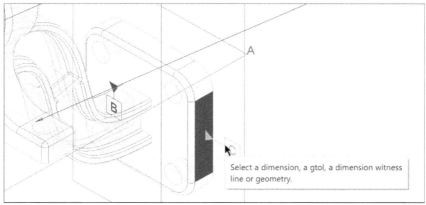

Figure 17.12(m) Place the symbol

593

Select the **B** footed datum symbol **> RMB > Change Orientation** [Fig. 17.13(a)] > Annotation Plane dialog box displays [Fig. 17.13(b)]

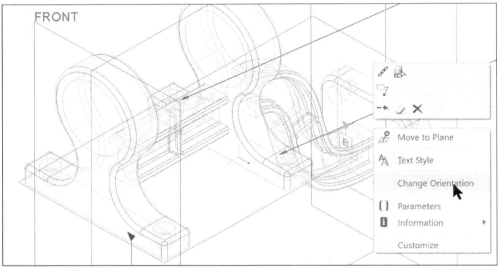

Figure 17.13(a) Change Orientation

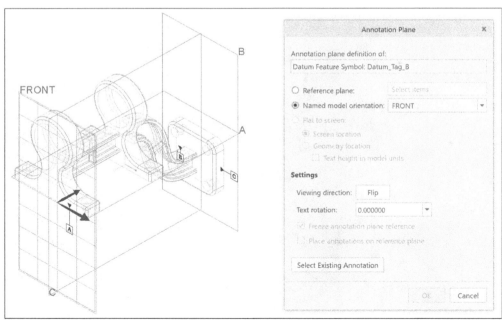

Figure 17.13(b) Annotation Plane Dialog Box

Reference Plane > select plane [Fig. 17.13(c)] > **Ctrl+D** > Text rotation > **270** > **Enter** [Fig. 17.13(d)] > **OK** > **Ctrl+3** > **Ctrl+S**

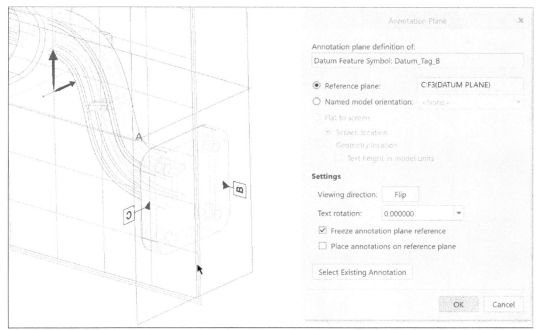

Figure 17.13(c) Select reference plane

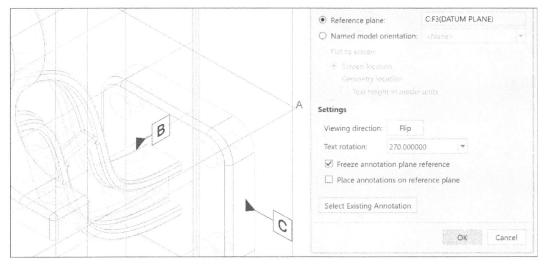

Figure 17.13(d) Text rotation: 270

Figure 17.14 Workshop Scene

Quiz

1. What is a Mirror Plane?
2. Name 5 shapes available in the Sketcher Palette.
3. What two sketches are required for a swept feature?
4. How do you change a Section Orientation?
5. When you create a feature using an internal datum what does it display as in the Model Tree? Does it display in the model?
6. What are the three options available for a Shape for a Trajectory rib?

This completes Chapter 17.

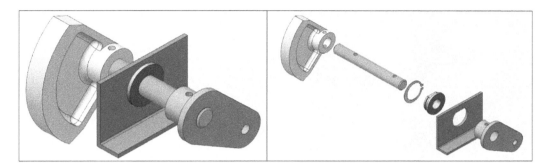

Objectives

1. Use Assembly commands
2. Establish and edit Units
3. Apply Analysis to determine Global Interference and Global Clearance
4. Measure features to analyze components fit
5. Use Edit Definition features to resolve design problems

Resources

- Chapter Lecture

- Choose **commercial** or **academic** Gear Assembly for parts .

Chapter 18 Steps

- Watch Chapter Lecture
- Create the assembly using the available parts
- Check your Units
- Use Measure and Analysis on the assembly model

This completes Chapter 18.

CHAPTER 19: **Valve Assembly** (video chapter)

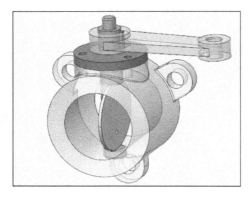

Objectives

1. Use Assembly commands
2. Establish and edit Units
3. Apply Analysis to determine Global Interference and Global Clearance
4. Measure features to analyze components fit
5. Use Edit Definition features to resolve design problems
6. Use Top-Down Design to create the component

Resources

- Chapter Lecture

- Choose **commercial** or **academic** Valve Assembly for parts .

Chapter 19 Steps

- Watch the Chapter Lecture
- Create the assembly using the available parts
- Check your Units
- Use Top-Down Design to create the Key component

This completes Chapter 19.

CHAPTER 20: **Final Project- Pulley using Top Down Design**
(video chapter)

A sweep will be used in the modeling of one of the assembly's components using top-down-design and referencing external component features to determine and control the belt's geometry. The Pulley will also be created using top-down design methods.

Objectives
1. Use Assembly commands
2. Establish and edit Units
3. Apply Analysis to determine Global Interference and Global Clearance
4. Use Top-Down Design to create the Pulley and Belt components

Resources
- Chapter Lecture
- Choose **commercial** or **academic** Pulley Assembly for parts.

Chapter 20 Steps

Follow the Steps to complete the lesson:

- Watch the Chapter Lecture and follow the procedures
- Use Top-Down Design to create the Pulley and Belt components

This completes Chapter 20.

Index